Samuel Davies Baldwin

Armageddon or, the Overthrow of Romanism and Monarchy

The Existence of the United States Foretold in the Bible

Samuel Davies Baldwin

Armageddon or, the Overthrow of Romanism and Monarchy
The Existence of the United States Foretold in the Bible

ISBN/EAN: 9783744622141

Printed in Europe, USA, Canada, Australia, Japan

Cover: Foto ©ninafisch / pixelio.de

More available books at **www.hansebooks.com**

ARMAGEDDON:

OR

The Overthrow of Romanism and Monarchy;

THE

EXISTENCE OF THE UNITED STATES

FORETOLD IN THE BIBLE,

ITS FUTURE GREATNESS; INVASION BY ALLIED EUROPE; ANNIHILATION OF MONARCHY; EXPANSION INTO THE MILLENNIAL REPUBLIC, AND ITS DOMINION OVER THE WHOLE WORLD.

REVISED EDITION.

BY S. D. BALDWIN, A. M.,
PRESIDENT OF SOULE FEMALE COLLEGE.

CINCINNATI:
APPLEGATE & CO., PUBLISHERS.
1864

CONTENTS.

INTRODUCTION 13

PART FIRST.

PROPHETIC HISTORY OF THE WHOLE WORLD.

CHAPTER I.

THE FIRST SPIRITUAL AND POLITICAL PROPHECY 17
SECTION I. Declaration of War.. 18
 " II. Mode of the World's Reduction—First Curse 24
 " III. The Principles of God's Government..................... 26
 " IV. The Last Contest 28

CHAPTER II.

SECOND GENERAL PROPHECY... 29
SECTION I. Course of Empire 31
 " II. Millennial Empire 32
 " III. The Second Curse 33

CHAPTER III.

PANORAMA OF CHRISTIANITY AND OF THE WORLD 35
SECTION I. Hebrew System Typical of Christianity and the World...... 35
 " II. Philosophy of the Hebrew System 53
 " III. Collateral Types 62

CHAPTER IV.

ISRAEL RESTORED IDENTICAL WITH THE UNITED STATES 64

SECTION I. Absurdity of the Common Theory 65
" II. The Common Theory Unscriptural 72
" III. The United States is Israel Restored 78
" IV. Parallel Prophecies of Israel 91

CHAPTER V.

EZEKIEL'S SYMBOLIC PROPHECIES OF AMERICA 92

SECTION I. Israel Restored—America............................. 93
" II. The great Battle and Destruction of Monarchy by Israel, or Gog and his Allies—Invasion of the United States...... 95

Paragraph I. Thirty-eighth Chapter 95
II. Thirty-ninth Chapter................................... 103

CHAPTER VI.

NEBUCHADNEZZAR'S PANORAMIC VISION OF THE SIX KINGDOMS OF THE WORLD 108

SECTION I. Head of the Image—Babylon 113
" II. The Medo-Persian Empire—Arms and Breast of Silver... 113
" III. The Macedonian Empire—Belly and Thighs of Brass...... 115
" IV. The Fourth Kingdom—Rome 119

Paragraph I. First Period—Rome as a Unit..................... 120
" II. Second Period—Church and State Union and the Fall of Rome, or its Broken State, Iron and Clay................. 122

Clause I. Church and State Union 122
" II. Fall of Rome, or its Broken State 125

Paragraph III. Third Period—Reorganization of the Fourth Empire.. 127

SECTION V. The Fifth Kingdom, or United States of America............ 133
" VI. Sixth Kingdom—Reign of Messiah 167

CHAPTER VII.

DANIEL'S FIRST PANORAMIC VISION OF THE SIX KINGDOMS OF THE WORLD 169

SECTION I. The Lion—Empire of Babylon......................... 171
" II. The Bear—Medo-Persia............................... 172

CONTENTS. 7

	PAGE.
SECTION III. The Leopard—Macedonian Empire	173
" IV. Fourth Beast—Roman Empire	175
Paragraph I. First Period—Beast—Unity of Rome	175
" II. Second Period—Ten Horns and Little Horn, or Church and State Union, and the Broken State or Fall of Rome..	177
Clause I. The Ten Horns	178
" II. The Little Horn	180
Paragraph III. Third Period of Rome—Reorganization	199
SECTION V. Fifth Kingdom, or the Ancient of Days, or United States of America	200
" VI. The Sixth Empire, or Messiah's Kingdom	212

CHAPTER VIII.

SECOND VISION OF DANIEL.—FIVE KINGDOMS	215
SECTION I. The Persian Empire—Ram	215
" II. Four-horned Goat—The Macedonian Empire	216
" III. Little—The Roman Empire	217
" IV. Israel	221
" V. Doom of Monarchy	223

CHAPTER IX.

DANIEL'S THIRD VISION OF THE WORLD	224
SECTION I. The Persian Empire	225
" II. The Grecian Empire	225
" III. Roman Empire	226
Paragraph I. Ships of Chittim, or Rome	227
" II. Arms, or the Roman Military Power	228
" III. The Willful King—Rome and Russia	231
SECTION IV. Michael—United States	243
" V. The Final Kingdom of Messiah	248
" VI. The Sealing of the Vision and the Discovery	249
" VII. Length of the "Indignation"	252
Paragraph I. Three and a half Times	252
" II. The 1290 and 1335 days	254
" III. Application of these Times	256
SECTION VIII. Epitome of Daniel's Prophecies, and their Mutual Coincidence	258

CHAPTER X.

THE SPIRITUAL WORLD IN THE APOCALYPSE 260
SECTION I. Seat of Spiritual Prophecy.................................... 261
" II. The Prophecies 265

CHAPTER XI.

POLITICAL PROPHECIES OF REVELATION 266
SECTION I. The Seat of Political Prophecy................................ 267
" II. The Book of Seals—First Panorama of the World 272
Paragraph I. The First Seal, or Church and State Union 273
" II. Second Seal, or Western Church 278
" III. Third Seal—Mohammedanism in the South 280
" IV. Fourth Seal—Deism and France 283
" V. Fifth Seal—Destruction of Churches and oppressions ... 287
" VI. Sixth Seal—Destruction of Monarchy 289
" VII. Seventh Seal 292

CHAPTER XII.

THE LITTLE BOOK OF INTERPRETATION 293
SECTION I. Holy City and the Gentiles—Church and State Union ... 294
" II. The Two Witnesses—Christianity Depressed............... 297
" III. The Woman with Twelve Stars, and her Man child, or the Christian Church and the United States 305
" IV. Roman and British Monarchy, or the Seven-headed Beast... 320
" V. The Beast from the Sea, or the Universal Imperial Church... 328
" VI. The Two-horned Beast, or Great Britain..................... 336

CHAPTER XIII.

THE SEVEN TRUMPETS—SECOND GREAT PANORAMA 348
SECTION I. First Trumpet—Goths, Germans, Vandals—Invasion of Europe 349
" II. Second Trumpet—Invasion of Atilla and the Huns 351
" III. Third Trumpet—Invasion of Genseric........................ 353
" IV. Fourth Trumpet—Fall of the Western Empire 354
" V. Fifth Trumpet—First Woe, or Saracenic Invasion 356

CONTENTS.

	PAGE.
Section VI. Sixth Trumpet, and Second Woe—Turkish Invasion......	359
VII. Seventh Trumpet—Rise of the United States, and Fall of Monarchy	363
Paragraph I. First Panorama of the Seventh Trumpet	365
Clause I. First View—United States	365
" II. Second View—The Church and State Free	367
" III. Third View—Fall of the Western or Latin Church.........	368
" IV. Fourth View—Threat against Great Britain	368
" V. Fifth View—Overthrow of Europe by America...............	369
" VI. Sixth View—Overthrow of Britain.............................	370
" VII. Seventh View—The Millennium................................	372
Paragraph II. Second Panorama	374
Clause I. First View—United States	374
" II. Second View—Babylon and the Beast, or the State and Church, and Russia and Europe................................	384
" III. Third View—The Man with Many Crowns, on a White Horse, or the United States of America........................	392
" IV. Fourth View—Third Woe	396
" V. Fifth View—Chaining of the Dragon	399
" VI. Sixth View—The Millennial Democracy	402
" VII. Seventh View—The Spiritual Judgment-day	405

CHAPTER XIV.

The New Heaven and Earth—The Victory 407

CONTENTS.

PART SECOND.

THE DISCOVERY—COMPLETED JANUARY, 1852.

	PAGE.
THE DISCOVERY	413

CHAPTER I.

INTERPRETATION OF THE SEVENTY WEEKS	421
SECTION I. The Decree of Restoration—Crucifixion—Fall of Judea	423
Paragraph I. The Decree of Cyrus	423
" II. Decree of Artaxerxes Longimanus	425
" III. Year of the Crucifixion	426
" IV. Year of Judea's Fall	430
SECTION II. Beginning of the Seventy Weeks	434
" III. Hebrew Divisions of Time	439
Paragraph I. Hebrew Weeks	439
" II. Spiritual and Civil Time	440
" III. Length of the Sacred and Secular Years	440
SECTION IV. Abbreviated Time and Full Time	445
" V. Application of Principles	448
Paragraph I. Seventy Weeks equal to Five Hundred and Sixty-four Years	449
" II. Seventy Weeks equal to Six Hundred and Three Years	453
" III. Seventy Weeks equal to Four Hundred and Eighty-three Years	457
" IV. Seventy Weeks equal to Five Hundred and Twenty-two Years	459
SECTION V. Four Hundred and Eighty and Four Hundred and Thirty Years	460
Paragraph I. Four Hundred and Thirty Years	460
" II. Four Hundred and Eighty Years	461

CHAPTER II.

DAYS, YEARS, MONTHS, AND TIMES 462

SECTION I. Twelve Hundred and Sixty Days 462

Paragraph I. Twelve Hundred and Sixty Days—Spiritual Lengths... 463
" II. Secular Length of the Twelve Hundred and Sixty Days.. 464

SECTION II. Twelve Hundred and Ninety Days—Seventeen Hundred and Eight Years 464
" III. Thirteen Hundred and Thirty-five Days 466
" IV. Forty-two Months 467
" V. Three and a half times—1243, 1451, 1708, 1810 469

Paragraph I. Spiritual Length of the Times.................................. 470
" II. Secular Length of the Three and a Half Times 471

SECTION VI. Twenty-three Hundred Evening Mornings 472

Paragraph I. The Epochs of their Beginning and Ending.............. 472
" II. The Exposition 475

SECTION VII. Fall and Rise of the Western Empire—One third of a Day and One third of a Night................................ 476
" VIII. Five Months—Duration of the Saracenic Invasions... 477
" IX. Day—Hour—Month—Year 477
" X. Synopsis of Days, Months, and Times 478

CONCLUSION 480

INTRODUCTION.

PRINCIPLES.

> "Hold my right hand, Almighty."
> "I here
> Invoke thy aid to my adventurous theme,
> That with no middle flight intends to soar
> Above the Aonian mount, while it pursues
> Things unattempted yet in prose or rhyme.
> * * * * What in me is dark,
> Illumine; what is low, raise and support;
> That to the hight of this great argument
> I may assert eternal providence,
> And justify the ways of God to man."

We lay down the following as our principles of interpreting symbolic prophecy.

First. Perfect coincidence of events with prophecy, is infallible proof of the fulfillment of prophecy. It was in accordance with this principle, that Jesus proved himself to be the Messiah.

Second. The definition of prophetic symbols is to be found in scripture, or to be determined by fulfillment. Where a symbol has more than one scriptural sense, which is rarely the case, its intended meaning must be determined either by its context or by fulfillment, or by both.

Third. All interpretations must coincide with the literal and evangelical doctrines of the bible.

Fourth. All the symbolic days, months, and times, are interpretable on the same principles as are the seventy weeks, and have a double, or twice doubled interpretation and fulfillment.

Fifth. All symbolic prophecy of great events is given in twice doubled forms, or is interpreted by symbols, or literally.

Sixth. The people of God are symbolized, always, in a dual character, coinciding with the spiritual and civil departments of government, growing out of the spiritual and social nature of man and the dual nature of the great law of love to God and love to man.

Seventh. The globe and mankind are to be freed from the curse, and the globe is not to be annihilated, but renewed with all the splendors in the gift of Deity, and be the tabernacle of God, the Holy of Holies forever and ever.

For our work, we ask the calm and charitable attention of the reader. We present it as a theory, a true theory, of the dealings of God with the nations of the world; but we would by no means compel any one to adopt our conclusions against his will; we would rather let the demonstrations be examined, and persuade by invincible and logical argument. Our deductions are not the result of fugitive thoughts, but of unceasing attention, by day and by night, without intermission, for more than twenty years. Our labors have been of the severest and most painful and patient character, in making the discovery of the principles of interpreting the seventy weeks : to ascertain them, we have made not less than fifty thousand numerical experiments. In addition to this, it may not be improper to remark, that daily, and more than daily, through a space of sixteen years, have we sought God for wisdom to understand the mystery which he said should be unsealed. Through the pity of some, the derision of others, the rebukes of many, and with the good wishes of but few, we have steadily pursued our course in quiet to the goal of our wishes; and we now return gratitude to God for our success. We commit the work we have written to the direction of Him who hears the prayer of the humble, and doubt not but that it will do some good to our country, the church, and world.

The style of our composition is not labored, though we have been long in preparing our book; our time has been devoted mainly to *systematizing* and harmonizing the prophets. In doing this we have re-written the substance of the work very many times over. We have tried to make every sentence plain; but still it will require time and patience on the reader's part to go through with it. It will be observed that our interpretations of the future coincide with the positions assumed by Hon. John Bell, on non-intervention; and the coincidence is the more singular, because our positions were taken in a course of lectures delivered some eight days sooner than the speech. This coincidence attracted the attention of many persons, and resulted in a written request, on their part, that our views should be published in a book form. That we both should entertain the same views, from positions differing so widely, is very remarkable, and is entitled to grave consideration.

Should we be found somewhat in error in some smaller points relating to the future, it is no more than would be naturally anticipated; but we feel assured that we are not, and can not be, mistaken about the conflict of our country with Europe in the battle of the great day. So far as the past is concerned, we feel assured that we are presenting to the public some of the most extraordinary proofs of the inspiration of the scriptures that have ever been in print. Being sustained, triumphantly, by the facts of the past, and judging the future by principles deduced from certain knowledge, we feel that our judgment, in most cases, will be found coincident with plain common sense views of things. That ill fed and wounded vanity may instigate the hostility to our work of small envy and jealousy, of pride of sect and self-inflated opinion, is what we expect to a small extent, and we rather court than shun such prejudiced enmity.

We have not combated the theories of other expositors to a great extent, because it was foreign to good manners, in some cases, to do so, and useless in others. In every instance where we differ from others, we do so because they do not strictly conform to past facts, and by consequence must err, proportionally, with reference to the future. In some cases, very exalted human authorities will be consulted against us; but we appeal, for support, to inspiration and to history, and refuse to yield to any sanctified human opinion that is not punctiliously in accordance with known truth. We claim to have discovered, that all old interpretations of one great era are either erroneous in whole or in part. Unknown to fame or to the famous, we appeal to common sense people, to read and decide our correctness, for on account of such we have written; we crave not the attention of chiefs and princes, but seek an humble place of consideration among the great Christian democratic PEOPLE throughout the world. Misfortune is the fate of discoverers and inventors generally, and we expect no exception will be made in our favor; yet, from a better sphere than this, we hope in triumph to descend at the appearing of the victory of God, and advent of that kingdom for which from infancy, each Christian child is daily taught to pray. If, then, some humble place be ours among the glorified, we shall be more than recompensed for all our years of bitter toil.

PART FIRST.

PROPHETIC HISTORY OF THE WHOLE WORLD.

CHAPTER I.

THE FIRST SPIRITUAL AND POLITICAL PROPHECY.

(This prophecy is found in the third chapter of Genesis.)

At the fall of the world, or rebellion of mankind against God, he determined upon their reduction to allegiance, and immediately declared war against his foes. From the nature of things, this war was of a double character, or spiritual and political. Man originally possessed, and still possesses, a spiritual nature, which makes him a religious creature, and also a social nature, which constitutes him a political being. From these two constitutional qualities has resulted the universality of some kind of religion and civil government. In a state of perfection, these two principles would have ultimated in true religion and true civil government. At the fall of man, the rejection of the true God as monarch in both of these departments, led to the wildest disorder and universal misery. It is also a truth, established by universal experience, that all civil governments among mankind have conformed in principle and practice to the genius of the prevailing religion of the people;

religion has controlled the politics of the world in all ages. If the religion has been mild, so has been the civil government; if it has been bloody and despotic, so has been the civil government; if it has been liberal and enlightened, so has been the civil policy. This has resulted from a law of nature, by which inferior things are controlled by superior; and as the spiritual nature of man exercises supreme power over his conduct in his individual capacity, so does it in his aggregated state. To subdue man, it was therefore necessary to subjugate his spiritual nature first; to regenerate him as a religious race, and then his political regeneration would follow inevitably.

A physical victory might have resulted in a moment from the weight of Omnipotence, but a moral victory could not thus speedily be obtained, from the eternal, and immutable, and self existent principles of moral agency. To the principles here stated, the great declaration of war by Jehovah is strictly conformed.

SECTION I.

Declaration of War.

"I will put enmity between thee and the woman; and between thy seed and her seed; HE* shall bruise thy head, and thou shalt bruise his heel."

This declaration is a generic history of the whole contest for dominion of the world, from the fall to the final victory of God. The serpent and the woman, though real persons, are nevertheless, in this passage, used as

---

* Clark's Comm.

metaphoric terms. Were this not so, the whole passage would be ridiculous. Six parties are embraced in the text. First, the serpent and the woman are placed antithetic to each other; second, the seed of the serpent, and seed of the woman, are also counterparts of each other; third, HE and the serpent's HEAD are also placed in antagonism to each other.

Between each of these antithetic pairs, direct hostility was to rage, and it is evident that the serpent, his head, and his seed, are all confederate; and that the woman, her seed, and HE, the Messiah, are also confederates. It is evident, also, that the head of the serpent controlled the powers represented by the serpent and his seed, and that HE, who stood opposed to the serpent's head, held also a similar supreme control over the powers represented by the woman and her seed. It will be granted, without any argument on our part, that the head of the serpent represented the great enemy of God, and seducer of man, called, in the New Testament, the Prince of the power of the air, and the Devil, and Satan. It will also be granted, that HE who was antithetic to Satan, was the second person of the Trinity, also called Immanuel, or Messiah. The serpent represents the false religion introduced by the Devil, and his seed represents the false system of civil government growing out of it. The woman represents the true religion introduced by Jehovah, and her seed represents the true system of civil government growing out of it. Our reasons for these positions are many, but chiefly the following:

First.—The terms, "serpent and his seed," and "woman and her seed," can not be understood literally. For this would make the serpent to be a generator of snakes, and bring Eve into a war with the serpent personally, and then her children and snakes would have a perpetual war, till Messiah should crush the head of the Father of Snakes. Such a view of the text would be the quintessence of absurdity. Again, the literal serpent who seduced Eve died long ago, but the text represents the serpent of which God spoke as existing at the final victory of Messiah.

Second.—As the head of the serpent was symbolic of something besides the symbolic serpent, this serpent differs from the Devil literally, and yet is called such from its paternal name, it being the creation of the real seducer of man. Now, as false religion is the first great scheme of the Devil, the serpent being next to its head is properly represented by it. And as the "seed" of the serpent is something different from the serpent itself, it must represent the civil polity generated from a false religion. No two things in the whole history of the world can be found to coincide with the serpent and his seed, but false religion, and false civil polity. Again, as the woman and her seed are antithetic counterparts of the serpent and his seed, they must coincide with the true church of God, and the true system of government arising from it. The utter impossibility of any other things being found to coincide with the woman and her seed, than those here stated, in consistency with the whole text, inevitably fastens the symbolic meaning of the text to them.

Third.—That the woman and her seed, and the serpent and his seed, severally represent the two departments of false and true government, is further evident from the consideration of the nature of all moral government. That man possesses a dual nature, a spiritual and a social, is a fact of which all are conscious. A sense of Deity exists naturally in all minds, and this becomes the basis of all religion. This sense does not necessarily imply a knowledge of the true God, but it leads all men to feel that themselves, and the world, are controlled by a superior power or powers. In enlightened countries it leads to the worship and acknowledgment of Jehovah, and in barbarous countries it is the source of endless superstition, a general belief in ghosts, witches, and inferior spirits, which men believe control them and their interests. The *dual law* of love supreme to God, and equal love of neighbors, called the great law of God, is conformed to these constitutional principles of all moral agents. This is the constitutional law of the universe, and the Decalogue based upon it is but the constitutional law of a single province of God's empire, as is our world. The great universal empire of God is therefore of a dual nature, and had not man sinned, this dual government would have prevailed in perfection in this world. In re-establishing the fallen empire of God on earth, these two departments would of course receive attention, and their existence, prophetically, would be recognized, and an elementary existence would necessarily be seen. The kingdom of Satan would also conform to the great dual nature of man, and antagonism to God's dual law, and would be manifested therefore in the dual form of Church and State, or spiritual and social government.

Fourth.—The Scriptures, from the beginning to the end, recognize the duality of God's kingdom, in its elementary stages, and prophetically in its triumphs; and also the duality of Satan's kingdom in the world. We will first trace those which coincide with the woman and her seed. These are seen in the persons of Shem and Japhet, one of whom was to give spiritual law, and the other to sway the political scepter of the world, under Christ. Next we see it in Sarah and Isaac; next in Moses and Aaron; next in the typical church of the Hebrews, and the civil government arising from it; next in Jachin and Boaz, the two typical pillars of Solomon's temple.

The prophets we find speaking of "the Lord's house, and the mountain of the Lord's house;" "Judah and Jerusalem;" "Judah and Ephraim;" Judah and Israel;" "Ariel," or "the double city, or two lions of God;" "the mountain and stone cut out of the mountain;" the Ancient of Days and his chariot throne; "the saints and people of the saints;" "the two olive branches;" "two candlesticks," or "two anointed ones," Joshua and Zerobabel; and the white horse and his rider receiving a crown; the temple and the altar; the holy city, or double city; the two witnesses, the two candlesticks, the two olive trees; the woman with twelve stars, and the sun and moon which clothed her, and her man child; "salvation and strength;" "the *kingdom* of our God, and *power* of his Christ;" "the Lamb and his company;" the company on the sea of *glass;* the man with a sickle on a white cloud; the man with many diadems on the white horse; the seven candlesticks and seven stars; the Lamb with seven horns and seven eyes; the four beasts and twenty-four wings; the twenty-four elders and twenty-four seats; the seven lamps and the sea of *glass;* and finally, the throne, covered with a rainbow, and him that sat upon the throne. Many other instances besides these might be quoted, but these suffice to show the fact we speak of. Next, the serpent and his seed have their coincidence in Ham and Canaan, Hagar and Ishmael, or the bondwoman and her son; the iron and clay of the great monarchy image; the ten horns and little horn of the fourth beast of Daniel; the willful king and the strange god; the seven-headed dragon and seven-headed beast; the great whore upon many waters; the Harlot Babylon upon the seven-headed beast from the pit; the beast from the pit and the old serpent; the false prophet and the image of the beast with the wounded head.

This double form of empire is seen wherever we look into political prophecy in the Bible, and this universality of its reference to church and state, shows that the woman and her seed and the serpent and his seed were antithetic symbols of religion and civil polity. As the serpent and his seed are antipodes of the woman and her seed, so Ham and Canaan are antipodes of Shem and Japhet; and the iron and clay are antipodes of the stone cut out of the mountain and the mountain itself; and the ten horns and little horn of the beast are antipodes of the Ancient of Days and his throne, or the saints and people of the saints; Hagar and Ishmael are antipodes of Sarah and Isaac; the dragon and beast with a wounded head are antipodes of the woman and her twelve stars; the spiritual and civil Gentiles are antipodes of the Holy City; and the beast and harlot are antipodes of the two witnesses.

Fifth.—A perpetual enmity has existed between true and false religion and between true and false civil government from the fall of man; and no such enmity has existed between any double correlated parties besides them; so that no significations can be assigned to the woman and her seed and the serpent and his seed other than those we ascribe to them. It has been supposed that the descent of Messiah from Eve was intended by the term "seed of the woman;" but this must be a mistake, for the term is antithetic to "seed of the serpent," and if the term implies but one person in the one case, it must imply the same in the other, which would make us look for a person descended from the serpent as an antipode to Messiah. The term HE, unquestionably refers to Messiah, and from its nature it indicates a connection with the human race, but no special promise of a Redeemer or atonement is found in the text, nor any injunction to offer sacrifices with prospective faith in a Redeemer. It therefore follows, in view of the sacrificial rites of Abel and his faith, that Adam's family received clear information of its duty, not recorded in the Bible, and the promise of God incarnate, must also have been given, yet no record is made of it by Moses.

SECTION II.

Mode of the World's Reduction — First Curse.

To reduce the world to allegiance, God determined upon a fourfold mode of warfare. The first was to afflict the material and animal creation. He therefore laid a curse upon the ground, and upon beasts, and upon woman, and the curse of severe labor upon man, and death upon all the human race. This curse or evil condition of the world must be carefully distinguished from the penalty annexed to transgression. A penalty can righteously be inflicted upon actual transgressors only but the curse falls upon animals, and infants, and idiots who are incapable of actual transgression. The pains of the penalty of spiritual death are suspended during man's probationary state. These temporal evils inflicted upon man's habitation were intended to produce the effect of repentance and return to God, just as want, woe, starvation, and humiliation led the prodigal son to return penitent to his father's house. This first curse not producing the desired effect sufficiently, a flood of waters destroyed the heavens and earth that remained, and man's days were greatly diminished. The second mode of warfare was the universal operation of God's spirit upon the minds of men, persuading them to obedience. St. Paul says of the universal world: " that which may be known of God is manifest in them, for God hath showed it unto them," and "the Gentiles which have not the (written) law do by nature the things contained in the law * * shew the work of the law written in their hearts." The third mode of warfare was by the preaching of the gospel, or by living oratory, persuading men to repent and unite themselves to God's cause. This last was added to the plan of war as soon as men were prepared by the experience of ages to profit by it. The fourth mode was to break down all barriers which might lie in the way of the preaching of the gospel. Here the agency of special providence is brought in, and the work of superintending nations, and confirming or breaking them to pieces, as the progress of God's cause might demand. A determination certainly was made to break down all civil governments not based upon the great laws of righteousness, and to supersede them by upright governments. This breaking down of unrighteous domination at the close of the war is a constant theme of the prophets, and is termed a day of judgment, or political doom, or the battle of the great day of God Almighty. It is an earlier period than the spiritual judgment, which succeeds it several centuries later.

SECTION III.

The Principles of God's Government.

God's government is essentially a theocratic democracy. Its principles necessitate in democracy among men, when disseminated and embraced. The great law of "love to neighbors as to self" is a law conferring equal rights among all citizens of the same government; it is diametrically opposed to human legitimacy, papacy, and absolutism; it is not conformable to hereditary aristocracy, nor can it be. It is democratic purely, and places all citizens of the same country upon a dead level as to right to rule, and confers exclusive favors upon none. God is, according to it, the only one that has a divine right to exercise kingship, and he is by consequence opposed to all human monarchy, and hates it as a feature of hell and the devil. In the first book of Samuel, we have the opinion of God and Israel about kings, and it is one of great repugnance on God's part and repentance on Israel's. Israel asked Samuel to make them a king, but he was displeased with the proposition, and prayed to God about it; and God replied to him, "they have not rejected thee but they have rejected me, that I should not reign over them. Now, therefore, hearken unto their voice; yet *protest* solemnly, and shew them the manner of the king that shall reign over them." After a king was chosen, God signified his displeasure by a terrible thunder storm in wheat harvest, and the people were greatly terrified. For Samuel said " I will call unto the Lord and he shall send thunder and rain, that ye may perceive and see that your wickedness is great, which ye have done in the sight of the Lord in asking you a king. * * And the people said unto Samuel, Pray for thy servants unto the Lord thy God that we die not; for we have added unto all our sins, this evil, to ask us a king."

By this choice of a king the Hebrew republic was changed into a hereditary monarchy, and God ceased to be their only king. From the passages of scripture just quoted, it is certain that God considers a human monarchy as exceedingly sinful, and as standing in direct hostility to himself, and he has but little patience with it. It is also obvious that in the recovery of the world to good government, in the progress of Christianity, that human monarchy will share no part or lot in the new organization. God is therefore hostile to human monarchy because the system is iniquitous in principle; and he will destroy it because of its wicked nature.

If it be replied, " the powers that be are ordained of God," we answer that this does not prove monarchy correct in principle, for God uses monarchy as he does other *curses*, for the sake of chastising evil people. Thus the king of Babylon punished the Tyrians, and Cyrus punished Babylon at God's instigation: and wicked nations need tyrants to punish them for their vice. God said "O, Israel, I will be thy king. I gave thee a king in mine *anger* and took him away in my wrath."—Joel 13. Monarchy is therefore a *curse* added to a vicious people, who are unworthy of freedom. In the spiritual and political redemption of the world, it therefore follows, that monarchy must be overthrown.

SECTION IV.

The Last Contest.

The text states that Messiah shall finally crush the head of the false system of worship and authority, or despotism, in church and state. This, of course, would end in the overthrow of the existing monarchies, and empire or state church establishments every where. In the progress of the war toward completion, it is reasonable to suppose that some one portion of the globe would be subdued to God before any other. The consequence of the prevalence of the gospel practically would be a government in such region, conformable to a bible democracy. As enmity was declared between false and true religion, and false and true government, such new organization would be hostile to all monarchy, and vice versa. It would also be the representative of bible democracy generally, and would be looked upon as its organic leader in the world, and when it became strong enough, it would be the belligerent representative of all true liberalists in the world, and espouse their cause. Such actually has been the case in the history of the war. In the progress of Christianity, in America, it has formed a great bible democratic constitution, which stands in belligerent attitude to all monarchy, and will strike for its oppressed brethren every where, and carry the great war to the bitter end.

CHAPTER II.

SECOND GENERAL PROPHECY.

This prophecy is found in the ninth chapter of Genesis: "And he said, cursed be Canaan, a servant of servants shall he be unto his brethren. Blessed be the Lord God of Shem; and Canaan shall be his servant. God shall enlarge Japheth; he shall dwell in the tents of Shem, and Canaan shall be his servant." This being a generic history of the world, it is descriptive of the state of mankind from the flood to the judgment. As these various curses and blessings could not transpire without the separate existence of the three races, their perpetual separateness is thereby guaranteed. When in the days of Peleg, "God divided to the nations their inheritance," we find that Asia fell to the Shemites, Europe to the Japhites, and Africa to the Hamites. These separate countries became great barriers to amalgamation. Additional ones of greater efficacy were ordered, as is seen in diversity of language, and in the three original colors, and other extreme anatomical differences of the races. The term Shem is used metonymically for the whole of his family, a part being put for the whole; and so, also, Japhet is put for all his race;

and Canaan, it would seem, in like manner, is also used as a metonymic representation of his father's house. As Japhet is called the elder, to him belonged birthright privileges. These were the scepter, the highest honors, and a double portion of the great estate of the world. Hence the Japhetic, or the white race, has been enlarged, and enjoys the gift of two continents, and is to control Asia. The great political sway of the world was also to be his. Neither Shem, nor Ham, were to share political equality in his dominion. Shem was to be next to Japhet as a blessed race, but to Ham no blessing was given, a general state of inferiority, and personal slavery in part, was to be his lot. The relation of Shem to Japhet was to be that of an inferior; and that of Ham, or a part of his family, was to be of a servant to two masters. The white race will never admit a general equality of political franchise to either Asiatics or Africans, and it would be ruinous for it to do so; and as for a general amalgamation, nature revolts at it, and God's providence has always prevented it, and will do so to the end. Indeed, political and social equality, without general amalgamation, would be impossible. In the physical features of the three great races, is seen a picture of the Trinity. In it the second race, or Hamitic, bears the form of a servant, as did the second person of the Godhead. In the moral features of Noah's family, Shem and Japhet coincide with the religion of truth and the civil law of uprightness; while Ham and Canaan coincide with the serpent and his seed, and with Hagar and Ishmael.*

---

* We had written some one hundred and fifty pages on these points, demonstrating by facts the positions here assumed, but find-

SECTION I.

Course of Empire.

In fulfillment of Noah's prediction, the scepter of empire, severally swayed by the three races, is now held by the Japhetic race. Nimrod, the grandson of Ham, refused to obey the order of settlement and dispersion given by God. He collected the people at Babel, and corrupted the religion of Shem, and became king of the state, and high priest of religion, and first instituted idolatry. He greatly oppressed the Shemites, seized upon their territories, and depressed the true religion. For a full account of these matters, see Clarke's Comm., Josephus, and Enc. R. K., &c. The Hamites, however, retained their ascendency for a little time only, for God at Babel confounded the language of *all* the earth, and dispersed the people in the directions originally ordered. The various tribes that were scattered existed under the sway of petty chiefs, who were dignified by the name of kings; their empire was often limited by the walls of an insignificant town; Egypt and Damascus are, at this period, most prominent in history. As population increased, the kings in Asia began to gain more extensive sway, till the empire of Nebuchadnezzar extended over three continents; its limits being the Atlantic on the west, India on the east, and Abyssinia on the south. His empire was followed by that of the Medes and

---

ing they would swell our work beyond its intended size, we concluded for the present to drop them out, and write a special work, devoted to these points alone.

Persians; the Medes being of Japhetic origin, and the Persians of Shemitic. This dominion was followed by the Grecian empire, and by the Roman, both of full blooded Japhetic origin. Thus the course of empire was from east to west. At the discovery of America, the north was settled by refugees from European tyranny, and principally by true Christians. A Christian empire has arisen here, with no king but God; and in the march of power has outstripped all nations, and will soon be the last seat of the world's empire. In this great contest of races for dominion, the black race and its varieties, all descended from Ham, early sunk into great inferiority and personal bondage to the other races, and so continues. The Shemitic, or yellow race, also, after it dropped the scepter of empire, ceased to improve, and is vastly inferior to the white race. Thus has the great prediction been thus far fulfilled with precision.

SECTION II.

The Millennial Empire.

As the Japhetic race was to be enlarged and blessed with dominion over the whole world, and as this prediction is not fully verified, something yet remains to be accomplished. Now, as the scriptures declare a Millennium shall exist before the final judgment, and as the prediction of Noah embraces the world up to that time, and as Japhet was to be ruler over all at some period, and as but about a thousand years remains, it follows that Japhet will sway the scepter during the Millenium. This position is further verified by later prophets whose political predictions are mostly limited to Europe and America. The position of the three races will be, Japhet first and head; Shem second; and Ham third. Equality of political rights will not be held in common by the three races during the Millennium. Japhetites will give political equality only to Japhetites; Shemites to Shemites; and Hamites to Hamites. This arrangement and no other will be indorsed by Providence. Perhaps some little variation from this order may obtain, but will not be general. The Millennium is a political era of Christian republicanism, confined mainly to the white race. As a government, it will extend over Europe and America, and control the rest of the world, and gradually elevate the other races.

SECTION III.

THE SECOND CURSE.

The first curse, consisting in deterioration of the ground, and in labor and death, not being adequate to repress great rebellion against God, he again cursed the earth by a flood of waters, and by a diminution of the length of mortal life, and by a new curse of labor upon one third of the human race. This general curse was however softened by a relief of labor to Shem and Japhet.

As the curse of labor was originally inflicted on the whole race to drive them to the rest of the Messiah, and as it was adapted to the character and constitution of man before the flood, so the heavier curse of labor, on a third part of the human race, was adapted to its constitution, and was needed by it to urge it to God and salvation. All evils inflicted on man are intended, in this life, to lead to reformation, so that no charge of injustice can be laid against God for inflicting greater evils upon one race than upon another, for God knows what is in man, and therefore knows what means are best to use to reform the world.

No doubt that much of the original curse upon the whole human race will be mitigated by Christianity and its effects upon art, science, intelligence, and liberality; and, by consequence, we may expect the black race ultimately to share in these blessings during the millennial state. The entire removal of the curse on the whole human family will not transpire until the heavens and earth are relieved from the original curses pronounced upon them. The resurrection will take place by the removal of the curse of death, and then all labor will cease forever, and all political inequality be dispensed with. But, until then, the curses, though softened, will still abide. Then the "voice from the throne" shall say, "Behold, I make all things new, and there shall be no more curse."

Japhet received the highest blessings from God; Shem was also blessed; and the voice of history has echoed the words of God, and declared that they were blessed; but Ham received *no blessing;* and earth repeats that he has been unblessed; to be unblessed of God is to be subject to his curse; a negative of God is equivalent to a positive with men.

CHAPTER III.

PANORAMA OF CHRISTIANITY AND OF THE WORLD.

SECTION I.

HEBREW SYSTEM TYPICAL OF CHRISTIANITY AND THE WORLD.

The whole Hebrew system is a typical one. It is chronologically divided into seven periods, beginning with the fathers, and ending with the kings. As a system of types, it possesses a double application. First: it represents the whole history of the world from Noah's times to the establishment of the final kingdom. Secondly: it represents the full history of Christianity from the first advent to the second, inclusive.

The first period is that of the fathers, embracing Isaac as a type of Christ; the second is that of the patriarchs, in which Judah was a type of Christ; the third is that of the descent into Egypt, and union of the Hebrew family with the throne, in which Joseph was a type of Christ; the fourth is the bondage of Israel, in which the infant Moses was a type of the infant Jesus; the fifth is the exodus and organization of a church and state in the wilderness, in which the lawgiver Moses was a type of the lawgiver Christ; the sixth is the conquest and settlement of Canaan, in which Joshua was a type of Christ; and the seventh is the period of royalty, in which David was a type of Christ.

1. To this picture, the seven periods of the world's

history sublimely correspond, or will correspond when the cycle of its woes and triumphs is complete.

The three fathers, Abraham, Isaac, and Jacob, coincide with Shem, Ham, and Japhet; the twelve patriarchs correspond with the twelve sons of Shem and Japhet, who were the heirs of the world; the descent into Egypt, and the regal association of the Hebrews, conform to the first great apostasy in the present earth, and the union of church and state at Babel under Nimrod, or the descent into spiritual Egypt and Sodom; the Hebrew bondage coincides with the universal bondage of the world under paganism, and its evils of political bondage. The exodus and giving of the law, and organization of the Levitical church under Moses, coincide with Jesus Christ, the call of the Gentiles to the liberty of the gospel, the gospel laws, and the organization of the church of the true Israel, or Christianity.

The conquest and republic in Canaan typified the conquest of absolutism, and the millennial republic in Europe and America, and its ascendency over the world. The completion of the conquest under the three kings, together with the royalty itself, coincide with the predicted conquest of the whole world, and the full establishment of the kingdom of God in the regenerated heavens and earth.

2. The three fathers typified the Holy Trinity, taught so plainly by the gospel; and the twelve patriarchs typified the twelve apostles.

The descent into Egypt and union with the Egyptian throne, coincide with the descent of spiritual Israel into spiritual Egypt, or the union of the church of Christ's Israel with the throne of the Roman empire.

The Hebrew bondage consequent upon the descent into Egypt coincides with the civil and spiritual bondage suffered by spiritual Israel, after the union of church and state. The exodus from typical Egypt, the crossing a sea, the overthrow of Pharaoh's host, the general thanksgiving, the organization of a republican confederacy of thirteen tribes, composed of three millions of people; the adoption of a written constitution by the tribes; the separation of the church and state departments, their freedom from control of one by the other; their laws of servitude and naturalization, and their full organization and deliverance under a noble leader, in a wilderness, have all a complete correspondence in the United States of America.

The conquest of Canaan, the overthrow of its monarchies in two great battles under Joshua, and the firm establishment of republicanism on both sides of Jordan, represent the conquest of Absolutism in Europe in two great battles, and the establishment of the millennial republic on both sides of the Atlantic, in the land promised to Japhet. The choice of a royalty by the Hebrews, and the full conquest of the land of promise, "from the river of Egypt to the Euphrates," coincide with that period predicted by Daniel, in which the saints shall take the kingdom, and give the kingdom and dominion to one like unto the Son of Man, who shall come to "the people of the saints" in the clouds of heaven.

These expositions will doubtless be new to every one, for no one has hitherto attempted to explain the Hebrew types as a system, and but few of the parts of the system have ever been interpreted and applied. The field before us, like others we have ventured to explore, is an untrodden one, and our views should therefore be neither received nor rejected without reason; they may be new, yet antiquity of opinions does not prove their truth, nor is novelty always proof of error. Our expositions here harmonize most beautifully with our expositions of the prophets and doctrines of the bible, which would be impossible unless they were correct in all points, for error can not be harmoniously systematized.

We are now in honor bound to show some fair reasons for these views, and we hope shall be as satisfactory to reasonable minds as the nature of the case will admit. In order to prove our points, we must possess some rule for testing a type, or of distinguishing it from an accidental resemblance.

"A type is an example, pattern, or general similitude to a person, event, or thing which is to come." The term type is sometimes synonymous with that of symbol. It then is "an abstract or compendium, a sign or representation of something moral by the figures or properties of natural things." Among theological writers we find no complete rule laid down by which to identify types. Some things have been written upon them, but nothing very satisfactory to a thorough inquirer. Having, therefore, no rule given us by others by which to be guided, we offer the following as truthful and sufficient:

1. Those things, persons, or events in the ages prior to Christianity which were expressly arranged by immediate divine interference, either by remarkable providences or by miracle, may be regarded as types or symbols.

2. It is, and has been universally conceded in all ages of Christianity, that the whole Hebrew dispensation,

together with the preceding dispensations to Noah and Adam, were typical dispensations, rather than realizing ones.

3. Those events, persons, and things in the dispensations prior to Christianity, and which have had their exact counterparts in the Christian dispensation, must be regarded as types. No accidental resemblances can ever be considered as types, for our principles require that the events or persons or things in the Christian age to be regarded as antitypes, must have resemblance not only in character but in the order of sequence. The typical dispensation being a system stretching over ages, its several types follow each other in regular order, and in the realizing age, the counterparts of the several types must follow each other in the same regular order.

4. Whatever the scriptures affirm to be a type, must be esteemed such.

With these principles, our interpretation will be found fully to coincide.

The three fathers were expressly arranged as a trinity by miraculous power or providence. Abram was divinely called to enter Canaan; Isaac was born by miraculous interposition; and Jacob was born in answer to the prayer of Isaac. Isaac, as the second person of this trinity of fathers, was offered as the only begotten son of his father on Mt. Moriah, and thus clearly typified the offering of the only begotten Son of God by his father. As Abram received Isaac as from the dead, and thus occurred the type of the resurrection of Christ, and of the dead in general, so God received Jesus from the dead, and he became the first fruits of them that slept.

The limiting of the fathers to the number three, shows that it was an intentional limitation, and being in a typical dispensation, plainly confirms the number as typical. Of course we are to look in the plan of redemption for the counterpart trinity of heads of a race. This counterpart or antitype is found only in the trinity of the three heads of the human race and in the divine trinity. The coincidence being perfect in each case, the type is realized in each. The humiliation of Ham, of Isaac, and of Christ is a trinal coincidence and wonderfully correct. The twelve patriarchs being a number clearly ordered by God, was unquestionably typical, and as every one subscribes to this truth, we need not argue the question. We therefore look into the plan of redemption to find its antitype, which must coincide in number of persons and in exact order of sequence after the three heads of a race. The sons of Shem, Ham, and Japhet were the natural inheritors of the promises to the three fathers, but as the sons of Ham were given to Japhet and Shem, as servants, the heirship of the world fell to the twelve sons of Shem and Japhet. The heirs of the three typical fathers in the above twelve heirs of the world find a striking coincidence. The twelve apostles chosen as the especial heirs of the kingdom of the Divine Trinity also plainly coincide with the twelve patriarchs. Christ said to the twelve apostles, that when his kingdom was fully established they should eat and drink at his table in his kingdom, and sit on twelve thrones judging the twelve tribes of Israel. The term *judging* here used, has the sense of ruling or administering government; and the term Israel, means all the seed of Abraham redeemed by Christ, or all of the redeemed of the world.

The descent into Egypt of the seventy souls of the patriarchs and families, finds its coincidence in order and character of events, in the submission of the true people of God to the sway of Nimrod, and of the union of church and state under Constantine and Justinian.

The union of Jacob's family with Pharaoh's in the throne of Egypt was divinely arranged, and it was really the union of the Hebrew Church with the Egyptian State: in this union the church was inferior to Pharaoh in the throne. The particulars of the coincidence between this union of church and state are not so clearly marked under the monarchy of Nimrod in history, but the fact of the subjection of God's people to him in the throne is as clear; and had we a full history of the matter, we might find the coincidence minutely perfect.

The empire of Rome, St. John says, is "spiritually called Sodom and Egypt," and the descent of the Christians into union with Rome is therefore a clear counterpart or antitype of the union of the Hebrew Church with Egyptian royalty. For the likeness is perfect as to events, and the chronological order of the events is relatively the same.

The bondage of the Hebrews in Egypt finds also a double coincidence in time and character in the world's great history and in the history of Christianity.

From the days of subjection to Nimrod, the people of the world have been in general bondage to regal governments and to Satan's spiritual power; and while one race of men have been bondmen, all have been servants of sin and Satan, as subjects of political and spiritual despotisms. The task-masters of the Hebrew heirs of promise, find their correspondence in the kings and princes of the earth.

In the union of church and state, true religion was soon at a discount, and all the true seed of Abraham were grievously persecuted or destroyed. The destruction of the Hebrew infants was comparative kindness to the extensive butcheries of the children of truth in spiritual Egypt and Sodom.

The deliverance from bondage, the constitutional law, and the journey or probation under the law in the wilderness, find a double and sublime counterpart: 1. In the appearance of Christ as a second Moses, the new constitutional law he promulgated, and the long wilderness-like probation of his people in past ages. 2. In the passage of the sea by Christ's people, to the land of enlargement promised by God to Japhet, the establishment of the Christian constitution of the United States, and the testing of the ability of the people to uphold it, and be happy under it.

The reader will not fail to note that the coincidence of the history of Israel with the world's general history, is seen principally in the larger features of the Hebrew system, and that in the narrower diameter of the Christian era the coincidence between Hebrew and Christian history is seen in a greater number of points. That Moses and Christ coincide, the scriptures affirm; and that the plan of the redemption of the world taught by Jesus Christ, began an exodus from spiritual and political bondage, which will ultimate in the release of the world, as Israel was released from Egypt, every one admits. The probation in the wilderness was needed to accustom the people to new laws based upon democratic principles, and the democratic principles of Christianity needed to be tried by the world a long season, in order to be appreciated, and ultimately adhered to with tenacity. Hence we read that "the woman fled into the wilderness from the face of the dragon for a time times and half a time."

The ceremonial law, given in connection with the moral and political law or constitution, is affirmed by scripture to have been typically illustrative of the Christian system. The book of Hebrews gives the philosophy of the ceremonial law, and teaches that the whole Hebrew economy was "a shadow of good things to come," "a figure for the time then present."

As therefore the bondage was followed by the scheme of Israel's redemption, so the universal bondage of the world was followed by the scheme of the world's redemption. When Israel sighed by reason of oppression, and was willing to change its condition, and called to mind the promises, then a deliverer came; and when the world sighed for relief, and was willing to hear of a change, then a calm filled the earth, and expectation looked for some great event; then angels heralded the "desire of all nations," and the star of the east hung over Bethlehem.

Secondly; the exodus from Egyptian bondage, the organization of a democratic confederacy, and the probation under it till the conquest of Canaan, were typical of the exodus of the Christians and liberalists from spiritual Egypt to America, their organization of the democratic confederacy of the United States, and their probation under a democracy up to the time of the conquest of absolutism and the Millennium.

The coincidences between these two great periods are more numerous than between any other typical and antitypical period whatever, excepting that of the same typical period and the epoch of Christianity. We may premise here, that it should be specially recollected that like things always typify their like: thus, a person used as a type typifies a person; an event typifies an event; a thing typifies a thing; a country typifies a country; a period typifies a period; a church typifies a church; a state typifies a state; a bondage typifies a bondage; a deliverance typifies a deliverance; a probation typifies a probation; a war typifies a war; a priest typifies a priest, and a king typifies a king.

We now notice, more at large, the points of correspondence between the Hebrew period of deliverance and the Christian period.

1. The children of "the free woman," or Hebrews, were freed by the exodus from the servitude of Egypt; and so the children of the free woman or Christian liberalists, were, by the great exodus to America, freed from the bondage of "spiritual Egypt and Sodom." Let it ever be fixed in the mind, that Christians are the seed of Abraham, or the free woman, and full heirs of the promises.

2. The Hebrews were pursued by the oppressor, and he was vanquished; and so the liberalists were pursued by the oppressor, and he was vanquished.

3. The Hebrews crossed a sea to get rid of bondage, and so did the Christians in coming to America.

4. The Hebrews sought the land promised to their paternal head, and so the Christians, in their exodus to America, came to the land promised to Japhet, their paternal head.

5. At the destruction of the Egyptian tyrant's forces, Israel decreed a general thanksgiving to God, and so when the modern Pharaoh was defeated, a general thanksgiving was decreed by the American Congress. Songs and shouts, and all the demonstrations of exultation, joined with Miriam to celebrate Jehovah's name, and so songs and shouts, bonfires, illuminations, ringing of bells, tears of rapture, devout worship, and lofty thanksgiving celebrated the same Jehovah's praise through all our land. The Hebrew exodus was a short period, but the American one extends from 1607 to 1783.

6. According to Dr. Adam Clarke, and others, the number of the Hebrews that escaped from bondage was about three millions; and the number of people in the revolutionary colonies, in 1776, was about three millions.

7. The sea was frozen when the Hebrews reached the safe side, and the Pilgrim Fathers found a frozen sea, and a snow covered shore, when they landed in America. This may or may not have been an accidental, and not a providential correspondence.

8. The Hebrews were organized as a confederacy of thirteen tribes, and so there were thirteen colonies providentially organized into a Christian confederacy. Israel's tribes are called twelve, but out of Joseph there sprung two tribes who received an inheritance, thus making thirteen. It is also remarkable, that William Penn was proprietor of two colonies, Pennsylvania and Delaware. As Joseph was imprisoned, and yet had a double and birthright portion on account of his virtue, so William Penn suffered imprisonment for his virtue,

and yet had a double portion of the great anti-typical Israel.

9. The Hebrew exodus was into a wilderness which was to be inherited as a part of the promised land; and so the exodus of the Christians was to a wilderness, which was a noble portion of Japhet's promised inheritance.

10. The Hebrew confederacy was organized into a "more perfect union" after the exodus, by adopting a written democratic constitution: and so the confederate colonies, after the war of independence, "in order to form a more perfect union," adopted a written representative democratic federative constitution. The Hebrew constitution was submitted to the tribes for acceptance and ratification; and so was the American constitution. It is not a little remarkable, that the Hebrew and American constitutions are the only two written ones ever known to have been adopted at the birth of any nationality, prior to 1776.

11. The Hebrew nationality grew out of the Hebrew church, or the seed of Abraham; and so the American nationality grew out of the Christian church, and the seed of Abraham. All of the Americans were not Christians at the framing of the constitution, and so were not all of the Hebrews pious, as their culpable unbelief shows. Yet the unbelieving Hebrews enjoyed the same political benefits as did the faithful, and so it was with the Americans. About one hundred and forty-four thousand Christians were in America at the Revolution, yet the prevalence of Christian maxims and principles was universal, and the virtuous political principles avowed by the Christians were adopted by all classes.

12. Church and state were disunited by the Hebrew constitution and placed in the relation of associates. The church was debarred, as a church, from exercising direct control in civil affairs, and so it was in the American constitution. Many persons have either ignorantly or willfully mistaken the relations which the Hebrew church and state held to each other. Some mistakes may have occurred on account of the fact, that, as some laws were alike political and spiritual, it was supposed consequently that all laws were so. The Sabbath, the Sabbatic and jubilee years, and the rite of circumcision, were regulations of both a spiritual and secular nature. But with us the Sabbath illustrates the case of these laws, for we regard it as both a sacred and a secular institution: as a secular institution, its observance is compelled as a day of repose to wearied nature, and to prevent oppressors from grinding the poor to death by ceaseless toil; and also to give vigor to the general operations of society by the universal refreshment it bestows. The civil arm has with us no right to compel its observance as a spiritual institution, and should have none. Precisely so was it in the Hebrew law. The civil power was not the head of the Hebrew church, as the monarchs of Rome, Russia, and England have been of the Roman, Greek, and English churches. Neither the Shaphetim nor kings of Israel could appoint a high priest of the church; nor could the priesthood compel the paying of tithes, or the offering of sacrifices, nor require the secular arm to do it. In spiritual matters the Hebrew was responsible only to God and to the ecclesiastical law of the church, and was in no way responsible to civil authority for his spiritual conduct.

Now the United States Constitution puts religion in just the same relation to civil authority that God ordered it, in the days of Moses.

The disunion of church and state is the great prophetic epoch of liberty and progress according to both Daniel and St. John. It is the beginning of the end of despotism, and when it fully prevails the "time of the end" will close, and despotism will forever cease on earth.

The two separate departments of religion and politics in the Hebrew confederacy exactly coincide with these two departments in our country.

13. The political offices of the Hebrews were elective, and not hereditary, and so it is in our government.

14. Their government was not originally an aristocratic republic; the people decided in general assembly all questions of war, treaties, and peace, and Moses always appealed to the whole, and not to the few aristocrats, to accept or reject his propositions. Josephus says it was an aristocratic republic, but it is plain that he must speak of the executive department of the government, and not of the legislative. We might in a similar manner call our government an aristocratic republic. The term aristocratic meant, anciently, the *best;* it now signifies, in an odious sense, the *worst.*

15. The people of Israel chose God as their only king, and renounced allegiance to all other monarchs by acclamation, and so did the people of the United States.

16. The Hebrew constitution recognized the institution of Hamitic bondage, and so does the American constitution.

17. The Hebrew constitution forbade foreigners ever becoming supreme magistrates, and so does the American

18. The Hebrew constitution provided for the naturalization of foreigners, and so does the American, but not so strictly.

These coincidences between the exodus of Israel and that of the Christians, are of the most extraordinary nature if we take them singly, but when taken together they are nothing less than miraculous.

The sixth period of Hebrew history, which includes the conquest of Canaan and establishment of the republic, coincides with the sixth period of the world, and the sixth of Christianity, or with the Millennium. The great points in this period particularly noticeable are these: first, the conquest of Canaan was completed by two great battles; secondly, the conquest of Canaan under Joshua and the Judges did not embrace all of the promised land. The promise extended from the river of Egypt to the Euphrates, and was not realized till the days of Solomon. The prophets assure us that the monarchies of the Japhetic race shall be broken in two great battles at the conquest by Liberty, and hence the war for possession of Canaan by republican Israel, coincides with the predicted war of the Christian republicans for possession of the territories of Japhet, and the two great battles and victories of Joshua coincide with the two predicted battles in the war for liberty. These two battles are pointed out by St. John in the 14th chapter of Revelation, and in other places.

The first is indicated by "One like unto the Son of Man" on a white cloud who "thrust in his sickle on the earth and the earth was reaped;" and the second by the reaping of the vine of the earth, and its being cast into the wine press without the city, and the blood coming out of it "even unto the horse bridles, by the space of sixteen hundred furlongs." And again John says, that three agencies went forth to gather all the kings of the earth to the battle of the great day of God Almighty, and that they assembled at a place called Armageddon. He then, after a short episode, describes the United States and the attack of the confederate kings upon it, and states that the beast or Russian power was taken, and that Great Britain or the False Prophet was taken at the same time. The reaping of the earth signifies the destruction of European monarchy, and the reaping of the vine indicates the dreadful flow of blood at the fall of the British throne. As all thrones in Canaan fell before carnal Israel to make room for the republic, so all thrones must fall before Christian Israel to make room for the great millennial republic.

Let sceptics smile at our simplicity in writing the doom of European thrones: yet let them be serious as they hear Daniel the prophet saying, "I beheld till the thrones were cast down," and "became like the chaff of the summer threshing-floors, and the wind carried them away, and there was no place found for them."

The world was promised to Abraham as truly as was Canaan, and Canaan was but typical of the world.

A country typifies a country, and a people typifies a people; and so the blacks of Canaan under a curse, represented mankind depraved and under a curse, and spread over the whole earth promised to "the children of the free woman." The conquest of a large part of Canaan was, therefore, typical of the conquest of a large portion of the earth; and as a republic typified a republic, the commonwealth established in a great part of

Canaan, typifies a commonwealth erected over a great part of the earth. Now, the Millennium is clearly a state of the world in which a portion of it only is embraced under the realizing blessings of civil and religious republicanism, as we shall hereafter show. The state of the world after the Millennium, has generally been confounded with it.

The seventh period of Hebrew history coincides with the seventh of the world and of Christianity. This period is that in which the republic was changed to a monarchy by the universal voice of the people. During the reign of a trinity of monarchs, the promised land was all taken from the foe, a capital of the kingdom was selected, and a temple of transcendent glory was raised, and the Hebrews attained the zenith of splendor.

As like typifies its like, this royalty typified a royalty, and the full conquest, under it, of all the typically promised land, typified the full conquest of the world under the final royalty of Christ.

Now, prophecy declares that the people shall at last give up the government of the world to the Son of Man, who shall come in the clouds of heaven, and that he shall destroy all the wicked, shall renew the world, and reign for ever among men. It further says that the capital of the redeemed world shall descend out of heaven to the earth; and it will hold the same relation to all the world that old Jerusalem did to Canaan.

We have now briefly pointed out the great coincidences between the seven periods of the world from Noah to the final redemption, and the seven periods of Christianity. We have by no means descended to notice the minute resemblances between Christianity and Hebraism as religious type and anti-type, which fully accord with our expositions; we have refrained from touching them for want of space, and because they have been largely set forth by others.

We might have gone further, perhaps, in pointing out the coincidence of the later Hebrew history with Christianity, but shall hereafter advert to it.

One point more and we shall close these coincidences. It may be inquired why we have a right to give seven periods to Hebrew history rather than any other number. To this query we reply, first, that the periods we have given are plainly great ones, and are marked out as such by nature or providence. Secondly, each of these periods is also marked by a clear type of Messiah. Thus in the first period, that of the fathers, Isaac was clearly a type of Christ. In the second, or that of the patriarchs, Judah was a type of Christ. The scepter was not to depart from Judah, nor a lawgiver, until Shiloh came, and he was to be the "Lion of the tribe of Judah." In the third period, Joseph is called "the Shepherd, the Stone of Israel," and is allowed by all to prefigure Christ most graphically. In the fourth period, the infant Moses prefigures the infant Jesus. As Pharaoh decreed the destruction of Hebrew infants, so did Herod; and as Moses was providentially preserved, so was Christ; and as Moses came unto his own and they received him not, so did Christ. In the fifth period, Moses, as a prophet, declares that he was a type of our Lord; and in the sixth period, Joshua prefigured Jesus according to St. Paul, and in the seventh period, David was certainly the type of his Son Jesus.

SECTION II.

Philosophy of the Hebrew System.

The Hebrew system being typical of the plan of the world's redemption, the philosophy of its history becomes the philosophy of the world's redemption.

The Hebrew system was the preparative of Christianity. It filled but a small space in the world, though it was long in its duration. It was not an aggressive system upon the world at large; its area of action was a mere patch of the great globe, a quiet oasis in the bosom of the limitless desert around it; it was a star, which in the darkened heavens moved slowly before the coming of the sun it presaged; it was the shadow thrown forward by the coming throne of God; the dim but true outline of the age that was approaching; it was the mirage picture of the world, through all ages. We may here observe that all Christians agree that the Hebrew dispensation was not a realizing one, excepting as it was such incidentally.

The land of Canaan was a land of promise, therefore, only as a type of the world; and as it was promised to Abram, so the world was promised to Christ. That Abram understood the promise of Palestine as a typical one, is evident from the nature of the case, and from the express declarations of scripture. St. Paul says, of Abram, Isaac, and Jacob, and multitudes of the ancient believers, that "These all died in the faith, not having received the promises. But now they desire a better country; wherefore God is not ashamed to be called their God, for he hath prepared for them a city.

For he (Abraham) looked for a city which hath foundations, whose builder and maker is God." Here the inheritance of Canaan is clearly seen not to be the realization of the promise of God to Abram and his seed, but a mere shadow of "an enduring substance," and of "a better inheritance." The modern writers on the prophecies claim that Palestine is all that God ever promised to Abram, and thus they circumscribe the promises of the world's regeneration within a nutshell, and carnalize them all. For such narrow and antiscriptural tenets we have no charity; they are earthy, sensual, supercilious, heady, and degrading; they are too derogatory to the character of the Savior of a *world* to be entertained for a moment.

As Abraham had a claim on Palestine when he had no family to occupy it, so Christ had a claim to the world when he had no seed as yet to possess it; and as the accursed seed of Ham in the mean time piratically occupied Canaan, so the accursed seed of the serpent possessed the world.

To occupy Canaan, the seed of Abraham must increase in numbers sufficient to be organized into a nation; and so to possess the world, the children of Messiah must increase in numbers sufficient to be organized into a nationality strong enough to conquer and govern it; and as God expressly promised nationality to Abraham's carnal seed, so did he equally promise nationality to the seed of Christ, or Abraham's spiritual seed. The division of Abraham's seed into a confederacy of twelve states, or tribes, seems to have conformed to the twelve divisions of the world, and of the material and spiritual universe, and of the final kingdom.

To keep the seed of Abraham unmixed with foreign blood, the rite of circumcision was instituted, and the race was of a fair, or white complexion.

A rapid increase of population was also desirable, and also a firm unity of the confederate tribes.

These two great ends were readily accomplished by the four hundred years' bondage in Egypt.

When the family of Abraham was small, and wandered in Palestine and claimed its territory, the hostility of powerful foes would easily be engendered, and they might easily have become the prey of powerful adversaries, or their unity might have been early lost. To prevent these evils, and "to save much people alive," God provided them a shelter and protector in the powerful monarchy of Egypt. In Egypt the climate was highly favorable to fecundity, and to the support of a large population; it being a tropical country, and luxuriant in food. In addition to these things, they were made the slaves of the country, and thus, from the effects of labor, they multiplied but the more rapidly.

Such was the rapidity of their increase, that seventy persons had a posterity of three millions in four hundred years. No other instance of such rapid multiplication of our species can be found in any age.

Again, as the Hebrews were originally shepherds, they were an abomination to the Egyptians, and, of course, an amalgamation of Hebrew and Egyptian blood would not take place while a mutual antipathy existed between them. In addition to this, as the Hebrews were foreigners, and spoke a different language, had a widely different religion, and rites, and mode of worship; as they hated idolatry, and were of a different color from the Egyptians, and as the Egyptians were exceedingly cruel to them, they must have despised each other most cordially, so that a common fusion between them was rendered morally impossible. The Hebrews being common sufferers, would naturally possess common sympathies, and, of course, would be confederated by the strongest of all human ties, and would be ready to make common cause against their oppressors. The very existence of the Hebrews having grown more and more bitter as they multiplied, they at length became ripe for revolt from bondage, and ready to set up an independent government of their own.

Had their condition been an easy one in Egypt they would never have consented to leave it for Canaan. We find that few of the Babylonian captives ever returned to Canaan, on account of the ease they enjoyed in Babylon. The Hebrews in Egypt had also learned to hate every thing in the shape of monarchy, and longed for unrestrained freedom, so that they were in a pretty good state of mind to embrace a democracy. Their religion had been very simple in its ordinances, and in connexion with their great exodus from bondage they were prepared to receive one that was more gorgeous and imposing than that of the hated Egyptians.

Prepared as they were in feeling and wishes for a free commonwealth, they were yet unfitted for it practically. It was therefore needful that a provisional republic should be established under a dictator, and that they should serve a probation under the new constitution and under the oversight of a wise and truly patriotic leader. Hence we easily see the reason for the forty years' probation in the wilderness.

In the early part of this period the people were wild and extravagant in their action, and were at times ready to return to Egyptian despotism, but in the end the ultraists were calmed down, and all found the new "yoke easy and its burden light." As soon as the experiment had proved successful they were ready to enter Canaan and sustain the republic permanently. As Canaan was full of squatters and land-pirates, its possession was necessarily to be gained by force. Now as Israel had a divine right to the soil, he had an unquestionable right to occupy it, and as there was no arbiter in the case, an appeal to force was right and expedient and absolutely necessary. When states belong to a common confederacy they must appeal to the general government to secure their rights, but when no such general government exists, then nations must gain their rights by their own arm; they must redress their wrongs by the sword when none will arbitrate justly. Israel had a right to the soil of Canaan, a divine and unrelinquished right; he had been forced by famine to quit it for a season, and while gone after bread he had been seized and enslaved, and therefore his title to Canaan was strictly valid, and as none would give him possession of his patrimony it was righteous in him to lay hold of it *vi et armis*.

To such as deny God's right in the soil, our view will seem preposterous: and some would say, "Let Israel do without his patrimony rather than go to war, and leave the matter with God and he will settle it at last." Such talk is all fustian. Nations are temporal existences, their rewards and rights and punishments are as nations, all this side hell and heaven, and as God pointed out the sword to Israel to gain his divine rights as a nation, so he points it out to all other nations in the same condition.

The bible teaches us as individuals under the same government to do good to our enemies, and yet it requires us to have them brought to punishment for the common good of society. To make an enemy do right is no evidence of a want of love to him, provided we do not do it from pure hatred of him, rather than of his wickedness. So to make wicked nations and tyrants do right is no proof of want of true love to their souls, even if we have to break their power to atoms. God commands us to sanctify war.

As the commonwealth of Israel was composed of two departments, viz., the church and the state, and as like typifies its like, the church of Israel typified the Christian church, and the Hebrew state typified the Christian state, and both together typified the Christian commonwealth that was to rise in 1776, and to be completed by the Millennium. If we trace the rise of Christianity into a great free government in America we shall find the philosophy of its history in a *fac-simile* of the rise of the Hebrew confederacy in its great elements.

As the Hebrew people were at first few and feeble, so were the Christians; as the twelve families of Jacob were united into a family confederacy, so were the different branches of the family of Christ united into a great confederacy as early as the third century, and as a social government existed in embryo among the Hebrew families, so did a great social government in like manner exist among the Christians.

As the Hebrews found protection from destruction, and enjoyed repose for a while from union with the throne of Egypt, so did the Christians find repose from the attack and destruction of their foes by a union with the throne of spiritual Egypt.

As the climate and soil of Egypt, together with its bondage, served to produce finally a numerous and hardy race of people, so the country of Europe especially was favorable soil for the growth of Christianity, and the hard bondage of spiritual Egypt served but to mold into the noblest form the souls of the advocates of liberty and true religion. As the customs of the Hebrews were an abomination to the Egyptians, so the religious rites and customs of the faithful and spiritual circumcision were, and still are, an abomination to spiritual Sodom. As common suffering in Egypt produced a common sympathy, and cemented the common brotherhood into a resolve to unite to sustain a common cause, so a common lot as sufferers led the faithful to sympathize with each other, and to coalesce in union to sustain common liberty and independence.

Freedom is but a common body, as truly as true religion; if you strike one member, all of the others sympathize with it. Let the cry of the oppressed in any portion of the old world reach America, and every one of its millions of nerves are agitated, and all its pulses beat with excitement and indignation.

As the climax of the sufferings of the Hebrews rallied them around their leader for deliverance, so the climax of oppression on the American colonies instantly united them by elective and electric affinity. It was then that separate and independent provinces were melted like ingots of gold into a state of common fusion, or were welded like bars of steel by the fire and the hammer of despotism. And as the pride of Pharaoh wrought unwittingly the release of Israel, so the pride of monarchy brought out the stars of the great western constellation into the heavens of liberty.

As Israel entered a wilderness to stand its probation under a new constitution, so the advocates of civil and religious freedom entered the American wilderness to try the fortunes of a great republic. As Israel elected God for its King, so did America; as Israel was prepared to conquer Canaan by its discipline, and to maintain a great republic, so the United States in the wilderness is preparing to dash the great image of autocracy to atoms, and to establish the Millennium. As Israel had its judges or shaphetim, or chief magistrates, nominated by God and allowed by the people, so the people of our country choose their own executives.

As many people in the American colonies were not pious, and yet approved of the liberty taught by Christianity, so many of the Hebrews were unbelieving in the religion of Moses, and yet approved and contended for the justness of constitutional liberty. Those who imagine that anti-typical Israel was to be composed of pure and holy men altogether, are greatly mistaken. On this principle, the Hebrew church, as a type, would have required that every member of the anti-typica. or Christian church should have been holy. As the church of typical Israel possessed true doctrine, though many who belonged to it were impure, so the commonwealth of anti-typical Israel possesses the true doctrine of human government, though many who enjoy its benefits are not true Christians. In the end of time the angels shall gather out of the government of anti-typical Israel, or "*out of the kingdom, all things that offend, and them that do iniquity.*"

The growth of freedom, spiritual and civil, is necessarily gradual, as is the growth of an oak from an acorn. Men generally over the world, in past ages, and two thirds of them in the present age, have been, and are, as unfit for republicanism as the wicked are for heaven. It is a received maxim, that "the best form of government for any people, *is the best that its present moral and social condition renders practicable.*" A democracy can not exist without a high state of morals and intelligence blended together; we repeat it, they must both exist together. Their general attainment, at the greatest speed, must be comparatively slow. The general prevalence of democracy over the whole earth, will, therefore, be gradual, and will be attended in its march with the total extinction of some inferior races, as for instance, the Mexicans, and islanders of the Pacific. Europe is in a better state to receive republicanism than Asia or Africa, and yet Europe is far below the standard of the requirements of the case. Morality and intelligence are there retarded by the union of church and state, or by civil and spiritual monarchy. These barriers must be broken before Europe can move another step toward republicanism. It must be fused by the melting bolts of universal revolution, and its dross be thrown off like the cinders of a blast furnace, before it can hope for much. It must then have a great leading power, in whom it can repose confidence, as a guide to republican exaltation. No guide in such a case can be safe, but one who has tried the experiment on a grand and successful scale. America, therefore, is the natural hope of European freedom. The pilgrims of liberty, crowned with fortune and glory, will return, freed from tears, and share their salvation with the brothers left in bondage behind them. The child of sorrows, in the day of his splendor, will send the wings of an eagle to cover the retreat of his orphan sister, from the serfdom of Sodom.

SECTION III.

COLLATERAL TYPES.

In the Hebrew system are several collateral types or symbols not unworthy of consideration.

Of these we mention specially, Hagar and Ishmael, Sarah and Isaac, Moses and Aaron, the Hebrew church and state associated, and the two pillars of the temple, Jachin and Boaz. These were dual types of the dual government to come on earth.

1. *Hagar and Ishmael.* These were typical of the serpent and his seed, or of the religious and civil power of Satan. "For it is written, Abraham had two sons; the one by a bondmaid, and the other by a free woman. He who was of the bondwoman was born after the flesh; but he of the free woman was by promise. Which things are an allegory; for these are the two covenants; the one from Mt. Sinai, which gendereth to bondage, which is Agar. For this Agar is Mt. Sinai in Arabia, which answereth to Jerusalem, which now is, and is in bondage with her children. Now we brethren, as Isaac was, are the children of promise. As then, he that was born after the flesh persecuted him that was born after the spirit, even so it is now."

Here the free and the bondwoman are said to figure the two covenants, or the religion of dead works, or of Satan, and the religion of faith in Christ.

The two sons of these women, also, are said to be figures; and of course are different in signification from the women. If we now look at the original affirmation of God to the serpent, we find that Sarah and Isaac coincide with "the woman and her seed," and that Hagar and Ishmael coincide with the serpent and his seed, and, by consequence, they severally represent the two departments of the kingdom of God, and the two departments of the kingdom of Satan.

2. We see again the two departments of the kingdom of God represented by Moses and Aaron, who were the respective heads of the two departments of the commonwealth of Israel. As the kingdom of Israel was really a kingdom of God, and as it was typical of the final kingdom of Israel, its two departments must have their respective parallels in the coming kingdom, otherwise the type would be an imperfect one, which would be an unanswerable supposition.

3. The two pillars of the porch of Solomon's temple were typical, for all the parts of the temple were so, and as there is nothing with which they coincide except the dual law and dual government of God, it follows that they represented these. Indeed, the duality of such a multitude of symbols, in the scripture, all referring to the plan of salvation, is an insuperable argument from analogy to prove that God intended prominently to present the dual character of his kingdom.

4. The bondage of the Hamitic race in the family of Abraham, and the Hebrew commonwealth, were alike

typical of the final inferiority of Satan's power at the possession of the world by Christianity.

Hagar and Eliezer, the one an Egyptian and the other a Damascene, were of the Hamitic, or accursed race, so were all the bondmen of the Hebrews. This truth is deducible from the fact, that Hagar, the Egyptian, was a bondmaid, and, with her son, typified the old covenant of works.

It is not a little remarkable, that the family of Ishmael, like that of Jacob, was divided into twelve branches, from his twelve sons. "Their hand against every man," is a faithful portraiture of the sin-power of Satan.

CHAPTER IV.

ISRAEL RESTORED IDENTICAL WITH THE UNITED STATES.

The proposition of the world's redemption was stated to Adam; the divisions of the subject were announced by Noah; the subdivisions were treated of by succeeding prophets; fulfillment has illustrated each point, and the trump of God and the voice of the archangel will eloquently close the subject. As our purpose is to outline the prophetic system, and to amplify on those themes only which are of deepest interest to our own times, we shall take up only the prophecies which affirm the restoration of Israel to nationality in the latter day.

The Jews and speculative theologians have for near eighteen hundred years, believed that Israel would be restored to nationality in Palestine, and that it would then become the head of the whole world, and be the great agent in its Christianization. We protest against this theory, because it is absurd, fanatical, and repugnant to scripture, as well as to common sense. We believe that the carnal Israel will be, to a certain extent, Christianized, and that it will re-settle in Palestine, and form an integral portion of the Millennial republic, but that it will have no superiority at all over the other Christian states of the Millennial confederacy; we think it will simply be a common beneficiary of good government, as all other Christian states will be. We further believe the United States to be the first fruits of the promised restoration of Israel, and that the Millennial republic will be the salvation of "all Israel," politically speaking. To confirm our views, we submit the following arguments.

SECTION I.

Absurdity of the Common Theory.

This theory, which we have briefly stated, is too well understood to require an enumeration of its points. It has been, and still is, advocated by many learned men; but "great men are not always wise," and "learned men, when they err, err egregiously." Our objections lie against the theory, however, and not against its supporters, and are as follows:

First. The geographical position of Palestine is not such as to favor its claim to be the ultimate capital of the world. The capital of the world should be so located as to be easy of access to all nations, and should be above them, or higher than all other portions of the globe.

This can by no means be said of Palestine, which is difficult of access, and has scarcely any one commanding natural feature to recommend it as the physical head of the globe. America is the only country on earth that can by possibility lay any claim to be its natural capital. The researches of Lieut. Maury have demonstrated that, by wind and wave, it is down stream from our country to all the world; and that all nations must ascend to it to reach it. With an ocean on either hand, its power can descend with celerity to every country on the sphere; and that, too, from even the deepest interior of our territory.

Second. It is absurd to suppose that Palestine can be the agricultural capital of the world. It is a very small country, say about the size of some of the counties of our own states; it is broken by mountains, and has but a very small tract of arable land, and under the highest state of cultivation could export comparatively few products, and no great variety even of them.

How could it therefore compare with America! how could the little valley of Jordan compete with the shores of the Amazon! or the vale of Jehoshaphat with the valley of the Mississippi! We need not argue this point any farther, for the very thought of Palestine being the agricultural head of the world is repugnant to common sense.

Third. It is absurd to suppose that Palestine can ever become the commercial capital of the world. In selecting Palestine as the type of the great Israel, God chose a country without temptations to commerce, lest the people should be scattered and amalgamated, and lose their Hebraic identity. A commercial head of the world, should be a country of great agricultural and mineral wealth; it should have fine harbors, and many of them, and should be accessible on all sides round. But none of these things can be said of Palestine. Sidon, and Acre, and Joppa are all on one side of its coast, and are comparatively insignificant havens. Without vast productiveness in a country, assisted by good harbors, a commercial headship is utterly impossible, and hence to talk of Old Canaan being the commercial center of the great nations of the earth is vanity.

Fourth. Palestine can not be the manufacturing head of the world, for it has no natural facilities for such an ascendency.

Fifth. It can not become the intellectual head of the world. Art and science can flourish only where the resources of a country demand their cultivation to develop its native wealth; and in proportion to the diameter of a country's natural advantages, so will be its intellectual advancement, under a free constitution. And certainly, then, little Palestine can not compete with Europe or the Americas.

Neither can it be claimed that the Jews are superior in native genius to the white race generally, since, unaided by inspiration, they have not been equal in intellectual manifestations of power to the Greeks, Romans, French, English, or Americans. Besides this, the white race has, and will continue to have, as great stimulus and as many collateral aids to intellectual culture as the Jews can ever hope to attain. We can think, and invent, and discover, and learn, and write, and print, and read as much as the Jews possibly can; and it is arrogance to talk otherwise.

Sixth. The Jews can not become the political head of the world in Palestine. It requires the greatest elements of power to hold the scepter of the world's dominion. Vast national resources, vast territory, commerce, agriculture, manufactures, and improvements, with great enterprise, must combine with the mightiest intelligence and the greatest moral power, to rule the world in its present state of advancement; and these, in the highest degree, Palestine, from the very nature of its locality, limits, and native qualities, can never possess. When the world was far less potent than it is now, and was more easy to be controlled, Judea possessed the most insignificant political influence in it; and if, under better advantages, it was a mere cipher in the political world, it certainly, under worse advantages, will not become the head of it. It is most ridiculous to think of such a thing. Will Russia, Britain, Germany, France, and America become the vassals of the Jews? will they give their scepter to a patch of country that could not supply the world with cabbage; and to a people that can never become their mental and political superiors? The very thought is full of absurdity and fanaticism.

If it be contended that this result of supremacy is to occur through miraculous agency, we answer that no promise of such agency exists, and the belief in it is a species of Millerism, and equally as fanatical, though a little more popular. It is averred by some advocates of the theory, who feel its absurdity, that Christ himself will appear and reign in person, in Palestine, and will come at the war of Armageddon. We reply, that Christ says no such thing, but, on the contrary, affirms that his second advent will not occur till "after that tribulation of those days be ended."

Seventh. It is claimed that the Jews, restored to Palestine, will be the spiritual head of the world. We reply that such a notion is chimerical, for Christians are to be the spiritual head of the world, and not carnal Israel. The Christians in America have all the revelation the Jews can have; they have the Bible, which contains all that God will reveal till the second advent; and they can know as much about it as the Jews can; they can print as much as the Jews in Palestine would be able to do; they pray as much, preach as much, and worship God as devoutly, and also possess as much zeal as the Jews ever did, or ever will; so that there is not a single chance for the Jews to become their superiors, much less their head.

Eighth. The theory of the carnal restoration requires that the ten lost tribes, as well as Judah and Benjamin, shall be reunited in Palestine, at the restoration. Now this is utterly impossible, without a resurrection of the dead; for the existence of the ten tribes, at the present day, can not by any means be proved. It is said that traces of them exist in Asia, but traces are not tribes, and the Jews in Asia are, no doubt, the descendants of the dispersed of the two tribes, and not of the ten.

The truth is, the ten tribes were prone to amalgamation with the heathen, and for this reason they were ejected altogether from Canaan; and were in a few centuries almost entirely lost by amalgamation, and certainly have lost their identity as ten tribes, long ago, by mingled blood.

Ninth. Were the Jews to be Christianized, then the Hebrew ceremonial law would cease to be a wall of separation between them and Gentile Christians. Circumcision, and other rites, and especially the law or custom forbidding marriage with Gentiles, would cease, and all essential difference between them and Gentile converts would have an end. Amalgamation would follow, and the distinctive ethnological character of Hebrews would also cease.

To all these things it is replied, that the word of God declares the restoration of Israel, and "every word of God standeth sure." We most cordially admit the proposition, but deny that prophecy ever proclaimed the occurrence of events that are repugnant to common sense. Indeed, any interpretation of God's word that brings from it a theory really at variance with the laws of nature and good sense, is, to say the best of it, a false interpretation.

The Hebrews were a typical people; typical of the Christians; and what purpose is to be subserved by the reconstruction of a typical people? The whole plan of the world's redemption to the judgment is revealed to us, and in that plan, the restoration of carnal Israel, as the head of the world, can be seen to answer no useful purpose. If it be said, as it is, by theorizers, that the Jews are to be the great instruments of the conversion of the world, we answer that such a position is the depth of absurdity. For St. Paul says: "Blindness in part is happened to Israel, until the fullness of the Gentiles be come in. And so all Israel shall be saved; as it is written, There shall come out of Sion the Deliverer, and shall turn away ungodliness from Jacob; for *this* is my covenant unto them."—Rom. xi. Here the conversion of the Gentile world is plainly seen to transpire before that of the Jews, and also that the church from among the Gentiles is to be the agent to convert the Jews; and the Jews are to be the last people converted to the gospel. How absurd, then, it must be, to say that the Jews, restored to Palestine, are to convert the Gentile world.

The covenant here stated, speaks only of the spiritual restoration of Israel, and not of a restoration to Palestine. The restoration to God is as different a thing from restoration to Palestine, as Palestine differs from heaven.

Again, as Christians have equal rights with the seed of Abraham, if the Jews are restored to Palestine by promise, then all the seed of Abraham must settle there also, and, by consequence, the whole Christian world must immigrate to it. But as such an immigration is too absurd for a moment's consideration, the theory is false, because of its absurdity.

It is objected to our views, that the Jews have been providentially preserved as a separate people, and that this argues their final restoration to Palestine. We reply, that we cheerfully concur with such an opinion, but deny that they are to be the head of the world. We sympathize with the Jews, in all their captivity and wanderings, but we sympathize more with the Christian Israel in all its red path of martyrdom. If carnal Israel has been a wanderer, and homeless, so has been Christian Israel; if carnal Israel has been providentially preserved, so has Christian Israel; carnal Israel is a captive for its iniquity, but Christian Israel for its innocence;

the former for its vice, the latter for its virtue; the one murdered the Prince of Life, the other worshiped him; the Jews have ever continued to hate Christ, and pull down his cause; the Christians have loved him, and have sealed their devotion with their blood. Now, should God place carnal Israel above spiritual Israel, should he give him superior honors, and wider dominion, and greater glory, then would God be seen to reward his inveterate foes, and degrade his fast friends; then would he encourage treason, and disgrace fidelity; then would he exalt vice, and condemn virtue; then iniquity would be at a premium, and righteousness at a fearful discount; then equal rights would cease from Christianity, and contentment would leave the world.

Carnal Israel can not become the capital of the world without a violation of every law of nature, good sense, justice, and good government; and the theory which teaches such a doctrine is, therefore, false, fanatical, and full of evil.

SECTION II.

The Common Theory Anti-Scriptural.

A theory repugnant to good sense, is repugnant to scripture; and we shall find every thing in the plain teachings of the New Testament to conflict with the restoration of carnal Israel. Were the restoration of Israel to Palestine taught by the prophets, it is absurd to suppose the great and important fact would not be mentioned, or at least alluded to, in the New Testament. The New Testament is the great expositor of the Old, but it never says that carnal Israel will be restored to

Palestine; never hints it, never implies it. Now, why this silence about Canaan? why this emphatic neglect of carnal Israel, and full attention to Christian Israel, if the carnal seed of Abraham were to be the heirs and inheritors of the world? The silence can be interpreted to mean nothing in favor of the carnal restoration, and must mean every thing against it. We shall now quote some few decisive passages on the subject, and leave them with the impartial for mature consideration.

That nationality was promised to Israel, in the latter day, can not be doubted. The prophets most unequivocally announce it, and it is fully and plainly inferable from the great promises of the world's redemption, and the promised blessedness to all nations through Christ. Did true Christianity universally prevail among men, Christian republicanism would also necessarily spring up universally. Now, in the progress of Christianity toward universality, it is obvious that some one part of the earth would first be Christianized, and by consequence a true Christian nationality would prevail in that Christianized portion, and that would be the restoration of nationality as far as it extended. In speaking of the restoration of Israel, no one imagines that the same identical Jews who formerly lived in Palestine are to be restored to it, and to nationality; the legitimate descendants of Abraham only can be those to whom the promise was made. The controversy will, therefore, be decided by determining who are the legitimate seed of Abraham. We affirm that the Christian seed of Israel are the only true heirs of all the promises, and that Christians of the Gentiles are as truly the heirs of the promises, as are Christians from among the Jews. We shall proceed with our arguments as follows: 1. Nationality was promised to the true seed of Abraham in the latter day. 2. The Christians are the true seed of Abraham.

First. Promised restoration to Nationality.—Some persons who oppose the restoration of Israel to Palestine have taken an extreme position, and have disbelieved in any national restoration whatever.

This position is as absurd as the theory it opposes, because unequivocal prophecies declare a restoration to nationality; and it must, also, transpire from the very nature of things. We shall quote, for the present, but two authoritative and decisive prophecies on the subject, out of a score that now lie open before us. 1. "And it shall come to pass in that day, that the Lord shall set his hand again the SECOND time to recover the remnant of his people, ... and shall assemble the outcasts of Israel, and gather together the dispersed of Judah from the four corners of the earth. * * They shall fly upon the shoulders of the Philistines toward the WEST."—Isa. xi. 2. "Surely the isles shall wait for me, and the ships of Tarshish (Spain) first, to bring thy sons from far. * * * * The nation and kingdom that will not serve thee shall utterly perish. * * Thy people shall be all righteous, they shall inherit the land forever."—Isa. lx. As it is utterly impossible to spiritualize these passages, and as they, without the shadow of a doubt, predict the latter day restoration of Israel, the national restoration of the seed of Abraham must be a conceded point on all hands. The terms "WEST," and "SHIPS OF TARSHISH," utterly refuse to be accommodated to a mere figurative, or to a spiritual meaning.

Second. The Christians are the true seed of Abraham, to whom the promises inure.

1. *Who are Jews?*—" He is not a Jew, which is one outwardly, neither is that circumcision, which is outward in the flesh. But he is a Jew which is one inwardly; and circumcision is that of the heart, in the spirit and not in the letter; whose praise is not of men but of God."—Rom. ii. 28, 29. " For they are not all Israel, which are of Israel; neither because they are the seed of Abraham are they all children, but in Isaac shall thy seed be called. That is they which are the children of the flesh, these are not the children of God; but the children of the promise are counted for the seed."—Rom. ix. 7–9.

" Know ye therefore that they which are of the faith, the same are the children of Abraham. So then, they which be of faith are blessed with faithful Abraham. That the blessing of Abraham might come on the Gentiles through Jesus Christ. There is neither Jew nor Greek, there is neither bond nor free, there is neither male nor female, for you are all ONE in Christ Jesus. And if ye be Christ's, ye are Abraham's seed, and heirs according to promise."—Gal. iii.

In these passages, the Jew who is to be the inheritor of the promises, is plainly stated to be one who is an heir, by faith in Christ, and by that only. It is also as plainly affirmed as language can express it, that there is no difference in equality of right between the Gentile and Hebrew seed of Christ. Those therefore who insist on the superiority of right to pre-eminent position of Hebrew Christians, are in direct conflict with the text. They affirm there is a difference, while the text affirms that "all are one in Christ," and that "there is *no difference* between the Jew and the Greek."—Rom. x. 12. That the carnal seed are not received among the heirs of the promises, is further manifest from the affirmation of Christ to the Jews. He said: "Ye are of your father the devil, and the lusts of your father ye will do." "If Abraham were your father ye would do the works of Abraham."—John viii.

2. *Heirship of the world.*—"The promise that he should be the heir of the world was not to Abraham or to his seed through the law, but through the righteousness of faith."—Rom. iv. 13.

"For if the *inheritance* be of the law, it is no more of promise; but God gave it to Abraham by promise."—Gal. iii. 18.

Here the inheritance to Abraham is plainly given to all believers in Christ without any distinction between Jewish or Gentile converts. All benefits conferred upon men in the latter day were to spring from the gospel, and the gospel confers equal rights upon all of its beneficiaries throughout the world, irrespective of carnal relation to Abraham, for God is no respector of persons.

3. *Promise sure to all the seed.*—"To Abraham and his seed were the promises made. He saith not, and to seeds, as of many but as of one, and to thy seed which is Christ." How differently this sounds from the "two-seed" doctrine of the restorers of carnal Israel. "Now we, brethren, as Isaac was, are children of promise."—Gal. iii and iv. "Therefore, it is of faith that it might be by grace; to the end the promise might be sure to all the seed; not to that only which is of the law, but to that also which is of the faith of Abraham, who is the

father of us all."—Rom. iv. 16. Many other pointed texts of similar import might be quoted, if demanded, but these are sufficient to annihilate the theory of the superiority of carnal Israel. This theory makes *two* Israels, differing in blessedness in the final heirship, the gospel affirms there is but *one;* it claims a wide *difference* between the privileges of Jewish and Gentile Christians, the gospel affirms "there is *no* difference;" it makes the promise sure to a *part* of the seed only, the gospel declares it "is sure to *all* the seed;" it blesses the Israel of Moses, but leaves the Israel of Christ under a curse. These things being so, is not the carnal theory of Israel altogether unscriptural and false?

SECTION III.

THE UNITED STATES IS ISRAEL RESTORED.

Having shown that nationality was unequivocally promised to Israel, in the Christian era, or "latter day," and having demonstrated, as we think, that the application of this promise to carnal Israel, is at utter variance with the gospel, its reference to Christians only, is an inevitable conclusion. The United States being

---

NOTE.—During the Sabbatic year, or Jubilee, every man returned to his own possessions; "God divided to the nations their inheritance," in the days of old; during the Millennium, the Jubilee, or Sabbatic year of the world, the races will return to their patrimony: Negroes will return to Africa, Shem will occupy his own portion, and Japhet his, and scattered Hebrews will return to their portion, originally divided to them; they may then form an integral part of the general republic of mankind, but will possess no domination over it, as the carnal theory proposes.

a late and extraordinary Christian people, we inquire, may it not be the veritable nationality of the prophets? If it is an Israel at all, if it coincides with all the great characteristics predicted of a Christian nationality, then all doubt must end, and our country rise into an importance and sublimity absolutely overwhelming. We assume the following positions:

1. *The United States is a Christian Israel.*—The name, Israel, literally signifies, "a prince with God, or wrestling or prevailing with God." It was a personal appellative of Jacob, and, by metonomy, of his descendants; in the Old Testament, when used *declaratively*, it refers either to the Hebrew nation, or to the ten tribes; in the New Testament, it is applied to Christians, as, for example, "the Israel of God."—Gal. vi.

With the literal sense, the United States coincides, for it wrestled with God in universal prayer and tears, in its great struggle for civil and religious liberty, and it prevailed.

It is also, in form, a dual nationality, as was Hebrew Israel, the specific difference being just that existing between the Mosaic and Christian dispensations.

It is composed of a vast body of Christians, and its nationality, the offspring of their principles and of themselves, is as legitimately entitled to their name of Christian Israel, as is the legitimate child to the name of its sire; at the transformation of the Hebrew church into a nationality at the exodus, the name Israel was properly transferred to the nation; so the name of Christ's Israel may, with equal propriety, be applied to a nationality into which this Israel is transformed, the cases being exactly similar.

The United States, from these several considerations, may, therefore, with strict propriety, be called an Israel

2. *All the great features predicted of Israel restored are possessed by the United States.*—The most complete and specific descriptions of the restoration, are given by Ezekiel and Isaiah; to these we shall devote most attention. To appreciate, in any degree, the arguments of our entire work, it must be kept constantly in view, that prophecy is of two kinds—the clear and the obscure. The former needs no explanation; to know the true import of the latter, demands the greatest skill, and its exact meaning can be known only by fulfillment, coinciding with some one of the plurality of legitimate expositions, of which the specific prediction is, *a priori*, susceptible. By far the greater portion of prophecy is *intentionally* obscure. The obscurity proceeds from the ambiguity of terms used, or from symbols; the language of symbols is always determinate and simple, but realization is essential to their application to their subjects; ambiguous terms, from the nature of the case, admit of a plurality of senses, *a priori*. To determine which of these meanings was the divine intention, and at the same time to show an unequivocal fulfillment in the end, necessitates the following rule: any *legitimate, a priori*, exposition of an obscure prophecy, with which future events clearly coincide, is thereby determined to be the intention of the prophecy, and such coincidence is fulfillment. The great point of importance, then, is to be certain that our *a priori* expositions are legitimate, and a rule to test such legitimacy is demanded. The rule is this: any exposition not opposed to the context, nor to the nature of things existing, before

fulfillment, must be considered legitimate.* With these positions stated to guide the inquirer, we proceed.

First. "*Surely the isles shall wait for me, and the ships of Tarshish first, to bring thy sons from far.*"—Isa. lx.

1. The term "isles," was applied anciently to Europe, and all countries west of Asia Minor. Those vast countries supposed to exist in the Atlantic, west of Gibraltar, are also termed isles, by both Plato and Diodorus Siculus.

2. "The waiting of the isles for God," implies either their delay in receiving the emigrating people of God, spoken of in the text, or of the gospel; the former is more likely the meaning, since the ships bringing emigrants are those the isles were waiting for; indeed, the consecutive coupling of isles waiting for God, and for the ships with emigrants, almost necessitates this meaning.

3. "The ships of Tarshish." Tarshish was the most ancient name of Spain; it is supposed to apply, also, to Tarsus in Cilicia.

4. "Tarshish first;" the word "first," was intended pointedly to specify the first people who would approach "the waiting isles." As prophecy notes only the greatest events of time, the term "first," must apply to some very stupendous and famous circumstance. Now we do not claim that our exposition is the only one of which the text is susceptible, but simply that it is legitimate; this claim must be admitted, because it is in accordance with the rule stated above, and therefore can not be denied. America answers to the term "isles," and "the ships of Tarshish first," to the discovery of America by

---

* See discovery

the ships of Spain, opening the way to the emigration of God's people, to form a nationality in "the isles." The events coinciding with the legitimate exposition given, the prophecy is seen to be realized, as we supposed, and our supposition is thus confirmed, as the real intention of the prophecy.

Second. "*In the latter years thou shalt come into the land that is brought back from the sword, and is gathered out of many nations against the mountains of Israel, which have been always waste.*"—Ezek. xxxviii. As the Israel restored was to be of Christians, this text must predict the nationality of Christians, gathered from various countries. The country "always waste," prior to their coming, was manifestly a wilderness, "from of old." America coincides with the country described, and the United States with the "gathered" nationality of Christian immigrants.

Third. "*Thine eyes shall see Jerusalem a quiet habitation, a tabernacle that shall not be taken down. But there the glorious Lord shall be unto us a place of broad rivers and streams; wherein shall go no galley with oars, neither shall gallant ship pass thereby.*"—Isa. xxxiii. The peace and permanency of Israel are elsewhere spoken of by the prophets, who affirm, that once restored, it shall never fall again. "*There*, the Lord being a place of broad rivers and streams," teaches that prosperity and peace in the land of Israel will spring from the gift of a place of broad rivers and streams, where the tabernacle of Israel's nationality shall be erected. It is common, in scripture, to embody a promise, or threat, in terms figurative, which, when taken literally, designate the very agencies by which the threat or promise is realized. Sword and fire may symbolize war; or rain may represent plenty, yet each is an essential agent in the realization. So broad rivers and streams may symbolize vast *inland* prosperity, and yet are essential means of effecting it, and may, therefore, be taken in a literal, as well as figurative sense. Galley and gallant ship, represent the greater and smaller classes of war vessels; their presence would indicate the vassalage of Jerusalem to foreigners, their absence, therefore, declares Israel's independence. Vast inland prosperity afforded by broad rivers and streams; a glorious independence of all nations, are mighty features of the great American people. Our exposition is, *a priori*, legitimate, and is endorsed by the facts, as the intention of the prophet.

Fourth. "*They shall bring thy sons in their arms, and thy daughters shall be carried upon their shoulders.*" —Isa. xlix. "*But they shall fly upon the shoulders of the Philistines toward the west.*" Bearing upon the shoulders plainly teaches the transportation of Israel by the Gentiles; and Moses teaches that flying *upon* another, means transportation; hence it might mean it here. The course of transportation would then be westward; and, as Philistia was west of Palestine, it is manifest that Palestine is not the country of restoration, and Philistia is a figure of the modern foes of God. Now, the great emigration of Christians to America, was westward, from the maritime Philistia of modern Europe.

Fifth. "*Ye shall inherit the land according to the twelve tribes of Israel; Joseph shall have two portions.*" —Ezek. xlvii. Joseph had two portions of old Israel, and thus there were thirteen tribes, and the same number was to exist at the rise of Christian Israel. In the forty eighth chapter, it is said, these divisions shall lie side by side, on a great sea, with their limits extending "from the east side unto the west side." A map of these is published in Clarke's Commentary. All prophecies of the modern restoration, relate to a Christian nation, and since the United States arose in thirteen collateral divisions, whose limits, in the language of the old charters, "extended westward, from sea to sea," we have overpowering evidence, that our country was intended by the prophet.

Sixth. "*Kings shall be thy nursing fathers, and queens thy nursing mothers.*"—Isa. xlix. Nursing applies to attentions in the infancy of the restoration. A word is sufficient. The memorial of nursing kings, and queens, and princes, will remain upon our rivers and waters, our counties and towns, our cities and states, while time shall last. Louisiana, Georgia, the Carolinas, Virginia, Maryland, Delaware, New York, New Jersey, and New Hampshire, will ever suggest the early interest of royalty in our colonial history.

Seventh. "*I will restore thy judges as at the first, and thy counsellors as at the beginning.*"—Isa. ii. Judges and counsellors were an essential part of Hebrew democracy, or of the *first* government, and their restoration implies republicanism. "Their nobles shall be of themselves, and their governor from the midst of them." —Jer. xxx. The selection of rulers from the masses of the people, is incidental to democracy only. "Thy destroyers, and they that made thee waste, shall go forth of thee."—Isa. xlix. Spiritual and civil monarchists were ever the destroyers of Christians, and the removal of their power, leaves only the alternative of freedom.

Eighth. "*Thou (Gog) shalt say, I will go up to the land of unwalled villages; I will go to them that are at rest, that dwell safely, all of them dwelling without walls, and having neither bars nor gates, to turn thy hand upon the desolate places that are now inhabited, upon the people that are gathered out of the nations.*"—Ezek. xxxviii. Our Israel was "gathered out of the nations;" "we dwell in the midst of the land;" we "are at rest in the desolate places now inhabited;" we "dwell safely in unwalled villages, with neither bars nor gates" to our cities.

Ninth. "*Thy waste and thy desolate places, and the land of thy destruction, shall even be too narrow, by reason of inhabitants. The children thou shalt have after thou hast lost the other,* (having lost carnal Israel,) *shall say again in thine ears, the place is too straight for me, give place to me that I may dwell.*"—Isa. xlix. Eighteen new states, added to the "Old Thirteen," have not mitigated the unceasing cry for "place, that I may dwell." Here is a coincidence that comes home personally to the experience of all of us.

Tenth. "*Thou shalt not see a fierce people, a people of deeper speech than thou canst perceive: of a stammering tongue that thou canst not understand.*"—Isa. xxxiii. The universality of one language is legitimately inferred from this passage, and the unity of the language of the American people, is one of the most extraordinary occurrences in the history of great empires.

Eleventh. "*All thy children shall be taught of the Lord,*" Is. liv. *A priori,* this may mean either conversion to God or universal Christian education. Our educational system is unparalleled in history; the Bible is its basis, and every child in our country is taught of God and the gospel.

Twelfth. "*The abundance of the sea shall be converted unto thee.*" That is, the commerce of the world. "*The forces of the Gentiles shall come unto thee; the multitude of camels shall cover thee.*" That is, vast multitudes of immigrants shall pour into the country. "*Who are these that fly as a cloud, and as doves to their windows?*" Is. lx. Clouds indicate multitudes, and doves returning show that wanderers are flying hither for rest, from the flood of sorrow on the earth.

More graphic accounts of the foreign immigration to our shores than Isaiah gives, (chs. xlix and lx) could not be written.

Thirteenth. "*In the last days the mountain (civil government) of the Lord's house, (church or Christians) shall be established in the top of the mountains, and all nations shall flow unto it. And many people shall go and say, come ye, and let us go up to the mountain of the Lord; (to the nationality) to the house of the God of Jacob;*" (to the Bible church, Is. iii.) The locality of the nation is represented higher than other places. Lieut. Maury shows that the whole earth, to reach us, is literally obliged to *come up* to *us*, because we are on the physical head of the world, and doubtless in the ancient Eden, with its four-headed river.

Fourteenth. "*These shall come from far; and lo, these from the north and west; and these from the land of Sinim,*" Is. xlix. Drs. Morison and Hagar affirm that Sinim is China, and the latter "undertakes the proof in two very learned tracts." How true this text of our country; how unlikely of Palestine; the Chinese are immigrating hither from the west.

Fifteenth. "*The sons of them that afflicted thee, shall come bending unto thee,*" Is. lx. Romanists were the great prosecutors of Bible Christians, and their heavy laden sons and daughters crowd by tens of thousands, to serve as menials, that people whom their fathers afflicted.

Sixteenth. "*The sons of strangers shall build thy walls,*" Is. lx. Our great systems of internal improvements are our walls of strength, and all their drudgery is performed by strangers to our religion and liberty. Ireland, and Germany, and Rome, respond to the prophecy.

Seventeenth. "*Ye shall divide it by lot for an inheritance to you, and to the strangers that sojourn among you, that shall beget children among you. They shall have inheritance with you,*" Ez. xlvii. The constitution tolerates all religions. The inheritance or citizenship is first to sojourners; then to those who raise families of native born children; and then to the children themselves. Ezekiel's suggestion is profoundly politic. To limit citizens' prerogatives to strangers, who are heads of native born families, is consonant with good sense, as such persons have strong motives to uphold good government.

Eighteenth. "*Unto two thousand and three hundred days, then shall the sanctuary be cleansed.*" "*It shall be for a time, times and a ha'f; and when he shall have accomplished, to scatter the power of the holy people all these things shall be finished.*" "*From the time the daily sacrifice shall be taken away, there shall be* 1290 *days,*" Daniel. These texts give, each, the length of

Israel's desolation. Their starting point is at the cessation of the daily sacrifice, on the 189th day of 68, A. D., and each period is exactly equal to 1708 years. The ending point is therefore on July 4th, 1776. On that day "a nation was born at once." (See discovery.)

Before closing the argument, we will consider a few objections to it.

1. Literalists object that we attribute a figurative sense to such towns as Israel, Judah, Canaan, &c. We deny the charge; we argue with all our strength to maintain that very ground. For instance, the word Israel, literally, is not the Jewish nation, as literalists would have us think; it signifies any one person who prevails with God, no matter who. Applied to a body of people, it is then used figuratively, and, as a figure, it may designate the Hebrew nation; the ten tribes; the scattered Jews of our time, or any single body of Christians, as the Waldenses, or "Israel of the Alps." The term is used by St. Paul to designate the true seed of Abraham, as, "they are not all Israel, who are of Israel;" "the Israel of God," &c. But even on the supposition that the term means carnal Israel literally, our position is still tenable. Terms are always either literal or figurative; if their literal sense stands opposed to plain testimony, and the figurative does not, then are they to be understood as figurative, and *vice versa*. There is no evading this position. Scriptural examples also sustain the use of literal terms as figures: thus Ezekiel uses the name of David in such a way as necessitates it to stand for Christ; so, also, does David himself, see Ezek. xxxvii, and Ps. cxxxii, 11. Further, the gospel unequivocally affirming that "if a man be circumcised Christ shall

profit him nothing," and positively limiting the fulfillment of the promises to Christians only, the figurative sense of the term Israel, as used in the promises, is required by inevitable necessity. The objection, though very grave with some, is really very trivial.

2. It is objected that the promise is so very specific, as to affirm that Israel restored is to "dwell in the land where their fathers dwelt." This, however, is only a seeming objection. The "promise being sure to all the seed," and the absurdity of supposing that "all the seed" can by possibility dwell in Palestine, compels this restoration to be understood as a figure. But the prophecy is really detailing the history of Israel after the final resurrection, and positively coincides with the New Heavens and Earth, described by Isaiah, St. Peter, and St. John. All, therefore, that can be inferred from it, is that the dwelling-place of Israel, after the resurrection, will be on the regenerated globe.

3. It is objected that God has preserved the Jews an isolated people, for the express purpose of restoration to Palestine. "We answer, had they heard (believed) Christ, as God commanded, (Deut. xv, 18, and Acts ii, 22,) the customs which isolate them abolished, they had lost their carnal identity, and been merged into the true Israel. The sole and simple secret of their existence, as a *distinct* people, is their *infidelity*. And God has no farther interfered, in this preservation, than may be implied in his making their sin their *curse*. Surely the literalist will not insist upon a theory which makes God the author of sin." Rev. L. D. Huston. But further, the great works of Providence are all designed to promote the single end of regenerating the world; Christianity is the chosen agent of accomplishing this end, and the providences of God are all intended to spread Christianity; now can any man see cause for the restoration of a merely typical people, after the ends of its existence have been accomplished? The Hebrew nation was a type of a regenerated world, a representation of happiness,

not to be enjoyed by itself alone, in the realizing age, but of the blessedness of all nations in Abraham, through Christ. Are not, then, those Christians and converted Jews, who labor to convert Jews to the Christian faith, by holding out motives of a carnal restoration, assuming untenable ground, and indirectly carnalizing Christianity, and fostering the very spirit which St. Paul denounced, when he proclaimed the Gentiles "fellow-heirs" of the promises to the seed of Abraham? Is not a false sympathy for the Jew thus engendered, which will prove disastrous in the end? Let Jewish sinners hear the gospel, and embrace it from the same motives presented in common to all mankind; let them be willing to allow to all Christians an equal right to all the blessings of the gospel; let them acknowledge that God looks only at moral character, and "is no respector of *persons*" on account of mere parentage; let them admit the fact, that God will not raise and sustain any aristocracy of persons on account of mere fleshly extraction, and that such extraction confers no virtue, no hereditary pre-emption, to royal supremacy; let them remember that the "joint-heir of Jesus Christ" is not necessarily by birth a Jew, but any one that is born of God, no matter who. The carnal theory is positively arrogant and intolerable, and should be rejected as a fanatical delusion.

We now epitomize our arguments and close. 1. We showed the carnal theory to be irrational and anti-scriptural. 2. That nationality in the latter day, was promised to Christians only. 3. That the United States, is a Christian Israel. 4. That America, coincides with the waiting isles. 5. That the ships of Spain, opening up America to the Christian emigration, coincide with "the ships of Tarshish first, to bring thy sons from far." 6. That America, a wilderness "from of old," coincides with the lands "which have been always waste." 7. That the United States, answers to the people gathered out of many nations in the country "always waste." 8. The great fluvial system of America, and our vast inland prosperity, answer to " there, a place of broad rivers and streams." 9. American independence, answers to " no galley with oars, neither gallant ship," &c. 10. Western emigration, by royal encouragement, answers to flying to the west on the shoulders of modern Philistia or maritime Europe. 11. " The Old Thirteen," answer to the thirteen divisions of the Christian nation, predicted by Ezekiel. 12. The royal proprietary and charter colonies, answer to " kings shall be thy nursing fathers, and queens thy nursing mothers." 13. Our republic, answers to " restoring thy judges as at first, and thy counsellors as at the beginning." 14. Our unwalled towns and villages, answer to Ezekiel's description of Israel's villages and cities. 15. Our unparalleled expansion, answer to the cry " the place is too straight; give place that I may dwell." 16. The universality of Christian education, answers to " all thy children shall be taught of the Lord." 17. The vast foreign immigration, answers to the 49th and 60th chapters of Isaiah. 18. America's location as head of the world, answers to the country to which all were to " go up." 19. The immigration from China, answers to " lo, these from the west, and from the land of Sinim." 20. The menial service of foreign Romanists, answers to the " bending of the sons of them that afflicted thee." 21. The drudgery of building canals, turnpikes, railroads, &c., &c., by foreign Catholics, answers to " the sons of strangers shall build thy walls." 22. Constitutional rights to foreigners, answer to an inheritance among us promised to strangers. 23. Universality and unity of language, answer to " thou shalt not see a people of a deeper speech than thou canst perceive," &c. 24. The birth day of our nation, July 4th, 1776, answers exactly to the day when Israel was to " be born at once." Now, then, as the legitimacy of our expositions, *a priori*, cannot be denied, and as they are all realized in America, it follows that the United States is the promised nationality to Christian Israel.

SECTION IV.

Parallel Prophecies of Israel.

The restoration of Israel and its fulfillment in the rise of the United States, has its parallels in the Hebrew escape from Egypt across a sea, and its erection of a republic in the wilderness; and in the stone cut out of the mountain, or fifth great empire of Nebuchadnezzar's vision; in the ancient of days, or fifth empire of Daniel's vision of empires; and in Michael, in his last vision; in the two witnesses; the woman and her twelve stars; in the woman and her man child; and the man with many diadems, on a white horse; and in the sealing of the twelve tribes of Revelation.

An Israel restored was promised by the prophets on a mighty scale, and it was to be a Christian Israel. If we look at our own glorious country, we see clearly a Christian Israel, enjoying the greatest and most glorious of all nationalities. Here is a coincidence with the prophets; and here then is their fulfillment.

Christ assured his disciples, that the restoration was to be a mystery, and Daniel told that its history, in prophecy, would be concealed, till just before the battle of the Kings; and the blindness on the subject hitherto, has resulted from the order of God. This concealment of our country as the Israel restored of the promises, every wise man can see was a prudent measure with reference both to our past and future history.

CHAPTER V.

Ezekiel's Symbolic Prophecies of America.

Ezekiel is both a literal and symbolic prophet, and in this he differs from Daniel and John. He also differs from them in this, that he does not give the history of the four great empires that were to precede the final triumphs of Christianity. He, however, coincides with them as to Israel's restoration, and the freeing of the earth from the curse. The parts of his prophecy which we take up, are those which relate to the close of the fourth monarchy by the battle of the great day; the rise of Israel; and the final empire of Christ on earth.

SECTION I.

Israel Restored—America.

We have already considered some prophecies of Ezekiel, which show that the Israel of Christ was to be restored in the latter day: we shall now add a few additional points of interest. From the forty-third to the forty-eighth chapter of Ezekiel, he gives a description of Christianity, in all its progress and triumphs after the rise of the Israel of Christ to nationality. He embraces all that Daniel does, beginning with the rise of the stone kingdom, and all that John does, beginning with the kingdom that sprung from the woman or church in the wilderness. We can not quote these chapters, and shall only give the strong points of coincidence between the three prophets mentioned. We say, that this vision coincides with Daniel's and John's descriptions of the same era.

1. This must be true, because they both describe the same era, and, of course, must coincide in the same subjects.

2. Both John and Daniel predict the universality of the empire of Christ, and Ezekiel does the same. The holy city of Ezekiel, and his trees of life, and river of the water of life, also coincide with the city New Jerusalem, the river and trees of life given by St. John. This shows that their descriptions of these things refer to the very same era.

3. Ezekiel, in addition to this, describes the rise of Israel, and his occupancy of the promised land. In this description it is plain that Israel did not, at the time of this settlement, possess the whole earth, but only a part of it, and thus it coincides with the descriptions of Isaiah, Jeremiah, Daniel, and John. In the forty-eighth chapter he says, the divisions of the promised land to the tribes, shall not be as in ancient times, but that they shall extend from east to west, and lie side by side of each other. He says, also, that there shall be a sea on the east side of the land, and a great sea on the west. "This shall be the border whereby ye shall inherit the land according to the twelve tribes of Israel; Joseph shall have two portions."—xlvii: 13. It this land, also, was to be an inheritance for strangers: ' And they shall be unto you as born in the country among the children of Israel, and they shall have inheritance with you

among the tribes of Israel."—v. 22. Joseph, having two portions, would, of course, make thirteen tribes or states when restored. Let it be borne in mind, that the whole of the vision of Ezekiel is given in the apparel of the ceremonial law of the Hebrews. This being so, the whole prophecy is certainly symbolic, because the Hebrew ceremonial law will never be restored. But as the ceremonial law was typical of Christianity, and as the whole Hebrew economy was typical of the Christian dispensation, it follows that all Jewish names and customs mentioned by Ezekiel, were figuratively used for coincident names and objects in the days of Christ, or Christianity. Of course, therefore, carnal Israel is put for Christ's Israel, and the restoration of thirteen tribes was to be realized by Christians; and Palestine was to coincide with the land promised to Japhetic Christians; and the boundaries by east and west seas, were to be realized by Christians in their restoration. Now, as the United States arose from a Christian people; as its borders are two great seas; as it arose in thirteen divisions lying side by side on a great sea; and as provision is made for the inheritance of strangers, it exactly coincides with Ezekiel's symbolic description of Israel restored, and, as perfect coincidence is fulfillment, the United States fulfills the prophecy of Israel's restoration.

SECTION II.

The Great Battle and Destruction of Monarchy by Israel; or Gog and his Allies—Invasion of the United States.

Paragraph I.—38th Chapter.

Ezekiel gave several descriptions of Israel's restoration, and we have just considered his last prediction on that subject. In the description prior to it, he tells us the condition of Israel restored, and announces a great invasion of its country by the allied powers of the world. His description of the battle is found in the thirty-eighth and thirty-ninth chapters, and is doubled. In John and Daniel, we have Russia, or the last head of the beast and willful king, described as the invader of Israel prior to the Millennium, and, as this invasion of Israel by Gog coincides chronologically with John and Daniel's descriptions, Gog and his allies coincide with Russia and confederate Europe. We shall, however, find in this prophecy of Ezekiel abundant proof that Gog coincides with Russia. We shall interpret minutely: first, "Son of man, set thy face against Gog, the land of Magog, the chief Prince of Meshech and Tubal, and prophesy against him."

1. The term *Gog*, is plainly derived from Magog, for Magog is as old as the days of Noah. Gog is called a prince, or head of many countries.

2. "The land of Magog." Magog was one of the seven sons of Japhet. His sons were Gomer, Magog, Maadai, Javan, Tubal, Meshech and Tiras. The sons

of Gomer, Japhet's oldest son, were Ashkenath, Riphath, and Togarmah. The sons of Javan, Japhet's fourth son, were Elisha, Tarshish, Kittim, and Dodanim. "By these were the isles of the Gentiles divided in their lands." Calmet, and most other investigators, prove that Europe and Asia Minor are to be understood by the term "isles of the Gentiles." The word rendered "isles," literally signifies settlements.—(*Calmet.*) The sons of Japhet, or the white race, undoubtedly settled the northwest of Asia, and all Europe; so that the land of Magog, the son of Japhet, must be found in these limits. Josephus says, that "Magogue founded the Magogæ, whom the Greeks then called Scythæ." Now, the Greeks called those people Scythians, or Scythæ, "who extended themselves in length from Hungary, Transylvania, and Wallachia on the westward, to the river Don on the east."—(*Rennel.*) This country forms a large part of the Russian empire in Europe and Asia.

3. "Gog—the chief prince of Meshech." Meshech was the sixth son of Japhet, and settled with his brother Tubal. They settled in the northeast angle of Asia Minor, from the shores of the Euxine along to the south of Caucasus; where were the Montes, Moschisi, and where, in after times, were the Moschi. There appears to have been in the same neighborhood, a river and country called Rosh, and a people called Rhossi. These Rhossi and Moschi dispersed their colonies jointly over the vast empire of Russia, and preserve their names in those of Russians and Muscovites. Muscovy is a name given by some geographers to Russia, and the terms Moscow, or Moskwa, Mosch, Mesce, Mesoch, and Mosc, are but variations of their primitive Meshech.

Watson says this passage under consideration, is, in the Septuagint, rendered "prince of Rosch, Meshech, and Tubal." These different translations are in harmony, because the Rhossi and Mosch were interchangeable terms, used to designate the same people.

These people and their country are now included in the Russian empire, and gave name to it, for Muscovy and Russia are derivative names from Rhossi and Moschi, or Meshech.

4. "Gog—prince of Tubal." Tubal was the fifth son of Japhet. Bochart very copiously proves that Meshech and Tubal are the Muscovites and Tibarenians, or Siberians. The river Tobol, or Tubal, that waters a large part of Asiatic Russia, still bears the ancient name of the son of Japhet. The city of Tobol-ski, or Tobolium, also retains the name in composition. The territory of this region is also in the Russian empire.

From these facts, it follows, that, as Meshech, Tubal, and Magog, compose the present Russian empire, that Gog, the prince of these, must represent the present Russian power.

Second. "Thus saith the Lord God, Behold I am against thee, O Gog, the chief prince of Meshech and Tubal; and I will turn thee back, and put hooks in thy jaws." Dr. Clarke says, "to turn him back" signifies hostility to him.

Third. "And I will bring thee forth, and all thine army, horses and horsemen, all of them clothed with all sorts of armor, even a great company, with bucklers and shields, all of them handling swords."

The horses and horsemen symbolize the national kind of soldiery employed in war by Gog. All sorts of armor, shows the promiscuous character of the troops to be brought into the field. Bucklers and shields, and swords, represent the fierce hostility of the troops prepared for war.

Fourth. " Persia, Ethiopia, and Libya with them, all of them with shield and helmet." Persia is here a representative of Asiatic power, or the Mongolian Asiatics, and Libya and Ethiopia represent the Africans, who will be enlisted in the war.

Fifth. " *Gomer*, and all his bands, the house of Togarmah, of the north quarters, and all his bands; and many people with thee."

The *Gomerians* spread from the regions north of Armenia and Bactriana, and extended westward over nearly the whole continent of Europe. They spread from the Black sea to the Western ocean ; from the Baltic to Italy, southward; and first planted the British isles. They have retained their paternal denomination slightly varied, as Cimmerians in Asia; Cimbri, and Umbri in Gaul and Italy; and Cymri and Cambri in Wales and Cumberland.

Togarmah was a son of Gomer, and his descendants may be traced in Trocmi of Strabo, the Trogmi of Cicero, and Trogmades of the council of Chalcedon, inhabiting the confines of Pontus and Cappadocia. Calmet says, Togarmah is to be placed in Scythia and Turcomania. "Many people with thee," shows that many allies of Gog would accompany Togarmah from the north, or from Russia.

Sixth. " Be thou prepared and prepare for thyself, thou, and all thy company that are assembled unto thee, and be thou a guard unto them." This is prophetic of the jurisdiction to be extended over these multitudes by Russia, and of the alliances it would make for the battle.

Seventh. "After many days thou shalt be visited; in the latter years thou shalt come unto the land that is brought back from the sword, and is gathered out of many people, against the mountains of Israel, which have been always waste; but is brought forth out of the nations, and they shall dwell safely all of them." Here the time of this great war is stated to be in the latter years, when Israel is restored. The "lands that have been always waste," and the people brought out of the nations, and all dwelling safely, coincide with the Christian Israel in the United States.

Eighth. "Thou shalt ascend and come like a storm, thou shalt be like a cloud to cover the land, thou and all thy bands and many people with thee." Here a mighty invasion is predicted. No gathering of people has ever yet equaled the sublime one here described; for the people that were to be with Gog, or Russia, embrace nearly all of Europe, and a great portion of Asia and Africa. The draught of men is from three continents. The invasion is likened to a storm, and a cloud, and is seen to enter the glorious land.

Ninth. "Thus saith the Lord God, it shall also come to pass, that at the same time shall things come into thy mind, and thou shalt think an evil thought, and thou shalt say, I will go up to the land of unwalled villages; I will go to them that are at rest, all of them dwelling without walls, and having neither bars nor gates, to take a spoil and to take a prey; to turn thine hand upon the desolate places that are now inhabited, and upon the people that are gathered out of the nations, which have gotten cattle and goods, that dwell in the midst of the land."

The invasion is here stated to be to take a prey, and to subdue the country and people to Russia. The people to be invaded are represented as one made up of emigrants from the nations, as dwelling in peace, plenty, and safety; as dwelling in cities having no defenses of any external character, in other words, as being easily accessible; and also as inhabiting a country never settled before it was by them. Now, no country on earth ever did or ever can coincide with this description, but the United States, and it meets the case exactly. The object of the invasion is to subjugate our power.

Tenth. " Sheba, and Dedan, and the merchants of Tarshish, with all the young lions thereof, shall say unto thee, Art thou come to take a spoil? hast thou gathered thy company to take a prey? to carry away silver and gold, to take away cattle and goods, to take a great spoil?" Sheba and Dedan, sons of Raamah, and grandsons of Cush, son of Ham, were famous traders in spices and ivory, ebony and fine cloth. Tarshish, the son of Javan and grand-son of Japhet, gave name to the commercial world, figuratively; he must have settled in or near his father's estate or division, which was in Ionia, or Greece, or Southern Europe. These various names are used figuratively for a mercantile people, and the term merchants is used to fasten the meaning in this direction. The words "art thou come," seem to imply that the coming was to them, or to a commercial country. Indeed, the question could not be properly propounded except by those to whom Gog had come. The question is not " are you *going* to take a spoil," but, " are you come;" that is, are you come to *us* to take a spoil from us. The term " young lions," which means young powers or states, is a question propounded by the states as well as by the merchants.

Eleventh. "Therefore, son of man, prophesy and say unto Gog: Thus saith the Lord God; in that day when my people of Israel dwell safely shalt thou not know it?" Here a repetition of the prophecy begins. It is interrogatively affirmed, that Russia shall be thoroughly acquainted with Israel restored.

Twelfth. "And thou shalt come from thy place out of the north parts, thou, and many people with thee, all of them riding upon horses, a great company and a mighty army."

The seat of Gog's empire is here shown to be relatively a north country, which again coincides with Russia. A mighty army and company is to attend the power of Russia at this great invasion. "All of them riding upon horses." This is figuratively put for the character of the invading host. The Cossack forces of Russia and Turcomania boast that they have furnished horsemen for war " by the million."—(*Gibbon.*)

Thirteenth. "And thou shalt come up against my people Israel, as a cloud to cover the land." This is a repetition of the same facts already stated, in almost the same words.

Fourteenth. " It shall be in the latter days." This fastens the time to the later ages of Christianity, for the words, " latter days," when used prophetically, always refer to that late period.—(*Faber.*)

Fifteenth. " And I will bring thee against my land, that the heathen may know me, when I shall be sanctified in thee, O Gog, before their eyes." Here God asserts that he brings Russia, and Europe, and the world to this war, to manifest his glory to the heathen, or wicked world.

Sixteenth. "Thus saith the Lord God, Art thou he of whom I have spoken in old time, by my servants, the prophets of Israel, which prophesied in those days many years, that I would bring thee against them." As this address is made at the very time of the invasion, the ancient prophets referred to, must be those who, in all past ages, had predicted the doom of monarchy by Israel restored. There is, indeed, scarcely a prophecy of Israel's restoration, in the Christian age, but treats also of the overthrow of monarchy, or the heathen, by the arm of Israel restored.

Seventeenth. "And it shall come to pass, at the same time when Gog shall come against the land of Israel, saith the Lord God, that my fury shall come up in my face, for in my jealousy, and in the fire of my wrath have I spoken." Here God declares he will aid Israel in battle, with tremendous passion. Certainly, no one supposes that God in person will appear at that time; for Christ says he will not appear till "the tribulation of those days be ended." The reference, therefore, must be to the anger of God's Israel, who are called by his name.

Eighteenth. "Surely in that day there shall be a great shaking in the land of Israel, so that the fishes of the sea, and the fowls of heaven, and the beasts of the field, and all creeping things that creep upon the earth, and all the men that are upon the face of the earth, shall shake at my presence, and the mountains shall be thrown down, and the steep places shall fall, and every wall shall fall to the ground." This is descriptive of the terrible wrath that will shake our nation, and set the world on fire with destruction. Heavens! what an hour that will be!

Nineteenth. "And I will call for a sword against him throughout all my mountains, saith the Lord." Calling for a sword is a tremendous call for slaughter. The term mountains is used figuratively for governments or states, and shows that all the states of our Union will rally to a man in the dreadful fray.

Twentieth. "And every man's sword shall be against his brother." This indicates, that in Europe, at the time of this invasion, great insurrections will transpire, and that revolts among Russian troops may be generally expected.

Twenty-first. "And I will plead against him with pestilence and with blood; and I will rain upon him, and upon his bands, and upon the many people that are with him, an overflowing rain and great hail stones, fire and brimstone." Here dreadful war and sickness are to afflict the invading host. The rain and hail, and fire and brimstone, indicate great destruction by powder and bullets, and cannon balls. "Thus will I magnify myself; and will I be known in the eyes of many nations, and they shall know that I am the Lord."

Paragraph II.—39th Chapter.

This chapter twice repeats the destruction of the European invaders of America.

1. "Therefore thou son of man prophesy against Gog and say, Thus saith the Lord God; Behold I am against

thee, O Gog, the prince of Rosc, Meshech, and Tubal."— *Septuagint.*

2. "I will turn thee back, and leave but the sixth part of thee (or smite thee with six plagues), and will cause thee to come up from the north parts, and will bring thee upon the mountains of Israel; and I will smite thy bow out of thy left hand, and will cause thine arrows to fall out of thy right hand." As God is said to bring Russia to the United States, he will do it instrumentally. No clue is given to the occasion of the invasion in the prophecy.

3. "Thou shalt fall upon the mountains of Israel, thou, and all thy bands, and the people that is with thee." This determines the place of the battle to be in the United States, and shows that monarchy shall here meet its doom.

4. "I will give thee unto the ravenous birds of every sort, and to the beasts of the field, to be devoured. Thou shalt fall upon the open field, for I the Lord have spoken it." This shows that monarchy will have a most inglorious close.

5. "And I will send a fire on Magog, and upon them that dwell carelessly in the isles, and they shall know that I am the Lord." This shows that there shall be fire or war in Europe at the same time. The isles seem to refer to Great Britain. This is indeed confirmed by John, who, at the time he describes the overthrow of Europe by Israel, or the man on the cloud, describes also the treading of the vine or conquest of Britain. He also says Britain, or the false Prophet, shall be taken with the beast, or Russia. "So will I make my holy name known in the midst of my people Israel; and I will not

let them pollute my holy name any more; and the heathen shall know that I am the Lord, the Holy One of Israel."

6. "Behold, it is come, it is done, saith the Lord God, this is the day whereof I have spoken." This is the very language used by John when the seventh vial was poured out, in which Russia and Britain were to be overthrown. "It is done."

"And they that dwell in the cities of Israel shall go forth, and set on fire and burn the weapons, &c., and they shall burn them with fire seven years," &c. This indicates the terrible nature of the victory we shall obtain.

7. "And it shall come to pass, that I will give unto Gog a place there of graves in Israel, &c., and seven months shall the house of Israel be burying of them." This and several succeeding verses, show further the awful nature of the slaughter.

8. The seventeenth verse renews the declaration of the battle: "And thou son of man, thus saith the Lord God, Speak unto every feathered fowl, and every beast of the field, Assemble yourselves and come; gather yourselves together on every side, to my sacrifice, that I do sacrifice for you, even a great sacrifice upon the mountains of Israel, that ye may eat flesh and drink blood. Ye shall eat the flesh of the mighty, and drink the blood of the princes of the earth, of rams, of lambs, and of goats, and of bullocks, all of them fatlings of Bashan. Ye shall eat fat till ye be full, and drink blood till ye be drunken, of my sacrifice which I have sacrificed for you. Thus shall ye be filled at my table, with chariots, with mighty men, and with all men of war, saith the Lord

God. And I will set my glory among the heathen, and all the heathen shall see my judgment which I have executed, and my hand that I have laid upon them." This coincides with the political judgment day of the ancient of days, described by Daniel. A parallel call to beasts and birds to the supper of God, is found in the seventeenth verse of the nineteenth chapter of Revelations.

CONCLUSION.

In this prediction we see all the great forces of Europe, Asia, and Africa, conjoined to invade Israel restored, and they are all allied with Russia. A greater force is assembled, and more millions of men are brought to the contest, and from a broader field, than were ever before assembled. Now, in the name of all that is rational, is it probable or possible to excite and muster such a force, to pull down a few feeble Jews restored to Palestine. What is there, again, that could induce the ruling powers to grant Palestine to carnal Israel, and then bring all creation together to pull them down again. Surely nothing but wild enthusiasm can believe that the great statesmen of Europe and mighty warriors would combine to effect so small a work as the conquest of Palestine. Surely men must be beside themselves who believe such a thing will take place. But if we turn to the United States, the Christian Israel of the latter day, we see a foeman that bids defiance to all their steel, and that would demand such a confederacy as the prophet describes to create even a hope of success in the contest.

If, in addition to this, we take Ezekiel's description of the country and people of Israel which Russia invades, and compare it with our own, the coincidence is perfect. So that common sense and revelation both coincide in determining the United States as the Israel to be invaded by confederate Europe.

This destruction of European monarchy by Israel, coincides with the smiting of the great monarchy image by the stone kingdom; the "casting down of the thrones by the people of the saints;" the destruction of the "willful king between the seas in the glorious holy mountain;" "the reaping of the earth and vine;" and the taking of "the beast and false prophet," before **the** Millennium.

CHAPTER VI.

NEBUCHADNEZZAR'S PANORAMIC VISION OF THE SIX KINGDOMS OF THE WORLD.

The history of the world, and of Israel, as detailed by the literal or metonymic prophets, is repeated by symbolic predictions. It is obvious that prophecies of the same ages in the future, must agree in describing the same events; they can not disagree on the same subjects and points; but, as they give views of the same fields, they must shed light upon each other. Symbolic prophecy is more systematic in its arrangement, more vivid in its pictures, and more exact in its chronology, and has enlisted more efforts of exposition than metonymic prophecy.

Thick darkness has hung over all attempts to unseal that portion of them descriptive of the world from the fall of Jerusalem to the present time.

The learned, and the world at large, have been perplexed greatly at this mystery and blindness, and so complete has been the blindness on the subject, that men have not even seen that Daniel affirmed that the prophets were all sealed from the fall of Jerusalem " to the time of the end." The wise have been divinely and purposely hindered in the work of interpretation of this great era. If, however, our age is " the time of the end " of Israel's wandering, we may anticipate the meaning of "the words closed up and sealed," and we may cautiously examine all theories proposing the solution of the great riddle of the prophets. All theories of the meaning of it must certainly be fraught with some dominant error, if they have been proclaimed before the beginning of the time of the end. And as all theories now in vogue adopt the basis of interpretation projected ages ago, they must drive to the same conclusions and be imperfect, from the same errors. Much may have been done to prepare the way for the final unsealing, yet none has hitherto accomplished the stupendous achievement. With a becoming modesty, we trust we approach a work where a thousand giants have failed to scale the ladder of observation, and view the hidden mansions and golden streets within the secluded city of full revelation. Let us not be charged with presumption in undertaking what was to be accomplished by some common mortal, without the aid of miracle. May not a child discover a priceless gem? did not a timid slave discover the wealth of Peru? and may not one, as insignificant as either, by some strange providence, discover the lost key of the prophetic temple, as readily as the wise in their ermine and glasses? Neither proof nor presumption of our error can be based upon our early years, our humility of station, or unknown scholarship or abilities; these must be judged alone by the nature of our logic, and the realization of our interpretations. Good sense must test the one, and future events the other; facts already known will certify whether we are correct as to the past, and give presumptive testimony of our future accuracy. All we ask is an unbiassed judgment in the mind of the examiner.

We begin our expositions by taking the for, *four* general prophecies of the world's history, related by Daniel.

These prophecies were given between the years 607 and 530 B. C. The first was given in the days of Nebuchadnezzar, and is an interpretation of a vision of that monarch; the second was given in the first year of Belshazzar; the third in the third year of the same king; and the fourth in the first year of Darius the Mede. Each prophecy contains the history of the world from the date when it was given. We begin with

Nebuchadnezzar's vision of the six kingdoms.— "Thou, O king, sawest, and behold a great image. This great image, whose brightness was excellent, stood before thee; and the form thereof was terrible. This image's head was of fine gold, his breast and arms of silver, his belly and his thighs of brass, his legs of iron, his feet part of iron and part of clay. Thou sawest *till that* a stone was cut out without hands, which smote the image upon his feet, that were of iron and clay, and brake them to pieces.

"Then was the iron, the clay, the brass, the silver, and the gold broken to pieces together, and became like the chaff of the summer threshing floors; and the wind carried them away, that no place was found for them; and the stone that smote the image, became a great mountain, and filled the whole earth. This is the dream: and we will tell the interpretation thereof before the king. Thou, O king, art a king of kings; for the God of heaven hath given thee a kingdom, power, and strength, and glory. And wheresoever the children of men dwell, the beasts of the field and the fowls of heaven hath he given into thine hand, and hath made thee ruler over them all. Thou art this head of gold.

"And after thee shall arise another kingdom inferior to thee, and another third kingdom of brass, which shall bear rule over all the earth.

"And the fourth kingdom shall be strong as iron, forasmuch as iron breaketh in pieces and subdueth all things; and as iron that breaketh all these, shall it break in pieces and bruise.

"And whereas, thou sawest the feet and toes part of iron, the kingdom shall be divided, forasmuch as thou sawest the iron mixed with miry clay. And as the toes of the feet were part of iron and part of clay, so the kingdom shall be partly strong and partly broken. And whereas, thou sawest the iron mixed with miry clay,* they shall mingle themselves with the seed of men; but they shall not cleave one to another, even as iron is not mixed with clay. And in the days of these kings shall the God of heaven set up a kingdom, which shall never be destroyed, and the kingdom shall not be left to other people, but it shall break in pieces and consume all these kingdoms, and it shall stand forever.

"Forasmuch as thou sawest that the stone was cut out of the mountain without hands, and that it broke in pieces the iron, the brass, the clay, the silver, and the gold: the great God hath made known to the king what shall come to pass hereafter; the dream is certain, and the interpretation thereof sure."—Ch. ii.

There is one peculiarity in the symbolic prophecies which must be noted; that is, that the vision of the

---

* Baked clay.—(*Bush.*)

future is generally accompanied by an interpretation, so that in fact, each prophecy is doubled to us; and each complex part of the prophecy receives also an especial interpretation in addition to the general one.

This vision comprehends the great spiritual and political history of the world, divided into great periods, definitely marked. The image is the embodiment of all the great monarchical governments that were ever to exist, for so the prophet affirms. These monarchies are said, by the text, to be four in number; and expositors generally agree that they were the Babylonian, Medo-Persian, Macedonian, and Roman empires, and are by them commonly called the four universal empires, though they were not, strictly speaking, entirely universal. The fifth empire is reckoned to be Christianity, and the sixth the final kingdom of Messiah.

To this general interpretation we agree, with but one exception, and that is, the interpretation of the fifth to be Christianity. We have already adverted to the fact, that Daniel affirmed that his prophecies of the period under consideration were not to be clearly understood, "until the time of the end;" and, of course, all systems of interpretation of this period, must be liable to some capital defect which prevents the proper understanding of his words. The first and most important thing that can be done, is to ascertain where the error lies. We affirm that it exists in the interpretation given to the stone cut out of the mountain, or to the fifth kingdom of the vision. We shall undertake the proof of this by proceeding with a regular interpretation of the whole vision, beginning with the first, and proceeding to the final kingdom in chronological order.

SECTION I.

Head of the Image—Babylon.

"This image's head was of fine gold." "Thou art this head of gold." Here we have both the vision and the interpretation. The kingdom of Nebuchadnezzar is thus promptly explained to be represented by the golden head of the image, and the term Nebuchadnezzar is put metonymically for the Babylonian empire. This empire is said to embrace the earth, " wheresoever the children of men dwell," and may properly be called a universal empire. Its capital was in Asia, yet it subdued a portion of Africa, by the reduction of Egypt and Libya. Europe, at that time, seems also to have offered temptations to conquest, and Megasthenes affirms that even Spain was subjected by Nebuchadnezzar.

SECTION II.

The Medo-Persian Empire—Arms and Breast of Silver.

"This image's head was of fine gold, his breast and his arms of silver." "Thou art this head of gold, and after thee shall arise another kingdom inferior to thee."

As the first kingdom coincided with the gold, or first division of the image, so the second kingdom must coincide with the second division of the image, which was the breast and arms of silver. The *name* of the second kingdom is not given, but the means of ascertaining its name are fully sufficient to determine it as soon as it makes its appearance; for the name of the first kingdom being given, as soon as the second kingdom arises, its name must be known. It is as easy to identify objects by the numbers they bear, as it is to identify them by names upon them. These four great kingdoms are numbered severally, by four numerals in categorical or chronological succession, beginning with number one, and proceeding regularly onward in the consecutive order of one, two, three, four. The names of the four kingdoms are to be found, with the numbers they bear in prophecy, the name of the first in the series being given. If we number four consecutive letters of the alphabet, one, two, three, and four, and state that the first in the series is A, every one knows that number two will coincide with the letter B, and that B is the name of number two, and so C and D will, in like manner, coincide with numbers three and four. And just so the Medo-Persian empire must be the name of the second kingdom in the series presented by Daniel, since the first in the series is named Babylon, because the Medo-Persian empire was the next in order to Babylon chronologically. How any one could mistake so plain a mode of identifying the four kingdoms is hard to divine, unless we allow that they were judicially blinded.

Media and Persia were originally provinces of the Assyrian empire, and in the days of Cyrus they were united in one monarchy, and overturned the Babylonian empire; and of course this was the second empire intended by Daniel, since it removed the first and raised itself upon its ruins. It was to be inferior to the Babylonian empire. This may be understood in the sense of being less extensive in territory, or inferior in moral force, in both of which it was inferior to the Babylonian kingdom. "Neither Cyrus, nor any of his successors, carried their arms into Africa and Spain so far as Nebuchadnezzar is reported to have done."—(*Newton*.) Dr. Prideaux says, the kings of Persia "were the worst race of men that ever governed an empire."

The two arms of the breast, may properly represent the two kingdoms of Media and Persia conjoined; the silver, being less valuable than gold, may represent the moral inferiority of the Persian empire to the Babylonian.

SECTION III.

The Macedonian Empire — Belly and Thighs of Brass.

Text.—"This image's head was of fine gold, his breast and his arms of silver, his belly and his thighs of brass."

Interpretation.—"Thou art this head of gold. And after thee shall arise another kingdom inferior to thee, and another third kingdom of brass, which shall bear rule over all the earth."

In the vision we now see three parts of the image; the head, the breast and arms, and belly and thighs; these are composed each of a different metal, and each metal represents a different kingdom. Now, as the gold head represents the Babylonian, and the silver breast and arms represent the Medo-Persian kingdom, the brass must represent the third kingdom; and the interpretation says the third kingdom was of brass, and that it should bear rule over all the earth. We have then three great marks, by which to identify the name of the third kingdom: 1. It was to be the third in the order of the four empires. 2. Its character was to differ from the other three. 3. It was to bear rule over all the earth. 4. It was finally to exist in two parts. With these four marks the Macedonian empire agrees, and no other empire does, and therefore it must be the empire predicted. For it is infallibly true, that perfect coincidence of events with prophecy is a perfect fulfillment of prophecy.

Coincidence First.—Alexander the Great subverted the Persian empire and founded the Macedonian on its ruins, so that the third kingdom in chronological order from the Babylonian, inclusive, that appeared in the world, was the Macedonian. It is plain that these four several empires could not rise simultaneously into their *fullness* of strength, since all were to occupy the very same territories. Each successor was, therefore, to overthrow its predecessor, to make room for itself.

Coincidence Second.—Bishop Newton says, the Macedonian empire was fitly represented by brass, for the Greeks were famous for their brazen armor, their usual epithet being, *the brazen-coated Greeks.*

St. Jerome in commenting on this point, says, "they may rightly be said to be of brass. For among all metals, brass is more sonorous, tinkles loudest, and its sound is diffused far and wide, and so it shows not only the fame and power of the kingdom, but also of the Greek tongue." While these things may have had some influence in determining the name of brass to the Macedonian empire, we think that more extensive qualities were indicated. The gold of the head indicated the refined character, and splendor, and value of the Babylonian empire; and the silver the inferior value and splendor of the Persian power; and the brass, being baser, yet stronger than gold or silver, may indicate a baser moral character of government, but of greater energy and capabilities in war. The Macedonian empire being compared to the belly and thighs, shows not only its position chronologically, but appropriately denotes its beastly sensuality. Alexander's moral character was that of the vilest and most lustful sensualist on the page of history, and his kingdom took its cue from its founder. The moral history of the Seleucidæ and Lagidæ, or Syria and Egypt, which coincide with the two thighs, is one that might, in licentiousness, outvie the manners of Sodom.

Coincidence Third.—The third kingdom was to bear rule over all the earth. The term *all the earth* has a variety of meanings, but generally signifies only a very large portion of the world, but more especially the civilized world. Alexander commanded that he should be called, "king of all the world," not that he literally ruled every individual man, woman, and child on earth, but that his kingdom was so large as to be commonly spoken of, in that age, as embracing all the world. His kingdom comprehended Europe, Africa, and Asia as largely as any empire ever did, except the Roman.

Coincidence Fourth.—The later existence of the third kingdom was to be marked by a division into two branches. This is indicated by the two thighs of brass. One kind of metal indicates only one kingdom, prophetically, or one dynasty. The gold indicates but one kingdom, the silver, though divided into three parts, the breast, and two arms, nevertheless indicates prophetically but one compound kingdom, and the same must hold good of the brass. As the image expresses chronology, from the head downward, the thighs must represent the later stage of the kingdom of brass, just as the arms at the upper part of the breast indicate the duality and union of the Medo-Persian empire, in its early history. As the thighs were less than the belly, they by this indicated that these two divisions of the kingdom would be less extensive than the kingdom in its first organization.

Now, the Macedonian empire, soon after the death of Alexander, was divided into four parts, at the heads of which were Cassander, Lysymachus, Ptolemy, and Seleucus. But out of these four, but two divisions at length remained; these two were those of the Lagidæ and Seleucidæ, reigning in Egypt and Syria. Newton says, "their kingdom was no more a different kingdom, than the parts differ from the whole. It was the same government still continued. They who governed were still Macedonians. The metal was the same, and the nation was the same; nor is the same nation ever represented by different metals, but the different metals always signify different nations. All ancient authors speak of the kingdom of Alexander and his successors as one and the same kingdom. The thing is implied in the very name by which they are called, 'the successors of Alexander.' There is one insuperable objection against the kingdoms of the Lagidæ and Seleucidæ being a different one from that of Alexander, because if they are not considered as parts of Alexander's dominion, they can not be counted as one kingdom, but constitute two separate and distinct kingdoms." As, therefore, the Macedonian empire coincides with all the marks given in prophecy by which to identify the third great monarchy, and as no other nation does, it follows infallibly that it was predicted by the vision.

SECTION IV.

THE FOURTH KINGDOM—ROME.

Vision.—"The image's head was of fine gold; his breast and his arms of silver; his belly and thighs of brass; his legs of iron, his feet part of iron and part of clay."

Interpretation.—"And the fourth kingdom shall be strong as iron; forasmuch as iron breaketh, all these shall it break in pieces and bruise. And whereas thou sawest the feet and toes, part of potter's clay, and part of iron, the kingdom shall be divided; but there shall be in it of the strength of the iron, forasmuch as thou sawest the iron mixed with miry clay. And as the toes of the feet were part of iron and part of clay, so the kingdom shall be partly strong and partly broken. And whereas thou sawest iron mixed with clay, THEY shall mingle themselves with the seed of men; but they shall not cleave to one another, even as iron is not mixed with clay. Thou sawest till that a stone was cut out without hands, which smote the image upon his *feet*, that were of iron and clay, and brake them to pieces." We have here a prediction of the Roman empire. It is represented as existing in three distinct forms, or periods, and as perishing under the last. We will consider each of these forms separately.

Paragraph I.

First Period. Rome as a Unit.—"His legs were of iron." "And the fourth kingdom shall be strong as iron; forasmuch as iron breaketh in pieces and subdueth all things; and as iron that breaketh all these shall it break in pieces and bruise." This represents the first period of the fourth empire.

1. We have seen that the Babylonian empire was represented by the gold, the Medo-Persian, by silver, and that the Macedonian, including the Lagidæ and Seleucidæ, were symbolized by the belly and thighs of brass, and of course the fourth great empire was to follow the kingdom of brass, and to succeed the kingdoms of Egypt and Syria in chronological order.

We are thus particular, because some expositors have, in their blindness, interpreted the *two* kingdoms of Syria and Egypt to be the ONE fourth kingdom. Porphyry, the ancient foe of prophecy, asserted this, and some moderns have sided with him. Bishop Newton says, that they who follow this infidel, do so from an innate love of disputation, rather than from any love of truth. Now, as the Roman empire was the fourth that followed from the Babylonian, it is identical with the fourth empire of this vision.

2. The strength of the fourth empire.

Each of the metals of the image plainly represented by its qualities the political character of the empire it symbolized. The gold indicated the splendor, but comparative weakness of Babylon; and easily fell before the silver empire of Medo-Persia, which, though a less splendid, was yet a stronger power, as silver is less splendid, yet comparatively stronger than gold. Silver is a more splendid, yet feebler metal than brass, and the Persian empire was more excellent than the Macedonian, yet was too feeble to resist the impetuosity of the brazen-coated Greeks. In like manner as brass, silver, and gold all yield to the superior strength of iron, so the fourth empire was to break up and subdue, by superior strength, all of the preceding dynasties that remained before it. Rome has the best claim to this iron character of any nation that ever existed. Whether consolidated or in fragments, it has wielded greater power and commanded a larger measure of influence, been more resistless in war and endured more lastingly, than any other empire whatever. It was a vast kingdom of warriors, and that, too, for ages, and Mars was its tutelary deity; its codes of jurisprudence, also, have yielded a commanding influence in the earth for near two thousand years. As iron is the strongest of metals, so Rome has been the strongest of all nations.

3. The fourth kingdom was to crush all other nations.

Rome conquered all nations, and, in our Saviour's time, the terms Rome and the whole earth were generally used as synonymous terms. The riches and glory of three continents were either embraced in its limits or its tributaries; it comprehended all of the civilized world, and much of the barbarous. It existed as an iron unit down to the days of Theodosius, or for a thousand years.

Paragraph II.

Second Period. Church and State Union and the fall of Rome, or its broken state, iron and clay.—The text affirms two things with regard to the history of the fourth great empire. It says of it, that it shall be divided, and then it says it shall be broken. The divided and the broken states spoken of, are two totally different matters; the division into iron and clay is what is meant by the term *division*, and refers to a double political character of the empire; and the broken state refers to the fall of the empire, or its fragmentary condition indicated by the toes. We shall consider these two points separately.

CLAUSE I.

Church and State Union.—A division of the political power of the fourth empire into two great departments of church and state, is what is predicted by the iron and clay of the feet and toes. The text says "whereas thou sawest the feet and toes part of potter's (baked) clay, and part of iron, the kingdom shall be divided; but there shall be in it of the strength of the iron, forasmuch as thou sawest the iron mixed with baked clay."

In the final vision of Daniel, in which the previous visions are interpreted, we find it said that the visions embracing the period from the captivity by the Romans to the restoration of Israel, was to be a veiled one. And as the text before us relates to events during that period, its mystery was guarantied by the Divine will, and of course all expositions of it during that era must be imperfect.

However, not an expositor, to our knowledge, among the many we have examined, has considered with any proper and critical attention, the division of the fourth empire into iron and clay. Now, not a word of holy writ is unimportant, or can be overlooked, without detriment to its proper understanding; and in a prophecy which in a very few sentences describes the history of the world for thousands of years, not one jot or tittle can be overlooked, for each minute point of the graphic miniature must possess a sublime importance when expanded into its full life size. It is, therefore, of vital importance to a correct interpretation of the prophecy before us, that the divisions of the fourth empire should be most carefully noticed and explained. We therefore call emphatic attention to the following points, on which hinges a full and harmonious view of the whole vision.

1. The empire was to possess a dual political character. This dual character is symbolized by the iron and clay in the feet, and also in the toes of the image. As the iron unquestionably represented the political character of the empire, and as the clay comes in and mixes with the iron in about equal proportions, they must conjointly represent the political character of the empire after this union.

2. The prophet's interpretation still further confirms its signification to be political. He says, "Whereas thou sawest the iron mixed with miry clay, they shall mingle themselves with the seed of men; but they shall not cleave to one another, even as iron is not mixed with clay." Here the term iron is plainly seen to represent men, and the clay being interpreted by the term "they," is seen to represent men also; or two orders of men

in the state are indicated by the terms " iron and clay." The want of harmony between the iron and clay, shows a want of political harmony in the state. Again the text says, "there shall be in it of the strength of the iron, forasmuch as thou sawest the iron mixed with miry clay." Here strength of national power is represented by iron, and comparative feebleness by the clay.

3. This division in the fourth empire was not to occur until the empire had stood for some time as an iron kingdom only; after a season this division was to begin and to continue through that period of the history of the empire represented by the toes. The division begins in the feet, and continues till the feet are smitten by the stone.

4. There were to be two classes of men, in the fourth empire, between whom the political power was to be divided. The class represented by the iron certainly possessed civil authority, and the other class possessed it to a certain extent. The term, "seed of men," coincides with the term iron, and the term iron coincides with civil power or nationality, represented by the iron legs; hence the term "clay," which is synonymous with the term "they," which is here a pronoun of multitude, must represent also a great class of men associated in the general government with that class designated by "iron" or "seed of men."

5. Again; the term "they," is antithetic to the term "seed of men," and is therefore expressive of a class of people antithetic in character to those represented by iron. The term "they shall mingle themselves with the seed of men," conveys, with great clearness, the idea of the degradation of a superior class of persons by the

mingling with the seed of men in national affairs. It is very similar to a passage in Genesis, which speaks of the corruption of the sons of God, by uniting with the daughters of men. The "mingling with the seed of men," by this superior class, also conveys plainly the notion of a spiritual people uniting with a political power. Indeed, as no two classes of men can be found in the world, corresponding to the two in the text, except spiritual and carnal people, the union of these two classes in the fourth empire, must represent church and state union in it; and as in the Roman, or fourth great empire, such a union did exist, the case is a very clear one, that the mingled clay represented the church of Christ, corrupted by union with the civil power of Rome, represented by the iron.

6. This political union of civil and ecclesiastical polity, was to be perpetual. This is manifested by the symbols and interpretations. The clay continued during that portion of Roman history represented by the feet, during which time, Rome was still a territorial unit; after the breaking up of this territorial unity, it continued to exist in the toes or various nations of Europe represented by them; and finally, when the feet are broken, the clay is found existing in them, and shares the fate of the iron.

CLAUSE II.

Fall of Rome or its broken State.—" And the toes of the feet, part of iron, and part of clay—the kingdom shall be partly strong and partly broken." The words, *as*, *were*, and *so*, which are found in the common text, were supplied by translators, and are not in the original. This text shows, that the breaking up of the iron and clay was to take place; and the term "*broken*," differs materially from the term "*division*" in signification. In this text, the feet are not mentioned, the toes only are treated of, and, of course, the interpretation is of the toes only; the clay and iron are mentioned to show that in the broken state, the divisions, or fragmentary nations, would still retain the double political organization of church and state union. The legs, for the time being, represented the Roman empire; and, in like manner, the toes represented it, also. Now, mark this point with attention: historians, in speaking of the Roman empire, always now speak of it as having ceased to exist; but the prophetic historian regards its broken state as still continuing to be the fourth empire; the former do not anticipate a reorganization, but the latter predict a reunion of the fragments into a great empire. The number of toes in the feet of the image being ten, each toe would naturally signify a kingdom itself. That there might be more than ten, during the long period of the broken state, is neither affirmed nor contradicted, but we can look for no more than ten at the time when the breaking up of the unity of government was to take place. In a succeeding vision of Daniel, coinciding with this, ten is distinctly stated as the number into which Rome in Europe was to be divided. The text before us, however, simply affirms, that the ten toes indicate the disruption or fall of Rome. The Roman empire in Europe was broken up, and there soon appeared ten coeval kingdoms. In the Apocalypse it is said, that just prior to the organization of the empire again, that there shall be ten kingdoms. Newton says, that whatever was their subsequent number, all of them are called ten, from their original number. The whole of the disorganized period of the empire will, therefore, be properly represented by ten toes or ten horns, no matter what number may coexist in any age after the first, in which the original ten appeared.

The breaking of the empire began about 396, and the empire still exists in that state, the prophecy recognizing the broken state as continuing to be the fourth empire, and history looking upon it as ended.

Paragraph III.

Third Period. Reorganization of the Fourth Empire.—But few prophetic expositors have looked far enough to see the whole truth of the fourth empire. It is clear that the fourth empire is to be reorganized. By this we mean, that a large portion of the empire represented by the ten toes in Europe, and by the broken state in Asia and Africa, will combine again; that is, the reorganized empire will embrace a portion of three continents.

The facts by which the third territorial form is proved, are few, but conclusive.

1. It is said the stone struck the image upon his feet, which were of iron and clay, and destroyed it. Now, as the image is strictly chronological in its symbols, it is evident that the toes represented a later period of time than the feet, just as the fall of Rome was later than the beginning of church and state union.

It is also as evident, as the sun at mid-day, that the smiting of the feet, and the instant fall of the great image of monarchy, was a later time than that of the ten toes, or broken state of the empire. If this last were not true, then the broken state, represented by the toes, could never have existed; for the feet, aside from the toes, represented the empire as a unit, divided into civil and ecclesiastical government, and the toes represented a later period than the feet. As, therefore, the state of the empire represented by the feet, was obliged to exist before that represented by the toes could exist, and as both could not simultaneously exist, and, as the image was smitten on the consolidated and broken state represented by both feet and toes, it is obvious that the empire to be smitten thus, must assume a form of unity, such as was represented by the feet. The symbols being expressive of territorial form as well as of chronology, make this understanding of them reasonable, and indeed imperative.

2. When the feet of the image were smitten by the stone, THEN it broke in pieces the iron, gold, clay, brass, and silver, altogether. Now, as the gold represented the Assyrian government, and the silver the Persian, and the brass the Grecian, it is evident that an empire in which these existed, together with the iron and clay, must have been smitten by the stone, or they could not have been broken together by a single stroke.

3. The time when they were broken was not to be a long period, but a short one. The whole image fell, the moment it was smitten. It was struck with violence, and, the vision says, "then" the image was broken. The term "then" has but one brief signification; it means "at that time," and not at some other time, nor during a long period of time. At the very time, then, that the image was struck, it fell to atoms; it did not wait and fall some other time; its metals all perished then; they did not wait to be worn away by any slow moral process of decomposition.

4. In all the other symbolic prophecies of the fourth empire, it is represented as being reconstituted for a very short period before its annihilation; this general uniformity must, therefore, be confirmatory of our position here.

We have given every point of character the fourth empire was to possess, together with the time of its rise; the empire, therefore, which coincides with all these points, must be the one predicted by the vision and the interpretation, for perfect coincidence between events and prophecy is infallibly perfect fulfillment.

Coincidence First. Repetition.—The fourth kingdom of iron was to follow the one of brass. The brass being the Macedonian empire, the next empire which followed it must be the iron one. Now, nothing is plainer than that the Roman empire followed the Macedonian.

Coincidence Second. Political strength.—The fourth empire was to be politically as strong as iron, and as much stronger than the empires which preceded it, as iron is stronger than brass, or gold, or silver. To this character the Roman empire has the fullest of claims. Whether consolidated, or in fragments, it has wielded greater power, and commanded a larger measure of influence, and endured more lastingly than any other empire ever did. The Roman empire was a kingdom of mighty warriors for ages, and its codes of jurisprudence have wielded a commanding sway over the nations for near two thousand years. As iron is the strongest of metals, so Rome was the strongest of human empires.

Coincidence Third.—The fourth kingdom was to crush all other nations, and become universal. Rome conquered all nations, and the term applied to the Roman empire was the common term used in our Saviour's day to represent the whole world; the riches and glory of three continents were tributary to it, or embraced in its limits. It comprehended all the civilized world, and much of the barbarous.

Coincidence Fourth.—The political complexion of the fourth kingdom, after a given period of time had elapsed, was to be of a dual character, in which the church was to be mixed or united with the political iron power, and was to continue to the end of the empire, in all its territorial forms. Not quite four hundred years after the extinction of the Macedonian power, the Christian church was united to the Roman political power, and, in every stage of the history of the empire, since the days of Constantine, this mixture has continued. In the broken state of the empire in Modern Europe, this union still abides, and seems likely to abide while monarchy endures. As the clay is a base material, so the Christian church, by this union with the state, has been grossly corrupted; and they who mingled themselves with the seed of men, have become baser than the iron of the world. As the clay and iron were not to cleave closely to each other, so has been this debased alloy of church and state. The exact relationship of the church to the state has never been generally agreed upon; and there has been, through past ages, a constant struggle between them for political supremacy, the iron generally prevailing over the clay. Popes have arrogated supremacy, and absolved nations from allegiance to kings and princes; but kings and princes have generally carried the day. So that while they have remained, and do remain combined, they have never been chemically united; even "as iron is not (chemically united, or) mixed with clay." They have had conflicting interests, and, from the nature of the case, they always will have. Nothing can exceed the accuracy of the brief description the prophet gives of church and state union in the Roman empire, since its institution. Nothing in fact could be more perfect.

Coincidence Fifth. First Territorial Form.—The first *territorial* form of the fourth empire, was to be that of a unit. The Roman empire was a unit territorially, down to the days of Theodosius, in the year 395; and after his death it began to be broken up by the northern migrations.

Coincidence Sixth.—The second territorial form of the fourth empire, was to be a broken one, and one part was to be divided into ten kingdoms. The Roman empire, or at least that portion of it which was in Europe, was broken to pieces by the inroads of the Germans, Goths, Vandals, and Huns; and ten kingdoms, in less than two hundred years, made their appearance. The Eastern empire existed up to this time; but, after Justinian, it declined, till all its light was extinguished. These ten Roman kingdoms, though not exactly simultaneous in origin, were just enough so to accord with the symbol which represented them and the empire. It is observable, that the toes of the feet do not project from the foot in a right line across the foot, and that the foot is longer on one side than on the other. And so, a large part of the original empire represented by the feet, still existed, after some of the smaller toe kingdoms began to project; and so, also, some of these ten kingdoms sprung up a very little in advance of others, yet all in the same era.

Coincidence Seventh.—These fragments of the fourth kingdom, were again to confederate. This has not yet taken place, and we can not, therefore, claim a certain coincidence here. The signs of the times, however, indicate, so it is thought by those who know best the state of eastern Europe, that Russia will effect a subserviency of Europe to its power. The exiled Hungarian affirmed upon this subject, the following bold, yet not improbable things. "I predict (and the eternal God hears my prediction), that there can be no freedom for Europe, and that the Cossacks from the shores of the Don, will water their steeds in the Rhine, unless liberty be restored to Hungary." Indeed, we can not entertain a doubt of the supremacy of Russia over all Europe, for such is clearly to be understood from the book of Revelation and Ezekiel.

The conclusion we draw from these most extensive and complete coincidences of the Roman empire with the fourth kingdom is, that the Roman empire was meant by the prophecy; indeed, it is infallibly certain; for a full and perfect coincidence of prophecy and events, is, infallibly, a clear fulfillment.

Newton says, "All ancient writers, both Jewish and Christian, agree with Jerome, in explaining the fourth kingdom to be the Roman." Mede says, "The Roman empire, to be the fourth kingdom of Daniel, was believed by the church of Israel, both before and in our Saviour's time; received by the disciples of the apostles, and the whole Christian church, for the first three hundred years, without any known contradictions. And I confess, having so good ground in scripture, it is with me, *tantum non est articulus fidei,* little less than an article of faith."

SECTION V.

The Fifth Kingdom, or United States of America.

" Westward the course of empire takes its way,
The *first four acts* already passed,
The fifth shall close the drama with the day:
Time's noblest empire is its last "

Vision.—" Thou sawest till that a stone was cut out without hands, which smote the image upon his feet, that were of iron and clay, and broke them to pieces."

Interpretation.—"And in the days of these kings shall the God of heaven set up a kingdom, which shall never be destroyed: and the kingdom shall not be left to other people, but it shall break in pieces and consume all these kingdoms, and it shall stand forever."

. It is but right for us to observe, that our discoveries in interpreting scripture, have compelled us to affirm that this fifth kingdom which the vision presents, and which Daniel interprets, is no other, and can be no other, than the restoration of Israel to nationality, or, in other words, it is the United States of America. Our arguments to prove it, shall be as fair and candid as they have been on the preceding kingdoms. As we shall be candid and honest, we insist that the same correctness of courtesy shall be shown to our arguments, that are shown, or ought to be shown, to every investigator, and especially to one treading a new path for truth. The difficulties under which we shall labor here, we know are great, but we are confident they do not arise from the subject, nor from the trouble of logically demonstrating our position; but they lie altogether in the preconceived opinions of men upon the subject, and the firm and settled error of those opinions, and the determined hostility to any argument that would overthrow or unsettle them. Some persons have never fully formed an opinion on the subject; while others have satisfied themselves that some one has made a great mistake in explaining prophecy somehow, and are consequently distrustful of the ability of any man to throw any new light upon the subject. Others, and of the smaller class, are ever ready fairly to examine all honorable argument, and to decide justly. As the decisions of this class will ultimately prevail, we appeal to them to see that justice is done us; if we are wrong, we crave no mercy; if we are logically true, we claim a candid support. Is not this fair? Let the prejudiced remember, that perhaps their opinions are not infallible, and that, after all, they may be just a little wrong, if no more. For the captious, we have not a word; not the first favor have we to ask of them, except—that they will be kind enough to take exceptions to some things, and to all things, we propose.

Two classes of opinions about the signification of the fifth kingdom, have gained considerable ascendency in the world. One class of expositors hold, that the stone is a political power, and another that it is purely a spiritual power, and that it is no other than Christianity. The former suppose that it represents Jesus Christ in his kingdom, suddenly appearing to break the political powers of the earth to pieces, and the latter suppose it to represent the gradual consuming of wicked governments by the prevalence of piety. We hold, that neither system of exposition is exactly correct, and that the truth lies between them. We do not propose to answer the arguments in favor of either theory, directly. We shall explain the fifth kingdom by the exact description given, and let the *arguments in favor of our scheme* be a sufficient proof of the erroneousness of the other theories. We shall proceed to particularize, with severe discrimination, each point in the description of the stone kingdom, and, having minutely developed all that is said, we shall look then for a corresponding kingdom in history. Understand us: we will admit no loose or vague opinion upon any point here; and every point in the coincidence must match with the prophecy, as regularly as each letter upon a newspaper matches with the types of the form upon which the impression was made.

The following are all the points which are given to identify the fifth kingdom:

1. The time of its rise. 2. The character and mode of its origin. 3. Its character and its work of demolition, and the manner of it. 4. Its change of character. 5. Its perpetuity. 6. Its character as a theocratic republic and royalty.

First. The Time of its Rise.—The time of its rise is expressed and implied in the positive words of the vision, and in those of the interpretation, and in the time when the destruction of the image was to take place.

To render the matter plain, we shall quote the text carefully. "This image's head was of fine gold, his breast and his arms of silver, his belly and thighs of brass, his legs of iron, his feet part of iron and part of clay. *Thou sawest till that a stone was cut out without hands."*

Now, mark earnestly the following facts: It is certain that the image was a chronological one, and represented successive kingdoms, and successive periods in those kingdoms, from the Babylonian to the broken state of the Roman empire, represented by toes of iron and clay. In seeing these several kingdoms, it is certain that Nebuchadnezzar saw the history of the world, down to the subversion of the Roman empire. It is certain that he saw a period of time, extending from the days of Nebuchadnezzar down to the fifth century. It is certain, that after he had seen the whole era of the image down to the broken stages of Rome, that he continued to look prospectively into the future. It is certain that he did not see the empire of the stone, until he had seen the whole history of the world, from his own days to those of the broken empire. It is certain that he saw the stone kingdom, by looking beyond the period of the broken state of Rome, and that he did not see it by any retrospective view. These statements are plainly comprehended, and explicitly stated in the text. 1. The prophet expressly told the king, that *after* he had seen the whole prophetic and chronological image, down to the *toes*, that then, he continued to look *forward*, and that in looking *forward*, his attention was arrested by the sight of a stone cut out of the mountain without hands. The expression, " thou sawest till that a stone was cut out," indubitably signifies a looking into the future, and a looking into the future from the toe period, on which his attention had last rested. The term, "thou sawest till," has an expressiveness of futurity in it absolutely, as well as relatively. The word *till*, says Mr. Webster, signifies " to the time of, or to the time, as, I will wait *till* next week," or "occupy *till* I come, "saying they would neither eat nor drink *till* they had slain Paul." The term, " thou sawest," signifies, that he continued to look upon events. Now, as all the events in the vision beside the stone, occurred chronologically, the expression " thou *sawest till that* a stone was cut out," shows that the looking was chronologically into the future.

This view is further confirmed, as well as illustrated, by a parallel and fac-simile passage found in Daniel's vision of the very same events. After Daniel had seen the fourth beast, or kingdom, and its broken state represented by ten horns, and dwelt for awhile upon the broken state of Rome, he says, " I *beheld* or *saw till* the thrones were cast down." The fourth kingdom of the image, and the fourth kingdom represented by the anomalous beast in Daniel's vision, are synonymous ; and the ten toes are synonymous with the ten horns ; and the term, " thou *sawest till* the stone was cut out," and broke the kingdoms to pieces, falls in precisely the same relative position as does the term, " I *saw*, or *beheld till* the thrones were cast down ;" they relate to the same events, and therefore synchronize, and are synonymous, not only in words, but in signification. The meaning of the latter term can not be mistaken, it plainly looks to the destruction of the kingdoms before it by the ancient of days, and to the rise of the ancient of days ; and what IT means, must also be understood by the former term.

2. The interpretation of the vision by the prophet himself, drives us to the same conclusion, irresistibly.

The period of the rise of the fifth kingdom is stated again so circumstantially, as to leave no doubt when it was to occur. The text says, "they shall mingle themselves with the seed of men, but they shall not cleave to one another, even as iron is not mixed with clay. And in the days of these kings shall the God of heaven set up a kingdom."—v. 43, 44. The phrase, "in the days of these kings," is in the Hebrew original, "*beyomahon*," signifying, literally, "in *their* days," and "*dimalchayyah innun*," signifying, "of those kings."—(*Dr. Thomas.*) Now it is a principle of logic that, "relative words should be referred to the nearest, rather than to a remote antecedent."—(*Hedge's Logic.*) Hence the term, "in *their* days, and of *these* kings," must either refer to the persons or kingdoms expressed in the preceding sentence, by the words, "they," "themselves," or of the corrupt church; and by the two kingdoms of iron and clay, or to the kingdoms of the broken state of the empire. We can not, therefore, without a palpable violation of a plain, logical rule, make the terms in, "*their* days, and of those kings," refer to the great period of the whole four kingdoms. Again, the terms in *their* days, and of *those* kings are plural, and doubly imply the existence of a plurality of kings at the time of the setting up of the stone kingdom. Whereas, if this kingdom had arisen in the days of Rome, before it was broken into a plurality of kingdoms, it is a plain case that it would have been set up in the days of *one* king, or kingdom, and not, "in *their* days of *these* kings," as the text says it should be.

In Daniel's vision of the same great period, he presents us with precisely the same number of kingdoms as are found in Nebuchadnezzar's vision. The four kingdoms represented by the four metals, are represented by four beasts; the final, or sixth kingdom, is represented by a mountain in one vision, and by the Son of Man in the other. Now, between the divided state of the Roman empire, and the universal kingdom of Christ, Daniel predicts a fifth kingdom; and the fifth kingdom of Daniel's vision coincides with the fifth of Nebuchadnezzar's, in number, character, work, and final triumph, and, therefore, they are but one and the same kingdom.

Daniel calls his fifth kingdom, "the ancient of days," and says, that it was to arise after the broken state of the Roman empire, and that it would consist of the saints, or Christians, and people of the saints or Christians. He says that it should fully destroy the fourth empire; and as he had said the stone should do that veritable work in full, it follows that the *stone* and the ancient of days represented the same veritable empire. Now then, as Daniel says the ancient of days was to rise after the broken state of Rome, it follows that the stone was also to rise after it, they being but the same identical kingdom.

Second. The Origin of the Stone Kingdom.—No writer we ever heard of, has ever interpreted one vastly important symbol, which we now bring forward. It is the mountain origin of the stone kingdom. The vision says, "thou sawest till a stone was cut out without hands." Here it is very plain that the stone was inherent in something; otherwise it would not have been "cut out." The interpretation says, "Forasmuch as thou sawest that the stone was cut out of the *mountain* without hands." As the stone symbolically represented a kingdom, it is plain that the kingdom was derived from some pre-existent power, from which a kingdom could be formed. Again; as all the symbols were prophetic, the mountain was a *prophetic* one also. The term mountain, when used as a symbol, has a definite meaning, and always signifies a government of some kind, either political or ecclesiastical. Now, the fifth kingdom being cut out of a prophetic kingdom, we must inquire what kind of government it was to be. It is evident, from the nature of the case, that it was a kingdom totally different from any in the image represented by the gold, silver, clay, iron, or brass. It is further clear, that as the stone would partake of the nature of its original composition, that the mountain would be opposed in character to the kingdoms in the image, because the stone kingdom hated and destroyed the other kingdoms. Now, the only great organization in the world that hates corrupt religion and corrupt civil government, is pure and free Christianity, and therefore the mountain must represent the true church, or kingdom, of Christ. Again; as the stone was to be cut out of the mountain in the later, or broken state of Rome, or time of church and state union, it is plain that it was to be composed of a body of Christian people, though perhaps not of all of them, until it was changed into a mountain.

What else the kingdom of the stone could be cut out of, than the church of God, it is hard to divine, since the new kingdom was to be set up by God. The term, "cut out of the mountain," does not imply a part *cut off* from the mountain, as a stone cut off from a cliff, or ledge of rocks composing a mountain, but the change of the mountain substance into a double nature, just as we say a statue is cut out of a block of marble, or a vase is cut out of alabaster. In these cases the marble and alabaster still remain as they were in substance, while, at the same time, they are changed into another character which is essentially distinct from the original material. It is a truth, which forces itself upon us irresistibly, that since Christianity is to spread over the world; in its prevalence, the political constitutions of the tyrannical world must be subverted, and be substituted by a governmental policy growing up out of, and embracing Christianity and Christians. The position can not be denied by any rational and intelligent mind. The cutting, or forming of the stone empire out of the mountain, is, therefore, a most beautiful symbol of the forming of a Christian government out of a Christian people; and it is not less beautiful than truthful.

Third. The Political Character of the Fifth Kingdom.—The fifth empire was to possess a mighty political strength of character. This view was most ably vindicated by Tillinghast, whose work was published in 1654; and has also been, by able Scotch divines of the present century.

Tillinghast says, "The kingdom of the stone is a kingdom, in respect of nature, the same with the kingdoms represented by the great image, i. e., it is Outward as they are Outward; which appears: (1.) From the general scope and drift of the prophecy, which runs upon Outward kingdoms. All the first four kingdoms, or monarchies, are Outward, as none can deny; why, then, the Holy Ghost, in speaking of the fifth and last, should so far vary the scope as to glide from the Outward kingdom to the Inward, ought (besides the bare say-so) to have some solid and substantial reason brought for it by those, *whosoever* they are, that either do or shall assert it. (2.) Because it is not proper to say, that a bare spiritual kingdom, considered only as spiritual, should break in pieces, beat to very chaff, grind to powder the great image, i. e., destroy the very being of worldly kingdoms, which work is yet, notwithstanding, done by the stone. Indeed, Christ's spiritual kingdom may, by that light and life which it gives forth, much refine and reform outward kingdoms; but when once the work comes to breaking, and breaking to pieces, i. e., subverting kingdoms, razing their very foundations and destroying their very being, as they are the kings of this world here, unless we conceive God to do it by a miracle, must we also conceive some other hand, besides a spiritual, to be put to the work. (3.) Because the stone, to the end there might not be a vacancy in the world, comes straightway in the place and room of the great image, so soon as the same is totally broken. For as the great image, while standing, bears rule over all the earth, so the same being broken, the stone becomes a mountain, and fills the whole earth, therefore must the kingdom of the stone be such a kingdom as was that of the great image, viz., Outward; or otherwise, the coming of that, in the place of the other now taken away, could not supply the want of the other."

We arrange our arguments as follows:

1. The nature of the work to be accomplished by the stone was of a purely political, or rather martial character: it was to break up the four great monarchies, and utterly annihilate them. No monarchy was ever broken down, except by martial or political violence: and

no kingdom was ever overthrown by another, without great bloodshed. The vision says, the fifth kingdom shall break the four kingdoms to pieces, and they should become as chaff; the interpretation says, " it shall break in pieces and consume all these kingdoms." Here the stone is stated to perform the work of annihilation of the political fabrics before it, in two ways: first, by breaking them to pieces; and, secondly, by consuming them. The term, " breaking to pieces," must be understood in the same sense in which the prophet uses it in other parts of the prophecy. Now, he said of the fourth kingdom of iron, that it should " break in pieces" all the kingdoms before it. Then, as the Roman, or fourth kingdom, broke in pieces all the nations before it, by the most bloody and devastating wars, it follows, that as the fourth kingdom should be " broken to pieces" by the stone, that the breaking would, in its case, be by dreadful war, as in the other cases. There is no room to evade this conclusion, without violating a plain rule of interpretation : that is, by assigning a different sense to an author's words than he himself has given.

The terms, " became chaff," and " consuming," are obviously somewhat different in signification from that of " breaking to pieces." They imply that the empire was first divided into large masses, and that these were then subjugated, and utterly wasted away by conquest.

St. John, in describing the destruction of the Roman power in the last battles, by the fifth kingdom, says the beast and false prophet were first taken, and then the remnant were slain. The beast corresponds to the fourth kingdom; and his being taken coincides with the breaking up of the image into fragments; and the slaying of the remnant coincides with the consuming process upon the fragments of the broken image.

2. The breaking of the image was by a single and sudden stroke of the stone. Dr. Adam Clarke says, the falling of the stone upon the feet of the image, was like the stroke of a stone discharged violently from a Roman catapult. There was but one stroke of the stone on the feet. It was plainly a swift stroke, and, therefore, a sudden one; there was no protracted effort on its part to break up monarchy; there was no repetition of the blow by the stone, for the image fell the very instant its feet felt the force of the single disrupting blow. The text says, it "smote the image upon his feet, which were of iron and clay, and broke them to pieces;" and it adds, "THEN was the iron, the clay, the brass, the silver, and the gold broken to pieces together." One sudden stroke of the stone broke the feet to pieces, and THEN, at that very time, for such is the meaning of the term then, the whole material fell to pieces.

The sudden dashing of the Roman empire to pieces by a single stroke, absolutely implies great and unprecedented political or martial power. And, again, the existence of the empire in fragments, implies that this state was produced by political power; and its comminution into chaff is still further expressive of it.

3. The time when this smiting was to transpire, is further proof that the fifth kingdom was to be a political power. The feet were to be broken by the stone, and then every vestige of Rome was to disappear. The *toes* were not to be smitten, but the *feet*, the prophet says. Now, as the image was chronological, the Roman empire represented by the toes, was not simultaneous with that

state of it represented by the feet, nor could the image be smitten in that state represented by the feet prior to that represented by the toes; for if it had been, the toe, or broken state, would never have appeared at all, because the image was all to dissolve at only one stroke of the stone.

The only way to reconcile the matter, is, by allowing a reunion of the broken empire represented by the feet of iron and clay. St. John very clearly states, that the ten kingdoms should agree together, to give their power to the beast, and that, in this confederacy, they should be broken by the fifth empire; he, therefore, fully confirms our positions here. No man of any brains can imagine, that the European states, when confederated, can ever be broken to pieces by an extraneous power, unless that extraneous power be a civil government with martial power.

4. The Roman empire, or fourth kingdom, was to be demolished by a power without its borders. The stone was not in any wise attached to the image; it was not generated in it, and did not operate upon the image internally; it smote the image outside, and moved toward it from a distance. It was, therefore, a kingdom that did not grow up in the bounds of the Roman empire at all; it did not foment discord in its territories, nor secretly and silently work its ruin by *moral suasion*. On the contrary, as it grew in strength, Rome grew in strength; for as it originated in the broken state of Rome, and did not smite it till Rome was reunited, it is evident that both grew stronger simultaneously. It was an external, foreign power to Rome or Europe, and its country was not in the limits of the old Roman empire.

5 The kingdom of the mountain, into which the stone was to grow, every one admits, will be a government in which every thing will be Christianized. From the very nature of the case, the civil and spiritual departments of good government will never be blended. Christ will ultimately be priest of the one and king of the other; but this does not imply that they will ever be blended, but just the contrary. The Millennial government, or mountain, will, therefore, possess a civil department. Now, as the kingdom of the stone is simply to expand into the Millennial government, it follows that it must be possessed of a civil department of government.

Those persons who fancy a universal church on earth, with no civil code, have very crude notions of the matter, to say the least of it. The gospel will never admit of any such universal salmagundi.

Fourth. Change of Character.—The stone was to grow into a mountain after it had destroyed the political powers of Roman Europe. It was to fill the whole earth. This power, external to the Roman Europe, was to break up its kingdoms, root them out, and extend its own government over them. Nothing can be plainer than the fact now stated. The powers first broken by the stone, were those of the Japhetic race; and the government of the stone would, therefore, include Europe first, and thenceforward extend to Asia and Africa. The improbability of a general government for the white race, seems chimerical to some politicians, but God has said it shall be, and that all nations shall be included in it; and, of course, the existence of such a great confederacy, is not dependent upon the notions of short-sighted philosophy.

Fifth. The Perpetuity of the Fifth Empire.—The text says, the kingdom of the stone shall change into a mountain form, and "shall never be destroyed." All of the political empires before it had been destroyed by physical violence, but this one was not thus to be moved. "The kingdom shall not be left to other people." The empire of the world had passed from people to people, but, according to this, the people of the fifth kingdom were to hold the scepter of empire perpetually. Other political powers were to be wholly removed, " no place was found for them," "they became like chaff of the summer thrashing floor, and the wind carried them away;" but this empire stood up in everlasting continuance. It stood on earth; it stood where the Roman, the Grecian, the Persian, and the Assyrian empires stood; and there it stood, and stood forever. The judgment and the resurrection, and the regeneration of the heavens and earth by fire, did not move it; it shall stand and not be removed forever. In its progress of glory, its territories may be cleansed by fire; its inhabitants may be purified by the judgment; the angels may "gather out of it all things that offend, and them which do iniquity," but the kingdom shall remain standing where it was originally established. It will be remembered, that the promise of perpetuity to the stone kingdom is precisely that made to Israel, when restored to *nationality* in the latter day, of which, it is said, they shall never be removed, but shall abide forever.

Sixth. The Stone was to be a Political Theocratic Republic.—This position, though not stated in so many words, in the vision and interpretation, is yet fully deducible from them, and from the very nature of things.

According to the constitution of man, there can be but two genuine kinds of civil or spiritual government. All governments must either be republics or monarchies; there may be various kinds of each, but there is no harmonious medium kind, nor can be. There may be absolute, limited, constitutional, or hereditary monarchies, but they all agree in asserting or practicing the doctrine that the right of governing does not exist in the consent of the governed. There may be aristocratic, democratic, representative, and confederative republics, but they all agree that there is no right of government except by the expressed consent of the governed. These two can never exist in a blended state harmoniously, because their principles are essentially and originally antagonistic.

Now, it is an undeniable fact, that the great image represented all the human monarchy that was ever to be universal on earth; and it is also undeniable, that not one fragment of their political character was to remain, for "there was no place found for them." In the annihilation of these monarchies, it follows that the divine right of kings, claimed by them, was swept forever from the earth. Now, as the stone removed all of the political fabric of monarchy, and filled its place with another kind of government, it is evident that the government must be a republican one, because it could be of no other kind. Again; no reason is assigned in the text for the hostility of the stone to the whole system of monarchy; yet it is plain, that it purposed to break up and totally extirpate not one part of the system of monarchy, but it was terribly hostile to the minutest fragment of it. This again indicates its republican character; for there is an innate hostility in republicanism to monarchy, nor can it ever rest satisfied while it sees a monarchy in existence. It is belligerent to the very name of a human king, and its highest indignation is never reached, unless it is roused on account of monarchy.

We have already shown that God hates monarchy, and loves a theocratic democracy, such as that of republican Israel; and, as he establishes the stone kingdom, it is evident that he would conform it to his notions of a true government, which is that of a democracy, with himself as the chosen head. The fifth kingdom or government would, therefore, be a Christian democracy.

The stone, it is observable, did not incorporate one particle of clay or of the metals with itself; it preserved its lithological nature, unmixed by any affinity with the political qualities of clay or metal; it must, therefore, have been a republic. But as God was its founder, he must have been acknowledged as its head, so that it was just such a republic as that which entered Canaan under Joshua.

We have now considered all the points of character which the fifth kingdom was to possess; we therefore proceed to identify its realization, by presenting a nation which coincides with the description down to the present age.

The fifth kingdom can not represent simple Christianity, and it is strange any one could ever be induced to think so. The reason why it does not predict simple Christianity is, that Christianity does not coincide with it. For the satisfaction of inquirers, we will try the analogy, and let it be seen how signally it fails.

1. The stone kingdom was to rise in the broken state of the Roman empire, indicated by the toes of the image,

and this state did not even begin before the last part of the fourth century after Christianity had made its full appearance.

2. The stone was to be formed from the mountain kingdom at first. Now Christianity itself is the kingdom of the mountain, and it was not cut out of anything. It was primarily instituted by God, who says, his kingdom is not meat and drink, but righteousness, and peace, and joy in the Holy Ghost.

3. The stone was to possess a political department of government, which the Christian church does not possess.

4. The whole body of monarchy was to be broken by a single, sudden, and violent stroke of the stone. The work of suddenly breaking down monarchy by such violence is forbidden to the church. Christianity overturned Paganism in the Roman empire, and this fact has been adduced as proof, that by this act the smiting of the stone was realized. Certainly no exposition can be less worthy of confidence than this. For, in the first place, paganism was not the fourth monarchy, nor is paganism once referred to by Daniel, in the vision. The whole body of human monarchy, and especially of the Roman monarchy, was the thing the stone was to demolish, and not its religion only. Now, instead of Christianity breaking up the empire, by changing the religion of the empire, it rather cemented the empire; and the broken state of the empire, represented by the toes, was produced by northern barbarians, and not by Christianity at all.

5. The time when the empire was to be broken by the stone, was a later period than that of the breaking

assigned to Christianity. It was to be after the toe period of time, or later than the fourth century, and at the time when the broken fragments should be reunited into a confederacy. Now, Christianity does not coincide with the prophecy here at all.

6. The stone was to be a kingdom entirely without the pale of the Roman empire, and removed to a distance from it. This can not be said of Christianity, which arose in the very midst of the Roman empire.

7. The stone was not to destroy the Roman power by any internal agency at all; it was to be altogether an outward attack. But Christianity, to overthrow the Roman empire, could only act gradually upon the elements within, and not from without. The consuming power is all that Christianity constitutionally possesses; but the stone was not only to consume, but it was first to break monarchy, and then was to consume it. There were to be two periods in the destruction by the stone: the sudden and violent breaking of the monarchy, and then that of the comminuting of the fragments. Christianity might coincide with the latter in some sense, but in no sense with the former.

8. The attack upon all monarchy, by the stone, was direct and intentional; but the church makes no attack upon monarchy, nor is it directed to do so: so that the church does not again coincide with the stone.

9. The stone was to abide as a perpetual organization, with a change of form. The church will abide forever, and in this respect it will coincide forever; but then the church will not change its radical character, it will be a spiritual organization, without material change. Now, as Israel, when restored to nationality, will abide forever,

as truly as the church, and as nationality can change its form, it is plain that there is not a full coincidence in Christianity with the point of character under consideration, while there is with Israel restored. As, therefore, the Christian church does not fully coincide with a single point of character in the stone kingdom, much less with all the points, the stone kingdom and Christianity can not in any wise be identical. We have already observed, that Daniel said, that the period comprehended in the three and a half times, should not be understood till a late period in Christian history. As, therefore, all of his prophecy would have been understood, if the application of the stone to Christianity had been a correct interpretation, it follows that the application was and is erroneous.

We will now bring a nation that exactly coincides with the stone in all points, from its incipiency down to the present day. We affirm that the stone corresponds to the restoration of Israel to nationality; and that the nationality was to be that of Christian Israel, and not of the Jewish.

It is unreasonable to suppose, that, in a great prophecy, detailing the world's great history, that the restoration of Israel to nationality should have no place; for one great theme of the major and minor prophets was the glory of Israel restored, in the latter day. Indeed, as it was to be one of the greatest events of modern times, it could not have been left out of the vision, according to Daniel's own words; for he said to Nebuchadnezzar, " thy thoughts came into thy mind upon thy bed, what should come to pass hereafter; and he that revealeth secrets, maketh known to thee what shall come to pass;" and, "The Great God hath made known to the king what shall come to pass hereafter." The vision plainly shows, that all the great nations that were to rise, down to the end of the world, and the great events of it, were all presented to the king. Now, if Israel restored was not among these nations, then one of the most important features of modern history was not seen by him: which is too absurd to suppose.

Every point in the character of the stone finds a full coincidence in the nationality of Israel restored, as the reader can see at a single glance of thought. Now, we have shown that the restoration of Israel was to be that of Christian Israel; and we will now show that the Christian Israel, or stone spoken of, coincides exactly with the United States of America.

As some may think the notion an absurd one, we may be allowed to offer a few remarks upon the probability, that the United States would be a theme of prophecy.

Prophecy was given for various objects. To the church it was given for encouragement, and to the world it was given to dismay the foes of God, and to be a perpetually recurring proof of the providence of God, and of the divinity of the plan of redemption unfolded by revelation. The whole history of the world is, therefore, given prophetically at different times, and all points of great interest to the church are embraced in prophecy. There is not a single age since the oral prophets, but is the subject of their predictions; nor is any great nation whose existence vitally affects the church, neglected by them, unless the United States be the nation. Indeed, every great epoch of the Christian world, and every era is duly chronicled and described. Now, among all the epochs, and eras, and nationalities, that have ever appeared on earth, before and since Christianity, none has ever been so replete with good to man and blessings to the church, as the epoch and era of the United States. Its rise was the great epoch of the freedom of Christianity. Never before, from the days of Christ, was the church freed from foreign domination; never before, since its union with the state, was the control over its purity taken away, and temptation to impurity and corruption removed. The severance of church and state, is one of the greatest and most blessed events with which the church was ever favored. Volumes might be written on the benefits accruing to piety from it; and it is one of the great features of our organization which distinguishes us from all the nationalities, except the Jewish, that ever preceded our own.

The rise of the United States began the great era of national humanity in the world. Cruelty and blood had been the principal features in the governments, from Babylon down to the Declaration; and the Declaration enumerates a catalogue of abuses and cruelties, on the part of England, for which rebellion was the only remedy.

The successful example of a rebellion on the part of oppressed subjects, soon taught monarchies to lighten the pressure of their iron heel upon the necks of the crushed. Hence, the cessation of inquisitions, *auto de fes*, and the general and bloody massacres of the good. The rise of the United States was the era of a national morality. Bad as many of our people are, our plague spots are purity compared to the corruptive courts of other lands.

Humanity arose at our dawn; and the wars of our country have been less liquid with blood, than the municipal sword in time of peace, among Europeans. Never did a nation have such a feeling heart as ours. The cry of starving Ireland, wakens no chord in the heart of the Lion and Unicorn; but it thrills the bosoms of our millions, and they give with a free and full hand to the fainting *slaves* of *British* FREEDOM. The despairing cry of liberty from Hungary, stirs all, from ocean to ocean; and they nurse the moan upon the breast of memory, till the day of vengeance comes. They open wide their gates, and with outstretched arms, invite the weary and heavy laden to tarry with them and be refreshed, and sharpen their sword till the hour to strike for the world's release. They say, "whosoever will, let him come;" they say to the starving, "we have bread enough and to spare;" they say to the poor, "come, share our rich inheritance;" they say to the oppressed, "take shelter under the stars of our banner;" and, while millions crowd the way, they say "there's room for millions more." Our kind hearted country is "the desire of all nations;" and to it the nations come.

Our rising, was the epoch of knowledge among men; the realization of the prediction, "that many should run to and fro, and knowledge should be increased." With us, the press, that luminary of liberty, arose like a splendid sun from the deeps of chaos, and, through the rifted clouds, flashed a bewildering brightness on the unused eyes of the world. The press was chained before; now it is free. Unnumbered millions of books and printed truths, each year, and month, and day, like bars, and beams, and rays of "massy light" pour their fair splendors on the immortal mind, through all our hemisphere.

Here burns "the lamp of eternity" on every table of the rich, and in every cottage of the lowly; lighting the soul with the knowledge of its sublimity, and the luster of Christianized humanity. Here, science and art have sowed seed of perennial fruit, to grow and blossom now, and ripen early in the approaching millennial summer. Like fountains of worth and beauty, schools are among the hills and vales, and everywhere; and "all our children are taught of the Lord."

Our rise was the epoch of agriculture, commerce, manufactures, and trade. Land had been tilled from Adam, to be sure, but when an empire was at once put under tribute by improved modes of production, then was an epoch. Cotton rules the world; and cotton makes an era in the world's prosperity; and with us its culture fully began. Commerce was but a fishing smack, before our union; now it is a navy on all the seas around the globe. Navigation then was a snail, now it is a tempest; then it was a galley with oars, now it is a palace driven by superhuman and invisible force; then it was toil, now an exquisite luxury. Then manufactories were mere crudities, now they darken and deafen kingdoms with smoke and roar. Then all were poor, now all are independent. Then all was sluggish, now all is motion. Then all was ignorance, now all is information. Then a pillar of cloud led the world, but now a pillar of fire.

But again, our rise was the birth of organized and democratic liberty. For such an event the nations had groaned, but never hoped to see. Philosophy had pronounced it impossible, and kings had scouted it as an idle conceit; yet it is realized at last. Its country, like a throne, is seated above all lands, upon the highest region of the globe. Its temple, like itself, is new, and free, and glorious. Its dome is the great open sky, adorned by God's own fingers, and lighted by lamps of his own kindling; circled with a cornice of his own painting, and animated with clouds moved, and gilded, by his own skill. Its floor is the great continent, bordered by seas on either side; its altar is the nation's heart; its music is the cheerful voice of the myriads of the free; its worship is the praise of God; and there is no image of a god within its mountain walls, for the true God is there in spirit. Our nation was "a nation born to God in a day,"—born on Independence day.

Upon the world the effects of our birth have been, "life from the dead." Every part of the civilized world, and especially the religious world, has felt our existence as if we had been a universal galvanic battery. Our influence abroad can not be expressed by volumes of words; it can not be measured by a guage, nor be estimated by balances, nor computed by figures. Revolutions are stirred by it; and every throne trembles on account of it; kings feel it, and the people are inspired by it; religion brightens through it, and apostate papacy shrinks from its touch. Blot us from the world, with all the influence we have exerted upon it, directly and indirectly, and how dark the globe would be! Hell would celebrate the catastrophe, and monarchs would invite all hell to a feast of thanksgiving at an event so delightful to iniquity! Pope and Pagan would leap to youth from decrepitude; and Despotism would embrace them again in its loving and confraternal arms; and all would dance with delight over their common and dreaded foe.

No country ever existed that, in so short a space, affected the world so much, and did so much for the good of the cause of God and humanity; and yet ours is but the state of infancy. Now, then, we ask a question: How can it be, that all other nations affecting the cause of God, and man, should be specifically and repeatedly predicted by prophets, and our country, which has done more good than all others, be unmentioned by the prophets. The prophets mention the minutest facts, and the smallest countries and villages that affected God's ancient and his modern Israel; and how happens it that not a word is said of America? Egypt and Greece, Edom and Moab, and Tyre, and Damascus, and Sidon, and all the little towns of Asia Minor, and the Levant, come in for a share of notice, and all the mighty empires affecting the church are carefully enumerated; the divisions of the Roman empire were specially noticed, down to the end of them all, and yet no notice given of a Christian country that gives more comfort and relief to the Christians and the distressed, than was ever given by all the world put together? How can it be possible that this country was left out of prophecy? how came it to be the alone proscribed nation in all the prophetic calendar? You may talk largely of reformations in church and state, but no great and organic reformations were, or are, complete and free elsewhere. And can the greatest epoch, the brightest era in the history of Christianity, be unnoticed in the scriptures, while all others of minor note are emphasized with a will? Surely no. Right where the prophets place the rise of Israel; right where the stone, or fifth, kingdom was to appear; right at that appointed time our Christian country arose, and it must be the fifth predicted kingdom; if so, it will coincide in character with every quality predicted of the stone. We proceed to the identification.

Coincidence First.—The stone was to rise after the broken state of the Roman empire represented by the toes, and before their reunion, and after church and state union.

The United States arose in this identical period, and, therefore, coincides with the rise of the stone. No other nation but the United States did arise in this period, except it was represented by the toes of the image, or such as grew up from fragments of the Roman empire, or in the empire.

Coincidence Second.—The stone was to be produced from the mountain, which was identical with Christianity. It was, therefore, to possess the dual character so often specified by the prophets, and which is an essential element of civil government.

Washington, in his farewell address, says, " with slight shades of difference, you have the same religion, manners, habits, and political principles." As the United States possess the double nature of a Christian religion and a Christian civil government, it coincides with the double character of the stone. Again; it is indisputable that the United States government arose out of a Christian people, and that the constitution is essentially Christian, but not sectarian. It recognizes all the great virtues and customs of true Christianity, and especially the sacredness of the Christian Sabbath. And in all our history, the God of history has been authoritatively proclaimed as the king, and the only king of our people. The declaration, the constitution, the statute laws, the executive, the judiciary, and the legislative powers of our country, have manifested uniformly and decidedly, that Christianity was the basis of our political structure. It is not necessary to quote documents by the cart load to establish this position, for it has always been agreed to, and none will take the thankless pains to dispute it.

Coincidence Third.—The stone, or fifth kingdom, was to possess a political structure. This, of course, will apply fully to the United States.

Coincidence Fourth.—The kingdom of the stone, or fifth empire, was to be a power that should arise external to the Roman empire; it was not to be within its limits, and was to attack it externally.

Now, the Roman empire's limits embraced all of civilized Europe, Asia, and Africa, or the whole of the old world; and, by consequence, the stone kingdom was to be in some portion of the new world, or America. To this conclusion we are logically and inevitably coerced. Now, the United States was the fifth empire; was erected external to the Roman empire, and is the only continent out of it, where a great empire could arise.

Coincidence Fifth.—The fifth empire was to be a republic; and to this characteristic the United States corresponds.

Coincidence Sixth.—The fifth, or stone kingdom, was to break up the whole fabric of monarchy by war, and was then to annihilate the fragments. It must be remembered, that the image represented all of human monarchy that was ever to exist; and the image was smitten by the stone upon its feet, thus showing that the whole body of monarchy was to be smitten, as well as that particular kind specially represented by the feet. The feet were of iron and clay, and not of gold, and silver, and brass. The inference, therefore, to be made, is, that all the monarchies were finally to be embodied under an Assyrian head of gold.

As the events here predicted have not transpired, of course no coincidence, by fulfillment, can be affirmed between the fifth kingdom and any power whatever. But, while these things are so, we nevertheless can show that the United States will doubtless engage with monarchy for its destruction, and that it will never rest while a monarchy remains.

In all ages of the world, there has been a contest between the democratic and despotic element. Since the prevalence of Christianity, with the art of printing, every revolt among European kingdoms has arisen from the conflict for rights between kings and the people.

The spread of Christianity is, indeed, essentially the spread of liberalism; and, since the days of Luther in Europe, and of John Knox and Wickliffe in Britain, the democratic element has increased with great rapidity. The spread of the Bible has inflamed the minds of men, and they have grown restless and revolutionary in servitude, and have again and again given evidence of what democracy will do when its locks are grown.

Since the origin and success of organized democracy in America, the liberal principle has accumulated and grown with unprecedented rapidity in Europe. The innate hostility between it and monarchy, will, from the very nature of the case, lead to exterminating hostility of one party or the other; both can not exist together in the world, on a large scale, and be at peace. Democracy is a sympathising element, which, in addition to its common interest, will never let monarchy alone. Sympathy is the strongest excitant of our nature; and liberalism sympathises with all true liberalists, as brother with brother.

The democratic element must inevitably harmonize and organize. Now, the United States is the first successful organization of democracy in the world, and it is the representative of the world-wide democracy. It is inseparably allied to democracy every where, from the very nature of things, and must make common cause with it, when it strikes for the great Millennial release. We are not yet ready for an issue with monarchy, on democratic principles; it has been our proper and steady aim to mind our own particular business. We have never committed ourselves to any unholy alliance with Egypt and Edom; we have left our way clear to act just as we please, and when we please; and, because we have never joined issue upon democracy, is no reason that we will not, but a premonitory symptom that we will do so at our earliest convenience.

With all the governmental efforts to curb the inborn tendency to become implicated in the democratic strife with monarchy, among our people, it is impossible to repress the growth of a universal desire to crush monarchy. The ebullition of the feeling in "fillibustering," and public speeches, secret organizations, in resolutions of conventions, and in the press, reveals a national itching to extend the area of freedom on the ruins of thrones.

But this is not all that indicates a collision. The same tendency that directs democracy to engage in an annihilating strife, exists also in as strong, if not in a stronger degree in autocracy. Its antipathy to democracy grows daily more intense, as it is obliged to be more and more watchful of its interests. America it regards as the great crater of melted lava, whose streams are reaching its hemisphere; and it would be a matter of intoxicating delight to it, if we were out of the way; and this feeling would lead it to put us out of the way, if it could. It views with surly jealousy all our sympathy for the restless democracy struggling beneath it; and it is fully aware, that to possess a steady throne, America must be disorganized. In view of these very things, a proposition to destroy the American republic was proposed in Russia as early as 1818.

Again; it is evident that monarchy will cease during the Millennium, because the prophet says, "the thrones were cast down," before that period. Now the thrones must have been overturned by the universal democracy of the world in organic form; because no power, less than that, could at once demolish so vast an establishment simultaneously. How such a brush could take place without our having a hand in the *jubilate* it is impossible to imagine.

Sound philosophy teaches that we can not avoid a collision with monarchy in general.

This collision with monarchy is more clearly foretold in succeeding descriptions of the fifth kingdom, and in all the predictions of Israel restored. The destruction of monarchy by Israel restored is fully predicted by Ezekiel in the destruction of Gog. Daniel also predicts it in the political judgment day of the ancient of days, and in the fall of the willful king in Israel's country. John repeats the same thing in the sixth seal: in the reaping of the earth, and in the taking of the beast and prophet by the man on the white horse.

Coincidence Seventh.—The fifth kingdom was to spread over the whole earth, after the destruction of monarchy. Of course, no full coincidence can here be shown, as no fulfillment has been realized. The capacity of our government for unlimited expansion is a quality inherent in its federative structure and representative policy. Its tendency is, also, to accumulate territorial power. This tendency, not arising from individual lust of power, can not be mischievous, as when it springs from the monarchal power of aggrandizement. The tendency springs from a desire to fulfill a divine command; to fill the earth, to till it, and subdue, or civilize and refine, and bless it. The easy yoke and gentle burden of our government is desired by almost all people, in preference to the chains of anarchy and iron collar of oppression. Our doctrine is, that "if the people wish a government, they should have it in spite of kings; and if any people wish to be annexed to us, they should have their wishes gratified in spite of the hellish despotisms that crush them."

Coincidence Eighth.—The fifth empire was to be established by the God of heaven. This does not imply any miraculous power at all, but simply providential care in its origin and progress. All "the powers that be are ordained of God," as well as the fifth empire. Yet the language plainly conveys the notion that it would be one that God would approve as proper. Now when we remember that America was kept from the world, till an intelligent Christian people were ready to occupy it; when we see it made use of as a Christian refuge, till millions of a Christian people were ready to organize a government in it; and then remember the commitment of their cause to God universally as a people, and as a government; their choice of God as king; their days of humiliation, fasting, and prayer for civil and religious redemption, the conviction is irresistible, that God especially looked to the United States as a government peculiarly his own.

The acts of congress were in the name of God; and, at its first session it adjourned, and on a solemn day of fasting and prayer, dedicated themselves and their country to God; and on that memorable day, the people pledged themselves to God and liberty. Individuals and families, churches and colonies prayed to God to establish a Christian nation of freemen: for this, old men and children prayed; for this, sisters, and wives, and weeping mothers prayed; for this, soldiers, and statesmen, and generals, and Washington, all humbly bowed in prayer to God,—in long and agonizing prayer. From Lexington to the last victory, tears flowed, and prayers ascended in one universal undying cry all over the land, for the salvation of God.

"The bannered host inscribed upon their standards, "*Nil desperandum Christo Duce;*" "He that brought us over will help us through;" "Our appeal is to Heaven."

The great Declaration says, "Relying on Divine Providence, we pledge our lives."

When "God had gone forth with our hosts," and Yorktown had closed the war, said Washington to con gress, "I consider it an indispensable duty to close the last solemn act of my official life, by commending the interests of our dearest country to the protection of *Almighty God*, and those who have the superintendence of them, to his *holy keeping*."

To whom the president of Congress, in behalf of that body, replied: "We join you in commending the interests of our dearest country to the protection of ALMIGHTY GOD, beseeching him to dispose the hearts and minds of its citizens to improve the opportunity afforded them, of becoming a happy and respectable nation." Nothing in the valedictories of Moses or Joshua, is replete with nobler or sincerer consecration to Jehovah.

The people of the United States in the Revolutionary war, abandoned human monarchy forever, and chose God for their king; and God accepted the office, and "set their feet upon a rock and established their goings, and put a song of praise in their mouth, and a two-edged sword in their hand."

Coincidence Ninth.—The fifth kingdom was furiously hostile to monarchy. This we all know is exactly descriptive of the character of the United States. We detest the very name of king, and have no sort of respect for human crowns or scepters.

It will be seen that the United States coincides with every characteristic of which the fifth kingdom was to be possessed, down to the present time. The great and essential points which are given to identify it, are the time of its rise, the source from which it was to come, the political character it was to possess, its locality outside the limits of monarchy, and its direct hostility to

Roman monarchy. With all these great marks of identity the United States perfectly coincides; and, as perfect coincidence of persons, events, and objects, with prophecy, is a perfect fulfillment of prophecy, it follows that the United States is the fulfillment of the fifth kingdom predicted by Nebuchadnezzar's vision.

SECTION VI.

Sixth Kingdom—Reign of Messiah.

Vision.—" The stone which smote the image became a great mountain and filled the whole earth."

Interpretation.—" It shall break in pieces and consume all these kingdoms, and it shall stand forever."

The fifth empire was to spread over all the earth, and remain forever. This coincides with all the declarations of the prophets of the finality of the great war for the conquest of the world. God made oath to Moses, that the whole earth should be filled with his glory. The same thing was also, in substance, uttered in the first declaration of war; was repeated to the fathers; announced by Isaiah and all the prophets of the latter day, without exception. The state of the world described by John during the Millennium, and after the renewal of the heavens and earth, coincides with this sixth empire. Ezekiel's vision of Israel's final restoration and his holy land, temple, and city, predict the same thing; Isaiah's new heaven and earth, also coincide with it; as does Daniel's kingdom of one like the Son of Man, and the resurrection of the dead.

It is objected by some, that no civil organization can by possibility endure forever; but we see not why it can not, when God says it can. He says, Israel restored to nationality shall abide forever. (See Ezek. 37 ch. and other places.) The Israel restored being a Christian Israel, there can be no trouble on the point, except in dull minds. At the sixth kingdom the republic will be changed to a royalty, as the republic of Israel was changed to a royalty. No resurrection, or Millennium, is here mentioned; doubtless, because the prophecy was mostly a political one, and gives only the great outline of the eternal history of the world.

CHAPTER VII.

DANIEL'S FIRST PANORAMIC VISION OF THE SIX KINGDOMS OF THE WORLD.

We have remarked that every very important prophetic event is twice repeated, or twice doubled, and that the symbolic prophecies are mostly accompanied additionally with an interpretation. This principle is especially exhibited in the universal prophecies of the political world, recorded by Daniel. For we find that every character of the whole panorama of the political history of the world, exhibited in Nebuchadnezzar's vision, is repeated and enlarged upon by Daniel's vision of the very same field.

Joseph, before Pharaoh, interpreting his double vision of the seven fat, and lean kine, and the seven full, and blasted ears, said the dream was *one*, and that the dream was "*doubled twice*," because the dream was established by God. We understand by this, that the second vision was to interpret the first, or throw more light upon it. The seven full ears explain why the kine were fat, and the seven blasted ones why the kine were lean; and the twice doubling of seven emphasizes the periods of seven years. And so we understand one of Daniel's visions to be an exponent of the other, and the emphasizer of the certain realization of its events.

We may therefore anticipate that the second vision of the same great succession of empires, will give us additional light in determining their characters, and identifying their names.

This second panorama of the six empires is recorded in the seventh chapter of Daniel. It is prefaced with a prophetic introduction, which shows the entire compass of the prophecy. "I saw in my vision by night, and behold the four winds of heaven strove upon the great sea, and four great beasts came up from the sea, diverse from one another."

As the four beasts were four empires, and as they came up in different ages of the world, it is plain that the term sea embraces the whole world during their history, or the history of the people. The striving of the winds upon the sea, represents commotions in the political world, and the striving of the *four* winds represents the universality of these changes and agitations. All of those symbols having the number four added to them, represent universality. Jeremiah explains the term, "four winds," in his forty-ninth chapter,

> "I will bring against Elam, *four winds*,
> From the *four extremities of the heavens.*"

The universality of agencies, or providence, operating among men, throughout all ages, is, therefore, symbolized by the four winds striving on the great sea.

Vision.—"And four great beasts came up from the sea, diverse from one another."

Interpretation—"These great beasts, which are four, are four kings which shall arise."

The term kings, here represents kingdoms, or governments, and would have been as properly translated kingdoms as kings, from the original text. We shall now find that these four kingdoms coincide with the four of Nebuchadnezzar's vision. We will consider them in order.

SECTION I.

The Lion—Empire of Babylon.

Vision.—" The first was like a lion, and had eagle's wings; I beheld till the wings thereof were plucked, and it was lifted up from the earth, and made to stand upon the feet as a man, and a man's heart was given to it."

In the fourth chapter of Jeremiah, the Babylonian kingdom is described as a lion. "The lion is come up from his thicket, and the destroyer of the Gentiles is on his way." This is a passage of Hebrew poetry, and a feature of it is, that every object delineated in it is mentioned twice, the latter statement always explaining or emphasizing the former; so that the lion and the destroyer of the Gentiles are synonymous. Ezekiel said of Babylon, "He shall fly as an eagle, and shall spread his wings over Moab."—Ezek. xvii. He also calls it "a great eagle with great wings."

The word wings symbolizes *various* things, as armies, velocity, protection; but, in all cases, eagle's wings imply power and velocity. The plucking of the wings of the lion will, therefore, represent the diminution of national power.

The lifting up of the lion from the earth, is translated in the septuagint, "it was removed from the earth."

The standing on the feet as a man, and receiving a man's heart after it was lifted up, shows a change of character in the government, from a beastly to a human character, after the king's conversion. These characteristics are agreed to by all writers, as identifying the winged lion with the first of the four great empires; and it is unnecessary to give a detailed list of the points of coincidence.

SECTION II.

THE BEAR—MEDO-PERSIA.

"And behold another beast, a second, like unto a bear, and it raised itself on one side; and it had three ribs in the mouth of it, between the teeth of it; and they said unto it, Arise, devour much flesh."

The points in this empire are as follows:

1. It was the second in the series of the four. 2. It raised itself on one side. 3. It had three ribs in its mouth. 4. It was to be very destructive.

The coincidences between the bear and the Medo-Persian empire are plainly seen:

1. The Medo-Persian was the second great universal empire, in the series of universal empires of the world.

2. The double dynasty of Medes and Persians coincides with the two sides of the bear; and the final superiority and ascendency of the Persians over the Medes, coincides with the raising of one side of the bear.

3. The three ribs in the mouth of the bear, finds their coincidence in the three vice-royalties into which this empire was divided, and of which Daniel speaks. He

says, "it pleased Darius to set over the kingdom a hundred and twenty princes, which should be over the whole kingdom, and over *these* THREE PRESIDENTS."

4. The conquests of the Medes and Persians were very extensive, and very cruel and destructive; and in this respect they jointly coincide with "the devouring of much flesh."

As complete coincidence is complete fulfillment, it follows that the Persian empire is symbolized by the second beast. The bear with two sides, coincides with the breast and arms of silver, in Nebuchadnezzar's vision.

SECTION III.

THE LEOPARD—MACEDONIAN EMPIRE.

"After this I beheld, and, lo! another, like a leopard, which had upon the back of it four wings of a fowl; the beast had also four heads; and dominion was given to it."

The points of character by which to identify the third great monarchy, are as follows:

1. It was the third beast, or kingdom.
2. It had four wings. The four corners of the earth signify also the four wings of the earth; and wings signify powers or governments, and velocity. The four wings may, therefore, signify four governments, and also the velocity of their movements.
3. The leopard being a spotted beast, represents a mottled or mixed kingdom.
4. The leopard had four heads. Of course the kingdom was to be divided into four parts. This, with the

four wings, is a double indication of the quadruple character the third kingdom was to exhibit. A head signifies a kind of government, as we learn in the Apocalypse. With these characteristics the Macedonian empire perfectly coincides:

1. As the leopard represents the third body of monarchy, so the Macedonian empire was the third universal embodiment of monarchy in the world.

2. As the leopard was to be a rapid kingdom in its conquests, so the Macedonian empire was amazingly rapid in its establishment, and swift in its conquests. In these respects it was unparalleled.

3. The third kingdom was to be motley in its composition, and so was the Macedonian empire.

4. The leopard kingdom was to be divided into four kingdoms, and so was the Macedonian.

After Alexander's death, it was parted among his four captains, Cassander, Lysimachus, Ptolemy, and Seleucus. Cassander had, for his portion, Macedon and Greece; Lysimachus, Thrace and Bithynia; Seleucus had Syria, and Ptolemy had Egypt. And "dominion (over the earth) was given to" this empire. As coincidence is fulfillment, the Macedonian empire was predicted by the third beast. This beast coincides with the belly and thighs of brass in the preceding vision.

SECTION IV.

Fourth Beast—Roman Empire.

The description of this kingdom is very lengthy, and is naturally divided into three periods, and we shall treat of each part separately. There are, properly, three reviews of it, all of which are important: first, the description of it in the vision; second, the interrogative description; and, third, the interpretation.

Paragraph I.

First Period—Beast—Unity of Rome.

Vision.—"After this I saw in the night visions, and behold a fourth beast, dreadful, and terrible, and strong exceedingly; and it had great iron teeth; it devoured and brake in pieces, and stamped the residue with the feet of it; and it was diverse from all the beasts that were before it; and it had ten horns."

Interrogation.—"Then I would know the truth of the fourth beast, which was diverse from all the others, exceeding dreadful, whose teeth were of iron and his nails of brass; which devoured, brake in pieces, and stamped the residue with his feet."

Interpretation.—"Thus he said, the fourth beast shall be the fourth kingdom upon earth, which shall be diverse from all kingdoms, and shall devour the whole earth, and shall tread it down and break it in pieces."

The points of character given in this period of the fourth kingdom to identify it are very full.

1. It was to be the fourth universal empire.
2. It was to be exceeding powerful above all nations before it.
3. It was to differ from all the other kingdoms.
4. It was to subdue the whole earth by violence.
5. Its political complexion was to be of iron teeth and nails of brass. With these characteristics the Roman empire fully coincides:

1. The Roman empire was the fourth great kingdom that existed after the Babylonian empire.
2. It was the most powerful nation that ever existed.
3. It differed from all the great kingdoms before it in almost every great point of excellence; in systematic government, and warfare, and power, durability, greatness and extent of dominion, it had no rival. Gibbon's Roman History is the smallest work that gives even any tolerable epitome of Roman character.
4. It subdued all nations, and made them tributary to its power. Its vocation, for a thousand years, was that of war for conquest, and it triumphed over all opposition.
5. Its political complexion was Roman and Grecian, or iron and brass. The iron of the legs in the great image in this vision, compose the teeth or destroying policy; the brass toes indicate a Grecian admixture of character. Rome adopted the polish and learning of the Grecians, and appeared with the strength of military power, polished with Grecian learning. The fourth beast of this vision coincides with the iron legs of Nebuchadnezzar's vision in unity and chronology.

Paragraph II.

SECOND PERIOD—TEN HORNS AND LITTLE HORN, OR CHURCH AND STATE UNION, AND THE BROKEN STATE OR FALL OF ROME.

Vision.—"I considered the horns, and behold there came up behind* them another little horn, before whom there were three of the first horns plucked up by the roots; and behold in this horn were eyes like the eyes of a man, and a mouth speaking great things."

Interrogation.—Then I would know the truth of the fourth beast, and of the ten horns that were in his head, and of the other horn which came up, and before whom three fell; even of that horn that had eyes, and a mouth that spake very great things, whose look was more stout than his fellows.

Interpretation.—"Thus he said * * the ten horns out of this kingdom, are ten kings (or kingdoms) that shall arise; and another shall arise behind them; and he shall be diverse from the first, and shall subdue three kings. And he shall speak great words against the Most High, and shall wear out the saints of the Most High, and think to change times and laws, and they shall be given into his hand, until a time, and times, and the dividing of a time. But the judgment shall sit, and they shall take away his dominion, to consume and destroy it unto the end."

The period embraced by these passages, is naturally divided into two characteristic parts; the first describing the ten horns, and the second, the little horn. We shall, therefore, consider them separately.

---

* Mede, Faber, and others.

CLAUSE I.

The Ten Horns.—The vision before us, is plainly a chronological one; and the body of the fourth beast represents the fourth kingdom in a united state; the horns represent a later and divided state of the kingdom, and, coming out of the head of the empire, they plainly indicate, that the divisions were to occur in that part of the kingdom represented by the head. The horns, it is said, were to represent ten kings. The term king, is metonymically put for a kingdom, or, the term rendered king, may be literally translated kingdom. The ten toes in the image, are said to represent the broken state of the fourth kingdom; and, as they coincide with the ten horns, the ten horns must also represent the broken state of the kingdom generally, as well as specifically, and its being broken into ten parts. Sir Isaac Newton remarks, that "whatever was their number afterward, they are still called the ten kingdoms from their first number."

With this general division into various kingdoms, and also into ten specifically, the Roman empire corresponds, for it has been broken into various kingdoms in Asia, Africa, and Europe. Europe was the head of the Roman empire; and as out of the head of the fourth beast, or kingdom, the ten horns or ten kingdoms grew, so, out of Roman Europe, grew up the specific number of ten kingdoms, immediately after the days of Theodosius. Bishop Newton says, that "Eberhard, bishop of Saltzburg, noticed it in the diet of Ratisbon, in 1240. At the Reformation it was also ten." Mr. Whiston says, that in 456, the number of kingdoms was exactly *ten;* and, that in 1706, it had nearly returned to that number again. Sir Isaac Newton enumerated ten; and Bishop Lloyd and Machiavel, also enumerated ten; and Dr. Thomas enumerates ten, now existing in the bounds of the old Roman empire in Europe. But in Europe, there are now just ten great ethnological, or compound and simple nationalities, corresponding to "people, nations, and tongues." We now give the kingdoms as enumerated by the historian Machiavel, who "is considered the best, because the most unprejudiced judge of the manner in which the Roman empire was originally divided. He very undesignedly, and (as Bishop Chandler remarks) little thinking what he was doing, reckons up the *ten primary kingdoms*, as follows: 1st, the Ostrogoths in Misia, 377; 2d, the Visigoths in Pannonia, 378; 3d, the Suaves and Alans in Gasgoigne and Spain, 407; 4th, the Vandals in Africa, 407; 5th, the Franks in France, 407; 6th, the Burgundians in Burgundy, 407; 7th, the Heruli and Turingi in Italy, 476; 8th, the Saxons and Angles in Britain, 476; 9th, the Huns in Hungary, 356; 10th, the Lombards upon the Danube, afterward in Italy, 483 and 526. The dates are given by Bishop Lloyd, an excellent chronologer."— (*Faber and Newton*.)

As the ten horns were to be found in the head of the beast, of course, they were all to be in Europe; and, as we find the kingdom of the Vandals was in Africa, we must look for another kingdom in Europe, not mentioned in the above catalogue. It will be perceived, that Machiavel gives only the new kingdoms, established in the empire by foreigners. Now, during this same period of the erection of new kingdoms in Europe, the kingdom of Rome, or that of the western empire, still existed in

Italy, and just completes the number of the ten kingdoms in Europe. The two Newtons, Mede, and Faber, all agree, and for reasons differing from each other and our own, that these ten kingdoms were to be in Europe, and all the reasons are valid. Some persons have contended for the rise of ten *Gothic* kingdoms in Europe; but we think it nonsense to talk so, unless all the folks in Europe are to be called Goths. The kingdoms were composed of Huns, Goths, Germans, Vandals, and Romans.

CLAUSE II.

The Little Horn.—In the divided state of Rome, and among the ten kingdoms, another horn, of a different and remarkable character, was to arise. The points in its character are very important, and clearly delineated, and we shall carefully distinguish them.

1. We consider, first, the time of its rise. The text says, "another horn shall rise *behind* them." We have here adopted the rendering of the text given by Mr. Mede, and highly approved by Mr. Faber. The text says, also, "the other which came up;" "there came up among them another little horn." As the prophecy is altogether chronological, events in it which are said to be before any others, are, of course, later in time, and, those which are *behind*, or after such event, are anterior, or before it, in point of time, and farther back than the other events. Mr. Faber and Mr. Mede both agree, and say, that, "in reality, the little horn did not spring up posterior, in point of time, to the *other horns*." How much farther back the little horn arose, is not *here* stated, but its influence in the state seems not to have been very great at first, as it was called a "*little* horn,"

though afterward it became greater than all the other horns, or kingdoms, or "stouter than its fellows." It seems plainly to coincide with that power in the fourth kingdom of the image, designated as the *clay*, in the feet and toes, and which we have shown was called a kingdom.

2. Three of the first kingdoms were to be removed before it. The text says, "before whom there were three of the *first* horns plucked up by the roots;" "before whom three fell;" "he shall subdue three kings." The term, *before*, plainly applied to a future state in the history of the little horn, as the term "*after*, or *behind*," applied to a previous or anterior event, or to the rise of the little horn anterior to the ten. The three kingdoms that were to be plucked up were to be of the *first* horns. This may mean, as Newton thinks, three of the other, or first and differing class of kingdoms; or, as Mr. Faber thinks, three of the original kingdoms among the ten. They were to be totally extirpated, or plucked up by the roots.

3. The little horn was to differ in political nature from the other horns. "He shall be diverse from the first."

4. The little horn was to be a spiritual power, as well as political. "Behold in this horn were eyes, like the eyes of a man, and a mouth speaking great things." "That horn that had eyes, and a mouth that spake very great things, whose look was more stout than his fellows." "He shall speak great words against the Most High, and shall wear out the saints of the Most High, and think to change times and laws, and they shall be given into his hand."

Eyes, used as a symbol, denote government and oversight. This is a customary figure to denote supervision. "The eyes of the Lord" signify his governmental oversight of the world. Isaac Newton says, "By its eyes it was a seer; and by its mouth, speaking great things, and changing times and laws, it was a prophet. A seer, *Episkopos*, is a bishop in the literal sense of the word; and the empire church of Europe claims the universal bishoprick." It had two eyes as a man, denoting that as a man sees but one object, through a double medium, so this horn had but one object in its mind, and attained its view through a dual organization of policy.

It was to speak great things, and great words against the Most High, and the saints were to be given into its hand. From this special oversight of the saints, and its political character diverse from the other powers, and its eyes and mouth of a prophet, directing words against God, it is evident that this horn was principally a spiritual power, though blended with the political, as is indicated by the union of the two eyes in the horn or head.

5. He was to "think to change times and laws." This is plainly expressive of a will on his part, to change political or spiritual policy, or both. The fact of the horn being a spiritual power, inclines us to the opinion that the laws and times given to it were of a spiritual nature, rather than political.

6. The "times and laws *were given* into its hand." This implies that it received control over times and laws, from some established authority that controlled them. It therefore appears that the little horn was really an inferior power, to the beast, or empire, a sub-controller of delegated authority, and was not possessed of original

and sovereign jurisdiction. As it arose before the other ten horns did, it must have received its power while the fourth kingdom was yet entire.

7. It was to " wear out the saints." The term saints, in the Old Testament, is synonymous with Christians in the New. It is remarkable, that in all Daniel's prophecies of the latter day, he never mentions the name of Israel or Judah, or any thing about Jews after the destruction of Jerusalem. The wearing out of the saints implies general persecuted condition; hence, the little horn was a persecuting ecclesiastical power.

8. The period or epoch of the giving of the "times and laws" into his hand is not stated in the text, and is left to be ascertained by the facts. Of course as each point in the miniature description of the prophet, embraces a large and emphatic epoch or characteristic in the realization of his prediction, the epoch of giving times and laws into the hands of the spiritual will be by no means an obscure or minute one. Those who look to small matters in detail, will never find a realization; for "no prophecy is of any private (or obscure) interpretation," or applies to obscure events.

9. The length of the era during which these laws and times were to be under control of the horn, is said to be "time, times, and the dividing of a time," or three and a half times; or just half a week of years, or of years of years, for twice three and a half make seven times or years. This is a Hebrew expression of the exact length of time the little horn was to have "dominion" over the laws, and times, and Christians.

It is also stated, that there would be two distinct epochal periods at which the jurisdiction of the little horn should terminate. Expositors have never noticed them; but Daniel gives them. He says: "I beheld, and the same horn made war with the saints, and prevailed against them, until the ancient of days *came*, and *judgment* was given to the saints of the Most High; and the *time* came that the saints *possessed the kingdom*."

Here two distinct points of time are mentioned, which are some distance apart; for, in addition to the separateness of them in this sentence, the prophet shows us that the ancient of days came sometime before the kingdom was possessed; and also shows that the ancient of days conquered the beast before the kingdom of the world was possessed by the kingdom. It therefore follows that the three and a half times must also have a double ending.

Our discovery shows that three and a half times have from two to four distinct lengths. Two of them are certainly applicable here, and the others may possibly be; and these two we mention. The first is 1,451 years and 17 days long, or 529,984 days; the second is one-seventh less, and 1,243 years and 277 days long, or 454,272 days.

10. The little horn was also to be a political power. The text says, "they shall take away his dominion to consume and destroy it unto the end." The term dominion implies authority, and the fact that he was to be "more stout than his fellows," indicates that he was to exercise superior authority as a secular ruler.

11. The dominion of the little horn was to be in Europe. This follows from this fact: the head of the beast represents the head of the kingdom, and the head

of the beast, or Roman empire, was altogether in Europe. As, therefore, the ten horns were confined to Europe, the little horn is confined there also, because all were in the head of the beast.

We have now given all the points by which to identify the little horn; we proceed to identify it with the papal power in Europe.

Coincidence First.—The little horn, we have seen, was to rise in advance of the ten kingdoms, and of course prior to the year 356, for, in that year the first of the ten kingdoms arose. Now, it so happens, that the Roman patriarchate was joined with the patriarchates of Constantinople, Antioch, and others, and made up the great Roman church of Christians. Each of these patriarchates had its own well-defined limits, and the patriarchate of Rome had its own jurisdiction separate from all other jurisdictions. To each of these patriarchates was assigned the control of its own ecclesiastical affairs; and each was amenable to the church head, or emperor, and not one to another. The emperor was head of all the churches, in name and in fact. There has been a world of disputation about the time when the Pope was made head of all the churches. If this point had been settled to the satisfaction of the parties, nothing would be gained by it that would interpret the prophecy; for nothing is said about the universal headship of the Pope throughout the Roman empire; but simply the headship of the little horn in Europe, or among the ten horns, is all that is referred to. Now, the Pope never was made head of all the churches in the Roman empire. In the days of Justinian a decree was passed to the effect that he should bear that title; but, in the first place, Justinian did not have jurisdiction over the original Roman empire, for the Western empire was far gone in its decadence in his day; and, in the second place, Justinian retained all power over the church in his part of the old empire, in his own hands, and the Pope only enjoyed a delegated power, for which he was responsible to the emperor. This subject has been reviewed, within a few months past, by the Royal Society of Literature.

It was agreed that the theories of Mr. Elliot, and Mr. Faber, making epochs in papal universal supremacy in the days of Justinian and Phocas, were not sustained by history. They affirm, that the power of the papacy was far greater before these dates than for some time subsequently.

They say that, "the eastern emperors gave the title of universal bishop to the patriarchs of Constantinople, while they maintained their own autocratic supremacy; and the western emperors, on the other hand, fully admitted the spiritual claim, but withheld the specific title." "If Justinian intended to confer exclusive powers on the papacy, yet those powers had already been conferred on it by Theodosius, A. D., 380, by the exertions of Leo the Great, and by the decree of Valentinian III." "It is clear that Justinian held that the imperial sanction was necessary to impart the power of law even to ecclesiastical ordinances." "Again, the character of Justinian as a legislator, is against it, (the supremacy of the Pope). Of his own will he drew up a complete code of laws for the universal church, entering into all the minutiæ of doctrine, discipline, &c. Such a ruler may have disregarded, but almost certainly did not intend to promote the power of the Roman bishop."—(*Epochal*

Periods Papal History.) With these statements we cordially agree, for they are exactly accordant with our own deductions from history. We now quote from Eusebius, proving that the Roman patriarchate was not above any other in authority, and that Constantine was head of the churches, and no one else, except by delegated power.

"CANON VI.—*Of the distinguished honors which were decreed to the Chief Bishops in Ecclesiastical Government.*—Let the ancient usage prevail of Egypt, Libya, and Pentapolis, that the bishop of Alexandria have jurisdiction over all these provinces, since *this is the custom* with regard to the bishop of Rome. In like manner at Antioch, and in the other provinces, let the churches preserve their privileges. It is very clear that if any one be made a bishop without the consent of the metropolitan, the great council has decreed he ought not to be a bishop."

This decree of Constantine clearly shows that all final authority was vested in himself, and that the bishop, or patriarch of Rome was not president over the other patriarchates, and that he endorsed the acts of the Council of Nice. The truth of the whole matter of the papal power in Europe, is this: the church was united to the state in the year 325, A. D., on the 19th of June, on the thirteenth of the kalends of July;* and Constantine

---

* We place church and state union on the opening day of the Council of Nice, because it was on that day that the first great ecclesiastical assembly met by order of the imperial decree; and in the morning the emperor appeared in the assembly, and in an oration, proclaimed formally the powers he conferred upon them in the state. He stated, impliedly, that the decisions of that assembly should be

was a priest, and was the real head of the church, and controller of it, and the supreme legislator, executive, and judge in it. The church was divided into large districts called sees, or patriarchates, and the district, or patriarchate, of the Roman bishop comprehended all of Europe. Each patriarch controlled as supreme executive, legislator, and judge, in his own great district, and was responsible to the emperor, and not to the bishop of Rome; and no independent control, free from imperial oversight, was ever given to any bishop, or patriarch, in the Roman empire. The Roman patriarchate was, however, more honorable, influential, and wealthy, than any other, and accumulated greater power, subsequently. A claim to supremacy was made by the Roman bishop, but was resisted by the other patriarchs, and a controversy and severance of the Greek and Latin churches, was the result; and the contest still goes on between them about it, and will yet be the ruin of Rome.

Neither in law nor fact, was the Latin church ever made head of the church throughout all the patriarchates by an imperial decree of the Roman empire.

The power of the Roman See was greatly augmented

---

respected as law in the empire, by imperial sanction; and from that day to this that speech he made has been the understood basis of church and state union. He proposed to settle church differences, and enforce unity of faith; "hoping, (says he,) by MY INTERFERENCE, a remedy might be applied to the evil, I SENT FOR YOU all without delay."

The various decrees of that beginning of iniquitous councils, were sanctioned by imperial authority; and on the first day of the council was formally begun a system of ecclesiastical despotism under which millions have suffered martyrdom. It was the first formal meeting of civil and ecclesiastical power in union.

by several emperors, after Constantine, down to the days of Justinian. He reorganized all Roman law, and in doing so, he reorganized the civil and ecclesiastical departments of government, generally. His code of laws settles distinctively the powers of the church, and of the several patriarchates, and of that of Rome in particular. He gave it its limits, and its prerogatives, and distinguished them from those of his own and others; and let it be understood that he was the first head in the church in Europe, and that the bishop of Rome was second. Justinian, in these laws, certainly gave precedence to the Roman bishop, over the bishop of Constantinople and over other patriarchates, but this precedency he had enjoyed before; it was a precedency of honor, and not of power; for Justinian says, he gives him only that which had been allowed by the councils. "*Sancimus, secundum (sacrarum synodorum) definitiones, sanctisimum senioris Romæ papam priorum esse omnium sacerdotum: beatissimum autem archiepiscopum Constantinopollos novæ Romæ secundum habere locum post sanctam apostolicam senioris Romæ sedem; alies autem omnibus sedibus proponatur.*"—(*Justin. Novell.*—Tit. 14, Constitut. cxxxi: cap. 2.)

The decree of Phocas, so much dwelt upon by many, as given in 604, 6, or 8, A. D., gave no new power to the papacy. The very existence of any such decree, is now generally doubted; it certainly can not be proved to have existed. The reorganization and *full* consummation of church and state union, transpired in the days of Justinian, and between the years 529 and 534. The work of reorganization of Roman law, was begun by Tribonian, in consequence of a decree of Justinian to that effect, dated February 3d, 528. "In little more than a year the new code, containing in twelve books all the imperial laws, from the accession of the Emperor Adrian, was ready to appear. Justinian affixed the imperial seal to the new constitution in A. D., 529."

In three years more, the digest or pandects were completed, and invested with the authority of law, December 16th, 533.

A revised code was published in 534, November 16th. In these, the laws of church government are embraced, and "laws and times" in Europe, were given to the empire church. The beginning of this union was in the days of Constantine. No critical historian will impeach our historical account of the papal power, unless he is a prejudiced person. It is unquestionably true, that the papal *power*, as such, took its rise from the decrees of Constantine, and from the union of church and state; for then it received delegated power from the civil government, for the first time, and has held it ever since.

Papal control being always nearly limited to Europe, it agrees well with the little horn kingdom, which was limited to the head of the beast.

Coincidence Second.—Three kingdoms were to be removed before the little horn kingdom, and these were to be of the first horns or kingdoms. Of course, the little horn was to have come up antecedent to them.

As Rome, since its broken state began, has been filled with a great succession of kingdoms, far exceeding the number, ten, which were to arise, it is evident that there must be a particular era in which these first ten are to be found. No expositor has ever touched this point, and here we are unaided by co-laborers.

The limit of this period of the first ten kingdoms, we suppose common sense will decide. It must be supposed to be finished as soon as ten kingdoms made their appearance in Europe. The first ten kingdoms in Europe, after the broken state of the Western empire began, we reckon as follows: 1. Visigoths; 2. Suaves; 3. Franks; 4. Burgundians; 5. Britons; 6. Huns; 7. Saxons; 8. *Lombards;* 9. *Ostrogoths;* 10. *Western* empire in Italy.

This list comprises the first ten kingdoms that existed simultaneously in Europe, just as the horns are represented on the head of the beast. It is not therefore liable to the objections to which any other list, that has ever been presented, must be. The last *three*, were of the first list of ten kingdoms that appeared in Europe; and these *three* were all removed before the papal power in Italy. It is true, the Ostrogoths were located first in Moesia; but they removed to Italy and conquered it, and were themselves conquered and uprooted there.

The Western empire, which lingered as a small state, ceased to exist under Augustulus, in 476. The Lombards, whose kingdom was first on the Danube, removed to Italy, and possessed it; but were subdued by Pepin, and their territories given to St. Peter.

Bishop Newton has presented another list, differing from ours; and Mr. Faber, another. But they are objectionable on various grounds. Bishop Newton, to make up his list of the three that were uprooted, has made a list of a second set of ten kingdoms, which appeared later than the first ten, which seems improper. Mr. Faber makes the kingdom of the Heruli and Rugii, or of Odoacer, one of the horns; but as this kingdom was of only seventeen years continuance over Rome, we have not counted it, it not corresponding with the general scope of the prophecy which notices only the larger features of history. Ours may be thought not to coincide with the text, which says, "he shall subdue three kingdoms." But it will be remembered, that it is once affirmed, that three shall fall before the little horn, and that before it, three of the *first* were plucked up by the roots, and then, that it shall subdue three. Now, a king is said to subdue a people when he does it instrumentally, or through other agencies; and such is the case here. We have here shown that three of the first fell before the papal power; and Bishop Newton shows, that three others, not of the first ten, but of a second ten, were overthrown at the instigation of the papal power. So, that we are both correct; and the prophet meant two sets of "three kingdoms."

This double showing of coincidences between the little horn and papacy, is a double proof of the fulfillment of the prophecy in the papacy. The minute accuracy of this description of papacy is very remarkable. Sir Isaac and Bishop Newton both show that the Lombards, the state of Rome, and Ravenna, were removed at the instigation of the Roman See, and that the Roman See then became a political power in the territories occupied by these several kingdoms.

Coincidence Third.—The little horn was to be different from all of its ten associates. This is true of the papal power, which, in its double nature of a politico-ecclesiastical government, was diverse from all the kingdoms of Europe.

Coincidence Fourth.—The little horn was to be an

ecclesiastical power. This is what the empire church was from the beginning, and still claims to be.

Coincidence Fifth.—The little horn was to speak great swelling words against the Most High.

The blasphemy of the papal power has been echoed, in papal thunder, in all of its history. No government ever erected on earth, has been such a pure embodiment of great swelling claims, arrogant pretensions, and Godlike expressions, and lordly assumptions, as the empire church. Its self-adulation has been its fame; and it has consented to be called the Lord God; its glory has been to bestow empire on kings, as a God; and its claims to be the vicegerent of Jehovah, and to dispense favors, and to receive worship, are as notorious as its existence. Massive volumes of its bulls and thunder lie open before us; and its history is one of blasphemy against God. Those who believe in the divinity of its claims, regard all of its character as proper and consistent; but they who deny them, can not but consider them as making the ecclesiastical power equal with God, and of setting up a rival deityship to the Almighty.

Coincidence Sixth.—He was to think to change times and laws.

"The appointing fasts and feasts; granting absolution and indulgences for sin; instituting new modes of worship; imposing new articles of faith; enjoining new rules of practice, and reversing at pleasure the laws both of God and of men," are parts of the changes introduced into primitive Christianity by the church power; it has claimed supremacy and infallibility in these and all of its acts and changes. The empire church power, in spiritual matters, has been emphatically a law and time changing power, and freely claims the authority to make these changes.

Coincidence Seventh.—Times, and laws, and Christians, in Europe, were given into its hand.

These were ecclesiastical laws and times. Now, papal power claims to have its spiritual power from St. Peter; yet, what it claims in this respect, it was not allowed to make use of until the union of church and state. At that time supreme ecclesiastical power in Europe was granted to the Roman See by Constantine, and by his successors. By virtue of this authority the papacy could decide who were heretics, and hand them over to the civil authority to be punished; and by virtue of this very authority, millions of the pious suffered torture, privation, and death, on account of their religion.

The Council of Nice, which met on the 19th of June, 325, was the first great common council to which authority to change "times" was given; and in it, the legate of the Pope presided. The Roman church being the European part of this council, received its pro-rata share to change the times and laws of Christianity.

"The question relating to the observance of Easter was still undecided. It was one of the principal reasons for convoking the Council of Nice; being the most important subject to be considered after the Arian controversy. It was decreed to celebrate Easter on the same day, and the Oriental prelates promised to conform to the practice of Rome and of all the west."—(*Eusebius, Ec. II.*)

The various canons and decisions of this most famous of all councils, have resulted in vast persecutions. In this council it "was proposed that bishops, priests, deacons, and sub-deacons, should abstain from cohabitation with the wives they had married while laymen." This infamous proposition, together with the more infamous one of the celibacy of the clergy, was enacted by the papacy.—(*See History Council of Nice.*)

The decisions of these councils were those of the church united to the state, and became authoritative by civil reaffirmation, and each patriarch was bound to see the decisions of the councils carried out.

Times and *laws* were given to the hands of the patriarchs, at the union of church and state, in general, but to each the control of them in his own district; and of course, at that time, Rome had the times and laws of the church in Europe given into its hand, for it presided over Europe.

Coincidence Eighth.—The little horn was to wear out the saints.

It is universally agreed, that "the persecution of Christians, by those of the same name, began almost as soon as the corrupt alliance of the Catholic church with the state."—(*Encyc. R. K.*) To compute the endless numbers of professed Christians who have been destroyed by the instrumentality of the established Roman church, is impossible: massacres, judicial murders, fires, chains, axes, racks, gibbets, bayonets, wheels, knives, swords, guns, powder, water, prisons, dungeons, famine, wild beasts, inquisitions, wars, and crusades, have been used as general and particular agents by the *Roman* Christians, to wear out the professed followers of Jesus Christ, ever since church and state were united. We appeal to the page of impartial history, to confirm, and more than establish our position, that the empire church of Europe has worn out the saints of the Most High.

Coincidence Ninth.—The period of the giving the laws and times into the hand of the little horn.

If we trace the history of the ecclesiastical power of papacy, we find its authoritative power, to enforce its decrees by the civil arm, begins with the Council of Nice and the decrees of Constantine; and that they were ratified by Justinian, in his reorganization of the Roman law.

Coincidence Tenth.—The little horn was to continue in power over the Christians, while church and state union continued, or for three and a half times. This was to be for 529,984 days, and for 1,243 years, and 277 days.

Now, if we date the origin of the papal power on the 19th of June. 325 A. D., the day of the session of the Council of Nice, and its opening by the emperor; and then add to it 529,984 days, and it brings us down exactly to the 4th of July, 1776. On that very day the United States declared their independence of civil and ecclesiastical monarchy, and that day was the first on which the church had been freed from the domination of civil and ecclesiastical power from the days of Constantine. If we now date the end of the other period of 1,243 years, and 277 days, at the 4th of July, 1776, we are carried back to the year 532, and the month of October. Now, it is well known, that just at this very point of time, Justinian's laws, confirming and completely establishing the papal jurisdiction over the church in Europe, were made. For explanation of these times, see discovery.

There were to be two ending epochs to the power of the little horn; the first was when a Christian nation, called the Ancient of Days, was to rise, and the second when it was to conquer Europe. But we consider those points, which relate to the future, in their proper place; here we are simply adducing proofs of our correctness. There never was a religious persecution in the United States. Since its rise, the papal power in Europe has been almost shorn of its persecuting power, but still it possesses it to a certain extent.

Coincidence Eleventh.—The little horn was to continue in power over Christians in the west, while church and state union continued; and this was to last for three and a half times. We have already seen that there were to be two ending epochs to these times. Now, three and a half times equal 529,984 days, and 1,243 years, and 277 days, and also 1,539 years, 312 days. Dating these at the 19th of June, 325, and at 532, when church and state union began, and we are landed at the 4th of July, 1776, exactly; and carried further down to 1865. (*See discovery.*) Now, on the fourth day of July, 1776, the first great epoch of church and state union in the west took place, at the rise of the United States of America. On that very day, independence of church and state monarchy was proclaimed to the world. This was the first day that the church had been free from civil domination since the reign of Constantine. The fulfillment of the "*times*" was thus realized to a day. As to the future date of 1865, we can not be positive, for the times have four interpretations, and the last one ends in 1878. The interpretation which ends in 1865, is purely from analogy.

No coincidence of events with prophecy was ever more accurate than the one here shown to end in July,

1776. It settles the question of our accuracy with mathematical precision, and we challenge the whole world to overthrow it. It was predicted that church and state union should begin to be dissolved three and a half, or 529,984 days after it began; and just exactly this number of days from its beginning, on June 19th, 325, it began to cease, at the rise of the United States, July 4th, 1776. Can any thing be more astonishingly correct than this?

We may look for the last epoch soon.

Coincidence Twelfth.—The little horn was to be confined properly to the west, or to the region generally occupied by the broken powers of the empire. This has also been true of the western church. It has claimed much beyond this diameter, but it has never enjoyed dominion out of the range of the west. It has been limited mainly to Europe.

Coincidence Thirteenth.—The little horn was to possess political dominion. The western church existed, as an ecclesiastical kingdom, from 325 to 754 or 800, when Pepin and Charlemagne conferred political power upon it as a settled country, and definite seat of empire.

We now claim that we have shown a perfect and minute coincidence between the little horn and the western, or Latin church, and that we have not failed in a single point; and as a perfect coincidence of history and prophecy is infallibly a perfect fulfillment, we claim to have shown, *infallibly*, that the little horn among the ten, predicted the western, or Latin, church, in Europe, as distinct from the Greek church.

Paragraph III.

THIRD PERIOD OF ROME—REORGANIZATION.

Vision.—"I beheld even till the beast was slain, and his body destroyed, and given to the burning flame. As for the rest of the beasts, they had their dominion taken away; yet their lives were prolonged for a season and a time."

It is remarkable that no interpretation of this point is given by the prophets. The other parts of the vision being understood, there will be no trouble in understanding this. As the vision was a chronological one, and as it is plain that the fourth beast was the Roman empire, it is also equally plain, that the broken state represented by the horns, is an entirely different one from that represented by the beast after the coming of the ancient of days. The *body* of the empire having been broken up, it must of course exist again, in order to realize the prediction, which says, "the *beast* was slain and his *body* destroyed, and given to the burning flame." The reorganization of the fourth kingdom seems, therefore, inevitable, in order to its final and total destruction as described.

The taking away of the dominion of those beasts, or empires, whose capitals were in Asia, and the prolongation of their lives for some period beyond the destruction of Europe, coincides with the other prophets, who show the Millennial government first to embrace America and Europe, or the white race, and allow Asia to remain pretty much in its former condition. Ancient Rome was an empire in three continents, and so at its reconstruction it will embrace similar portions of three continents. This coincides with the feet, gold, silver, and brass, of the former vision, with the willful king, who possesses portions of Europe, Asia, and Africa, and with the eighth head of the beast, allied with the kings, who is to be taken with the false prophet, as related by St. John.

SECTION V.

Fifth Kingdom, or the Ancient of Days, or United States of America.

This vision of Daniel, coincides throughout, with that of Nebuchadnezzar; the one presents us with six kingdoms, so does the other. The final kingdom of the mountain, in the first, corresponds with the final kingdom of the Son of Man, in the second; and the four kingdoms of gold, silver, brass, and iron, coincide with the four kingdoms of the beasts; and the remaining fifth kingdom of stone, in the former, coincides with the fifth kingdom of the ancient of days in the latter.

We may remark, that no regular and systematic *interpretation* of the ancient of days, has ever been attempted. *Opinions*, as to its signification, have been given, but the best expositors have passed over it as inexplicable in their day. We affirm, that it symbolizes the United States of America. Our proofs will be, the coincidence of our country with every point of character the ancient of days was to possess. We now quote Daniel's description:

Vision.—" I beheld till the thrones were cast down, and the ancient of days did sit, whose garment was white as snow, and the hair of his head like the pure wool: his throne was like the fiery flame, and his wheels as burning fire. A fiery stream issued and came forth before him; thousand thousands ministered unto him, and ten thousand times ten thousand stood before him; the judgment was set, and the books were opened."

Interrogation.—"The same horn made war with the saints, and prevailed against them, until the ancient of days *came*, and judgment was given to the saints; and the *time* came that the saints *possessed* the *kingdom.*"

Interpretation.—"But the judgment shall sit, and they shall take away his dominion, to consume and destroy it unto the end."

We shall now show that these passages predict the rise, and progress, and triumph of a Christian empire, or Israel outside of Europe; and, that it was to rise just 1,451 years after church and state union, or on the 4th of July, 1776. Some persons have said, that the ancient of days, was God the Father. Dr. Clarke says, "He is never so called in the scripture elsewhere, nor ever represented as incarnate." This bare assertion by wise men, is by no means sufficient proof of its truth, and the very fact, that no proof of its truthfulness was ever pretended, is prima facie evidence of its error. Indeed, nothing can be farther from the truth. We shall not, however, spend time in combating unsustained opinion, but proceed at once, to interpret the vision, and let logical exposition stand opposed to blind conjecture.

1. The ancient of days and his chariot throne, are symbols of a Christian people with a dual nationality. That this man and his throne are symbols, is presumable, because all the rest of the vision is symbolic, and this

part must be so, also, to preserve the harmony of the prophecy. Again; the very fact of its being interpreted to Daniel, shows that it was not literal, but symbolic; and, again, the interpretation itself, shows plainly that it was symbolic.

The whole vision was interpreted in two brief sentences, in which the four beasts are said to be four monarchies, and all the rest of the vision is said to predict the triumphs of the saints or Christians. "These great beasts, which are four, are four kings which shall arise out of the earth. But the saints of the Most High shall take the kingdom, and possess the kingdom forever, even forever and ever."

As, therefore, the ancient of days was symbolic, we inquire what it symbolizes. The answer is, that a man as a symbol, always represents a government of some kind or other. Thus, Judah is put for the Jewish nation; so, also, is Israel, and Ephraim, and Jacob. The great image of Nebuchadnezzar's vision, also, represents a body of government; and so, also, does the "Man of sin." The two horned beast, or false prophet in the book of Revelation, also symbolizes a nation; so, also, a woman is put for an ecclesiastical government; and, in general, a human person represents any organized body of power.

The ancient of days, therefore, as a symbol, must represent a body of government. The *throne* upon which he sits, being also a symbol, represents a government of some kind. A throne, in scripture, is put for a kingdom; thus, Pharaoh said to Joseph, "only in the throne will I be greater than thou." Again; kingdom and throne are used synonymously; thus, "to translate the *kingdom* from the house of Saul; and to set up the throne of David over Israel."—2 Sam. iii. 10. By all the oneirocritics, a throne is explained of power. These two symbols representing governments, must, as they are united, represent a dual government. And this dual character exactly coincides with the two departments of Israel that were to be restored in the latter day, called Judah and Israel, or the Christian church, and the civil government arising from it.

Again; as the ancient of days coincides with the stone kingdom, his throne must coincide with the mountain, out of which the stone was carved. This position is further proved by the text itself.

The vision represents the ancient of days as destroying Roman Europe; this is a clear case. It also represents him as giving the kingdom to the Son of Man, after he had taken it. Now, the interpretation says, the saints shall take the kingdom, and the people of the saints shall possess it: the saints and the people of the saints are represented as synonymous with the throne and the ancient upon it. Again; the vision emphatically shows that these people of saints, existed in a terrible and glorious organization; for all of the imagery representing them is most vividly organic. Again; the thousand thousands that ministered to the ancient, shows that an organic mass of people were united to execute one single design. But farther still; the work which the ancient had on hand, shows that he represents a nationality: his work was to destroy a mighty empire; to overthrow Europe; to cast down thrones; to sit in judgment on a hundred millions of people, and to annihilate the empire church, as well as the Roman state of Europe. Such a work necessitates him to be a political fabric, as well as a spiritual one. Having shown briefly, but truly, that the fifth symbol predicted the rise of a great and good people, as a nation in the latter day, we shall particularize all of its prophetic biography.

2. *The purity and nobleness of the national character of the ancient of days.* These are represented by his garment and his hair; "whose garment was white as snow, and the hair of his head like the pure wool." The garment of dignity and honor, worn by ancient priests and princes, was white. The hoary head represents honor, age, and great superiority and wisdom.—(*Sym. Dic.*)

3. *The nature of his throne.* 1. "His throne was like the fiery flame." The word of God is represented as a fire: as, "behold, I will make my words in thy mouth fire."—Jer. v. 14. Fire is also used as the symbol of energy, and purity, and strength: as, "he maketh his angels winds, his ministers a flaming fire." This fiery throne, therefore, represents the purity and energy of God's church. 2. "His wheels as burning fire." These wheels represent locomotion, and the speed with which the nation progresses. Being of fire, and burning fiercely, shows that its progress was irresistible; that its velocity was incalculable; and, that it was a progressive nation. No symbol could more impressively and appropriately express the nature of a lightning age; nor better symbolize expansion over the world. The throne was not to be stationary; it was on wheels; it was to travel; it was to do so rapidly; it was to do so irresistibly; it was to roll forward in terror and fury upon Roman monarchy in Europe and everywhere. 3. The

diffusiveness and destructiveness of his external influence on Europe. This is vividly symbolized. "A fiery stream issued and came forth before him." Fire signifies destructiveness to all impurity; it denotes war and furious vengeance; and also light and truth. A river of lava not only lights up the darkness of the night, but devastates all before it; it removes forests and towns, disrupts hills and mountains, and is utterly resistless. This "fiery stream issuing from, and going before, this Christian nationality, and rolling as a river of lava, indicates not only light and heat, but the terrible revolutions it was to instigate by its influences that went before it. This stream went out against the world, before the nation engaged in judging the world.

4. The number of people that waited upon the ancient, as ministering servants, plainly represent the people who composed this new nationality, and adhered to its Christian principles. Their number is distinctly stated to be "thousand thousands;" this sum is just three millions. It does not say there were thousand OR thousands; the word OF would have implied multiplication, and as it is left out, the addition of these is rather to be implied. The phrase "time times" is just three times, and so "thousand thousands" is just three thousand. Each thousand, it would seem, should be multiplied into itself, as "the ten thousand times ten thousand" of the wicked are who stood before the judge. Now, multiply each thousand by itself, and add the sums, and they are equal to just three millions.

5. *The number that were to be judged.* Those who stood before the ancient, were plainly they who were to be judged, and their number is "ten thousand times

ten thousand." This is just equal to a hundred millions of people.

6. The persons to be judged were Europeans. These facts are seen from the very nature of the case. The ancient of days destroyed the beast and the little horn, which represent Roman Europe, church and state together. The judgment when it was set, and the books when they were opened, were set and opened on account of the great words spoken by the little horn, and the ravenous character of the beast.

7. The ancient of days was to have two epochs in his history. The first is that of his rise, or coming; and, the second, that of his destruction of the beast. These facts are seen in the text. "Until the ancient of days came, and judgment was given to the saints," is plainly one epoch; and "the time came that the saints possessed the kingdom," is plainly another. The sitting of the ancient of days, is also a different epoch from that in which "the judgment was set and the books were opened."

8. *The judgment was to be a political one.* This is manifest in the work the ancient accomplishes, which is the destruction of the fourth monarchy. Again; as "all judgment is committed to the Son," and as the Son of Man is represented as coming *after* the judgment of the ancient of days was over, it is plain that the spiritual judgment is not here implied, but a judgment day of a political nature only. This judgment of the ancient corresponds clearly with the one which St. John mentions as occurring at the beginning of the Millennium, for both occur immediately after the destruction of Rome, or after "the thrones were cast down."

9. The government of the ancient of days is expressly stated to be a government of the Christians, or a Christian democracy. The term, "the ancient of days and JUDGMENT was given to the saints of the Most High, and the saints possessed the kingdom," is full proof of this. The strength of our affirmation rests in the true definition of the term "judgment given to the saints." The term saints, when the latter day is spoken of, or the Christian dispensation, signifies Christians, for so the Apostles all applied the term. The term *judgment*, signifies authority to rule or govern, as well as interpret law, or to condemn. We commonly, in our country, give it the specific meaning of the law-interpreting power. But, in scripture, it has a generic sense, and signifies both interpreting and executive power; for, among the Israelites, the shaphetim, or chief executive officer, was called the judge; and these judges interpreted and executed law. Christ says also of the Apostles, that they should sit on twelve thrones, judging the twelve tribes of Israel. Here the term judging plainly signifies executive or governmental authority. The "judgments of the Lord," are used by Moses and David, repeatedly, as synonymous with statute law. Indeed, nothing can be plainer, than that the term judgment, as used in the Bible, signifies executive and legislative, as well as interpreting power; it signifies the whole body of government. Governmental authority being, therefore, given into the hands of the saints, or Christians, is, from the nature of the case, synonymous with a democracy.

Again; the very antagonism of the ancient of days to the whole system of monarchy which he destroys, is prima facie evidence that he was a democracy; and, as his forces were Christians, he represents a Christian democracy.

10. The sitting of the judgment on the beast, represents the decision of the ancient to destroy monarchy, and the accomplishment of it. The opening of the books shows, that the democracy brought up all the history of monarchy, and, on account of its universal character in history, it determined its doom; it represents the actual beginning of the political judgment on Europe.

11. The ancient was plainly a nation beyond the limits of the Roman empire. For a universal monarchy and a great Christian republic, could not exist upon the same territory.

12. The name of the ancient of days, implies its priority of existence, as a nationality in kind. It had ceased to exist, but now rises into being again; indeed, the very coming of the *ancient*, implies his absence from a position he once occupied. As it was in a Christian dress, it is evident that it must have existed previously in a different style. As there was no democracy in olden times, with which the ancient could be compared except the Hebrew republic of ancient days, it is clear that the allusion is to that. And, as the restoration of Israel to nationality in the latter day, was promised, and, as that nationality was to be a Christian one, it is conclusive, that the ancient of days was the promised nationality of Israel restored—the democracy of Israel in a Christian dress.

13. The exact time of the rise of the ancient of days, is seen in the statement, that three and a half times after the union of church and state in Europe, this Christian

nationality was to appear. That is, it was to arise just exactly 529,984 days after this union of church and state took place, or on July 4th, 1776.

14. The ancient was to destroy church and state, and overturn every throne. No statement is plainer than that the monarchies of Europe were to be utterly annihilated by him. "The judgment shall sit, and they shall take away his dominion." The term "they," plainly refers to the people represented by the ancient, for it can refer to nothing else. Those persons who are so silly as to suppose the ancient was a single person, will see by the term "*they*," that the ancient represented a great plurality of persons. Again; "I beheld till the thrones were cast down." This refers to the Roman empire, or monarchies of the fourth beast; and indicates, that not one throne only, but many, were confederated in it. To this, St. John agrees. After the overthrow, the ancient is represented as possessing the kingdom, just as the stone kingdom is represented as changing into a mountain.

We have now pointed out all the characteristics of the ancient of days, and proceed to show that the United States coincides with every point of its character.

Coincidence First.—The ancient of days, was a dual Christian nationality. With this character the United States coincides. The church is not united in corrupt alliance with the state, but the religion of Christ is free and pure; it exists in conjunction with the state department as a legitimate partner, but not as its incestuous paramour, as it does in Europe.

Coincidence Second.—The political character of the ancient of days, was just and noble. It is useless to say, that the constitution of the United States gives the
18

best and most righteous government the world ever knew. The character of our country as a nation, has never been sullied by a single act of national injustice. Charges of injustice have been brought, but they have never been sustained. For humanity, for benevolence, for enterprise, for sympathy for the good, and for pure religion and undefiled, our name is justly celebrated, and ever has been. For every ennobling trait of national character, we have been distinguished from the beginning.

Coincidence Third.—The religion of the fifth kingdom, or ancient of days, was to be pure and energetic. The purity, energy, and prosperity of the Christian religion in our country, has been unexampled. Man can not write the deep and wide worth of its progress; heaven alone, can properly portray its true history.

Coincidence Fourth.—The fifth empire, or the ancient of days, was to affect Europe and the world, before it attacked monarchy. The continued flood of information that has rolled upon printed pages, from our country to Europe, has gone like a flood of lava; and revolution after revolution, by consequence, has filled Europe with dismay. Historians date the great period of revolutions in Europe, from the rise of our country, and its successful establishment of Christian democracy. The French revolution, the first in the great series of political earthquakes in Europe, was generated by the tide of democratic fire that rolled thither from America.

Coincidence Fifth.—The fifth empire, or ancient of days, was to sit in judgment on one hundred millions of people in Europe. At the rise of the United States, Europe's population was just about a hundred millions.

Coincidence Sixth.—The fifth kingdom was to judge, or overthrow, the European thrones. This has not yet been done; but every shadow on the political horizon indicates its approach; and unseen lightnings in the moral atmosphere, are affecting the great barometer of the world's politics, and its pointer is turned toward the region of hurricanes. The peace of the past generation is the lull before the great tornado that shall tear down all the kingdoms of the world in its angry march.

Coincidence Seventh.—The fifth empire was to be a Christian democracy. This is the precise character of the United States.

Coincidence Eighth.—The fifth empire was to be erected beyond the limits of the fourth monarchy, and out of Europe, Asia, and Africa. The United States is in America, and far removed from the old empire of Rome.

Coincidence Ninth.—The ancient of days, or fifth empire, was to be like the democracy of ancient Israel. The United States, at its rise, was exactly such a democracy as that of ancient Israel, except, that it was in a Christian rather than a Hebrew dress. The number of its states was the very same; its confederacy was like it; and its principles were identical. The Christian difference was, that the United States, like Christianity itself, was constructed to embrace the world. Hence, in its constitution, provision was made for the addition of new states, and the principle of *representative* democracy was incorporated. By these, its universal expansion was provided for.

The fifth empire, or ancient of days, was to rise 529,984 days after the union of church and state, or on the 4th of July, 1776. Now, on this veritable day and year, the United States arose.

We have now shown, that every characteristic the fifth empire of Daniel's vision was to possess, finds a full coincidence in the United States of America, excepting one, and that one belongs to the future, and is by no means necessary to the identification. We therefore claim, that as perfect coincidence between prophecy and history is infallibly a fulfillment of prophecy, that the United States was predicted by the ancient of days, or fifth empire of Daniel's vision of the world.

SECTION VI.

The Sixth Empire, or Messiah's Kingdom.

Vision.—"I saw in the night visions, and behold, one like the Son of Man, came with the clouds of heaven, and came to the ancient of days, and they brought him near before him. And there was given him dominion, and glory, and a kingdom, that all people, nations, and languages, should serve him; his dominion is an everlasting dominion, which shall not pass away, and his kingdom that shall not be destroyed."

Interrogatory.—"The time came that the saints possessed the kingdom."

Interpretation.—"The kingdom and dominion, and the greatness of the kingdom under the whole heaven, shall be given to the people of the saints of the Most High, whose kingdom is an everlasting kingdom, and all dominions shall serve and obey him."

This vision of a single person, in the likeness of Messiah, is symbolic of the revelation of the veritable Son of God with his holy angels, at "his appearing and his kingdom." All the exposition given of its meaning is, that the people of the Christians shall possess the world, regenerated forever. The term, "people of the saints," is clearly an expression for a Christian nation. If this were not so, it is impossible to account for the expression; for the term, saints, alone, would have expressed Christians generally, without any special nationality. It is coincident with the stone kingdom, which was to possess the kingdom of the world. No spiritual judgment day, or removal of the heavens and earth, are here alluded to at all. The reason seems to be, that the vision prominently embraced only political kingdoms, and departments of kingdoms; and the spiritual department of government was only mentioned incidentally, when mentioned at all.

This sixth empire embraced all the globe, and it was never to pass away, or be removed from it—never—never—never. As soon as the Roman empire was out of the way, the fifth empire, or the Christian Israel, filled its place, and dominion over the world was given to it. At the coming of the Son of Man, we learn that he shall gather out of his kingdom all things that offend, and them which do iniquity. This implies that many, spiritually wicked, would exist among the people of the saints.

The Millennial period, mentioned by St. John, is not noticed here as being a separate degree in the sixth kingdom, but is blended with it. The Millennium of John is, however, plainly the beginning of the world-wide dominion of the Christian democracy. The fifth empire was the Elias of Messiah's kingdom. The text affirms that the likeness of the Son of Man came to the ancient of days, or fifth empire, after its conquest of

Europe: that is, the dominion represented by it, came to the United States, or the Son of Man came to it in person. "They gave him dominion and a kingdom." The term "they," again refers to the ancient of days, or Christian nation. They gave the kingdom to the Messiah; that is, they chose him as their chief; for the reins of government had been given to them as a democracy. The United States chose Jehovah for its king, at its very inception; and when He shall be revealed, the original choice will be ratified by the Christians. The residence of Christ, will, from these things, be on this globe eternally, for so the text affirms.

CONCLUSION—THE FUTURE.

We have now interpreted each vision separately, and have separately seen their coincidence with the four kingdoms, and the United States. It also can not fail of being seen that they each coincide throughout in the minutest particulars, and yet they each interpret each other. What interests us more than all, is the fifth political power in each vision, and the martial work that lies before it. We see, from both visions, that the kingdoms of Europe are to confederate again under one head, and that the United States is to dash them all to pieces, and utterly annihilate them. The Millennial epoch will begin in 1878, and this conquest of Europe must come within the space of twenty-six years, perhaps in ten or fifteen. There are some persons who will give our theory no credit, and who do not believe in Christianity at all; to such, we have a proposition to make. It is this: if our calculations, drawn from scripture, are realized, will you embrace Christianity?

CHAPTER VIII.

SECOND VISION OF DANIEL.—FIVE KINGDOMS.

This vision is recorded in the eighth chapter of Daniel, and was given in the reign of Belshazzar. It contains a view of the whole world, from that time, leaving out the Babylonian kingdom, which was about to fall.

It contains a history of Persia, the Macedonian, and Roman empires, and the destruction of Rome, and the re-establishment of the nationality of God's Israel. It, therefore, goes over the same ground already viewed by the two preceding visions, and adds some things of importance, not contained in them; it has also an interpretation, as the preceding ones have. We give the vision and the interpretation of each power separately.

SECTION I.

THE PERSIAN EMPIRE—RAM.

Vision.—"Behold there stood before the river a ram which had two horns; and the two horns were high; but one was higher than the other, and the higher came up last. I saw the ram pushing westward, and northward, and southward; so that no beast might stand before him, neither was any that could deliver out of his hand; but he did according to his will, and became great."

Interpretation.—"The ram thou sawest are the kings of Media and Persia."

No interpretation of ours is requisite here. It may be noticed, that the two horns of different lengths coincide with the two arms of silver and the two sides of the bear, one of which was raised higher than the other The term king represents a kingdom.

SECTION II.

Four Horned Goat—The Macedonian Empire.

Vision.—" Behold, an he-goat came from the west on the face of the whole earth, and touched not the ground; and the goat had a notable horn between his eyes. And he came to the ram that had two horns, and ran unto him in the fury of his power. And I saw him come close unto the ram, and he was moved with choler against him, and smote the ram. Therefore the he-goat waxed very great, and when he was strong the great horn was broken, and for it came up *four* notable ones toward the four winds of heaven."

Interpretation.—" The rough goat is the king (kingdom) of Grecia, and the great horn is the first king. Now, that being broken, whereas four kingdoms shall stand up out of the nation, but not in his power."

Here is a declaration that the goat is the kingdom of Macedonia. The four horns represent the same kingdoms as the four heads in the preceding vision; that is, the kingdoms of Cassander, Lysimachus, Ptolemy, and Seleucus; and, as they ultimated in the kingdoms of Syria, and Egypt, this kingdom coincides with the brass kingdom of the great image.

SECTION III.

Little Horn—The Roman Empire.

Vision.—"And out of one (of these four) came forth a little horn, which waxed exceeding great toward the south, and toward the east, and toward the pleasant land. And it waxed great even to the host of heaven; and it cast down some of the host and of the stars to the ground, and stamped upon them. Yea, he magnified himself even to the prince of the host, and by him the daily sacrifice was taken away, and the place of his sanctuary was cast down. And an host was given him against the daily sacrifice, by reason of transgression; and it cast down the truth to the ground; and it practised and prospered."

Interpretation.—"And in the latter times of their kingdom, when the transgressors are come to the full, a king of fierce countenance, and understanding dark sentences, shall stand up. And in his power shall he be mighty, but not by his own power: and he shall destroy wonderfully, and shall prosper and practise, and destroy the mighty, and the holy people. And through his policy, he shall cause craft to prosper in his hand; and he shall magnify himself in his heart, and by peace shall destroy many; he shall stand up against the Prince of princes; but he shall be broken without hand."

That this *little horn* that becomes so great, is the Roman power, we shall briefly, but clearly prove. Many expositors have understood this little horn to indicate Antiochus Epiphanes, a great Syrian persecutor of the

Jews. Sir Isaac, and Bishop Newton have both shown that there are very strong characteristics in this horn that can not, in any wise, agree with Epiphanes, and of course it is certain that this horn can not predict him. The Newtons, and most moderns, say it was Rome.

First characteristic and coincidence of Rome with the little horn.

Vision.—" And out of one of them (one of the four horns) came forth a little horn."

Interpretation.—" And in the latter time (or last time) of their kingdom, when the transgressors are come to the full, a king of fierce countenance, and understanding dark sentences, shall stand up."

Here, a horn and a king, are said to be synonymous. Now these must represent a kingdom, just as the little horn represented one, for a king symbolizes a kingdom usually, and a horn always. No instance is found where a horn is used as a symbol, where it represents a single person. Of course Antiochus can not be designated by this little horn.

Again; this horn was to rise out of one of the four. It must here be remembered, that the prophet had been describing, hitherto, in previous visions, the Roman empire, and its particular manifestations in Europe, rather than in the Asiatic and African portions. He now, in this vision, describes the progress of the Roman power, in these latter directions. The horn was to rise out of one of the preceding four, and it was to rise in the latter end, or last end of their kingdom. Now, the Roman power arose in an *easterly* direction, by the conquest of Macedon, one of the four horns mentioned, and n the last stages of the dominion of the four horns; and thence extended over Syria, in the east; Egypt, in the south, and conquered Judea, or "the pleasant land." It did this, too, when the "transgressors were come to the full;" for, at that time, the Jewish state and people had become more corrupted than at any previous period.

This kingdom was to be very powerful and martial; for such is indicated by the words, "a king of fierce countenance." This kingdom was also to be very politic; for such is to be understood by the words, "understanding dark sentences."—(*Bishop Newton.*)

In all these respects, the Roman power coincides with the little horn. Mr. Faber thinks this last expression refers to a spiritual power, possessed by the little horn; and with his exposition we fully agree, as it harmonizes with all of the preceding descriptions of Rome, and with the facts of the case.

Coincidence Second.—"It waxed great, even to the host of heaven, and it cast down some of the stars to the ground, and stamped upon them."

Interpretation.—"And his power shall be mighty, but not by his own power, and he shall destroy wonderfully, and shall prosper and practise, and shall destroy the mighty and the holy people. And through his policy he shall cause craft to prosper in his hand; and he shall magnify himself in his heart, and shall destroy many in negligent security."

"It waxed great," &c. The Roman power was never very great, until the conquest of Macedon; previously, it had been comparatively small. As the little horn among the ten became more stout than his fellows, so this little horn became, after it gained Greece, the greatest power ever in the world. "But not by his own power."

The destruction of Judea, we have seen, was to be when "the transgressors were come to the full," and this event did not transpire until our Saviour's day. He said to his enemies, "Fill ye up, then, the measure of your fathers, that upon you may come all the righteous blood shed upon earth." Christ, also, said to the Roman governor, "Thou couldest have no power at all against me, except it were given thee from above."

Here, we learn, that the Roman power was sustained by God, to do his will among the nations.

The waxing great, against the host of heaven, and the casting down the stars, is interpreted to mean the destruction of the holy ones among God's people. All of the descriptions in the passages, have been so fully shown to coincide with the Romans, by Newton, that it is needless for us to particularize further.

Coincidence Third.—"Yea, he magnified himself, even to the prince of the host, and by him the daily sacrifice was taken away, and the place of his sanctuary was cast down."

Interpretation.—"He shall also stand up against the Prince of princes."

The terms Prince of the host, and Prince of princes, is, plainly, the Messiah; for such terms are applicable to him only. Beside this, it is said, the sanctuary of the prince of the host was cast down; and as the sanctuary was the Lord's only, the Lord, or Messiah, must be the person meant. Now, the Prince of princes, or Christ, was put to death by the Roman power, and by its decree.

Coincidence Fourth. Vision.—"By him the daily sacrifice was taken away, and the place of his sanctuary was cast down. And an host was given him against the daily sacrifice, by reason of transgression, and it cast down the truth to the ground, and it practised and prospered."

No interpretation of this is given, because it was a literal prophecy. Three things are here specially predicted:

1. The cessation of the daily sacrifice. 2. The destruction of the temple, and of Jerusalem; and 3. The casting down of the truth.

The first two were accomplished by the Romans, and by no other power.

The truth, spoken of, evidently refers to the gospel, which was cast down by the Romans, as well as was Judaism.

This little horn coincides, chronologically, with the iron, or fourth kingdom of the great image, and with the fourth beast, or fourth kingdom, of the preceding vision.

SECTION IV.

Israel.

Vision.—"Then I heard one saint speaking, and another saint said unto that certain saint which spake, "How long a time shall the vision last, the daily sacrifice be taken away, and the transgression of desolation continue to give both the sanctuary and the host to be trodden under foot."—(*Lowth's Translation. Arabic and Vulgar Versions. Bishop Newton.*)

"And he said unto me, unto two thousand three hundred evenings and mornings, then shall the sanctuary be cleansed."—*Ib.* The "sanctuary and host," are evidently metonymic terms, because the Jewish temple or Mosaic sanctuary, will never be rebuilt. They coincide with the two departments of the nationality of God's people: the sanctuary being put for the worshipers or church, and the host for the civil department of the nationality, and with them only.

The desolation of the nationality of Israel, was accompanied with the domination of a foreign and unclean power over the church of God. It is said, that this was not to be removed for twenty-three hundred evenings and mornings; or, as some versions have it, 2400. It is likely that both numbers are correct, as this cleansing was to have two epochs, as we have seen in the other visions.

As Israel's restoration is here affirmed; and as it was to be a Christian nation when restored; and as it was to be 2300 evenings and mornings from the destruction of the Jews and the cessation of the daily sacrifice, to this restoration, it is evident, that the nation of Christians arising at the end of this period must be the one predicted. The destruction of Jerusalem took place in 68, A. D., and the daily sacrifice ceased on the 9th of July; and the 2300 evenings and mornings are just 1708 years long; and this added to the 8th of July, 68, just brings us to the Declaration of Independence, in 1776, when a Christian democracy was organized, and the church or sanctuary was cleansed from all foreign domination. It therefore follows, that the United States is Israel restored.

SECTION V

Doom of Monarchy.

Interpretation.—"He shall be broken without hand." This indicates the final destruction of the Roman power on earth. The term "broken without hand," signifies, not that it will be broken without means, but without help or succor afforded at the time of his destruction. The term, cut out of the mountain "without hands," signifies an organization without foreign influence, as the American constitution. The term, "broken without hands," is also equivalent to a description of the doom of Rome in the eleventh chapter of Daniel, which says, "he shall come to his end and, none shall help him."

The final triumph of Christianity, is indicated in the prophecy. Rome being the world-wide obstacle to the triumph of pure Christianity, and being entirely removed, and the sanctuary being fully cleansed, show that the cause of Christianity would prevail universally.

CONCLUSION.

This vision, it will be seen, coincides with the two which precede it, and shows additional particulars of the works of the Roman empire in Asia. The notion that Antiochus Epiphanes coincides with the little horn, is preposterous; as he meets the case in but a very few unimportant particulars, while, with the most important he does not coincide at all. For a fuller exhibition of this subject, we refer anxious inquirers to Bishop Newton's excellent work. In this vision, Persia, or the two-horned ram, coincides with the silver breast and arms of the image, and with the bear of Daniel's first vision; Macedonia, or the goat with four horns, coincides with the third kingdom of brass, and the four-winged and four-headed leopard; and the little horn coincides with the iron and clay; and with the fourth beast, or fourth kingdom; and the host and sanctuary restored, coincide with the stone cut out of the mountain, and with the ancient of days and his throne; the destruction of the little horn, or king of fierce countenance, coincides with the fall of the great image of monarchy, and taking of the beast or fall of the fourth empire.

CHAPTER IX.

DANIEL'S THIRD VISION OF THE WORLD.

This vision extends from the beginning of the eleventh chapter of Daniel to the end of the twelfth. It is the explanation of all the previous universal visions to Daniel, and is made by some angel, perhaps Gabriel. It appears that Daniel had a vision in the third year of Cyrus, and that he had set himself to study to understand it, and had been engaged in prayer for that purpose. An angel came to him while he was thus engaged, and told he would show what was "noted in the scriptures of truth." By this we understand, that the angel was further to explain the visions before given and recorded; and, also, to explain his last vision. The object of the angel was to explain Daniel's last vision; and, as he proposes to explain all that had occurred before it, it is presumable that they all signified about the same things. It must, however, be recollected, that the explanations of visions, while they cover the ground of the vision, often add particulars which are only given in a general manner by the vision. This interpretation was given in the third year of Cyrus.

SECTION I.

The Persian Empire.

Interpretation.—" Behold there shall stand up yet, three kings in Persia; and the fourth shall be far richer than they all; and by his strength through his riches, he shall stir up all against the realm of Grecia."

As this was stated in the days of Cyrus, the four kings mentioned must succeed him. These were, Cambyses the son of Cyrus, Smerdes the Magian, Darius Hystaspes, and Xerxes. Of Xerxes, Justin says, " You may praise his riches, not the general; of which, there was so great abundance in his kingdom, that when rivers were dried up by his army, yet his wealth remained unexhausted." Xerxes' invasion of Greece, is one of the most memorable events of history.

SECTION II.

The Grecian Empire.

"And a mighty king shall stand up, that shall rule with great dominion, and do according to his will. And when he shall stand up, his kingdom shall be broken, and shall be divided toward the four winds of heaven:

and not to his posterity, nor according to his dominion which he ruled; for his kingdom shall be plucked up, even for others beside those."

That this describes Alexander and his kingdom, every one can see. Alexander died in Babylon, and in fifteen years his posterity was extinct, and his kingdom was divided into four parts, to the four winds. Macedon and Greece formed the western part; Thrace and Bithynia, the northern; Syria, the eastern; and Egypt, the southern part; and each was ruled by persons not of Alexander's family. The angel, after these declarations, proceeds to describe the history of the two principal branches into which the Macedonian empire was divided, under the name of north and south, or kings of Syria and Egypt. He proceeds with this description very minutely, and gives a better history than any other ever written of them. At the latter time of their kingdom, he introduces the Roman power. As his description of Syria and Egypt is minute and lengthy, we shall not interpret it, but refer the inquisitive to the perfect interpretation of Bishop Newton. We begin our next exposition at the appearance of the Roman power in Asia, which is mentioned in the thirtieth verse.

SECTION III.

Roman Empire.

The succeeding portion of the prophecy is symbolic, and, of course, doubled. It gives a history of the Roman power coinciding with the iron legs of the great image, and with the iron and clay, and follows it by the great restoration of Israel, and the resurrection of the dead.

Paragraph I.

SHIPS OF CHITTIM, OR ROME.

"For the ships of Chittim shall come against him, (that is, against Antiochus Epiphanes, the Syrian king,) therefore, shall he be grieved, and have indignation against the holy covenant; so shall he do."

The ships of Chittim are the ships of Rome. The prophet Balaam had predicted this very event. He said, "Ships shall come from the coast of Chittim, and shall afflict Asshur, and shall afflict Eber, and he, also, shall perish forever." Chittim, or Kittim, was one of the grandsons of Japhet, and settled in the south of Europe, and the Romans were, most probably, his descendants; at any rate, his name was given to south Europe, according to ancient scholars. Bishop Newton, in his fifth dissertation, has shown this fully.

In Balaam's prediction, Asshur and Eber are put for their posterity: Eber standing for the Hebrews, for they received their name from him. Balaam makes the term *he* refer to the ships of Chittim, and thus it becomes a prophetic term of multitude, and denotes one embodied people, or nation. As no doubt of our exposition can be entertained here, we pass on. Antiochus, in his last descent into Egypt, was grieved at interferences with his plans, by ambassadors, who came in ships from Rome, and peremptorily ordered him to desist from his designs. He complied, reluctantly, with their demands, and returned homeward.

On his way back, he vented his indignation upon the Jews. He detached Appolonius with 20,000 men, who went to Jerusalem, slew great multitudes, plundered the city, set it on fire, and shed blood on every side of the sanctuary, and defiled it. Josephus ascribes these calamities to the factions who communicated with Antiochus, and persuaded him to invade Judea. Thus, "he had intelligence with them that forsook the holy covenant."

Paragraph II.

ARMS, OR THE ROMAN MILITARY POWER.

1. "And after him (Antiochus) ARMS shall stand up." Bishop Newton says, this is the literal rendering of the original term *mimmdu*. Arms are always used to represent the military power of a kingdom.—Ezek. xxx. 21; Jer. xlviii. 25. As a symbol of a great power, it must properly represent a military nation, and thus coincides with Rome, which was, emphatically, a military empire. At this period of history, Rome conquered Macedon, one of the four horns of the he goat, in the preceding vision, and then grew up out of it in the east, and expanded toward Asshur and Eber. The countries of Illyricum, and Pergamos, soon became theirs; so that they " stood up" in the east, as far as the Taurus. All Egypt and Syria, including the Jews, also, soon fell to them. "Arms standing up," after "Antiochus in Asia," must refer to the Romans, who succeeded him in Asia and Egypt. This prophecy of Rome in Asia, matches the preceding vision.

2. "They (arms) shall pollute the sanctuary of strength, and shall take away the daily sacrifice." The Romans polluted the temple with the blood of thousands; and they, by war, caused the daily worship in the temple to cease, by the interruption of the daily offerings.

3 "And place the abomination that maketh desolate." We understand this not to refer to the standards of the soldiers, as some do, because it gives prominency to things entirely too small to be noticed in a prophecy about great objects only. The Roman power itself, as represented by the armies and their standards around Jerusalem, seems only that which can be understood. "To place the desolation," signifies to establish it permanently. To this passage Christ plainly refers, when he says, "when ye see the abomination of desolation spoken of by Daniel, standing where it ought not, then let them that be in Judea flee to the mountains." He here plainly refers to the desolating and unholy army of Rome, which encamped in the suburbs of Jerusalem, or on holy ground, on the 14th of Nisam, A. D. 68.

4. "And such as do wickedly against the covenant, shall he corrupt by flatteries; but the people that do know their God, shall be strong and do exploits." Two classes are here mentioned; the first, who were averse to the covenant, and those who favored it. As at this time the old covenant had passed away, and the new covenant succeeded it, the term covenant here used must represent the gospel, or Christianity. They who did wickedly against it, and were corrupted by the Romans, must be those Jews who rejected it, or those who, having embraced it, apostatized. Many great offers were made to the primitive Christians to forsake their religion, and many were induced to comply by flatteries.

The other class remained firm to their profession, and performed miracles, and suffered martyrdom gloriously. This period seems to refer exclusively to the Apostolic age.

5. "They that understand among the people shall instruct many; yet they shall fall by the sword, and by captivity, and by flame, and by spoil, many days." This embraces the era from the apostles to Constantine. The "men of understanding" are plainly put for Christians generally, who, after Jerusalem's destruction, went every where preaching the word. During the ten persecutions of pagan Rome, they fell in multitudes, by sword, fire, captivity, and by the joyful spoiling of their goods.

6. "Now when they shall fall they shall be holpen with a little help, but many shall cleave to them with flatteries." This clearly coincides with church and state union under Constantine. During the ten great universal persecutions, the last of which was desolating, and immediately prior to Constantine, the Christians had fallen as if their fall was irrecoverable. The union of church and state gave them some relief for awhile; but it is properly termed, "holpen with a *little* help." This very rest proved, ultimately, most disastrous to the piety of the church; for many adhered to it, or to the Christian power, allured by the flattering prospects of preferment; so that the state church became a most wicked and worldly political establishment.

During this state, it is said, "some of them of understanding shall fall, to try them, and to purge them, and to make them white." Notwithstanding this "help," still many true Christians were to fall, and their sufferings were to continue down to "the time of the end," says the text. This has been most fearfully true, as all know.

7. "To the time of the end, because it is yet for a time appointed." This period, therefore, of falling, was

to continue from the time of the "little help," down to an appointed time. This era is called "the time of the end," and is, of course, a considerable era, as it is called a "time," and not the end itself. It is the period between the two endings of the three and a half times, or that between the 1,290 days and the 1,335 days. The first of these ended at the rise of the United States. Now, it is remarkable, that persecution and death for religion's sake ceased at the rise of the United States; and we have since heard of few judicial murders for religion's sake. The prisons that before were crowded with victims, are moldering and empty. An occasional sufferer is dragged to prison for conscience sake, but the beast is careful not to draw blood. It was not so before the *Declaration*.

Paragraph III.

THE WILLFUL KING—ROME AND RUSSIA.

"The king shall do according to his will." Two principal interpretations of this power have been given to this kingdom; one by Bishop Newton, and another by Mr. Faber. Newton thinks it was the Roman church in Europe; but Faber tries to identify it with France. Bishop Newton is partially right, and only so; for it is impossible to explain this power of the church only, for the willful king was, without doubt, one of the mightiest *political* powers on earth, as we shall see.

We shall identify it with the Roman empire in all the stages of its history, and also see that it coincides with the iron and clay, or church and state united in the Roman empire; and also with the restoration of the empire under Russia. We shall sift the subject thoroughly.

First. Our reasons for identifying the willful king with Rome, are these; the word ARMS is proved to be the Roman empire; and, it is plain, that the pronoun HE, which follows it in the thirty-second verse, refers to ARMS, or the Roman empire, as its antecedent, for it has no other antecedent; and, it is also equally plain, that the term king, which follows the term HE, has no other antecedent; and, therefore, it is the very same power as that indicated by the terms HE and ARMS.

Again; the description of the Roman power previously given by the angel, was symbolic, and the other descriptions had been literal; and it is an invariable principle in Daniel's visions, that symbols all receive an interpretation, so that this repetition of the description of Rome was to be expected, as interpretative of the first or symbolic description of Rome.

Again; this power must be the Roman empire, because it is described as perishing on the mountains of Israel, and at the last end of the indignation, or late during the period of the time of the end.

In addition, he is represented as conquering Europe, Asia, and Africa, and then passing beyond their limits, and meeting his doom. Now, these things can not be said of the Roman church, for it is not anything like the national organization requisite to such immense conquests.

Besides these things, he is said to give all those things to that power which Newton identifies as the church; and, of course, he existed as a superior power, because he was the bestower of these favors. Indeed, the Roman empire was a consolidated government of church and state, and the emperor was head of both, and, in describing the empire, the description of its religion would be a natural part of its history.

Lastly; the interpreting angel promised to interpret the substance of all Daniel's visions at this time; and unless this is a vision of the Roman empire, as represented by the iron, and iron and clay, and fourth beast, and king of fierce countenance, the angel does not fulfill his promise.

Second. "He shall magnify himself above every god, and shall speak marvellous things against the God of gods." The term, "every god," implies a plurality of gods, and therefore must be applicable only to such deities as are called gods by men. Indeed, the scripture does not always confine the term to the Almighty, as we learn from the words of Moses and of Christ; thus, "Is it not said in your law, ye are gods? If he called them gods, to whom the word of God came, and the scripture can not be broken," &c. "Ye shall not revile the gods, nor curse the ruler of thy people." Here the chief persons of Israel are called by this name. The "magnifying himself above every god," indicates, therefore, that he would claim superiority over all persons high in office in the church. "He shall speak marvellous things against the God of gods." Here the Almighty Ruler is plainly distinguished from all inferior sovereignties. This power was even to arrogate to himself divine honors, and, of course, was to be a religious as well as political power.

St. Paul's description of the "Man of sin," so perfectly coincides, not only with this very character, but

20

with the very words used by Daniel, that he must have described the same identical power. He says, "that man of sin (shall) be revealed, who opposeth and exalteth himself above all that is called God, or that is worshipped; so that he as God, sitteth in the temple of God, showing that he is God."

It is well known that the Roman emperors claimed divine honors, and that the Roman church claims, and has claimed, that the Pope is in the room of God on earth: and it is certain that he has received honors as a god, and that he claims to be above every earthly priest, ruler, king, and potentate, in the world, and claims infallibility equal to God in heaven.

Third. "He shall prosper till the indignation be accomplished." This coincides with the very words spoken of the little horn that was to arise out of one of the horns of the Macedonian kingdom, or the rise of Rome in Asia. "It cast down the truth to the ground, and practised and prospered." "I will make thee to know what shall be in the last end of the indignation, for at the time appointed the end shall be."

This domination was to last, also, "even to the time of the end; for it is for a time appointed."—v. 35. As it still subsists, the last end of the indignation is not yet reached.

Fourth. "Neither shall he regard the God* of his fathers." The Roman empire renounced its ancient

---

* The term, God of his fathers, is here so plainly a figure used to designate the religion of his fathers, as to need no illustration. It therefore follows, that the strange God he embraced, and which is spoken of antithetically to the God of his fathers, must also represent **a new or strange religion which the empire was to embrace.**

religion, and adopted Christianity, which it soon corrupted. As this great change was to be the great act or law of an empire, it must be a matter of vast notoriety. A change of national religion is clearly indicated by the terms used in the text, nor can they find any coincidence in the world, but in that we have noticed. The rejection of the God of his fathers, was the rejection of Roman paganism by the Roman empire.

Fifth. "Nor the desire of women." This expression indicates a disregard of marriage, or rejection of it. The desire of women is spoken of in the curse on woman: "Thy desire shall be to thy husband," or on account of a husband. Conjugal affection is a primary law of nature. The Roman power first deprived its priesthood of second marriage, and finally of any at all, at least in Europe. It also encouraged vast orders of monks and nuns, and so organized them, that the mother of harlots was naturally an appropriate name for the Roman church, over the whole empire, in three continents.

Sixth. "Nor regard any God, for he shall magnify himself above all." The history of the ecclesiastical department of the Roman power has been but a regular systematized effort to exalt itself above all other authorities, nor has it ever respected any religion, or ministers, or governors, or gods, not of its own order. It has assumed unequaled authority, has claimed supremacy over kings, and nations, and churches, and has made unceasing efforts to raise itself to a level with its claims. It has truly magnified ITSELF.

Seventh. "And the God Mahuzzim in his estate shall he honor." The septuagint reads, "He shall glorify Maodzim in his place." The word forces is properly expressive of the meaning of Mahuzzim; it signifies munitions, bulwarks, fortresses, or, as abstracts are used by the Hebrews for concretes, it may signify protectors, defenders, and guardians.

The God of guardians, plainly signifies a consolidated power. The term God, is not only used for a prince, but plainly for one of a spiritual character; hence, the power represented is a spiritual power of guardians. Now, the worship of saints and angels was established by the secular, as well as ecclesiastical, power of Rome. The Roman church is very properly a church of monasteries and guardianships. This spiritual power was to be honored by the political; for the term "*he*," represents this. The honoring of the church after it became a great community of monkeries, and nunneries, and a worshiper of saints and angels, as protectors and defenders, was a peculiar and general characteristic of the civil power of the Roman empire, after church and state union. Bishop Newton has argued this point extensively.

"In his estate as a God of forces," implies his jurisdiction.

Eighth. "A God, whom his fathers know not, shall he honor with gold and silver and precious stones, and pleasant things." * We have before seen that the empire had changed its religion, and now the fact is repeated, and the character of its deportment to the new religion is designated. The church establishment has

---

* Gibbon says, "Constantine, while he influenced the debates, humbly professed that he was the minister, and not the judge, of the successors of the apostles, who had been established as priests, and as gods upon the earth."—Vol. I. 434.

received as gifts from the state, the greatest of wealth and honors. The best lands, the noblest buildings, the richest endowments, and the most extraordinary revenues, legacies, and gifts, have been bestowed on the church by the civil power. Nothing can equal the costly gems, or the gold and silver ornaments and treasures with which the whole empire church has been favored. Its saints of silver, and shrines of gold, and gems, and pearls, are but an index of the mighty wealth heaped upon it by the kings and princes of the empire, through many ages. The god Mahuzzim, represented a corrupt Christianity; and thus this corrupted religion has been honored by the ruling power of Rome, in all ages since Constantine.

Ninth. "Thus shall he do in the most strong holds with a strange god, whom he shall acknowledge and increase with glory." Here is a reiteration of the change of religion, and the honors that were to be conferred upon it. The repetition is made, as in all similar cases, to emphasize the important fact, that the church was to become exceedingly rich, by political influence. The very states over which the Pope rules were a gift of the state.

Tenth. "He shall cause them to rule over many." The pronoun "them," refers to the strange god, which further shows that that term was symbolic of a body of men; and this is additionally seen in the fact, that this god, or "they" were to rule over many. Of course the term applies to an organized body of men. The bishops, cardinals, popes, abbots, monks, and jesuits, who together form the government of the state church, were constituted by law, the governors in ecclesiastical matters, over millions of men; and they received their executive authority from the state, originally, and it has been perpetuated to them by the state authority. The term, "*he*," shows a different power from the term "they," yet both are plainly united.

Eleventh. "And shall divide the land for gain." This division was, of course, to be co-extensive with their jurisdiction; it was to be made by the church in addition to its ruling power conferred on it.

Now, the whole empire of Rome was divided into *dignities* and *benefices*. "The name *dignity*, applies only to bishoprics, deaneries, archdeaconries, and prebends; benefices apply to all ecclesiastical preferments under these degrees, as rectories and vicarages. Benefices are also divided into regular and secular: regular benefices are those held by monks of any order, abbeys, priories, or convents; secular ones, are those held by secular cures."—(*Enc. R. K.*) The revenues derived to the church from these divisions have been incalculable. In addition to this, the crime of simony, or sale of benefices, has prevailed to an unlimited extent in Europe.

We have now shown a minute coincidence between the willful king and the Roman power, in all its phases, to the present time. It is very plain that the political power of Rome is here treated of as erecting and glorifying the Roman church, for it is utterly impossible, logically, to interpret it of the church alone. Now, history teaches us that the civil power of Rome was head of the church, and that the church derived its glory and authority from it; and prophecy teaches us the same things. Though the unity of the Roman empire was broken, yet prophecy does not regard this as vitiating its existence, but teaches us that it was to have a representative existence down to the very end of monarchy. Thus Daniel said, that though the empire should be broken, the strength of iron should abide in it until the destruction of the reconstructed empire should transpire; and John says, it should have a representative existence in seven heads and ten horns, or in ten great empires and many small kingdoms. These empires have been the Western, Charlemagne's, the Papal, the empire of Charles V., the British, the French, and now Russia is the seventh, or eighth. Eight empires are found, by counting in the Roman before its disruption, and seven since that time.

Russia, being the last power of the seven, is to go into destruction, and is the one at which the king of the south is to " push."

The ships of Chittim, and arms, and the willful king, and the strange god, of this prophecy, coincide with the iron, and iron and clay, of the great image; with the fourth beast, his ten horns, and little horn; and with the little horn from one of the four horns of the he goat, and the king of fierce countenance. The willful king is, also, synonymous with arms, and Chittim.

Twelfth. "And at the time of the end." This period was to be that between the first and last endings of the three and a half times, or between 1776 and 1878, or between the 1290 and 1335 days. During this period, this willful king was to come to his end; but, before his end, he was to engage in war for some outlying countries, and was to be interrupted by two great powers, but was to conquer and prosper, till the "last end of the indignation." As this was to be the great monarchy power represented by the image that was to be broken by the stones, (since it was Rome,) it is evident that its head must be in Europe, and must be the empire represented by the septimo-octave head of the beast in Revelation. Now, the great power which fills half of Europe and overshadows and controls the rest, is the rising colossus Russia; Russia, therefore, must be the power intended, as falling in the holy mountain. Now, as Ezekiel, almost literally, describes Russia as falling on the mountains of Israel, in the latter day, he furnishes further evidence that the fourth kingdom, in the time of the end, was to be resurrected in, or by, Russia. The willful kingdom, was an autocrat among nations, and so is the Russian kingdom.

Thirteenth. "The king of the south, shall push or butt at him; and the king of the north, shall come against him like a whirlwind, with chariots, and with horsemen, and with many ships."

The two kingdoms, under the names north and south, are to be identified by their relative positions to the Russian power, or to each other. The king, or kingdom of the south, would, very naturally, apply to Turkey, on the south of Russia, but as Turkey exists by the sufferance of France and England, it is possible, that the two great western powers, which hold to each other the relation of north and south, may be intended. At any rate, the southern king makes a short fight of it, if any thing is to be understood by the figure of butting at the willful king, or he brings on the fight. The kingdoms of Syria and Egypt, called the kingdoms of the north and south, held about the same close relation to each other, and to Rome, that England and France do to each other and to

Russia; only, they were on the east of Rome, and the case is now just reversed. The king of the north, is Great Britain. This is evident from its northern position, as a great power, and from the immense naval, as well as land forces, it possesses. No nation, but a very great one, would attack the autocratic king; and no nation has such a navy as Britain. This north nation was to come like a whirlwind, with his great naval and land forces, which are indicated by "many ships," and "chariots, and horsemen." The attack was to be great and furious, but, finally, unsuccessful; for the autocrat moves right on to his purpose, and more than gains it, according to the prophet.

Fourteenth. "He shall enter into the countries, and shall overflow, and pass over."

His entering the countries, intimates that this was his original design, in which he had been interrupted by the two great powers that had confederated against him. England and France, or England and Turkey, will unite against Russia. And it seems as if a considerable effort was to be made to check Russia's designs; yet Russia is to take the countries this side the crossings, and is then to pass over into Asia, it would seem. The word "overflow," signifies the great increase of his armies, and triumphs. To "pass over," implies the advancement of conquest, by some great crossing, into a new scene of warfare.

Fifteenth. "He shall enter into the glorious land." This at once reveals his advancement into Palestine, and shows that the passing over related to the conquest of Asia Minor, and the Turkish empire generally.

Sixteenth. "Many countries shall be overthrown; but these shall escape out of his hand, even Edom and Moab, and the chief of the children of Ammon." This would literally imply the conquest of a great portion of Asiatic Turkey, with some exceptions. These were conquests in Asia.

Seventeenth. "He shall stretch forth his hand also upon the countries, and the land of Egypt shall not escape." This expression implies the exertion of severe sovereignty. African countries are here referred to, as Egypt is used as a specific for a generic term, or a part for the whole. "He shall have power over the treasures of gold and silver, and over all the precious things of Egypt."

Eighteenth. "The Libyans and Ethiopians shall be at his steps." This still further teaches the unlimited dominion over Africa in the west and south. Thus having obtained nearly all Europe, Asia, and Africa, he becomes indomitable, and his empire almost limitless; it emulates old Rome, as the possessor of three continents.

Nineteenth. "But tidings out of the east and out of the north shall trouble him." While engaged in these southern conquests, he hears news, from two directions, which enrages him. The eastern news may be from Asia or America, and the northern news is from Europe or Britain.

Twentieth. "Therefore shall he go forth with great fury to destroy, and utterly to make away many." The Russian empire has two great final works to do; the first is to destroy the Roman church in Europe, and the other is to attack the United States. The tidings from the east and north, may be the news of the disaffection of the papal power on account of the superiority which Russia gives to the Greek church, and on account of holy places in Judea. The word tidings seems also to indicate great insurrections.

Twenty-first. "He shall plant the tabernacles of his palace between the seas in the glorious holy mountain." As the Roman power restored was to attack Israel restored, and be overthrown, so the willful king, or autocrat, is here seen planting his imperial tents for battle in the land of Israel restored. The term "holy mountain," signifies the Christian country and government. The term "between the seas," is most graphically expressive of the situation of our Christian democracy between the Atlantic and the Pacific; and, we doubt not but the description here is to the same effect as that given by Ezekiel, when he says Russia shall fall on the mountains of Israel: "He shall come to his end, and none shall help him."

SECTION IV.

Michael—United States.

"And at that time shall Michael stand up the great prince, which standeth for the children of thy people." We shall now show that the United States is represented by Michael, and that the time of trouble is the destruction of monarchy by our country.

First. The time of the standing up of Michael, is the time of the destruction of the willful king, which we have seen was to be in "the time of the end," and at "the last end of the indignation," and the time of the invasion of Israel represented by the planting of the tabernacles of the willful king between the two seas; for the text definitely states, that "Michael shall stand up at that time," and that the willful king, or great monarchy, shall then be destroyed by Michael.

We have already seen, that this very body of monarchy was to be destroyed by the Christian democracy that was to rise in 1776, and that it was to extend over the whole world; it therefore follows, that Michael, who stands up for the Christians, is synonymous with the Christian Israel, or United States.

That angels take charge of kingdoms, and that Michael takes charge of God's Israel, is shown in the Bible clearly; but Michael is never visible, as is the power that destroys monarchy; hence, the term is symbolic, or metonymic. Again; in the Apocalypse, this very Michael is, with his angels, represented at the end of the three and a half times as fighting with the dragon and his angels, and driving the dragon out of the dominions of the Christian democracy into Europe. The dragon, with his seven heads and his angels, are no other than Roman monarchy and its armies; and Michael and his angels are the opposing Christian powers. As he is, therefore, a Christian power in the one case, he must be in the other.

Again; as the prophecy is plainly symbolic, the term Michael must be so, also; and as it is unquestionably such in the Apocalypse, it must be so here; for they both coincide. It is not, by any means, an improper symbol of Israel restored, for, in the Apocalypse, this very power is represented as "one like the son of man on a white cloud"

Again; "Michael, the great prince, shall stand up for the children of thy people," is synonymous with the stone kingdom, and the ancient of days; and these we have seen represented a Christian democracy, that would stand up for the Christian democracy throughout the whole world, and break down all oppressive powers and deliver them.

That the United States will ultimately make the cause of true Christian democracy its own cause throughout the world, is as certain as it exists; for its tendencies to this end are inevitable.

Again; this strife comes on before the Millennium, and coincides with the smiting of the stone, the taking of the beast, and the taking of the beast and false prophet; and, therefore, to expect a literal revelation of an archangel, is fanatical. To expect a literal and visible archangel on earth at this time of trouble, is fanatical; for Christ says, he (and his angels) will not come till "after that tribulation of those days."

Second. "Then shall be a time of trouble, such as never was since there was a nation even to that same time." From a misunderstanding of the similar words of Christ, in the gospels, this period has been applied exclusively to the destruction of Jerusalem. Christ said, "in those days shall be affliction, such as was not from the beginning of the creation which God created unto this time, neither shall be." Now, as Daniel places these troubles at the final doom of monarchy, he and Christ must coincide in reference to the same events. Now, if we remember that Christ said, "these things (the destruction of Jerusalem and the captivity) were the beginning of sorrows," and also, that he said, "they shall fall by the edge of the sword, and shall be led away captive into all nations; and Jerusalem shall be trodden down of the Gentiles, until the times of the Gentiles be fulfilled," and that he said, "these be the days of vengeance, that all things which are written may be fulfilled;" we shall then see that both Christ and Daniel referred this great distress to the close of the times of the Gentiles.

But again; as the destruction of the corrupt Jewish government, civil and ecclesiastical, may be regarded as typical of the corrupt Roman church and state, it follows, that what is said of the type and not realized by it, must be completed in the antitype.

This time of trouble plainly coincides with the "battle of the great day of God Almighty." How fearful will be the sufferings of that day! what national calamities will we endure! yet, we shall come off conquerors. The "powers of heaven shall be shaken" then, by the awful onset of the world in arms against us; but "God shall be the hope of his people."

We are poorly prepared as a nation, by defenses, to resist the invader; we are careless about them; and to be urged by prophetic warning, is considered preposterous. We would as soon exhort the man in the moon, as to exhort our nation to be ready for the danger before it; they would consider us as affected with lunacy, to preach for truth the prediction of the scriptures.

Third. "And at that time, thy people shall be delivered, every one that shall be found written in the book." The people of Daniel, or the "holy people," as he often calls them, when speaking of the latter day, are not synonymous with carnal Israel, but with Christians. St. Peter speaks of Christians, in language expressive of this fact, when he says to them, "ye are a chosen generation, a royal priesthood, an holy nation, a peculiar people, which in time past were not a people, but are now *the people* of God." The deliverance here promised is a political one, from the very nature of the case; and is identical with the deliverance promised in all ages to the Christians, and which now transpires, because the beast, or Roman empire, is destroyed, and the saints possess the kingdom and dominion of the world. We do not understand by this, mere personal salvation, but the universal deliverance of Christianity from worldly alliance and domination.

Fourth. "Every one that shall be found written in the book." As the ancient of days coincides with Michael, and, as their destruction of the fourth monarchy and deliverance of Christians coincide, so the books of the ancient of days and the books of Michael coincide. A book in judgment, represents the laws or principles of the judge; and a record book of names with the judge, represents those who subscribe to, and abide by, the laws of the judge. As the judge is a Christian democracy, when he sits in judgment or war, he will destroy all those who oppose his principles, and favor and assist with deliverance all who subscribe to his law of liberty.

The fall of the willful king, and the deliverance by Michael, coincide with the fall of the monarchy image, by the smiting of the stone; with the destruction of the fourth beast, by the people of the saints, and the judgment of the ancient of days upon 100,000,000 of people; with the breaking of the fierce king without hand; with the destruction of the willful king on the holy mountain between the seas; and with the destruction of Gog on the mountains of Israel.

SECTION V.

The Final Kingdom of Messiah.

Almost all of the prophecies of the latter day, whether political or spiritual, close with an account of Messiah's kingdom. The first two in Daniel, close with the kingdom of the mountain and of the Son of Man; and here, the angel, in interpreting all the visions, gives a further and particular account of other things connected with it.

As the stone smites monarchy, and becomes a mountain; as the ancient destroys monarchy, and receives the Son of Man, so Michael destroys the great autocracy, and then comes the final kingdom, ushered in complete by the resurrection of the dead. We will notice the points, given here, carefully:

First. "And many of them that sleep in the dust of the earth, shall awake; some to everlasting life, and some to shame and everlasting contempt."

As no interpretation is given of this passage, we take it to be literal; and as it coincides with the "resurrection of the just and unjust," we take it to be spiritual. How soon it will occur, after the last great war, is not stated, and we must look elsewhere to find its mode and time. In the close of the vision, Daniel is told, that all the war shall be finished at the end of a certain number of years; and that he shall then stand in his lot. John tells us, that as soon as the war closed, there was a first resurrection, and he then describes a final one, occurring a thousand years later. The resurrection, occurring immediately after the days of great tribulation, coincides with the words of Christ. He says, "*immediately* after the tribulation of those days, shall the sun be darkened, * * and the powers of heaven be shaken, and then shall appear the sign of the Son of Man, in heaven."

Second. "And they that be wise, shall shine as the brightness of the firmament, (or the sun) and they that turn many to righteousness, as the stars forever and ever." This is explained and enforced by the Saviour's words, "The Son of Man shall send forth his angels, and they shall gather out of his kingdom (on earth) all things that offend, and them which do iniquity, and shall cast them into a furnace of fire. Then shall the righteous shine forth as the sun, in the kingdom of their Father."

SECTION VI.

The Sealing of the Vision, and the Discovery.

"But thou, O Daniel, shut up the words, and seal the book, even to the time of the end; many shall run to and fro, and knowledge shall be increased. Go thy way, Daniel, for the words are closed up and sealed till the time of the end."

First. The words to be sealed were those which related to the willful king, and the history of the world, during his existence, down to the time of his destruction.

This must be so, because, a part of the interpretation is expressly literal, and it is almost perfectly so, in every word, down to the destruction of the Hebrews by the willful king, or by ARMS. Here it changes into symbolic prophecy, or interpretation, and we are left altogether in the dark about both. As the prophecy of this period is said, by the angel, to be an interpretation of all the others, of the same period, it is evident, that if this was understood, all the rest could be; and if any others, of the same period, could be interpreted, this could be also; hence, it follows, that all prophecy of that period of the world, from the destruction of Jerusalem, was to be clearly understood by no one, " till the time of the end." Of the truth of this affirmation we need not write, for the whole Christian world agrees to the proposition, and all hold the book of Revelation, itself, to be a mystery, and yet all know that it predicts the great features of this period. Who has written a clear explanation of Daniel's visions of this period? Who has explained the times, and days, and months of the prophets? Who, that has adhered to prophetic expositions of this period, but has been obliged to hold his views as mere speculations, for want of any certain evidence upon which to ground them? Every thing, on all sides, has proved that the words relating to this great era were closed up and sealed.

Since the German reformation, many men have applied to the study of these predictions, yet they have seldom agreed together, and have done little more than to prepare the way for a final discovery; in some cases, they were very nearly right, yet he who follows them, will find he is following as much error as he is truth, for the words were to be sealed until a later period, and in the age of the Medes and Newtons, there was still a vail over the law and the prophets.

Second. The words were to be sealed until a certain period, called "the time of the end." This appears, very plainly, to be the period between the 1290 and 1335 days. That the signification of the prophecy was then to be understood, seems not to be doubted, since the sealing "*till*" the time of the end, leads us to imply, necessarily, that their mystery would be then understood. Again, it is also stated, that they shall be understood by the wise, and not by the wicked. These terms are to be taken in their widest sense, and, of course, refer to nations, for they are prophetic terms of multitude. They seem to affirm that Israel restored will understand them, and Christian democracy generally, but that the monarchy system will not; and that they will not, because they are so wicked that they shall still be blinded, and shall hasten to their ruin.

They were to be understood in an age of "running to and fro;" that is, in an age of great travel, and trade, and emigration, and discovery; such as the present.

They were to be understood in an enlightened age, or one of great knowledge, as is the present.

Lastly; it was to be made by somebody, and not by chance, and its very delay was to be promotive of immense good to the church and the world. Its benefits will be without limit. The discovery of the mystery of this period we profess fully to have made; and if we are not mistaken, the great mass of people in our country will agree to our views.

SECTION VII.

Length of the "Indignation."

We now come to the exact number of years during which the willful king was to domineer over the people of God. This number of years is affirmed in the vision, and is then repeated in an interpretation. Their beginning and ending are each distinctly stated, so that no difficulty can possibly occur on these points. We shall first take up the vision, and then the interpretation.

Paragraph I.

THREE AND A HALF TIMES.

First. Period of Wonders.

Vision.—" And one said to the man clothed in linen * * How long shall it be to the end of these wonders?"

The wonders here spoken of, can not date farther back in the vision than the destruction of Jerusalem by "ARMS," or the Romans, for all the previous part of the vision is literal, and not mystic, or wonderful. This is proved, also, by the passage which immediately follows, explanatory of the term wonders, which says, "and when he shall have accomplished to scatter the POWER of the holy people, all these things shall be finished." In this passage, the pronoun "he" is represented as the scatterer of Israel's power, and plainly refers to the willful king, or ARMS; and, of course, the period of the Roman power from the destruction of Jerusalem is referred to, because the first we hear of this power of ARMS, is when he is casting down the sanctuary Again;

the period of the destruction of the nationality of God's people is expressly affirmed to be the period of the wonders. The term, *power*, as here used, represents nationality; for it can have no other sense. "The *powers* that be, are ordained of God," means the governments ordained of God; and in the above passage the word is used in the very same sense.

This period, also, plainly coincides with that which is called the period of "indignation," which is so frequently repeated, and which all know is synonymous with the destruction and desolation of Israel's nationality, or with the "times of the Gentiles upon Jerusalem."

Second. Exact length of the period of the scattering of the nationality of Israel.

Vision.—"He held up his right hand and his left hand unto heaven, and sware by him that liveth forever and ever, that it shall be for a time times and a half."

The solemnity of this oath leads us to consider how very definite the length of this period was to be, and how important an era would transpire at its close.

The end of it was to be signalized by the cessation of the broken condition of the POWER or nationality of the saints or Christians. Of course, the reorganization of God's Israel into nationality is plainly taught; for the cessation of scattering is the beginning of union, and also the consummation of it. This gathering is also synonymous with the deliverance, by Michael, of those written in the book; and coincides with the great predictions of Israel's restoration.

The restoration to nationality must require considerable time, and is called "the last end of the indignation, or time of the end." It would, therefore, seem natural to suppose that the three and a half times would mark the limits of this period, when explained.

Now, our discovery shows that it has a double signification, or has two distinct lengths; and that one of them is 1,708 years long, and the other is 1,810; and one ended in 1776, and the other will end in 1878.

Paragraph II.

TWELVE HUNDRED AND NINETY AND THIRTEEN HUNDRED AND THIRTY-FIVE DAYS.

As each symbolic vision has an interpretation, so has the vision of the length of the desolation of the nationality of God's Israel. And it will confirm our views above given.

1. *Interpretation.*—" And I heard, but I understood not; then said, O my Lord, how long shall be these latter times, or latter wonders?" Such is Bishop Newton's translation of the passage, and it is very accurate.

Daniel had seen and heard what was to be upon the people of God, and the exact length of the time of their sufferings is now emphasized in his ears, but he does not understand the terms used, and he asks for an explanation, and the explanation of the times is given. The reply to him is, that the words are closed up and sealed till the period of their fulfillment; but still the whole vision is briefly repeated, and the times explained in a different form.

2. *Interpretation.*—" The words are closed up and sealed till the time of the end. Many shall be purified and made white; but the wicked (kingdom) shall do

wickedly; and none of the wicked (kingdoms) shall understand, but the wise (nation) shall understand. And from the time the daily sacrifice shall be taken away, and the abomination that maketh desolate set up, there shall be a thousand two hundred and ninety days. Blessed is he that waiteth and cometh to the thousand three hundred and five and thirty days." In these pasages are repeated: first, the fact that there is to be a period at the close of the sufferings of God's people, called the time of the end. Secondly; the sufferings of God's people through this long period of depression, is again mentioned. Thirdly; the wickedness of Rome is reaffirmed. Fourthly; in the end the people of God are to understand the prophecy with great profit. Fifthly; the Roman monarchies are not to understand or to believe in it. Sixthly; the 1290 and 1335 days represent the very same periods as the three and a half times. This must be so, because they are given in explanation of these very three and a half times. One length of the three and a half times must, therefore, be equal to 1290 days; and the other to 1335 days. Here we see that the times are resolvable into days. Now, the 1290 days are equal to 1708 years, and the 1335 days to $1809\frac{2}{3}$ years.

3. The time when these days were to be dated, is plainly at the destruction of Jerusalem; for the text most emphatically and constantly, throughout the vision, pins the beginning of these days right down to that epoch. The "wonders;" the "time of scattering the *power* of the holy people," and "the indignation," all begin right there; and the interpretation reiterates that there is the place and time to begin the days; for they

are to begin at the *cessation* of the *daily sacrifice,* and at the setting up of the desolation over Israel.

How any expositor could venture to begin these days at any other epoch, away from the destruction of Jerusalem, is very singular, and demonstrates that the words were truly closed up and sealed to all such violators of the plain words of holy writ.

Paragraph III.

APPLICATION OF THESE TIMES.

The destruction of Jerusalem by the Romans, occurred in the year 68 A. D. On the 14th of the month Nisan, the Roman army encamped at Jerusalem, but had entered Palestine somewhat earlier. On the 7th of Jyar, or on the fifteenth day of the siege, the Romans got possession of the first wall. The whole city was encompassed by a wall some time within the months of Jyar or Sivan. This wall was the cause of the great desolation by famine. On the 17th of Panemus, the daily sacrifice ceased; on the 10th of Ab, the temple was burned; on the 8th of Elul, the city was burned, and, about the middle of Tisri, the walls and whole city were demolished. The period of the destruction of the daily sacrifice, and the setting up of the desolator, occupied, as near as can be estimated, about six months.

It will be allowed that the period represented by these days may begin within the limits of the time the Roman army entered Judea and finished its conquests. No reasonable person would require a more specific point than this to begin with.

Now, the 1290 days are equal to 1708 years, and if we add this to A. D. 68, it brings us down to the year 1776 A. D. And, as three and a half times also equal 1708, we are also brought by this down to 1776. These two, therefore, coincide, and point to 1776 as the beginning of the restoration of Israel, or restoration of the saints or Christians to nationality; and also the beginning of "the time of the end," or "last end of the indignation."

Again; the 1335 days are equal to $1809\frac{2}{3}$ years, and if we date these at the close of the Jewish war, or the time when the desolator was established, or $68\frac{2}{3}$ A. D., we are brought down to about A. D. $1878\frac{1}{3}$. Then, as the three and a half times are equal to 1810 years, if we date them at the beginning of the war, or $68\frac{1}{3}$ A. D., we are brought down to $1778\frac{1}{3}$ A. D. These coincidences must be esteemed wonderful, and we may look to 1878 as the close of the time of the end; as the finishing point of the indignation; as the victory over monarchy; as the possession of the world by the Christian democracy; and as the end of war forever, and the erection of the Millennial republic.

"Go thou thy way till the end be; for thou shalt rest and stand in thy lot at the *end* of the days."

SECTION VIII.

Epitome of Daniel's Prophecies and their Mutual Coincidence.

The four great visions of universal empire given by Daniel, all coincide with each other, point to point; the last two visions leaving out Babylon, which had passed away at the time they occurred. In the first two, the four metals and four beasts coincide in representing the four great monarchies; and after these two, leaving out Babylonia, they all agree together.

The gold head, and lion, both symbolize Babylon; the silver breast and arms, the bear with the two sides, the ram with the two horns, and the king of Persia, all coincide with the Medo-Persian empire; the belly and thighs of brass, the leopard with four wings and four heads, the he goat with one horn, divided into four horns, and the mighty king of Grecia, and the kingdoms of Syria and Egypt, all coincide with the Macedonian empire and its four divisions, ultimating in two.

The legs of iron, the fourth beast; the little horn from the he goat, or king of fierce countenance, and the willful king, or ARMS, all coincide with the Roman empire. The iron and clay, the little horn and ten horns, the fierce king understanding dark sentences, the willful king and his new god, all coincide with church and state union in the Roman empire. The ten toes and the ten horns coincide with the broken state of the Roman empire. The fall of the whole monarchy image, the taking of the fourth beast, the fall of the fierce king, and the breaking of the willful king on the mountains of Israel between the two seas, all coincide with the destruction of Gog by Israel, or with the general destruction of monarchy. The mountain, and stone cut out of the mountain, the ancient of days, and locomotive throne of fire, the saints and people of the saints; the sanctuary and host, the holy people and the POWER of the holy people, all coincide with the Christians and the government growing up from them in the United States of America. The 2300 evenings and mornings of the casting down of the sanctuary, the three and a half times of the scattering of the *power* of the holy people, and the 1290 days from the cessation of the daily sacrifice, coincide with 1708 years, in civil measure, and dated at the 17th of Panemus, or 189th day, 68 A. D., end on July 4th, 1776. In spiritual measure, they are 1451 years long, and agree with the *three and a half* times of the little horn of the fourth beast, and, dated on June 19th, 325, at church and state union, they end on the 4th of July, 1776. The *three and a half* times in civil measure, are also 1810 years and ten days long, and, dated at the last passover Nisan 14th or 97th day, 68 A. D., they end 1878 A. D., and 117th day. The 1335 days equal 1809 years and 244 days, and dated at the burning of Jerusalem the 8th of Elul or 239th day of 68 A. D., we are brought to 1878 and 117th day. Thus, do all four versions most wonderfully harmonize, even down to days, though they cover a field of vast ages. We now turn to Revelation, and shall find it harmonizing with Daniel's visions of the fourth, fifth and sixth empires.

CHAPTER X.

THE SPIRITUAL WORLD IN THE APOCALYPSE.

The book of Revelation was written by St. John in the days of Domitius Nero, and not in the days of Flavius Domitian, a later emperor.

It consists of a set of prophecies addressed to the Christian church, and containing its future history; and, also, of a complete history of the political world. The spiritual prophecies begin their accomplishment with the fall of Jerusalem, and the political with the union of church and state.

The style of the book is figurative in the most refined degree, and involved and inrolled in the most systematic, yet apparently complicated manner. Nothing can exceed the perfect symmetry of the whole book.

The proof that it contains the history of the church and of the Roman Empire, is found in the fact, that it is expressly stated that the events were close at hand; such is the signification of *Kairos enggus*, in the very opening of the book. And, also, in the facts, that at the close of the book, a full view of the final judgment is given, and that a consecutive series of events are represented, as filling the entire era between the beginning and end of the prophecies. Now, as Daniel's prophecies embrace all the greater features of this long era, it is plain that John must predict the same events as Daniel; but, as he is a later prophet, he must be expected to give more particulars than Daniel.

We now take up the two great classes of prophecy in this book, hoping that we shall be able to explain the great features of them, if not every minute shade of symbol and figure.

In our expositions we shall pay no sort of attention to the arbitrary and unauthorized divisions into chapters, but follow up each vision till it closes.

The introduction to the whole book of Revelation is couched in few words, by the apostle. He simply states that God gave Christ this Revelation, and that Christ sent his angel to tell the matter to him; saying, that they were things which must shortly begin to be fulfilled. He then addresses the churches, and communicates what things were expressly directed to them, by Christ, and tells the mode in which he received them.

SECTION I.

Seat of Spiritual Prophecy.

The seat of these spiritual prophecies, first claims our attention. John says, "I turned to see the voice that spake with me. And being turned, I saw seven golden candlesticks; and in the midst of the seven candlesticks, one like unto the Son of Man, clothed with a garment down to the feet, and girt about the paps with a golden girdle. His head and his hairs were white as snow, and his eyes were as a flame of fire, and his feet like unto fine brass, as if they burned in a furnace; and his voice as the sound of many waters. And he had in his right hand seven stars, and out of his mouth went a sharp two-edged sword; and his countenance was as the sun shineth in his strength. * * Write the things which thou hast seen, the things which are, and the things which shall be hereafter." This is, plainly, a symbolic representation of Christ, and not of his literal person; for various parts of the image are subsequently shown to be symbols; as " the mystery of the seven stars, and the seven golden candlesticks." It may be proper, here, to show the signification of all these symbols:

1. *The seven golden candlesticks.*—This symbol is a double figure: first, it represents the seven churches in Asia Minor; second, it represents the whole Christian church. These things are so, because, first, the text says, " The seven candlesticks which thou sawest, are the seven churches;" second, the seven churches are put by synecdoche, for the whole church. That this last is true, arises from several considerations, which may be named.

It stands to reason, that one part of the church of God, is as much the subject of God's promises and rebukes as another, for God is no respecter of persons; beside this, every Christian feels, that if he performs the commands of God, he has as much a claim to the rewards severally promised to these particular churches, as any individual member in them; since it is written, " Ye are all one in Christ Jesus," and, " What I say unto one I say unto all." Again; as the great intent of prophecy is for the general good of the church throughout the world. " no prophecy (to the churches) can be of any private interpretation," but embraces all. Again: the very language of promise and threatening is, plainly, not confined by the text to a specific portion of the church, but is generic, and embraces all; as, "He that overcometh," &c., "Be thou faithful unto death," &c., "He that hath an ear let him hear what the Spirit saith (not) unto (some, but unto) *the churches.*" Lastly, the style of the apocalypse being figurative throughout, the seven churches must also be so, to conform to the style of the book. It is, indeed, hardly necessary to advance these things, since the whole Christian world has regarded the address to the seven churches, as an address to a part as representatives of the whole; the number seven being the sacred number of perfection, seven churches are chosen to represent universality, rather than any other number.

Let it be constantly borne in mind, that almost every figure of speech used by John, has a double significancy, and must be translated twice, to reach its true import, or, that two symbols mean but one thing.

2. *The seven stars.*—"The seven stars are the angels of the seven churches." These, from the nature of coincidence, must also possess a double signification, as well as the seven candlesticks. These angels were the governors, or body of government, of the seven churches, and, hence, represent the body of the social government of the church, throughout the Christian world. Here we see the same dual power represented, which is recognizable in all descriptions of God's people throughout the Bible.

3. "One *like* unto the Son of Man." This is, therefore, only a resemblance, a symbol, of the person of

Christ, and through which form Christ manifests himself to a mortal.

4. "Clothed with a garment down to the feet." As celestials are not clothed in mortal apparel, which is a badge of human disgrace, this garment must signify the nature of the spotless character that wears it. A robe of white is a symbol of honor and dignity.

5. "His head and his hairs were white like wool, as white as snow." This, also, is emblematic of superior wisdom and glory; for, "a hoary head is a crown of glory."

6. "His feet like unto fine brass, as if they burned in a furnace." "How beautiful upon the mountains, are the feet of him that bringeth good tidings, that publisheth salvation, that saith unto Zion, Thy God reigneth."

7. "His voice as the sound of many waters." That is, as the voice of multitudes; it shows vast authority and fame.

8. "Out of his mouth went a sharp two-edged sword." A sword symbolizes authority, as, "He beareth not the sword in vain." Coming from the mouth, it is the word of God, which is called the sword of the Spirit, and "sharper than any two-edged sword."

9. "His countenance was as the sun shineth in his strength." A face symbolizes justice, severity, or favor; here it must represent the light of God's countenance, or favor to his people.

SECTION II.

The Prophecies.

"Write the things which thou *hast seen*, and the things which *are*, and the things which *shall be hereafter.*"

The address and prophecy to the churches, are plainly included together, under the terms, "which thou hast seen, and the things which are;" for when John is subsequently invited to receive a view of political prophecy, he is called to look only at the "things which shall be hereafter." Now, the temporal state of the churches predicted under the "things that are," seem limited to the period designated by ten days. "Ye shall have tribulation ten days." A day signifies a certain limited period, and is generally put for it. Now, these ten days of tribulation had their coincidence, and by consequence their fulfillment, in the ten great persecutions under the pagan emperors, and closed in the days of Constantine the Great. So that the prophecy of "the things *that are,*" seems clearly bounded by this ten days. This is further confirmed, by the fact, that the political prophecies began to be realized at the union of church and state.

The very expression, "things that are," seems to imply things that will transpire, while the church is under the then present pagan government, in the world.

CHAPTER XI.

POLITICAL PROPHECIES OF REVELATION.

The visions of John and Daniel, being in the same great field, they must coincide; and it is plain, that as Daniel prophesied in full of the political state of Rome, so John must also do the same, and that, in the principal features of the fourth kingdom, they must agree together. It will, therefore, be expected that there will be a similarity of the construction of their imagery; and such we shall find to be the case. As Daniel gives a twice doubled view of the world from his times, so does John, from his. John begins his political visions at the union of church and state, and thence proceeds to the final kingdom; but of the Roman world he gives four distinct views. The first view is that by seven seals, extending down to the Millennium; the second, is by seven trumpets, rehearsing great eras of the same period. He then gives a view of Rome, during the same great era, under the form of a dragon and a beast, and under the symbols of a beast and harlot.

In addition to this, he gives a double history of the dual Israel, through the same period, under the symbols of two witnesses, and the woman and her man child. Besides these, he gives two episodical descriptions; one of the destruction of the Roman church, and one of the destroyer of the Roman state.

We shall first interpret the seals, and then the episodical descriptions of Rome and Israel, and then of the seven trumpets.

The seat of prophecy, whence the book of seals is given, is worthy of attention, as it is a prophetic one.

SECTION I.

The Seat of Political Prophecy.

At the seat of spiritual prophecy, no throne was to be seen; but only Christ among the churches; here the scene is changed, and the symbols of civil dominion over the world are introduced. The imagery before us claims attention, as it is all of a dual character. We shall quote the descriptive text of the second seat of prophecy, as it may be needed.

1. "A door was opened in heaven." This was a symbolic heaven, as any one can see at a glance; for, in the "third heaven," no such objects as beasts or doors exist. The term, heaven, was originally applied by God to the atmosphere, or firmament, and is figuratively used as the etherial dwelling of the true Christians after death; and on earth it is used variously to represent sublimity, or exaltation; and, symbolically, it represents the place of the church on earth, or the dominion of God on earth, &c. Many passages of scripture teach us the figurative sense of the term.

2. "Come up hither, and I will show thee things hereafter." Here John changes his locality of view.

3. "Behold a throne was set in heaven, and one sat on the throne, and there was a rainbow round about the

throne, in sight like unto an emerald." God is a spirit; he can not be represented by any image; yet his ruling power and government can be, and these may represent himself. The worship, therefore, paid to this person, must be symbolic of the praise offered to the God who rules over the kingdoms of the world. The throne, and the person on it, represent the dual and supreme government of Jehovah; the throne, representing his spiritual supremacy, and the person upon it his civil or regal supremacy.

4. "And I beheld, and lo, in the midst of the throne, and of the four beasts, and in the midst of the elders stood a lamb as it had been slain, having seven horns and seven eyes, which are the seven spirits of God, sent forth into all the world." This lamb received the worship of countless millions. The lamb is, plainly, symbolic of the kingdom of Jesus Christ, for a beast, universally, in scripture, symbolizes a kingdom. The seven horns and seven eyes, further represent the dual and perfect nature of this kingdom. The whole, however, having a double significancy, must symbolize, not merely Christ's kingdom, but Christ himself; for, Christ's kingdom, when used as a symbol, must represent himself, just as we have seen that the throne and person upon it signify God's great kingdom; and that then, God's kingdom symbolizes himself. This double representation is the most beautiful imagery imaginable.

5. The seven eyes and seven spirits are representatives of the very same things as "the seven spirits of God and seven stars," which are synonymous with the seven candlesticks and seven stars, which represent the church and its social government, as we have seen

already. The duality of God's kingdom is preserved in all descriptions of it. The spirits, or eyes, sent into all the earth, represent the Christian church through the world. But here the double imagery must again be kept up, and, as the spirits represent the church, the church must represent the power that inspires it, which is the Holy Ghost. The seven horns, also representing the civil power, must represent God himself, as its author, so that the Trinity is represented in the lamb, and the unity of Godhead by the throne and him that sits upon it.

6. The rainbow symbolizes that God's throne is the seat of the promises, and represents its final establishment in the world.

7. "And round about the throne were four-and-twenty seats; and upon the seats I saw four-and-twenty elders sitting, clothed in white raiment, and they had on their heads crowns of gold."

1. *The seats.*—A seat represents, in symbolic language, a separate power. Twenty-four seats would symbolize twenty-four seats of dominion; but, as the figures in this scene are all double, the twenty-four will represent but twelve.

2. *The elders.*—A man represents a body of government. Twenty-four elders, therefore, as the symbols are double, will represent twelve governments.

3. *The crowns.*—There are two different words, in the original scripture text, which are translated crown; but one should be rendered diadem, and the other crown; for one word is *stephanos*, and the other *diadema*. The diadem is a symbol of independent power, and the stephanos of delegated power. The crowns of the elders

are of this latter class, and signify that their power or civil authority was received from a higher source, and was responsible to it. These twelve seats of delegated power and elders, doubly represented, perfectly coincide with the twelve dominions the apostles are to receive from Christ in the final kingdom.

8. "And in the midst of the throne, and round about the throne, were four beasts, full of eyes before and behind. And the first beast was like a lion, and the second like a calf, and the third beast had a face as a man, and the fourth beast was like a flying eagle. And the four beasts had each of them six wings, and they were full of eyes within." Some persons make a great ado about these living creatures being called beasts, but as one was a lion, and another an ox, our translators were tolerably correct.

1. *The beasts.*—A beast is always used to represent a civil power, and two of these four beasts are a lion and an ox. A man is, also, used to symbolize a government, as the willful king, the ancient of days, &c.; and one of these creatures was like a man. An eagle is often used, by the prophets, as a symbol of a civil power. These four beasts must, therefore, represent civil power; and as they are all blended together in the same work and throne, they must be a twice doubled representation of the very same power. "They had eyes before and behind." This shows that their power was external, or national, and that they watched over the exterior department of power.

It is remarkable, that the four national standards of Old Israel precisely coincided with these four beasts, and were the representatives of nationality. A lion was the standard of Judah and two tribes on the east of the camp of Israel; a calf, or ox, was the standard of Ephraim and two tribes on the west; a man's face was the standard of Reuben and two tribes on the south; and an eagle flying was the standard of Dan and two tribes on the north. To these the vision is plainly conformed.

2. *The twenty-four wings full of eyes.*—A wing is a symbol of a power. Isa. xviii. 1: "Wo, thou land shadowed with wings,"* or governments. As these twenty-four wings (each beast having six) were full of eyes within, a spiritual power must be represented, which looks to internal affairs, as the state looks to outward matters. The number twenty-four, is just a double symbol for twelve. As these wings give motion to the beasts, so the church of Israel gives velocity and power to its nationality.

9. "And there were seven lamps of fire burning before the throne, which are the seven Spirits of God. And before the throne there was a sea of glass like unto crystal." These two symbols are associated by their locality, and must be counterparts of each other. The seven spirits, we have already shown, symbolized the church and the Holy Spirit. The Holy Ghost is but one spirit, but a capital letter being used of the seven, seems directly to show a symbolic reference to divinity.

A sea denotes a body of people; and a sea of glass shows a pure people; and, as glass is of a thicker consistency than water, it would seem to represent the civil authority of Israel and of Christ; while the lamps represent the church and the Holy Ghost.

---

* Lowth's Isaiah.

In all this description, the supreme government and the Trinity are represented double by a single symbol; and the subsidiary kingdoms of God are represented by double symbols.

This doubling is in accordance with Joseph's dreams, and his declaration to Pharaoh, that the dream was twice doubled, because the dream was certain and the interpretation was sure. Now, as one of Pharaoh's visions was given to interpret the other, so in this vision there are double forms of the very same things, so blended as to make one glorious picture.

The worship of the redeemed millions before the throne, is prophetic; and, indeed, the whole vision of the heavens before John, was prophetic of the final and universal prevalence of God's kingdom on earth; and, as Christ's second advent is placed at the beginning of Revelation, so this final kingdom also comes before the prophecy is delivered, as indicative of what would result when prophecy was all ended.

SECTION II.

The Book of Seals—First Panorama of the World.

"I saw in the right hand of him that sat on the throne, a book written within and on the back side, sealed with seven seals." "And no man was able to open the book neither to look thereon." "And he (the Lamb) came and took the book out of the right hand of him that sat on the throne." "And they sung a new song, saying, Thou art worthy to take the book and to loose the seals thereof.

Before the giving of this prophecy to Christ, the history of the world was already in the hands of Israel; but Daniel had declared that it would be "a sealed vision, until the time of the end;" and this sealed book coincides with the declaration, "the words are closed up and sealed." As God gave the prophecy of the book of Revelation to Christ, and he to John, and John to the world; and as it, like Daniel's vision of the same great period, has ever been sealed to men, we can not understand the breaking of the seals by Christ, to refer merely to the giving a new prophetic history of the church and the world; but we understand it to be symbolic of the giving of the prophecy; and this, then, of the greater exercise of the power to bring the prophecies to a complete fulfillment, in the establishment of the throne of God and the Lamb forever among men. This interpretation is in accordance with the double symbolism of John's writings, and with a scriptural consistency of interpretation of the Old and New Testament prophecies. The seven seals show that the book contained seven great prophecies; and, being written without and within, shows other prophecies additionally.

Paragraph I.

THE FIRST SEAL—OR CHURCH AND STATE UNION.

"When the Lamb opened one of the seals, I heard as it were the voice of thunder,. one of four beasts saying, Come and see. And I saw, and behold a white horse; and he that sat on him had a bow; and a crown was given unto him; and he went forth conquering and to conquer."

Right here we must state the principles of interpretation essential to determining the meaning of symbolic prophecy. The principle is simple: first, the signification of a symbol must be determined by the Bible; and, secondly, by the fulfillment itself. Nor can the specific character of any event be determined from the symbolic text, until the agents engaged in the event have been shown to coincide with the symbols of the text. It, therefore follows, that not one of the great symbolic characters of prophecy could be known until they existed; and as ages were required to develop their historic character, it resulted naturally that Daniel's visions, and the apocalypse, have been sealed visions for ages past.

We now begin our exposition of the first seal.

1. The first beast, or lion, calls John's attention. As this beast coincides with Judah's station on the east, we might naturally expect the characters to which attention is called should be manifested on the east of Rome, or of the Christian Israel.

2. *The Horse.*—" I saw, and behold a white horse." We must now look to scripture for an interpretation of the symbol before us. The symbol is a horse, and his symbolic complexion is white. Zachariah says, that " God hath made Judah as his goodly horse in battle." Here Judah is figuratively represented by a horse, and Judah is a figure of speech for the Jewish nation. Isaiah says, " which bringeth forth the chariot and the horse, the army and the power." As it is a feature of Hebrew poetry to repeat the same idea in different words, the chariot, and the army, and the horse, are synonymous with power. Zachariah uses the term horse as a symbol. He says: " I saw, and behold a man riding upon a red

horse, and he stood among the myrtle-trees in the bottom, and behind him were red horses, speckled, and white. Then I said, O my Lord, what are these? And the man that stood among the myrtle-trees, answered and said, These are they whom the Lord sent to walk to and fro through the earth. And they answered the angel of the Lord that stood among the myrtle-trees, We have walked to and fro through the earth, and behold all the earth sitteth still and is at rest. Then answered the angel of the Lord and said, O Lord of hosts, how long wilt thou not have mercy on Jerusalem and the cities of Judah." Here the angel on horseback, praying for Israel's restoration from his wanderings, plainly represents Israel praying for deliverance from Babylonish captivity. Again; the horses without riders, are represented as conversing, which shows that they represented bodies of men; and their wanderings, while all else had rest, refers to the captivity and wanderings they suffered in Babylon; for God immediately says, "I am sore displeased with the heathen that are at rest." The various horses may properly represent the various tribes of Israel, but being without riders, shows a church without the state in their captivity. In the sixth chapter of Zachariah, it is stated that the four chariots, and four horses to each, represent the four spirits that stand before God, and that go into all the earth. As these were mere symbols, they represented great organizations; and, as they were symbolic spirits, or minds, they must represent organic bodies of power.

White color signifies prosperity and purity, or honor.— (*Sym. Dic.*) A white horse was therefore a symbol of an organic body of a pure character, and moving with the velocity of the war horse, whose neck is clothed with thunder. A horse being an organic symbol, must, from the very nature of symbols, represent an organic power or body of power.

3. *The Rider.*—A man, when used as a symbol, represents a government or organic body of some kind; and when riding symbolizes felicity and successful progress.—(*Sym. Dic.*)

4. *The Bow.*—This signifies anger or power to avenge or punish others. Thus, in Ps. vii, God is said to be " angry with the wicked every day. If he turn not, he will whet his sword; he hath bent his bow, and made it ready." It may also represent virtue; as Joseph's "*bow* abode in strength;" but it seems to denote warfare in the passage before us, ending in victory.—(*Sym. Dic.*)

5. *The Crown.*—This crown was not a diadem, and, therefore, represents the royalty conferred as a delegated, and not an independent one. The body of government represented by the man with the bow of victory, was not, at first, a royalty, but became such after victory, denoted by the bow. This vision, it must be remembered, filled the whole field of view, over the whole symbolic heavens, and nothing coexists with it to compare in magnitude.

We must now look for a coincidence to this seal, in the Roman empire, somewhere between John's day and this; and, properly, immediately after the ten persecutions. Now, we shall look in vain for any such a double character, crowned and victorious, before or after the days of Constantine. The white horse and his rider crowned will, therefore, represent the church of Christ, united to the state, after outriding the ten great persecutions.

Coincidence First.—The scene was to be in the east. Christianity first arose and conquered in the east.

Coincidence Second.—The horse represents a moving

body of warlike power, but of a pure character. Christianity was just such a moving body, in all respects.

Coincidence Third.—The horse and his rider represent a double organization, a body of moving principle, and a government, without regal power or sanction. Now, according to all history of the fourth century, it appears that the churches had gradually formed themselves, not merely into Christian societies, but had founded a great ecclesiastic or social confederate republic, which, however, had no legal power to enforce its rules of order.—*Gibbon.*

Coincidence Fourth.—It was to be a victorious power, as was indicated by the bow. Now, although the Christian confederacy was impaired by the persecutions, yet it rode through the ten great persecutions, or "ten days' tribulation," and exhibited a victorious strength after them all.

Coincidence Fifth.—The rider received a crown. So the Christian confederate church government received royal sanction; was united to the state and made second only in the throne of power, as the crown is second to the diadem. The time of the giving the crown, was the time the horse appeared, with his rider and bow; so that this seal is fixed to this epoch of church and state union as its goal. From that point it begins to move on.

Coincidence Sixth.—"And he went forth conquering and to conquer." Christianity, after its union with the state, soon prevailed over every thing, and paganism was soon routed from the empire, and finally renounced by imperial law, in the days of Theodosius. All the points to identify the first seal being found in Christianity in the fourth century, and being found in nothing else, and at no other time, it follows that this full coincidence is full proof of fulfillment.

Paragraph II.

SECOND SEAL, OR WESTERN CHURCH.

"And when he had opened the second seal, I heard the second beast say, Come and see. And there went out another horse that was red; and power was given unto him to take peace from the earth, and that they should kill one another; and there was given unto him a great sword." This represents the western politico-ecclesiastic power in Europe.

1. The station of the second beast was on the west, or Ephraim's place. Of course, then, we look for a manifestation of a religious power of a red cast, in the western empire. In this direction the empire church was manifested in all its mighty strength, as a corruption of Christianity, and a very much altered religion.

2. As the horse symbolizes a body of moving religion, so we find the Latin religion, in the west, made vast strides toward universality.

3. *The horse was red.*—Red and blood are explanatory of each other. "Though your sins be *red* like crimson." A bloody religion was, therefore, represented by this horse. Now, the Christian religion soon changed its character, after its union with the state. It immediately began a persecution of the Arians, and the blood of the people has flowed, like rivers, by its influence, ever since.

4. "Power was given him that sat thereon, to take peace from the earth." Ever since the overthrow of the Roman empire, and the rise of corrupt Christianity, the wars, that have extensively prevailed in Europe, have been on account of religion, and have been instigated, or inflamed, by the fanaticism of the church. The crusades are some instances of it.

5. "That they should kill one another." Here, the

term "they" shows that the rider represented a vast body of people. Their killing one another represents war among themselves, or civil wars. These were to be a consequence of taking religious peace from the earth. Now, if we look at the cause of civil wars in the western empire, we find they were generally of a religious character, and the wars have been almost without limit.

6. *The Rider.*—The man on the white horse represented the social organization of his religion; and the seven stars represented the ecclesiastical polity of the churches; and so this red, or bloody religion, has its polity, or ecclesiastical government, represented by a man, or rider. The church, after its union with the state, was, in polity, a great ecclesiastical despotism; but it had no supreme magisterial authority given it in the state, at first, but afterward it became the civil ruler of Europe, by usurpation.

7. "And there was given unto him a great sword." A sword is a symbol of magisterial authority; it represents a destroying executive power, and, also, war and slaughter by the civil arm.—Isa. xxxiv. 5; Ezek. xxi; Lev. xxvi. 25; Rom. xiii. 4. "For he (the civil magistracy) beareth not the sword in vain, for he is the minister of God, a revenger, to execute wrath upon him that doeth evil."

The corrupt, or Roman religion, in Europe, existed, for a long time, solely as a politico-ecclesiastical power, but afterward it received the civil sword, and it was a most powerful one; for it existed as the dominant power in Europe for more than two centuries. It destroyed thousands of thousands; it mustered the great crusades, and lorded it over God's heritage, with a mighty and vengeful hand. This power was to extend, by the symbol, over the whole west; and so this power, was chiefly manifested in the west the station of the second beast. We have now shown a perfect and full coincidence between the second seal and the western church; and, of course, we have shown a complete fulfillment.

Paragraph III.

THE THIRD SEAL—MOHAMMEDANISM IN THE SOUTH.

"And when he had opened the third seal, I heard the third beast say, Come and see. And I beheld, and lo! a black horse, and he that sat on him had a pair of balances in his hand. And I heard a voice, in the midst of the four beasts, say, A measure of wheat for a penny, and three measures of barley for a penny; and see thou hurt not the oil and the wine."

As these seals opened in chronological order, the subjects they disclose must occur chronologically. The first seal began with Constantine; and Justinian, in the early part of the second century afterward, fixed the whole establishment, represented by the red horse, upon a permanent foundation. The black horse must, therefore, represent a subsequent spiritual power, and the next great religious power that arose was the Mohammedan, or Saracenic. We shall criticise each point of this seal carefully.

1. "*A Black Horse.*"—A horse symbolizing a religion, a black horse must designate its moral character, since color designates moral character. " Black represents, in ancient prophecy, affliction, disaster, anguish." —(*Symbol. Dict.*) A black horse would, therefore, represent a destroying power, that would greatly afflict with anguish, as did the locusts, which also represent the Saracenic power.

2. "He that sat on him." This represents the ecclesiastical polity of the religion.

3. "Had a pair of balances in his hand." A balance is used to weigh things, and, of course, refers to the demands of conformity to the standard weight or measure of this ecclesiastical government, for the balances were in its hand, and it did the weighing according to its own standard.

4. "A voice from the four beasts." As these represented the Israel of God, the voice is a declaration from it, and relating to it, or an order from God's providence.

5. "A measure of wheat for a penny, and three measures of barley for a penny." Provisions were cheap at this rate, and many expositors have said so; but others say it means famine: the first are correct. For in the locust vision, the people who had the seal of God, were to be spared from devastation, and the corrupt Christians, only, were to be tormented. "They should not hurt the grass, nor the earth, nor any green thing." This coincides with plenty of corn, and barley, and grapes, and olive trees, or oil and wine. Let it also be remembered that the balances did not measure out the corn and barley, for they were among the four beasts, or pious Israel. The whole, therefore, teaches, that among the true Christians there would be no attack by the black horse, but only among the false Christians.

6. "See thou hurt not the oil and the wine." Now, these terms, and the corn and barley, may, if used as symbols, represent the choice people of God, who were to be preserved. As, however, a literal accomplishment is found, it is likely that both were intended; indeed, the preservation of the one would be attended naturally by the other. If we now look for a coincidence to this power, we shall find it only in the Mohammedan fanaticism.

Coincidence First.—"A black horse symbolizes an afflicting and disastrous religion. Every body knows that the Mohammedan imposture was one of this very character.

Coincidence Second.—This religion was to have a well organized ecclesiastical polity. Such was the character of the ecclesiastic organization of Mohammedanism, that it has had the tenacity to adhere together for ages.

Coincidence Third.—This religion was to bring every one to its own exact standard. Such was the character of Mohammedanism. It demanded exact agreement to its doctrines, or death. Abu-Beker, who, on the death of Mahomet, succeeded to his great authority, set out for conquest, and to convert the world by the sword and fire. His charge to his chief commander was couched in these words, "As for those members of the synagogue of Satan who shave their crowns, cleave their skulls, unless they embrace Islamism, or pay tribute." Death or Islamism was the watchword of the Saracenic host.

Observe, that the balances had nothing to do with the measuring of the corn, barley, wine, and oil, for they are not measured in balances, but in liquid and dry measures.

Coincidence Fourth.—The church of God was to remain intact, or, as the corn, and barley, and wine, and oil, in security. Now, the great body of the true evangelical Christians were found in the interior, and northwestern portions of the empire, and in Britain; and these countries were not seriously affected, and never overcome by the Saracens; while all of the great body of the corrupt Christians suffered terribly from the Saracens, for near two hundred years.

Coincidence Fifth.—The agricultural interests, among the true Christians, were not to be desolated by the invasion of the black horse and his rider. And none of the countries, where the true witnesses of God were most abundant, were invaded by the Saracenic armies. Spain, Italy, and the southern and south-western coasts of Europe, where the red horse had dominion, were invaded, and their inhabitants awfully scourged.

Coincidence Sixth.—The station of the third beast was on the three parts of the south, and the scene was to be in that direction. Now, the attack of Mohammedanism was in the east of the southern part of the Roman world, and thence extended all along its southern border, including all Africa and south Europe, and Spain, or the west portion of the south.

There being, therefore, a full coincidence between the Mohammedans and the fourth seal, in the time of its rise and all of its characteristics, we have a perfect fulfillment.

Paragraph IV.

FOURTH SEAL—DEISM AND FRANCE.

"And when he had opened the fourth seal, I heard the voice of the fourth beast say, Come and see. And I looked and beheld a pale horse; and his name that sat on him was Death, and Hell followed with him. And power was given unto them over the fourth part of the earth, to kill with sword, and with hunger, and with death, and with the beasts of the earth."

1. "The fourth seal." This represents, chronologically, another prophetic era in the religious and political world.

2. "The fourth beast." The station of the eagle was on the north parts, corresponding to Dan and the two tribes on the right and left of him.

3. "A pale horse." Here, another religion appears, and its moral character is represented by a pale color. "Pale color signifies mortality and affliction. It is a

usual epithet of death."—(*Sym. Dic.*) Applied to a religion, it must signify a ruinous one in spiritual things, and be the basis of ruin in political.

4. "His name that sat on him was Death." "Death symbolizes a destroyer, as a plague or pestilence."—(*Sym. Dic.*) As a man has symbolized the polity of a religion, and its distinctive political complexion has been symbolized by a bow and crown, a sword and balances, so, here, the political texture of the polity of this rider is represented by the term death. As Death is a destroyer, he must be, here, the representative of destruction to the existing state of affairs at his appearance. The name Death, and the paleness of his horse, are well adjusted to each other.

5. "And Hell followed with him." The word hell, or hades, signifies the grave of the soul or body. As it follows death, and is symbolic of earthly matters, it must refer to distinctive political effects that would naturally attend a church and soul-destroying religion. This living impersonation of death must symbolize destruction to all other spiritual powers beside itself; and the living personification of hell, or the grave, shows the state of ruin that would ensue.

6. "And power was given unto them over the fourth part of the earth." This shows that these symbols were to operate on earth, and were human agencies or embodiments of power. "The fourth part of the earth." This is the only place in prophecy, of Rome, that a fourth part of it is mentioned; in all other places a part is expressed by a third. As this power would not rise till very late, it may have reference to the new state of the world after the discovery of America. Before this event, the world consisted of three great parts, Europe, Asia, and Africa, but, on the discovery of America, it was said to consist of four parts. At any rate, it was to be

confined in its operations within one quarter of the earth, or to one continent.

7. "To kill with sword and with hunger, and with death, and with the beasts of the earth." This great destruction of men could not result but from great political strength; hence, the union of death and hell, in this work, shows the union of a destroying religion with the state, or its collusion with the state.

We now affirm that atheism, or French infidelity, and its polity, associated with France, are represented by the pale horse, by death, and by hell.

Coincidence First.—The fourth seal was the fourth great era in religions in chronological order; and the infidelity of France was the fourth great spiritual system of doctrine taught after the rise of Christianity. It was called Deism.

Coincidence Second.—This system was to be manifest in the north of the Roman empire; and France was in the west part of the north, and extended its doctrines all along the north of the old empire.

Coincidence Third.—A ruinous and dead religious system was to appear. With this, French infidelity most accurately coincides; for it denied life and immortality, and wrote upon its gateways to the grave, "Death an eternal sleep."

Coincidence Fourth.—The polity of this religion, or body of religious or rather irreligious doctrine, was to be destructive of all others within its range. With this, French infidelity corresponds; for it threw down all religions in France and in the countries it could control, and began a crusade against all systems of divinity except its own.

Coincidence Fifth.—The political power was to follow within the same track as the spiritual; hell was to accompany death Now, it is notorious that the French revolutionists of 1792 adopted the doctrines of infidelity; and that their political system was based upon infidel doctrines and theory of government, that the reign of terror, and all the great tides of blood of that day, and many since, were the results of this great deadly system of infidel religion. Liberty and equality were deified by the French, and all other gods were proscribed for a time.

Coincidence Sixth.—This system of doctrine and government was to have power to destroy or desolate a fourth part of the earth. Now, the French infidel system threw all Europe into the wildest confusion, and into the fiercest and most desolating wars; death to priests, and religion, and kings, and government, was their well-observed motto. They were fiercer and more destructive than the age of the Goths, or the barbarity of the Vandals. Their power, however, was confined to one fourth part of the earth, or to one continent. They troubled every nation in Europe, and made Europe a fresh graveyard. Their doctrines and their practice might well be called death and hell, from the vengeance they inflicted, and the millions they destroyed and tormented.

Coincidence Seventh.—The destruction of men was to be a political and real one, as is indicated by death, famine, sword, and beasts. In all of these ways, even literally, multiplied thousands upon thousands perished in the great wars instigated by infidel France; but figuratively the destruction was also as great.

As between French infidelity, its philosophic polity, and France and the pale horse, his rider and hell, there is a perfect coincidence; there is in them a fulfillment of the fourth seal.

Paragraph V.

THE FIFTH SEAL—DESTRUCTION OF CHURCHES, AND OPPRESSIONS.

"And when he had opened the fifth seal, I saw under the altar the souls of them which were slain for the word of God and the testimony they held. And they cried with a loud voice, saying, How long, O Lord, holy and true, dost thou not judge and avenge our blood upon them that dwell upon the earth? And white robes were given unto every one of them; and it was said unto them, that they should rest for a little season, until their fellow servants, also, and their brethren, that should be killed as they were, should be fulfilled."

This is the most difficult of all the seals to interpret; its locality, however, being fixed chronologically between the French reign of death, or terror, and the sixth seal, which coincides with the taking of the beast, or final destruction of the fourth monarchy by the Christians, we know the period in which to look for its symbolized realities.

1. We first take up the symbolic altar and souls; this symbolizes the gospel body, as we shall show in another place. The souls of the slain did coincide with the worshipers at the altar, in the imagery of the two witnesses; and they must represent church organization as it is represented by the angels of the churches, and the rider on the white horse, &c.

2. The slaying of these souls. Spirits, we have already been informed, represent the doctrines of the church, or the churches themselves; the souls, or spirits will, therefore, here represent the worshipers of God. The slaying will, therefore, represent the disorganization and scattering of the true Christians, and the impossibility of their resurrection, to perform the services of the

altar, or gospel, in their slain condition. The terms can not be understood literally, for it is against all reason to do so; for departed Christian spirits go to the third heaven, and are with Christ; and they are not placed under an altar there, but worship God; and there is no sacrificial altar there, and no complaint of sorrow.

3. They were slain for two things; one was for the word of God, and the other for the testimony which they held. These two things coincide with the principles represented by the two witnesses; that is, for religious and civil liberty; for religion and freedom; the "word of God" being put for the true religion, and "the testimony," representing the civil rights they claimed. Their being under the altar shows that they had become victims to their fidelity, and that they had ceased to be a visible organization. This coincides with the suppression and destruction of all the dissenting churches of true Christians, which had, for a long period, been crushed by the civil arm, in the dominions of the established church in Europe. Many true Christians have, during many centuries, existed in Europe, but have had their churches overthrown; many of them have been murdered, and others have been obliged to hide their worship from public observation, as if under the very altar of God.

4. They desired vengeance on their destroyers. This shows a struggle for independence, and an appeal to God for help. These struggles have been made, but hitherto, unsuccessfully.

5. They were clothed with white robes. This shows that they and their cause would be held in honor among men somewhere in the world.

6. They were to rest; that is, to cease to struggle, until the set time of the sufferings of their fellow

Christians, that should be also oppressed, should be fulfilled. This destroying of other Christian dissenting churches coincides with the slaying of the two witnesses, by the beast out of the pit. We can not but think this refers to the late suppression of Hungarian and Italian liberty by Russia, Austria, and the tyrants in other portions of Europe. We are, certainly, now living in the period of the fifth seal.

Paragraph VI.
SIXTH SEAL—DESTRUCTION OF MONARCHY.

"And I beheld, when he had opened the sixth seal, and lo! there was a great earthquake; and the sun became black as sackcloth of hair, and the moon became as blood; and the stars of heaven fell to the earth, even as a fig tree casteth her untimely figs, when she is shaken of a mighty wind. And the heaven departed as a scroll when it is rolled together; and every mountain and island were removed out of their places. And the kings of the earth, and the great men, and the rich men, and the chief captains, and the mighty men, and every bondman, and every freeman, hid themselves in the dens and in the rocks of the mountains; and said to the rocks and to the mountains, Fall on us, and hide us from the face of him that sitteth on the throne, and from the wrath of the Lamb; for the great day of his wrath is come, and who shall be able to stand?"

This sublime and extensive description reveals a period of vastly greater interest than has ever yet transpired in prophecy. It is, however, most clearly symbolic, as it comes with symbolic characteristics from the seat of symbols. We shall consider the symbols separately.

1. "*A great earthquake.*" An earthquake is a symbol of great revolutions and changes in the government

of the world.—Jer. iv. 23; Joel iii. 16; Haggai ii. 6-7. It is frequently used in the apocalypse in this sense.

2. "The sun became black." As the sun rules the day, so the civil government rules the kingdom, and it must here represent the whole civil power of monarchy, as this seal coincides with the destruction of the fourth empire.

3. "The moon became as blood." The moon is always used as the symbol of a church. As the sun, or civil power, disappears in great affliction, so the moon, becoming as blood, shows the dissolution of the empire church in great slaughter, since blood and carnage are synonims in prophecy.

4. "The stars of heaven fell unto the earth." A star symbolizes a prince, "as a star out of Jacob;" and, also, a deity, as "the star of your god Chiun;" "the eleven stars" represented eleven sons of Jacob, the heads of the tribes of Israel. The falling of the stars will represent the collateral fall of all princes, at the time of the fall of monarchy.

5. "And the heaven departed as a scroll when it is rolled together." This is a symbolic representation of the old political world; for after it is gone, we see men still on the earth running for shelter. The political world is here to be understood by the terms heaven and earth; they are so frequently used in the old prophets, in this sense, that every one is familiar with the proofs. Indeed, if any one doubts that these are symbolic heavens and earths, all we have to say is, that he is very simple, for the proofs that they are so, are as abundant as could be desired. We have here a double description of the same great events; the first by the sun, moon, and stars; and the second by the quaking earth, and removing heavens, and mountains, and islands. Moun

tains and islands symbolize the governments of the political heavens and earth. This removal of the heavens and earth, sun, moon, and stars, mountains, and islands, is further interpreted to be the overthrow of monarchy, for the kings of the earth, and princes, and all together, are represented as flying for shelter from the wrath of the Lamb.

6. "The wrath of the Lamb." As this represents a scene before the Millennium, the Lamb must represent some great power conformed to Christianity, for a Lamb must represent a kingdom of a kind like itself, or actuated by the gospel of Christ. Wrath is not a quality of a Lamb, but it must be remembered, that at the same time Christ is called a Lamb, he is called a Lion.

7. "The great day of his wrath is come." This must be a day that had been anticipated, because predicted. It conforms, in time and circumstances, to the smiting of the great image; the taking of the beast; the judgment-day of the ancient of days; and the predicted triumph of Israel; and must, therefore, represent the same general destruction of monarchy predicted by "the casting down of thrones," in Daniel; for it is just before the Millennium.

8. Immediately after this great victory, follows a description of the organization of the Millennial government, under the symbol of the sealing of Israel, and of the gathering together of the good of all nations. The twelve tribes coincide with Israel restored, before the other nations were received into confraternity. This period coincides with the changing of the stone into a mountain; the possession of the kingdom by the saints, and of the deliverance by Michael of those written in the book; and of the end of the time of the end; and with the marriage supper of the Lamb; and the first

resurrection. It must be kept in constant memory, that the prophets represent two general judgments; the one is a political judgment-day, and the other is a spiritual judgment-day; the first precedes the Millennium, the second succeeds it. The great day of the wrath of the Lamb symbolizes the former, and the great white throne symbolizes the latter. Christ certainly will not appear till after the first; he will appear on the throne at the second. There will also be two coincident resurrections; the first at the beginning of the Millennium, the other subsequent to it; the first *may* be purely political, and the next will be a literal one.

Paragraph VII.

SEVENTH SEAL.

"And when he had opened the seventh seal, there was silence in heaven about the space of half an hour." Silence signifies a cessation from action, and as this was a cessation in the heaven, it was a cessation of the vision in the temple, for a season, to be resumed again at another time. The apostle is next directed to a set of prophecies without the temple. Now, these other prophecies are not said to be in the seventh seal at all, but quite the contrary is seen to be true. John, within the temple, had been looking principally at the religious history of the world down to the Millennium, and he now views the scene outside, as the altar was outside; that is, the political prophecy of the same period embraced by the seals. The seven trumpets will be treated in regular order in another place; and we shall here bring in the interpretation of the period given in the little book. The seventh seal is renewed at the spiritual judgment-day, or at the Millennium.

CHAPTER XII.

THE LITTLE BOOK OF INTERPRETATION.

All symbolic prophecy is twice repeated, as we have before observed, and is also interpreted. The second vision of the same events is regarded as an interpretation of the first; and it generally adds some new particulars in the same symbolic language. This is stated by Joseph to Pharaoh, when he said, "the dream is twice doubled, because it is certain and the interpretation is sure." As no interpretation had been given when Joseph spoke, it is plain, that he referred to the second vision as the expositor of the first, though both needed a literal translation. Daniel's visions, while they are twice doubled, have each of them also an interpretation; and John's visions, being symbolic, must be expected to follow the general law of symbolic visions. John's receiving a little book which goes over the same field with that of the seals and trumpets, must be but a book of interpretation, since he inwardly digested it. This prophecy of this book, like all others, has a magnificent introduction, which, with the book itself, we shall now notice. We first quote the introductory text:

"And I saw another mighty angel come down from heaven clothed with a cloud, and a rainbow was upon his head, and his face was as it were the sun, and his feet as pillars of fire, and he had in his hand a little book open. And the voice which I heard from heaven spake unto me, saying, Go and take the book which is open in the hand of the angel. * * And I went unto the angel and said unto him, Give me the little book.

And he said unto me, Take it and eat it up; and it shall make thy belly bitter, but it shall be in thy mouth as sweet as honey."

This angel, it will be seen, is very much like the symbolic representation of Christ, given in the beginning, and must be that angel of Christ who was sent by Christ to signify to John the things which he received from his father. His symbolic dress is glorious, and he seems to attend John to the very last of the book after this, and, as he represents himself finally as one from earth, we may have some faint notions of the glory of the saints in heaven. As the first book of seals was a prophetic book, so this little book must be one also; and as it is open, it professes to contain an exposition of the events before related, by the seals and trumpets, down to the seventh trumpet, for it is introduced just at the sounding of the seventh trumpet. We introduce it here, so as not to interrupt the regular chronology of the trumpets by an episode. We shall take up the contents of this little book in regular order. It contains a vision of the temple and Gentiles; and one of two witnesses; one of a woman and twelve stars; one of a seven headed dragon; one of a seven headed beast; and one of a two horned beast.

SECTION I.

Holy City and the Gentiles—Church and State Union.

"And there was given me a reed, like unto a rod, and the angel (the one that had the little book) stood, saying, Rise, measure the temple of God, and the altar, and them that worship therein. But the court which is without the temple, leave out, and measure it not; for it is given unto the Gentiles, and the holy city shall they tread under foot forty and two months."

1. *The Measuring.*—To measure any thing, is symbolically equivalent to sealing it; as in Zech. ii. 2, to measure Jerusalem is equivalent to taking charge of it. It here plainly means that God would take special care of the temple, and altar, and worshipers, and that he would not take care of the outer court.

.2. *The Temple.*—The temple is here plainly used as a symbol. It is figuratively used by Paul to represent the church, but by the prophets it represents the civil power. Jeremiah twice speaks of the "vengeance of God's temple" going forth to destroy Babylon, and as such destruction could not go forth from the church proper, the temple must stand for the civil power of Israel. Again, it is said, that in the last days, the fallen tabernacle of David, or Israel's civil power, or nationality, shall be restored, and, as the temple and tabernacle are convertible terms, the temple, in prophecy, is used as symbolic of the government of Israel. That this is its sense here, is further obvious, from the fact that another symbol is conjointly used, which clearly stands for the church, and as Israel, on account of its dual nature, is always represented by two figures, so it is here; and one refers to the civil polity, and the other to the spiritual.

3. *The Altar and the Worshipers.*—The altar is used not only as an instrument of worship, but as a sanctuary, or place of refuge. It was surrounded by the court of Israel, and of the priests who brought their sacrifices to it, to be offered; and as the worshipers are represented as worshiping *in* the altar, it must, by synecdoche, represent the court of Israel, a part of the court being put for the whole. The worshipers, therefore, properly represent the organic church, and the altar their

religious system of faith and worship, or religion. This distinction between the church government and religion, is elsewhere clearly noticed among the symbols, as also the distinction between the church government, and the civil government of Israel.

4. *"The Court without the Altar."*—That is, the court outside of the court of Israel, in the temple, which was separated from it by a partition wall. In this court the Gentiles were allowed to worship, and their worship was considered inferior in character to that of Israel. As no altar was in it, it must stand for the church of the Gentiles, or for an impure church. This view is confirmed by the fact, that it was not measured or cared for by God.

5. *The Holy City.*—This, as a figure, represents the church, but as Jerusalem was called Ariel, that is, the double city, or two lions of God, and as the capital of Israel is put for the Jewish nation, by synecdoche, it must, as a symbol, represent the Christian Ariel.

6. *The Gentiles were to tread the Ariel of God under foot for forty-two months.*—As the Jerusalem here mentioned is not the literal Jerusalem, but the Christian Jerusalem, or Ariel of God, those who tread it down must be spiritual Gentiles.

7. *Forty-two months.*—These months amount to 529,984 days, or 1451 years and 17 days, and also to 1243 years and 277 days. As the true Israel of God was trodden down by spiritual Gentiles, from the days of church and state union till the rise of the United States, the 42 months must be the exact measure of the period between these two epochs. The length of this period, therefore, is the number of days between the 19th of June, 325, and July 4th, 1776; for church and state union began on the former date, and began to end gloriously at the latter. The length of this period is exactly

529,984 days, and thus it coincides exactly with the first length of the 42 months. Again; church and state union was completed, under Justinian, about 532 A. D. Now, from October 1st of this year, to July 4th, 1776, is just equal to the other length of the 42 months, or 1243 years 277 days. It is, however, obvious that the church of God is still trodden down in Europe; so that there must be another length of the 42 months to be fulfilled. That length ends as early as 1865 or 1878, but perhaps much earlier.—(*See discovery*.)

SECTION II.

The Two Witnesses—Christianity Depressed.

"And I will give power unto my two witnesses, and they shall prophesy a thousand two hundred and three score days, clothed in sackcloth. These are the two olive trees, and the two candlesticks, standing before the God of the earth."

1. *Two witnesses, two candlesticks, and two olive trees.*—These represent the same thing as Jerusalem, the double city; and the text refers, by implication expressed in the word "my," to Jerusalem, as the two witnesses; and as it is called by Isaiah, "Ariel," or the double city, it is the proper antecedent referred to as "my two witnesses." The two olive trees, mentioned by Zechariah, (fourth chap.) and their interpretation as the two anointed ones, plainly coincide with these two olive trees, for the text of Zechariah mentions two candlesticks, with seven branches, and seven bowls, and the two olive trees as standing together, and representing, doubly, the two anointed ones. These two anointed ones plainly represented the dual Israel or Ariel of God. The dual

character of God's law, and of man's nature as a spiritual and social creature; the necessary two kinds of government springing from them; the dual character of the Hebrew government; and the perpetual representation of this duality by figurative terms; and its perpetual recurrence in symbols applicable to the people of God, is full evidence that the two witnesses represent the dual character of the people of God, and can represent nothing else.

2. "*They were to prophesy in sackcloth.*"—The word prophet signifies a predictor, but means a teacher of religious obligation as often as it does any thing else. The prophecy of the witnesses must have been the teaching "the word of God, and the testimony they held." They were to teach in sackcloth. The ancient prophets were mostly clothed thus, and it was the habit of mourning and great humiliation. They were to be trodden down by the Gentiles. As the Gentiles destroyed and trampled upon the literal Jerusalem, the symbolic meaning of the term must be spiritual Gentiles, or unclean persons of a religious character. It was bad enough to be trodden down by the real Gentile, but to be trampled upon by spiritual Gentiles was to be wounded in the house of their friends, and was cause of double grief and humility. If we now look at God's people, ever since the unhallowed and incestuous marriage of church and state, we find that the truly pious have been obliged to suffer the greatest indignities, and to change the garment of praise for the spirit of heaviness, and lay aside the oil of joy for mourning, and beauty for ashes.

3. They were to prophecy for 1260 days, which are equivalent to 1451 years, or 529,984 days, and to 1243 years, 277 days. These begin and end with the 42 months, and partly await fulfillment.

4. "If any man will hurt them, fire proceedeth out of their mouth, and devoureth their enemies; and if any will hurt them, he must in the same manner be killed. These have power to shut heaven that it rain not in the days of their prophecy; and have power over waters to turn them to blood, and to smite the earth with plagues as often as they will." Elijah is the prophet who sits as the subject of this portraiture. As he destroyed his enemies by fire, so do they; as he shut the heavens from rain, so do they; and as he ascended to heaven by translation, so do they. The mouth symbolizes the words or doctrine of these witnesses, and the fire symbolizes its warlike and revolutionary, or destructive character. It is observable they both spoke with one mouth, or both taught the same doctrine. Now, it is certain that both departments of Israel teach the great doctrine of true liberty, and that this doctrine is inherent in Christianity, and it is revolutionary to monarchy in its very nature. The term *man*, is a term of multitude, and embraces their enemies, or organic power that hurts or oppresses them. Now, it is notorious, that all of the revolutions, for many centuries, in Europe and Britain, have originated from the attempts to gain civil and religious freedom; and the Bible has been, and is, a proscribed book, because of its revolutionary character in church and state. Though true Christians have not existed, organically, in Europe, in the two forms indicated by the two witnesses, yet it has virtually existed; and the very term "sackcloth," shows that they were not to exist in this dual organization independently, until the end of the forty-two months. These two departments, however, being essential departments of the people of God, when possessed of true rights, are properly represented, while they existed in a depressed state.

The shutting of the heaven, and turning waters to blood, "as often as they will," symbolizes the fact, that, whenever they have resolved to strike for liberty, they have produced the greatest of destruction. Now, this accords with the history of the causes of many of the revolutions. The doctrines which these witnesses proclaimed, have fired almost every throne and kingdom in past ages; and the smothered fires of a volcano, produced by their doctrine, is making Europe now tremble to its center, and will bring on the final shock of the great political earthquake of nations.

5. "And when they shall be about to finish (*Telesosi*) their testimony." This conforms to the "time of the end," spoken of by Daniel, and to the seventh trumpet period.

6. "The beast that ascendeth out of the bottomless pit." This beast is distinguished from the beast out of the sea, and from the two horned beast, and is the fourth empire restored under Russia, coming out of Asia, or from barbarism.

7. "Shall make war against them, and shall overcome them and kill them." As this event was to be in the time of the end, it must refer to something now existing. Now, when we remember that civil and religious liberty has lately been crushed in Hungary and south Europe, by the special agency of Russia, we see a very fair coincidence. Indeed, throughout Europe, since the year '49, the chain of despotism has been more strongly riveted than for many years.

8. "And their dead bodies shall lie in the street of the great city, which is spiritually called Sodom and Egypt, where also our Lord was crucified." The city is evidently put for Europe in general, and the street of a city may symbolize a kingdom of it.

The witnesses to be slain being chiefly in one part of Roman Europe, correspond most closely with the fall of the Hungarian witnesses in Austria, by the aid of Russia. Sodom and Egypt are apt representations of the Roman empire, but spiritually applied, they with great force describe Austria and Italy, where our Lord is daily crucified afresh. Austria is, doubtless, the street of Roman Europe referred to.

9. "And they of the people, kindreds, and tongues, and nations, shall see their dead bodies three days and a half, and shall not suffer them to be put in graves. And they that dwell on the earth shall rejoice over them, and make merry, and shall send gifts to one another, because these two prophets tormented them which dwelt upon the earth." It is well known that the monarchists of Europe have had great rejoicings and public thanksgivings over the suppression of liberalism in Europe, and especially in Hungary and Italy. These witnesses were to lie unburied. This, with the ancients, as all classic readers know, was considered a state of great misery. It is used in the scriptures to represent dishonor and disregard.— 2 K. xxiv. The king of Babylon, to dishonor Jehoiachin's memory, threw his dead body without the walls, without burial. The cause of the Hungarians is now a disreputed and dead cause; the two witnesses in the Austrian street lie quiet and cold, and no voice of consolation reaches their ear of death.

10. "And after three days and a half, the spirit of life, from God, entered into them, and they stood upon their feet; and great fear fell upon them which saw them." This resurrection in three days and a half is to occur about four or five years after their overthrow. We may, therefore, look for a great insurrection in Hungary, say in the course of two or three years. It will

cause great alarm to Austria, who will see them alive again, and ready for contest.

11. "And they heard a great voice from heaven, saying unto them, Come up hither." As this heaven is symbolic, it must represent either exaltation at the call of some power, represented by the voice, or a call to emigration to the place of the church. This call may be from our country.

12. "And they ascended to heaven in a cloud; and their enemies beheld them." This ascension seems not merely to imply exaltation, but an actual removal from the country. Clouds are the symbols of God's power and of protection; they also signify a great multitude, as "a great cloud of witnesses." "Their enemies beheld them;" but could not help themselves. It is very possible that there may be extended to the Hungarians, at their resurrection to life, an invitation to come to this country, under sure protection guaranteed to them, and that a large multitude may come, and that Austria may not be able to prevent it.

13. "And the same hour was there a great earthquake, and the tenth part of the city fell, and in the earthquake were slain of men seven thousand; and the remnant were affrighted, and gave glory to the God of heaven." An earthquake symbolizes an insurrection, or overthrow, and the destruction of the tenth part of the city is equivalent to the overthrow of a principal kingdom in Europe. This tenth part of Europe is plainly Turkey. This is evident from the fact, that after this tenth part fell, it was immediately announced that "the second wo is past." Now, as the rise, and progress, and duration of the Turks is called the second wo, the end of this wo is the end of Turkey. Its fall, therefore, synchronizes with the rise of Hungary, since it fell at the same hour with the rise of the witnesses.

The three and a half days of the witnesses may have two lengths. One of them is equal to four years two hundred and sixty-eight days, and the other to five years three hundred and eleven days. The end of these is close at hand, as well as the end of Turkey; 1854–6–61, are the points of time. We do not claim, absolutely, certainty here in time, but only in facts of other kinds. Should we be mistaken as to Hungary, it will follow that Russia will crush some Christian people, who will rise in three and a half days, and then, in a few years thereafter, Turkey will fall.

The slaying of seven thousand is symbolic of great destruction, and the glorifying of God by the rest is the admitting of the people to a decent privilege of civil rights, and, probably, giving up Islamism.

CONCLUSION.

1. The two witnesses being synonymous with Jerusalem, the double city, and representing the Israel of God, must represent Christianity, universally, in its depressed condition during the prevalence of church and state union.

2. As Jerusalem and the two witnesses are synonymous, and one is the interpretation or duplicate of the other, the 1260 days must be the duplicate or interpretation of the forty-two months.

3. The term Gentiles being a symbolic term, must represent the spiritual Gentiles of the church; and as they were set up over the witnesses at church and state union, the time of this union must be the epoch at which to date the 1260 days and 42 months. But as this epoch was a double one, or was an era from Constantine to Justinian, we must date them from both. The first epoch

of this era was June 19th, 325, and the second was in the year 532, as near as can be found.

4. The 42 months are an abbreviated year, and may represent a year of 42, or 49, or 52 months, and to these the 1260 days conform. Now, 1260 days and 42 months equal 454,272 days, and from the Justinian epoch of church and state union extends to the year 1776. Forty-nine months, or 1470 days, are equal to 529,984 days, and from the Constantine epoch, June 19th, 325, to July 4th, 1776, is exactly 529,984 days. Fifty-two months, or 1560 days, are equal to 562,432 days, and extend from the last epoch in 325 to 1865, June 15th or 16th. Now, at the rise of the United States, a part of the great body of true Christians ceased to be trodden under foot, and the rest, it appears, will cease to be in 1865. Babylon church will be destroyed before civil monarchy, and as that will transpire by 1878, this epoch of its destruction looks reasonable.

5. The witnesses to be slain were only those in one part of the great city, and not throughout the world; that is, those in the street of the city, or those in the great thoroughfare of the Roman church; the street meaning either one particular kingdom of Rome, or the whole of Roman Europe. At the rise of our country, the triumph of the witnesses began, but still they are not yet free in Europe, and will not be till the last end of the 42 months, or 1878.

SECTION III.

The Woman with Twelve Stars, and her Man Child, or the Christian Church and the United States.

This vision is the duplicate of the witnesses and, by consequence, aids in their explication. It has been called the *crux criticorum,* among expositors. It is not, in the first part, consecutively chronological; had it been, the apocalypse would have been tolerably easy to understand, for it is almost a key to it.

1. "And there appeared a great wonder in heaven; a woman clothed with the sun, and the moon under her feet, and upon her head a crown of twelve stars." These symbols are a twice doubled representation of Israel. A woman is a common symbol of the church of God, and stars are a representation of the twelve sons or tribes of Jacob, and represent the civil department of God's Israel. The moon is, also, a common symbol of the church, and the sun is always a symbol of civil power. This double set of symbols to represent one dual object, is seen also in Zechariah, where the two olive trees, and two candlesticks, represented the dual anointed one, or Israel.

2. "And the woman fled into the wilderness, where she hath a place prepared of God, that they should feed her there, a thousand two hundred and three score days." That is, the church went into obscurity; went into a mazy and dreary condition, and was mostly hidden from the world for 1260 years. These 1260 days are equal to 529,984 days, or to 454,272 days, or to 562,432 days, as we have seen already.

3. "And there appeared another wonder in heaven; and behold a great red dragon, having seven heads and

ten horns, and seven diadems upon his heads." This was the representation of Roman monarchy in Great Britain, and will hereafter be explained.

4. "And she being with child, cried, travailing in birth, and pained to be delivered." "And the dragon stood before the woman which was ready to be delivered, for to devour her child as soon as it was born. And she brought forth a man child, who was to rule all nations with a rod of iron; and her child was caught up unto God, and to his throne. And there was war in heaven; Michael and his angels fought against the dragon. And the dragon and his angels fought and prevailed not, neither was their place found any more in heaven. And the old dragon was cast out, that old serpent, called the Devil, and Satan, which deceiveth the whole world. He was cast out into the earth, and his angels were cast out with him. And I heard a loud voice saying in heaven, Now is come salvation, and strength, and the kingdom of our God, and the power of his Christ, for the accuser of our brethren is cast down, which accused them before God day and night. And they overcame him by the blood of the Lamb, and by the word of their testimony; and they loved not their lives unto death. Therefore, rejoice, ye heavens, and ye that dwell in them. Wo to the inhabiters of the earth, for the devil is come down unto you, having great wrath, because he knoweth he hath but a short time. And when the dragon saw that he was cast unto the earth, he persecuted the woman which brought forth the man child." This is a spiritual and political prophecy. It represents Christianity, in humility for 1451 years, at length striving for nationality. It represents the declaration and the confederacy; the revolutionary war and the victory over Great Britain; the formation of the Union and the banish-

ment of spiritual monarchy forever from the United States; and the subsequent violence of monarchy in Europe, because it saw poor prospect for long continuance, after the rise of so great a Christian democracy. This vision is further interpreted by a repetition of its principal features.

"And to the woman were given two wings of a great eagle, that she might fly into the wilderness, into her place, where she is nourished for a time times and a half, from the face of the serpent. And the serpent cast out of his mouth water as a flood, after the woman, that he might cause her to be carried away of the flood. And the earth helped the woman; and the earth opened her mouth and swallowed up the flood which the dragon cast out of his mouth. And the dragon was wroth with the woman, and went to make war with the remnant of her seed, which keep the commandments of God, and have the testimony of Jesus Christ." The point of trouble, with interpreters, in this vision is, the apparent want of harmony in its parts; and the reason of this difficulty lies in this, that they placed this birth of the man child before the 1260 days began; whereas, it did not occur till afterward. It is true the birth of the child is announced before the woman's probation is mentioned, but that proves nothing as to its being after the birth of the child, for, in the interpretation, the times of the woman are placed before the attack of the serpent. Again; no event in all history, prior to the end of the times of the woman, or church, coincides with the man child; so that it can not represent any thing in the early days of the church, nor for centuries in its history. With this premised we proceed.

1. "She being with child, cried, travailing in birth, and pained to be delivered." In Isaiah lxvi. 7, the travailing

pains of Zion, and her bringing forth a man child, is interpreted by the Targum of a king or deliverer; and Paul, Rom. viii. 22, compares the earnest desire of creation for the kingdom of Christ to the pains of a travailing woman.—(*Sym. Dic.*) As the woman was the church, her labor pains represent the struggles of a Christian people, at the close of the three and a half times, to establish or bring forth a delivering power.

2. "She brought forth a man child." As a man, when used as a symbol, represents a civil government, so this man child must represent an infant and feeble civil government, yet of noble character, as it was to rule all nations. It was to be the offspring of the church, and, therefore, different from the church; and this difference is further expressed by the gender of the two persons, the one being female, and the other male.

3. "Who was to rule all nations with a rod of iron." This infant government was to rise above all others, and give its own law to the nations, and enforce obedience with an iron will or rod. It will be remembered that this language, in the Psalms, is applied to Christ; and that Christ, in his address to the churches, promises that this power shall be given to the Christians; for he said, "He that overcometh, to him will I give power over the nations, (and he shall rule them with a rod of iron; as the vessels of a potter shall they be broken to shivers,) even as *I* have received of my Father." This ruling over the nations with an iron rod, is fully expressive of a political power over the nations. This government was, therefore, a political fabric of a Christian people. Again; this child of the woman, or church, is identical with the man on the white horse with many crowns, that is to destroy the beast, and false prophet, and kings of the earth; for he was to "smite the nations, and rule

them with a rod of iron." They are identical, because they fill the very same office, and because that office can be occupied by but one. As the three and a half times end at the beginning and end of the seventh trumpet, the beginning of this period is the infancy of this great ruler; and at the close of this trumpet he is a man grown, and on horseback, and just a hundred years old.

4. "And her child was caught up unto God, and to his throne." This symbolizes that the new government was specially cared for by Providence, and preserved from destruction.

5. "The dragon stood before the woman, to devour her child as soon as it was born." As the dragon represents Roman monarchy in some form, its waiting before the church to destroy the nationality to which it was about to give birth, shows that it anticipated the event, and was determined to prevent it, and to destroy it in its infancy. It was, however, foiled in its purposes, and the new government was preserved.

6. "And there was war in heaven." This was a symbolic heaven, for Roman monarchy, nor any dragon, ever had a foothold in the celestial world. It was, therefore, in the place where the church was principally gathered. Other Christians, however, were represented elsewhere on the earth, whom the dragon went to war with. War signifies a contest for dominion, and the contest between the monarchy and the church was about sovereignty.

7. "Michael and his angels fought against the dragon." As the dragon and his angels were symbols of monarchy and its armies, so Michael and his angels, must, also, be symbols. How any one can make this appear as a literal spirituality, is very singular. Michael is as much a symbol as any other angel, or person, in the book, and the whole context shows it. Angels are symbols of

active assistants, and legions of angels are armies of agents. As Michael is placed antithetic to the dragon, or civil power of monarchy, he must, from the very nature of symbolic language, represent a civil power also; and his angels must represent armies aiding his cause. The civil power of one party is represented by a dragon, and the civil power of the other by a good archangel, and the military power of both is represented by angels, for they are represented as fighting against each other. Michael was the guardian angel of Israel, and, of course, is the guard of the Christian church, and as he is invisible, his name is most appropriately chosen to represent the cause he superintends. As Christianity is liberty essentially, whether civil or religious, this contest between the Christians and monarchists was a war for freedom, and independence of the monarchial power. These symbols are so poetic, that people would prefer the mystery of poetry around them, rather than look at the plain matters of fact they symbolize. The symbols, however, are prophecies, and therefore belong to earth, and no where else, and must have a matter of fact fulfillment here. At the close of "the time of the end" here begun, we find Daniel stating that this very Michael shall stand up for all Christians, as he here stands up for a number at the beginning of the time of the end.

8. "And prevailed not." The monarchial power was defeated.

9. "Neither was their place found any more in heaven." As heaven symbolizes the place of the church, this passage shows that monarchy was driven out of the country forever.

10. "And the great dragon was cast out." The dragon with seven heads being defeated, a decision is made to eject the whole draconic system of principles.

The seven headed dragon was evidently the offspring of the great dragon, and was the seed of the old serpent.

11. "That old serpent, called the Devil, and Satan, which deceiveth the whole world." The old serpent, we have seen, represented the false religion of Satan, or the head of the serpent. It took its name from its sire, the devil. A false religion, in union with the civil power, had deceived all nations until our nation rose. Our people proclaimed a dissolution of that union, and rejected all pagan religion, all state religion, and embraced only a free Christianity. No doctrine is more devilish than that which claims that religion must be united with the state. It has been the cause of more misery than any other single doctrine ever broached, and has ever deceived the world into the belief that it was the will of God.

12. "He was cast out into the earth, and his angels were cast out with him." That is, all of the advocates of a national religion, and all who held office in consequence of it, either in church or state, were thrown out of their former position, and were never restored, and never will be.

The term earth, here used, is a symbol, for as the prophecy was to be fulfilled in this world, the heaven and earth used, must represent different portions of our world.

13 "And I heard a loud voice saying, in heaven, Now is come salvation and strength, and the kingdom of our God and the power of his Christ." This loud voice in the symbolic heaven, or place of the church, represents great exultation of the Christians at the close of the war, and at the rejection of all kinds of monarchy, and at the organization of a new government. The words uttered are a double representation of the new organization.

"Salvation" is applicable to the church, as freed from all human domination; "strength" applies to a new civil power of iron scepter. "The kingdom of our God," applies especially again to the new organization of Christianity under a new constitution; and the power of his Christ, most especially, refers to his full exercise of civil authority. Under the symbol of a stone cut from the church, Daniel had predicted that a kingdom would be set up by God, in "ten horned" state of the Roman empire, and that it should extend over the earth, and here it breaks into view, and the Christians are represented as rejoicing at an *expected* event; for they say *now is come* the *kingdom*. Now, observe it does not at its coming, fill the earth, just as the stone does not, but it proposes to rule all nations, as the stone will rule them.

14. "The accuser of the brethren is cast down, which accused them before (in the presence of) God, day and night." The church of Europe, and all pagan churches, claim that they never killed Christians, and they lay the blame on the civil power. The truth of the whole matter, however, is this, they accused the Christians before the civil tribunal, and that tribunal gave the religious decisions the sanction of law, and thus Christians were murdered by multitudes. The " casting down of the accuser of the brethren," was, therefore, the casting down of the state church, which had ever brought Christians to death by accusation before the civil courts and monarchs.

15. "And they overcame him by the blood of the Lamb, and by the word of their testimony, and they loved not their lives unto death." These expressions coincide with what is said of the souls under the altar, slain for the word of God and the testimony they held. The expression is a *dual* one, and is beautifully put for the

gospel and the social philosophy it teaches. The two witnesses had preached the same things; and the victory over monarchy, in church and state, was the result of doctrines proclaimed by multitudes of martyrs and sufferers for the gospel's sake. This new kingdom is, therefore, appropriately represented as the result of gospel doctrines, proclaimed and maintained even unto blood through many dark ages. A call is then made upon all the land, and especially upon all Christians, to rejoice that they enjoyed so highly favored an age. "Rejoice, ye heavens, and ye that dwell in them."

16. "Wo to the inhabitants of the earth and sea." These represent the rest of the world outside of this new kingdom. The term "wo," is a symbol of great distress to be endured by the people under the dominion of monarchy.

17. "For the devil is come down to you, having great wrath." The defeat which monarchy had experienced was a great one; and was very aggravating, for the dragon was in great fury.

18. "Because he knoweth he hath but a short time." This was the cause of the wrath of monarchy. It was easy to perceive that a successful rebellion against kings would be the precursor of final ruin to all. The strongest efforts would be put forth, therefore, to preserve their dominion, and great wrath would be exhibited towards every manifestation of a restless disposition among the people of Europe, where the dragon had his seat.

19. "And when the dragon saw that he was cast unto the earth, he persecuted the woman which brought forth the man child." A persecution is symbolic of war, or of an attempt to injure. The monarchy, therefore, was to make war upon the church or upon the country again. We have now gone through all the points of the first part

of the prophecy, and we take up its brief duplicate or interpretation.

Duplicate Vision.—1. "And to the woman were given two wings of a great eagle, that she might fly into the wilderness into her place, where she is nourished for a time times and a half from the face of the serpent." The woman and the serpent, or the Christian church and Roman monarchy, both appeared in heaven at the same time, but the church fled from him into the wilderness, and the monarchy saw it no more as an object of attention for many centuries. The time of this hiding of the church, was in the first statement said to be 1260 days, but in the interpretation it is said to be hid for three and a half times. This shows that they are convertible terms, and doubles the certainty of their having a definite meaning. As the 42 months were equivalent to 1260 days, and as 1260 days equal three and a half times, it follows that they are all convertible or synonymous terms.

2. "And the serpent cast out of his mouth water as a flood after the woman, that he might cause her to be carried away of the flood." This passage briefly comprehends the war against the woman with the twelve stars upon her head. A flood of water represents armies, and is so used by Isaiah. The translation of the symbol, therefore, is this: the monarchy sent out its armies to destroy the woman and her stars, or the church and its new nationality.

3. "And the earth helped the woman." The term earth must be understood as the place of the dragon as distinct from the place of the woman, and as Europe is the place of monarchy in general, it is evident that this help to the Christians, endeavoring to establish nationality, must come from Europe.

4. "And the earth opened her mouth and swallowed

up the flood which the dragon cast out of his mouth." This was the checking of the war against the church and its stars, by European aid; for the swallowing of the flood is the overthrow of the armies of the dragon, or the absorption of them by people living on the earth, or Europe.

5. "And the dragon was wroth with the woman." This shows that as the true church was the origin of the great disaffection towards monarchy, the dragon or monarchy system was opposed to the true church every where.

6. "And went to make war with the remnant of her seed, which keep the commandments of God and the testimony of Jesus Christ." As the woman was herself the church, the seed of the woman must represent the offspring of the church, and they must be of the same character with the man child who was her seed, and, of course, it represents the advocates of civil and religious liberty, that were not in the immediate territories of the man child or woman. This is well expressed by the phrase " the remnant of her seed." These are separated, too, from fanatical liberalists, for they are those who are true men and true Christians, who are known by keeping the commandments of God, and who have the testimony of Jesus Christ. These must be in Europe, for they can be found no where else outside of America.

It must now be remembered that the church was to be in the wilderness, before the rise of nationality, 1451 years, and that the kingdom which appeared at the end of this time, had been promised, and that at its rise, it did not fill the world, but that monarchy, or the serpent, was for a short time to be a joint tenant of the world with this kingdom. Its territory, also, was to be separate from that of monarchy, for monarchy was cast out of it.

Again; the twelve stars on the woman's head were prophetic, and as they represented the civil department of God's Israel, they prefigured that when the nationality of the church arrived, that it would exist as a confederacy of twelve states; for each star represents a tribe or state separate from any other, yet all united in a crown show that they were to be confederated. At the full growth of the man child, we see a diadem of many stars or states united on his head. The number of Israel's twelve tribes and of the twelve apostles was thirteen, but were always represented literally or symbolically as twelve; the birth-right tribe of Joseph, being composed of two tribes, counted as one. The development, therefore, of the church or woman into nationality, was to be signalized by a confederacy of thirteen governments confederated, two of them being reckoned as one or having been one; the stars showing the divided state of the government, and the sun, with which the woman was clothed, its unity.

COINCIDENCES.

Coincidence First.—The church was to be in the wilderness for 1451 years or 529,984 days before the rise of her nationality, and then it was to give birth to a Christian nation composed of 13 states. Now, the true church went into the obscurity represented by the wilderness, at the union of church and state, which took place on the 19th June, 325; and just exactly 529,984 days afterward, the American confederacy was declared independent, and it sprung from the Christian church, and was composed of thirteen states, two of which, Pennsylvania and Delaware, were originally but one state.

Coincidence Second.—The man child represented a new and immature system of government. Such was the American confederacy at the declaration. The several colonies had formed state organizations previous to the declaration; and in the same year, at the recommendation of Congress, they were allied to each other by a common interest, but by rather feeble articles of confederation.

Coincidence Third.—This new government was to be preserved by Providence, and become the ruler of all nations. The American confederacy, all agree, was protected in a most wonderful manner by Providence, and it now exists as the prospective ruler of the world.

Coincidence Fourth.—Monarchy anticipated the erection of the new confederacy, and stood ready to destroy it, as soon as it came into being. The monarchy of Great Britain anticipated the nationality of the colonies, and stood ready to destroy it as soon as it was developed: but the nationality was preserved.

Coincidence Fifth.—Monarchy, represented by Great Britain, was to make war upon the new nationality, and was to be met by its forces, and vanquished. Great Britain declared war against the confederacy, and hired mercenaries from Europe in legions, to carry on the war, but was vanquished.

Coincidence Sixth.—The European powers were to assist the woman, or Michael and his forces, and swallow them up. Now, it so happened, during the revolutionary war, that out of hatred to Britain, France and Spain acknowledged the independence of America, and their forces being engaged in the war, called the British forces to attend to them as well as to the forces of the colonies; and it was by their conjoint aid that the Yorktown victory was obtained. Denmark, Sweden, Holland and Russia, also joined in the famous league of the armed neutrality, and stood opposed to Britain in this war; so that Britain had those at home who rejoiced in her losing war with her colonies, and commenced war with her. Indeed, all Europe secretly or openly aided or favored the American cause, from hatred or jealousy of Britain; and destructive wars on the continent began on account of the revolution in America.

Coincidence Seventh.—The dragon, or monarchy, was cast out of the place of the church. This was done by the United States, after the revolution. Monarchy was held in utter execration, and not a. foothold has been left in the United States for it; not even the semblance of monarchy will be brooked by the people for an instant.

Coincidence Eighth.—The dragon, or monarchy, was to go forth in wrath against the democracy in Europe, feeling that its foundations were shaken. Since the time of American independence, has occurred the great era of revolutions in Europe; and these have been caused by republican institutions in America. And never has the wrath of monarchy been so hot against its own subjects as since then. Britain, in twenty years, spent 1,000,000,000 dollars, to establish legitimacy in Europe, beside unnumbered millions spent for the same purpose by other powers. Indeed, all the thrones of Europe leagued together to crush liberty; and such desolation to their subjects, on earth and sea, as has been produced in the space of seventy years, beggars description. Never was a period of such revolutions known before. And these wars and oppressions have been more severe because the dragon knows his throne will stand but a short time; monarchy feels the swell of a universal earthquake.

Coincidence Ninth.—The dragon was to persecute the woman after her victory; that is, he was to trouble her country with annoyances and war. Now, Britain, soon after the Revolution, began a series of grievous injuries toward our country, which were shameful and wicked, and renewed war with us, and has never yet forgiven us for our great victory. Indeed, not only the British government, but many of its people, have written and acted against us, and the church here, as if we were a gang of outlaws; and in spirituals they so esteem us.

Coincidence Tenth.—The dragon, or monarchy, was to make war upon the Christian republicans of Europe. That this has been done is a matter of history. Russia, at the head, and all other powers at the tail, formed an alliance, in 1816, to fight and put down all Christian republicanism in Europe; and they called their hellish league the "Holy Alliance." How fearfully it has worked the ruin of the noble and true-hearted, the page of fresh blood-stained history in Austria, Italy, and Hungary can tell.

Coincidence Eleventh.—This kingdom was to come and be established out of the limits of the European dragon. The United States was beyond these limits.

Coincidence Twelfth.—This new kingdom, predicted by Daniel and John, was to arise and fill but a part of the earth at first. This is true of the United States.

Coincidence Thirteenth.—The man child was born before the war with the dragon; and the kingdom, or government, came directly after the war. The confederate government of the colonies was, after the war, succeeded by the organization into a single nationality by the adoption of the present constitution. It was made up of the "*Old Thirteen.*" It was called a kingdom of God, because composed of a truly Christian people; and any government is, in ancient idiom, called a kingdom. It was called the power of his Christ, because it elected God as king by acclamation, and drove off the devil; and because, by it, Christ is to get "the heathen for an inheritance, and break them with a rod of iron;" because it was the stone that was "to dash them in pieces like a potter's vessel."

Coincidence Fourteenth.—Church and state union was to be dissolved, or the "old serpent, the accuser of the brethren," was to be discarded. How gloriously true this was, all the world knows. An article on this very point alone, fills a large space in the American constitution. As in all points, the history of the origin, character, and progress of the United States, coincides with the sun, and moon, and twelve stars, and woman and her man child, and the new kingdom, with the utmost precision, it is infallibly certain that the United States was predicted by them.

This man child, or new kingdom, coincides with the stone cut out of the mountain, or fifth kingdom of Daniel; with the ancient of days and his throne; with the saints, and people of the saints; with the sanctuary and host; with the holy people, and power of the holy people; and with Israel restored in a country always waste, without walls and gates to its cities; and with the exodus of Israel from Egypt, and its crossing a sea, and organization of a republic in the wilderness.

SECTION IV.

Roman and British Monarchy, or the Seven-Headed Dragon

"And there appeared another great wonder in heaven and behold a great red dragon having seven heads and ten horns, and seven diadems upon his heads. And his tail drew the third part of the stars of heaven, and did cast them to the earth." The description of this character is brief, yet amply full to identify its symbolic meaning. There seems to be but one opinion about its meaning among critics, for all take it as a symbol of the Roman empire. We agree to this in the main, but must dissent from some of the expositions, in their details of the proof of this great fact. We shall give our proofs on a much heavier scale than others have done.

The characteristic points of this vision are: 1. A dragon. 2. His color. 3. His seven heads. 4. His ten horns. 5. His destruction of one-third of the stars. 6. His tail.

1. *A dragon.*—This symbolizes a base tyranny, or monarchy. In Ps. lxiv, it is said, "Thou breakest the heads of the dragons in the waters." This passage, from its context, is seen to symbolize the powers of Egypt. Isaiah says, "Art thou not it that hath cut Rahab, and wounded the dragon?" Rahab is a name of Egypt, and the dragon is a name put for Pharaoh's government. "In that day the Lord, with his strong sword, shall punish Leviathan the piercing serpent; and he shall slay the dragon that is in the sea." Here, the dragon and serpent represent the persecuting powers. Ezekiel says, "I am against thee, Pharaoh, king of Egypt, the great dragon that lieth in the midst of the rivers." Here, Pharaoh is put for all Egypt, and the whole is called a dragon. Nebuchadnezzar is called, by Jeremiah, a dragon.—(chap. 51.) Indeed, any organic body, used as a symbol, always represents an organic body. The dragon, or serpent, in the very beginning, is seen to represent a body of religious doctrine and worship.

2. *A red dragon.*—That is, *purros*, or a fiery red dragon. This color represents his moral character, which is vengeful, and as destructive as fire. The common

distinguishing color of Roman royalty was a fiery red, or scarlet.

3. *The seven heads.*—As the red dragon represented a government, so the heads represent the forms into which it was to be divided. For the symbol was a prophetic one, and the body of the dragon represented the government in unity, and the heads, in a broken or divided state. A head is a symbol of a government, as we saw in Daniel. There, the four kingdoms into which the Macedonian empire was divided, were represented by the four heads of the mingled leopard. The head of the great image, also, represented the empire of Babylon. Each head of the dragon must, therefore, be an empire, and not a particular quality of an empire, or representation of any political quality of a government, such as regal, or consular, or imperial. The moral character of the head is, in the heads of the dragon, represented by color, as in the four horses. Whether these heads grew out of the serpent at the same point, or at different points, is not stated; so that it is impossible to determine whether these different head governments were to appear simultaneously or successively. In the vision of the beast from the pit, it is there stated that the heads were to be consecutive, and not coeval; and, as that beast and this dragon coincide, it is evident these heads were to be successive representations of the whole serpent's power, for each is called the whole beast, or empire, in turn.

4. *The crowns, or diadems.*—In the Greek, the word here translated crowns, is *diademata*, or diadems, and differs from the *stephanos*, also translated crown. Daubuz and Wemyss, in the Symbol Dictionary, show that the *stephanos* symbolized delegated power, and that "diadems are constantly the symbols of imperial or

autocratic power, extending itself over all sorts of power, civil and ecclesiastical." These diadems, on the several heads of the dragon, showed that the government represented by each, would be a dominant power, or possess supreme empire for the time being. It should be here noted, particularly, that the divided state of the Roman empire is represented, in Daniel, by ten toes and ten horns, but, in Revelation, it is represented by both horns and heads together, or by either separately. And though the empire is represented as divided, yet still its history is treated of as if it were a unit only.

5. The division into heads shows, that the original government would be broken, and that its imperial power would exist in successive empires that would rise out of the original body; the head being smaller than the body, indicates that the head governments would not be as extensive as the original government, but that each head would represent the original. The body and heads would represent the chronological history of the empire, and also its locality; the head and body occupying different places.

6. *The tail.*—Isaiah interprets the symbolic meaning of the tail to be a false religion, taught by false prophets. "The ancient and honorable, he is the head, and the prophet that teacheth lies, he is the tail."—Isa. ix. Here, by the ancient and honorable of Israel, is meant the civil power; and by the lying prophet, the corrupt religion of Judah. The tail of the dragon, therefore, represents a corrupt church, or impure and idolatrous religion.

7. *The third part of the stars of heaven.*—Heaven either symbolizes a church, or the place of the true church. The stars represent either spiritual or civil ruling powers, or authorities. The drawing of the third

part of the stars of heaven by the dragon's tail, and casting them to the earth, would represent the destruction of one third part of the true ministers, or churches of Christ, by the false doctrines of the government, or dragon. The term earth represents the empire of the dragon; and the casting down to the earth, shows that they were cast down in the dragon's dominions. We now look for an empire on earth, to coincide with the dragon empire. As the dragon appeared before the 1260 days of the woman began, of course, we must look for his matter-of-fact likeness before the year 325. Now, the Roman government is the only one under heaven that coincides with the dragon, and we will identify the truth of this statement.

Coincidence First.—The dragon symbolizes a great tyrannical autocracy. Such a government was the Roman.

Coincidence Second.—A red dragon symbolizes a great persecuting, or bloody power. Such a power was the Roman empire; and beside this, the imperial power was represented by a scarlet color.

Coincidence Third.—The draconic empire was to be broken, and seven great heads of government were successively to rise out of its ruins, and represent its iron power. Such has been the history of the Roman empire. It has been broken and divided, and seven great empires have arisen from it. Bishop Newton interprets these as the seven hills on which Rome was built; but this is simply ridiculous. For the prophecy is a miniature of only the mightiest occurrences in the world, and the comparatively infinitesimal piles of soil, in a single city, could have no such prominency here, as the heads of mighty empires do. He again interprets them of kings, consuls, dictators, decemvirs, military tribunes, and emperors; but this will not do either, for these existed while the empire was a unit, and were not empires either, which the symbolic head requires. But, again; these consuls and decemvirs, &c., belonged to an age anterior to the prophecy, whereas, the whole vision was prospective, and not retrospective: it predicted; it did not relate history back of John's day, for it asserts that the things seen were to "be hereafter." We must now look into history, from the days the woman fled into the wilderness, or from 325, and find the coincidences to these seven heads in great dominions that arose subsequently, in the Roman empire limits. We shall not look in vain. Every one acquainted with the history of Europe, even superficially, will instantly recognize the seven dominant empires of Europe, as soon as they are mentioned: 1st. The Western empire. The Roman empire was divided into east and west, in the days of Valentinian, about 365, and Milan was made the seat of government. This empire continued till about 475, when it was entirely overthrown. 2d. After the fall of the Western empire, the next great imperial empire that arose, was that of the Charlemagne, which had the autocratic sway of Europe. 3d. The next autocratic dominion, erected over Europe, was the papal. This arose to political supremacy in the days of Hildebrand, or Gregory VII, A. D. 1073, and held the scepter of empire down to Boniface VIII, about 1303. 4th. The next imperial supremacy in Europe, was that of Charles V, emperor of Spain and Germany, or the Spanish empire. 5th. The next great imperial dominant power, out of the old Roman territory, was the British empire. 6th. The next great dominant power, in the old Roman territory, was the French empire, under Bonaparte. 7th. The next head, according to John, in another vision, was to rise out of the Asian portion of the empire, and coincides with the autocracy of Russia in Europe. Russia is now the dominant power in Europe, and bids fair to absorb all its power.

We have placed these heads in Europe, because the original head-place of the serpent was there, and there all the heads must naturally be found. Another reason is, that this dragon coincides with the fourth beast of Daniel, as is seen in the correspondence of the ten horns in the beast and dragon. And as the head and horns of the fourth empire were in Europe in the one case, they must be in the other. Hence, it would have been wrong to have counted the eastern empire among the heads, for that was reckoned as the body of the beast and dragon. These seven empires, it will be seen, were not universal, but coincide with the dimensions represented only by the heads. They coincide also, with Daniel's description of the fourth kingdom in its broken state, where he says the strength of the iron should continue. Each, however, is, for the time, considered as the Roman monarchy continued, as will be seen in the description of the beast from the pit. The whole dragon, therefore, was represented by each head, so that Britain was properly called the dragon, since it was one of the heads, and grew up out of the Roman empire, and thus became its representative, or the representative of autocracy for a time.

Coincidence Fourth.—The *seven diadems* represented the supremacy of empire. To this, each of the empires, we have mentioned, corresponds; for each was for the time being a dominant empire, and did according to its will; and each was a monarchy, so that monarchy in general was represented by the head and body and tail of the dragon, for they embraced all. Now, it is remarkable that each of these empires had domination over the churches as well as the states in Europe, while they were in the ascendant.

Coincidence Fifth.—The ten horns upon one or all of the heads, shows that that head or heads would be divided into ten kingdoms. This coincides with the head of Daniel's fourth kingdom; and we have already shown that these were out of the western empire, or on the first head of the broken empire.

Coincidence Sixth.—The tail of the dragon represented the dominant or ruling religion in the draconic empire. In Daniel's vision of the ten horns and little horn, we have seen that the little horn represented the Roman imperial church; and here the tail of the dragon is seen to coincide with the little horn, as a corrupt and dominant religion. The appearing of the dragon before the woman, was, therefore, as late as the union of church and state.

Coincidence Seventh.—The corrupt imperial religion was to cast down one third of the true Christian churches in a third part of the original draconic or Roman empire. Now, Europe was one third of the old Roman world, for the empire was made up of three continents. And the state religion, throughout all Europe, cast down, persecuted and disorganized all of the churches of Christ, because they were not united to the state.

Coincidence Eighth.—The broken state of Rome, and its existence in successive empires, were represented by the division into heads. To this very state of things the Roman empire, since the union of church and state, has corresponded. As every prophetic characteristic of the seven-headed dragon has coincided with the Roman empire, since church and state union, to the present, the Roman empire must be intended by the dragon.

CONCLUSION.

It can not escape observation, that the woman and her seed, the man child, and the dragon and his armies, and the victory of Michael, were symbols drawn from the declaration of war in the garden of Eden. The woman and her seed coincide with the woman and her man child; the dragon and his tail coincide with the serpent and his seed; the dragon and his angels coincide with the head, body, and tail of the Roman dragon, and Michael and his angels coincide with the woman and her seed and HE that shall bruise the serpent's head. Surely these symbols are of divine origin. The visions of the seals gave a religious history of the world; and the visions of the witnesses and the woman and dragon, are mixed, and so are the visions of the next two powers; but those of the trumpets will be found almost purely political.

SECTION V.

THE BEAST FROM THE SEA, OR THE UNIVERSAL IMPERIAL CHURCH.

The next vision of the little interpreting book, is that of a beast from the sea, representing the imperial church organization throughout the Roman empire. "And I stood upon the sand of the sea, and saw a beast rise up out of the sea, having seven heads and ten horns, and upon his horns ten crowns, and upon his heads the name of blasphemy."

1. *The beast.*—This, as we have already seen, in Daniel, symbolizes a kingdom or government.

2. *It rose from the sea.*—It was therefore not in existence in John's days, for he saw it prophetically. It came from the sea. The sea is, by John, defined to be a multitude of people, and so also by Daniel. As this beast was a spiritual dominion, the sea must represent the religion from whence it sprung, and the earth the civil power of the empire.

3. *Seven heads.*—These are conformed to the seven heads of the dragon, or to the great empires that were to have dominion in later ages in Europe.

4. *The ten horns.*—These are conformed to the clay of ten toes of the great image; to the ten horns of Daniel's fourth beast; and to the ten of the dragon.

5. *Ten crowns on the horns.*—These crowns were diadems, or *diademata*, and therefore represented that the ten kingdoms were independent of any superior imperial power. The heads having no diadems, in this vision, show that this beast was not identical with the dragon, but only a counterpart of it.

6. "Upon his heads the name of blasphemy." The term blasphemy signifies, "to arrogate the prerogatives of God," as "this man blasphemeth; who can forgive sins but God only?"—Matt. ix. The heads having no diadems, but marked with blasphemy, show that this was a spiritual power, arrogating the prerogatives of God.

7. "And the beast which I saw was like unto a leopard." We have already seen that the leopard's colors marked great variety of characters in a kingdom.

8. "His feet like unto a bear." The feet symbolized adoration, or the worship of this kingdom.—Ez. iii. 5; Prov. vi. 13. Like unto a bear, signifies the mummery and rapacity of the worship. "We *groan* all of us like bears."—Isa. lix.

9. "His mouth as the mouth of a lion." A mouth commonly signifies doctrine and authority. A mouth as a lion, signifies great authoritativeness of doctrine.

10. "And the dragon gave him his power, and his seat, and great authority." The dragon, we have shown, was imperial Rome, and as he gives this beast a seat, it shows that the beast was a protege of his, and not the imperial power, as that was the dragon himself. The dragon did not give up his own seat to the beast, but he gave a seat of power to the new government, or beast. The text does not intimate any abandonment, by the dragon, of his own prerogatives, but he asserts the rights of the beast. The pronoun "his" refers to the beast, and *his* seat, and not to the dragon; the text says nothing about the dragon's seat at all. The dragon still continued to exist and to occupy his own throne, for, in the second sentence afterward, they are both represented as existing conjointly, and receiving honor together; and the dragon is represented as existing in all subsequent ages, and is chained before the Millennium, and thrown into hell afterward. The authority given was a spiritual authority, and the seat was a spiritual one, and they conjointly ruled and received honors together.

11. "And I saw one of his heads as it were wounded unto death, and his deadly wound was healed." As each head represented some one particular form of the existence of the government in its broken stages, this wounding shows that one of these seven governments would be nearly overthrown; but its being healed shows that it would survive and be strong again.

12. "All the world wondered after the beast." That is, the whole world would be surprised at its existence.

13. "And they worshiped the dragon which gave power unto the beast, and they worshiped the beast,

saying, Who is like unto the beast? Who is able to make war with him." This worship represents new and increased homage given to imperial Rome, for the establishment of this blasphemous power, as well as the honors heaped upon this power by the multitude. It shows that it was a dominant power of great coeval ability with the dragon, and that it received its strength from imperial authority.

14. "And there was given unto him a mouth speaking great things and blasphemies." This, again, shows that the power was a spiritual one; for mouth and blasphemy are never applied to a civil symbol of government.

15. "And power was given unto him to continue or make war, or prevail forty-two months." That is for 529,984 days, and for 1243 years 277 days, and for about 1540 years, or until the 4th of July, 1776, and until 1865, or thereabouts.

16. "And he opened his mouth in blasphemy against God, to blaspheme his name, and his tabernacle, and them that dwell in heaven." This blasphemy, we have seen, was the assumption of divine power generally. To blaspheme the tabernacle would, therefore, be asserting rights in the church of God, which belonged to God only; and blasphemy against those in heaven, would be assuming divine authority over Christians generally.

17. "And it was given unto him to make war with the saints, and to overcome them." That is, this spiritual government was to oppress Christians, and destroy them, and crush them almost out of existence.

18. "And power was given him over all kindreds, and tongues, and nations." The Roman empire extended over all nations, and its power was to be commensurate with its limits. This, however, seems to be a different

power from that just expressed as extending over Christians, and must be a civil jurisdiction over the empire; so that both sacred and secular matters were to be under its control, at some period in its history.

19. "And all that dwell upon the earth shall worship him, whose names are not written in the book of life of the Lamb." That is, the whole empire should honor it, excepting those who were true Christians.

COINCIDENCES.

We now affirm that this beast, or spiritual kingdom, is no other than the church united to the Roman empire, in all of its stages of being. We shall simply enumerate the identifying coincidences categorically:

1. The church united to the state was a spiritual empire, and was conformed, universally, to the imperial empire of Rome.—(*Eusebius*, *Gibbon*, *Hallam*.)

2. It arose from the sea, or the church which had already lost much of its savor, and was the mystery of iniquity that was working in the days of St. Paul, and which he describes as the man of sin.

3. It has been in all stages of the seven empires, conformed to them, and allied to them, and has had a seat with them in civil affairs. Bishops, in England, have civil power.

4. The church was also united to the ten kingdoms of Europe, for the barbarians who erected them adopted the religion of Rome.

5. The heads, or smaller successive empires, as well as the original empire, gave this blasphemous power no imperial sway, but kept it subservient to them. The papal power claimed supremacy, as the regent of God, over kingdoms, rather than as a church.

6. This church has had the most motley composition of tribes, nations, and tongues, and has been of the most mingled religious character of any spiritual body that ever existed. Its worship has been the most mystic and whining, groaning and chanting, that was ever known. Its doctrines have been asserted with as lion-like authority as that of God himself.

7. One of the heads of this power was wounded as if unto death, but it recovered: that was the veritable papal head of Europe. In the war between the papal and imperial powers for supremacy, or that of investitures, or of the Guelphs and Ghibelines, Henry of Germany degraded Gregory VII., defeated and slew Rodolph, whom the Pope had declared emperor; he entered Italy, laid siege to Rome for two years, and carried it by assault; deposed Gregory, and reduced the papal empire, by the sword, to the brink of ruin. Thus was one of the great imperial heads of the beast, or one of the prophetic empires, wounded to death. Gregory VII. was the founder of the papal empire, and " added a blasphemous claim of right, as Christ's vicar on earth, and inheritor of his visible throne."—(*Taylor's Hist.*) See on page 409, of this history, the tremendous claims he made upon all governments in the world to submit to the papal power. Gregory returned to Rome after Henry IV. had left it, and reduced it to a mass of ruins; he then retreated to Salerno and died, as he said himself, " in exile."

8. "And his deadly wound was healed." The victory over the papal power was of short duration. The cardinals elected Victor III., and in a short time the papal power arose afresh, to tremendous and supreme empire, and rested in the very same principles avowed by Gregory VII., at the organization of the empire. Thus was the wounded head restored to life.

9. The seat of the imperial and universal Roman church was given to it, with all its spiritual despotism, by Constantine, on the 19th June, 325; and it was renewed by Valentinian, by Theodosius, and, finally, was most minutely attached to the empire by Justinian.

10. The imperial power of Rome, on account of its union with the church, was, and is, lauded by millions; and the church has received the support and honor of princes, kings, and people, in Europe, Asia, and Africa, without any bounds, and the millions of multiplied millions of the people have worshiped at its shrine.

11. The state church, in the bounds of the empire, has claimed the attributes of dominion over men, and the church, and all Christians, and all nations and tribes, which belong only to God. It has set itself as the judge of conscience, and the arbiter of the spiritual state of all men, even beyond the tomb; and language is a feeble instrument to express the enormity of its claims in earth, hell, purgatory, and heaven.

12. The power of this church dominion was to exist over all nations 42 months, or for 529,984 days, and for about 1540 years; and just exactly 529,984 days from the union of church and state, the dominion of its power ceased over a vast continent, and has bright prospects of a perpetual cessation before long.

13. The state church of Rome, as was predicted, attained to political supremacy under Pope Gregory VII., and maintained it down to the year 1303. "The Pope of Rome became, through the dark ages, a king of kings; nay, more, he assumed to be in the place of God."—(*Willard's Universal History.*)

14. At the instigation of the imperial church, 200,000 men were employed at one single time, to destroy the Christian Vaudois, Albigenses, and Waldenses, and a

million of these pious Christians were destroyed. Besides these, millions throughout Spain, Italy, Germany, France and England, have been destroyed by the same great empire church establishment. Indeed, wherever it exists it has persecuting power, and exercises it as far as it can without producing resistance. In England, France, Germany, Italy, Austria and Russia, it has been the same great asserter of right over the conscience, and still has this right guaranteed to it by statute. Like the spots of the leopard, it may have different intensity in its color of power, but it is the same leopard establishment everywhere. In the United States no such power exists, and the conscience is given up to God, and he is acknowledged as its only lawgiver and judge. The church establishment, whether English, Lutheran, Scotch, Gallic, Greek, or Roman Catholic, is the same in kind, though the several kingdoms in which it is established may be more or less humane in the exercise of its prerogative. The monarch is head of the church in each, and has been from the inception of the church and state system of iniquity. Nothing of greater iniquity ever saw the light, than this unholy, ungodly, blasphemous, and hellish combination. Pious people have lived in the established church, but they have been pious in spite of its corruptions; and multitudes of them, for their righteousness, have perished in a thousand modes of Satanic cruelty.

From these full coincidences of the established church in Europe and Asia and Africa, with the beast from the sea, it is certain they match each other, and that the one was the prediction of the other.

SECTION VI.

The Two Horned Beast, or Great Britain.

Immediately after the vision of the imperial church, another vision of another kingdom is seen by the prophet. This new vision describes Great Britain in the clearest and most exact manner, and describes no other power that ever existed. The great disagreement among past expositors as to its application, is proof that they never rightly applied it. Indeed, all prophetic expositors being Englishmen, who could not conceive but that God held their country in as profound respect as they did, never thought that England's government was to fall among the monarchies as a foe of God. They have supposed this two-horned beast was the papal power, or the Turkish, or French, but never their own. But if the fulfillment of any prophecy of any nation was ever clearly seen, it is seen in the coincidence between the two-horned beast and the British Empire. We will critically analyze the description, and show how exactly it fits the lion and the unicorn.

1. "And I beheld another beast coming up out of the earth." A beast is, as we have seen, an empire; and, as John says, he saw another beast, he, of course, saw another empire, and one very different from the beast from the sea. He says this new empire came up out of the earth, and, of course, it was different in its origin from any kingdom he had described, except the same in the head of the dragon. The term earth is clearly symbolic; for this new kingdom came up out of it, which could not be done literally. The earth is also used as antithetic to the sea, from whence the seven-headed beast

came up. Now, as the imperial church came up out of a great religion in the Roman empire, it is plain that the sea whence it came, coincides with that general religion; and as the earth is antithetic to it, it must represent its counterpart, or the civil or territorial empire of Rome. The Roman empire was commonly called the whole earth, among the ancients. It was designated by the terms, "Lux orbis terrarum, terrarum Dea Gentium, Arx Omnium Gentium, Caput Orbis Terrarum, Caput Rerum," &c., which terms are, in the highest degree, expressive of universality. This new empire was, therefore, to arise from the limits of the Roman empire, and be of Roman character as well as origin. To this, all agree.

2. "He had two horns like a lamb, and he spake as a dragon." In this empire, the character of a lion and a lamb were to be blended together. A horn, we have seen, represents a government, and there is no variation from this rule; and these two horns, therefore, must represent two governments, growing out of the head or imperial power of this empire. These two governments or horns, were to be like a lamb. A lamb is an emblem of innocence, and we have seen that a lamb symbolizes Christianity, or the true church of Jesus Christ; these two horns, must, therefore, represent two ecclesiastical governments, very like to the true church of Christ, but only *like* it, a resemblance being all. No other interpretation can be put upon these two horns like a lamb. The two governments were to be like a lamb, that is, they were to be like Christian churches. "He spake as a dragon." A dragon, we have seen, represents an imperial power; and the speaking as a dragon, represents the exercise of great imperial authority, and power of command. He did not speak as a lamb, though his

horns were like one. The horns were not like the horns of a lamb, but they were to be like a lamb itself.

3. "He exerciseth all the power of the first beast before him." This empire was to exercise the power of the great Roman hierarchy, which was represented by the first beast before him. That is, it was to assume spiritual authority in its own dominion, as extensively as the Roman church did in its jurisdiction.

4. "And causeth the earth and them that dwell therein to worship the first beast, whose deadly wound was healed." The earth here is, by synecdoche, put for the earth in its own dominions; that is, the whole is put for a part. This is a common figure of speech. It could not be put for that out of his limits, for that was beyond his control. The worship was the honor which was to be paid to the Roman hierarchy generally. "The beast whose deadly wound was healed." This was that head of the beast that was wounded in the first beast. Here, as in John's vision of the beast from the pit, a head is put for a beast, or government. And, as the wounded head, or wounded beast, are shown to be the papal power in Europe, the honors here mentioned were to be conferred on the papal power.

5. "And he doeth great wonders, so that he maketh fire to come down from heaven on earth, in the sight of men." These expressions are plainly symbolic, since no human empire can perform these things literally. The wonders refer, as national matters, to extraordinary actions of the governing power. Fire from heaven symbolizes words of authority from the church; for heaven symbolizes the church, and fire symbolizes either wrath or doctrine. In Hab. iii. 5, it is said, "Burning coals went forth at his feet, *i. e.* the preaching of his word was accompanied with punishment against the disobedient."—

(*Sym. Dic.*) Jer. v. 14, says, "Behold I will make my words in thy mouth fire, and this people wood, and it shall devour them." Descending fire also represents new commotion in the world. All of these scriptural explanations of the term fire coincide as cause and effect. The text, therefore, represents that the doctrines or teachings of the church, shall descend, or conform, to the notions of the governing power, and that the result will be destructive to those who disobey them.

6. "And deceiveth them that dwell on the earth by the means of those miracles which he had power to do in the sight of the beast." This shall, in some way, deceive the people as to the designs of these miracles, and they shall be led into great errors as to the false prophet's future objects.

7. "Saying to them that dwell on the earth, that they should make an image unto the beast which had a wound by the sword and did live." As the beast with the wounded imperial head was the politico-ecclesiastic empire power of papacy, the command to make an image to it, was a command to conform the empire church and state of the dragon head into a politico-ecclesiastic establishment like the papacy. There is no escape from this conclusion. An image of the wounded head is a likeness of it; and as the wounded head was an ecclesiastic power principally, such must be the image; hence, the organization of a new church, in form and outline like the Roman, was predicted.

8. "And he had power to give life unto the image of the beast." That is, the imperial power gave vitality to the new ecclesiastical establishment, and "caused it to speak;" in other words, to utter its commands with the same authoritativeness as the church, after which it was modeled.

9. "And cause that as many as would not worship the image of the beast should be killed." The killing, doubtless, refers to the overturning and destroying those organizations that would not honor the new church establishment. The term "many" is a collective one, and properly symbolizes collective bodies of people. Their death would, therefore, be their overthrow, or suppression.

10. "And he causeth all, both small and great, rich and poor, free and bond, to receive a mark in their right hand, or in their foreheads." These collective terms, again, properly represent all portions of the empire. The mark was, plainly, some legal distinguishing characteristic, to which all were to conform. It is plainly symbolic, and of course does not mean a literal marking of the hand or forehead; such small distinctions are beneath the great scope of prophecy, which deals with general and extensive qualities and not with very little ones. Ezekiel speaks of the marking of the foreheads of the pious of Jerusalem; that is, a separation of them from others. This marking by the image, or church establishment, therefore, symbolizes a drawing of a distinction by law among the people of the empire. Marks in the hands or wrists were, anciently, tokens of servitude to some master, or false deity.—See Zech. xiii. 6. To have a mark in the forehead, also signifies to make an open profession of attachment to any party. Captives were sometimes stigmatized with forehead marks. The Jewish high priest had the name of God written in the plate on his forehead; and the followers of the Lamb are said to have his Father's name in their foreheads. Among the heathen there were three ways by which the devotees of false religion designated themselves: 1. By marking themselves with the name of their deity in their

hand or forehead. 2. Sometimes with the ensign of their god, as the *thunderbolt* of Jupiter, the *trident* of Neptune, or the *ivy* of Bacchus. 3. Sometimes they marked themselves with some mystical *number*, whereby the god's name was described; thus the sun was represented by XH, or 608, that is, by the Greek letters *chi* and *eta*.

11. "And that no man might buy or sell save he that had the mark, or the name of the beast, or the number of his name." In the previous passage we see that the law was to demand a profession of some kind throughout the empire; but in this we see that this profession was to be one or the other of three kinds. The name of the beast was one, his mark was another, and the number of his name was a third. There is a wide distinction drawn between these three kinds of professions, for they are repeated here and elsewhere with great emphasis and separateness. The name of the beast we have seen to be that of the Roman or Latin ecclesiastical kingdom, and, therefore, as one religion is designated by the name of the beast, another must be designated by the mark, and another by the number of his name. The refusing to allow buying and selling to any but those who adhered to one of these religions, symbolizes civil disabilities to exercise office in the empire generally by non-conformists. Literal buying and selling is by no means all that is included under these terms, nor can their signification be restricted to their literal sense.

These three religions, though different, as indicated by the modes of designating them, were yet of a common Latin original, as is seen in the resemblance of their inlices; they were "par nobile fratrum." They seem to have possessed a different moral character, as is indicated in the difference between the name, the mark, and the number of the Latin church. This empire was therefore to have three accredited religions; only two, however, were subsequently to be national, as is seen in the two ecclesiastical horns or churches growing up from the head of the beast, or from the governmental head of power. These two are further referred to, as the hand and forehead marks; for these coincide with the two horns in number, and in the attachment to the national institutions by profession.

12. "Here is wisdom. Let him that hath understanding count the number of the beast; for it is the number of a man; and his number is six hundred three score and six." A man symbolizes a kingdom, and the number of the name of the beast, is to be computed as the number of the name of a man. Now, as the number of a man's name was known by adding the numbers represented by the letters in his name, so, by adding the numbers represented by the letters in the name of the Latin kingdom, we shall get the number 666, if it be the kingdom designated. The number is to be found in Greek, since this number is represented by three Greek letters, and was the language used by the writer. We will show two modes of deducing this number from the name of the Latin kingdom. 1. Η ΛΑΤΙΝΗ ΒΑΣΙΛΕΙΑ. Here is one name of the Latin church and empire. Now, counting the letters according to their numbers in Greek, and we shall have Η=8, L=30, A=1, T=300, I=10, N=50, H=8, B=2, A=1, Σ, or sigma,=200, I=10, L=30, E=5, I=10, and A=1. Add these together and we have 666, the required number of the name. This will identify the beast, and his mark as well as his number.

2. Irenæus, the disciple of Polycarp, the disciple of John, says that "the name Lateinos contains the

number 666; and it is very likely, because the last kingdom is so called, for they are Latins who now reign." "Lateinos with *ei* is the true orthography, as the Greeks wrote the long *i* of the Latins, and as the Latins themselves wrote in former times."—(See *Ennius*, Book vi. Line 26. *Bp. Newton.*) "After the division of the empire, the Greeks and other orientals called the people of the Western church *Latins*, and they Latinize in everything. Mass, prayers, hymns, litanies, canons, decretals, and bulls are conceived in Latin. The papal councils speak in Latin. Women pray in Latin. Nor is the scripture read in any other than the Latin language, by the Roman church. The council of Trent commanded the vulgar Latin to be the only authentic version. In short, all things are Latin in the Roman church."—(*Newton.*) Lateinos, or the Latin Man, is the appropriate name of the Latin church. Now, the letters of this name make just the number 666. Thus $L=30$, $A=1$, $T=300$, $E=5$, $I=10$, $N=50$, $O=70$, and $S=200$, and all equal just 666. The Latin church is, therefore, the beast; for we have doubly shown the proof of it. Now, no other name of any kingdom in the world will, in Greek, amount to 666; so that the interpretation is pinned down to the Latin church by the absolute nature of things. This two-horned beast is elsewhere called the false prophet.

We shall now show, that the British empire coincides precisely with this kingdom from the earth, and that it coincides with no other kingdom under heaven.

Coincidence First.—The two-horned beast was to be another empire, different from the Latin politico-ecclesiastic power. The British empire was another empire.

Coincidence Second.—This other beast, or empire, was to arise out of the earth, or Roman territory. The

British empire arose out of the Roman empire, and was originally a part of it.

Coincidence Third.—This other beast or empire was to speak as a dragon, or to assume imperial power over the nations and people. If we look to the times of Henry VIII., we shall see that then the British empire broke off from the papal dominion, and acted as an independent empire, and spoke with the greatest and most draconic authority.

Coincidence Fourth.—This new empire was to exercise the same kind and extent of power in its dominions, that the papal power did in its dominions. How true this was accomplished by Henry, and how fully it has been since his day, by the British government, the full page of history records. Henry set himself up as possessed of authority equal to the papal, and used all his imperial strength to sustain the papacy. He murdered and overturned all that opposed his dictation, and compelled all to worship, or do homage to the Latin church; so that he caused all to worship the first beast. Every reader of English history is familiar with these things.

Coincidence Fifth.—The false prophet was to humble the word of the true church, and produce disaster to all that opposed him in his course. The monarch of England burnt all the copies of scripture that were first printed in English; and also burnt Tyndal, the translator and reformer. He summoned the universities to decide that he could divorce himself at pleasure, and they responded satisfactorily. He wrote, in reply to Luther, and in defense of the Pope, and was named by him the "Defender of the Faith;" a name which England's monarchs have inherited ever since. He destroyed all the reformers in his reach, and made his people worship at the shrine of the beast, or murdered them.

Coincidence Sixth.—This new government was to make an image to the Roman hierarchy. This was done, by Henry. Macaulay says, " Henry attempted to constitute the Anglican church, differing from the Roman on the point of supremacy alone, and his success was extraordinary." "He meant nothing in the world less than a *Reformation.*"—(*Worcester Hist.*) "He arrogated infallibility to himself, and caused the law of the six articles of religion, called 'the bloody statute,' to be enacted."—(*Ib.*) This law required implicit obedience to the doctrines of the Roman church, and death, or imprisonment, was the penalty of disobedience. This new church was, in all respects, an image of the papal, or of the beast with the wounded head.

Coincidence Seventh.—Power was to be given to this new church, to have a separate and authoritative life. The church of Henry, the image of the beast, has lived ever since his day with great authority.

Coincidence Eighth.—"And cause that as many as would not worship the image of the beast should be killed." Let any man read the statutes of conformity to the English church, from Henry to William, and read the accounts of the deaths of martyrs, and extensive persecutions, for non-conformity to the English church, and he will see this coincidence in fire, and blood, and tears; and hear it in groans and screams of the tortured and imprisoned.

Coincidence Ninth.—Each one was to receive in their hands, or foreheads, or to have the name, the mark, or the number of the name of the beast. As with the ancients, the name of a false god represented the God; and as his mark represented him, and also the number of his name, so the name of the beast, which was a state religion, represented that kind of religion, and the mark and number of the beast also represented a state religion. Hence, this new empire was to endorse three religions Now, this was the state of the case in England, and in no other country in the world. During the reigns of Henry's successors, acts were passed by the government, restricting all civil offices to Catholics, members of the churches of England and Scotland, which were all, by turns and together, endorsed by the government; and non-conformity was punished in the severest manner. We could quote act after act, from the statutes of England, proving these points; but we refer the reader to these universal laws of blood, as they are indelibly recorded in English history. Small readers can not appreciate the depth of these laws of iniquity. There was the strongest line of demarcation drawn between the three religions and dissenters, and it was drawn with " fire mingled with blood," for several generations.

Coincidence Tenth.—This empire was finally to have two horns, like a lamb, or two established religions much like the Christian. Such has been the case in the British empire. The Anglican church was much reformed after the fire that burned John Rogers, and was conformed to many evangelical doctrines of scripture. The kirk of Scotland was erected into a state religion, and approaches very near to true Christianity. The great antipathy of God to a state religion is, because it places a human being at its head, and allows the state to rule where He alone has a right to rule. All state religions are, from the nature of things, subject to the secular head of the state. In England, the oath of supremacy, as head of the church, is taken by the king; on the day of his coronation, he puts on a stole, a dalmatica, and a surplice. Religion in America differs from all religion in the world, for it never had, and never will have, a secular head. The two great state religions of Britain coincide with the two lamb-like horns of the beast from the earth.

Coincidence Eleventh.—The number of the name of the beast or Roman church, whose imperial character was to be borrowed by the beast, we have already seen, was the Roman church.

To recapitulate: the new empire was to rise from the Roman territory; it was to organize a church like the Roman; it was to give aid and comfort to three great religions; it was to persecute all others; it was ultimately to have two established religions. The British empire arose from the Roman; it organized a church like the papal; it gave aid and comfort, to the papal, English and Scotch imperial or empire churches; and finally, established two state religions, the church of England, and the kirk of Scotland.

We have now shown a mathematically exact coincidence between the two-horned beast and the British empire. And, as perfect coincidence is infallibly perfect fulfillment, the two-horned beast infallibly predicted the British empire. No clawing off here, gentlemen; the coincidence is perfect, and so is the fulfillment; receive the interpretation, or deny the infallible rule. This empire is to be overthrown, and it will be the last to fall of all the monarchies. We have now finished the interpretations given in the little book, and shall take up the seven trumpets in order.

CHAPTER XIII.

THE SEVEN TRUMPETS—SECOND GREAT PANORAMA.

These trumpets are announced as soon as the cessation of the revelations under the seals occurs; nothing being given by the seventh seal at the time of its opening Nothing is said of the seven trumpets occurring *after* the seals, and, the sixth seal and seventh vial of the seventh trumpet coinciding, is full proof that the seals and trumpets rehearse the history of the same great era of the bondage of the church. Besides this, the seals and trumpets are seen to coincide chronologically, throughout the whole field of vision. The introduction to seven trumpets is marked by seven angels standing before God, and an angel standing at the altar with a censer, offering the prayers of the saints to God. An angel always symbolizes an agent or agency, and, doubtless, also represents a real spirit, for one of the seven engaged in conversation with John. The prayers of the saints would certainly be offered for the " kingdom to come in earth as it is in heaven." The altar symbolizes religion; and the angel at it, seems to cast the fire from his censer, indicative of the curses earth is to feel in working out its great redemption through sufferings. The thunders, lightnings, voices, and earthquakes, are prophetic of, either the whole period of the seven trumpets, or, of their initiative at church and state union.

SECTION I.

First Trumpet—Goths, Germans, Vandals—Invasion of Europe.

" And the first angel sounded, and there followed hail and fire, mingled with blood, and they were cast upon the earth; and the third part of the trees was burnt up, and all the green grass was burnt up." A trumpet is plainly a symbol of a period of time, during which certain events were to transpire. The period announced, must coincide with some period of history, and as trumpets are collateral with the seals, it is proper to see if their primary periods will coincide in historic events, and, if they do, of course the fulfillment will be found.

1. *Hail.*—This term is used for divine vengeance. See Ez. ix.; Job iii., viii.; Ps. cv., lxxviii. Ezekiel xxxviii. represents blood, hail and fire, as the warfare of Israel against the latter day monarchy.

2. *Fire.*—This term, mingled with hail, signifies increased vengeance.

3. *Blood.*—This is always symbolic of slaughter, and being added to hail and fire, shows the vengeance was to be three-fold.

4. *The earth.*—This was a common name for the Roman empire; and as these prophecies related to it, as they go over the same field that Daniel traverses, the term earth properly symbolizes this empire. The term is plainly symbolic.

5. *The third part of the trees was burnt up.*—That is, of course, one third part of the trees of the symbolic earth. The Roman empire was composed out of three continents, and hence the term, the *third part*, will represent one of these continents.

6. *Trees.*—In Zech. xi., the term trees is used for men.   See also, Is. ii., x., and xix.—(*Lowth*, note, and *Sym. Dic.*)

7. *Burnt up.*—That is, destroyed, or reduced by the greatest devastation to lifelessness.

8. "All the green grass was burnt up."—Grass signifies men. They are called grass in the Old Testament repeatedly: Is. xl.; I. Pet. i.; I. Cor. iii. People are called hay or grass. As trees and grass both signify men, there must be a difference in their character, and the trees must signify princes and nobles, and the grass the common people. Indeed, we find trees in the old Testament expressly symbolizing princes; and a book must be interpreted according to its own definitions.

The exposition of this trumpet then amounts to exactly this: that a desolating war, of a three-fold character, was to desolate one third part, or one continent of the Roman empire, and overturn its princes, and destroy a large portion of the common people, about the time of church and state union. A little prior to the time of the accession of Constantine to the imperial diadem, the Roman empire was shaken to the verge of ruin; which may be symbolized by the earthquake before the trumpets sounded. The northern barbarians began to press toward the south, and the sound of warlike voices and thunder began to presage the approaching storm. In 395, at the death of Theodosius, by whose might the northern storm had been repressed, the invading hailstorm began in good earnest. The Goths, under Alaric, began their incursions at this time, and swept in terrific desolation over Greece, and filled Italy with awful destruction. Philostratus says, "The sword of the barbarians destroyed the greatest multitude of men : and, among other calamities, dry heats, with flashes of flame and whirlwinds of fire, occasioned intolerable terrors, and hail fell down of eight pounds weight." The princes of these countries were everywhere overthrown, and Rome was given up to fearful pillage. Scarcely was this part of the tempest spent, before the Germans, under Radagaisus, burst upon the banks of the Danube, and entered Italy. "The banks of the Rhine were crowned like those of the Tiber, with elegant houses and well-cultivated farms. This scene of peace and plenty was suddenly changed into a desert; the prospect of the smoking ruins could alone distinguish the solitude of nature from the desolations of man. Mentz, Worms, Spires, Rheims, Tournay, Arras, felt the German yoke. The consuming flames of war spread from the Rhine over the seventeen provinces of Gaul. That rich and extensive country as far as the ocean, Alps, and Apennines, was delivered to the barbarians, who drove before them, in a promiscuous crowd, the bishop, the senator, and the virgin, laden with the spoils of their houses and altars."—(*Gibbon's Rome.*)

Immediately after this, the Sueves, Vandals, and Alans swept like a tide of blood over Spain: and thus was the whole of Roman Europe destroyed by hail, fire, and blood, or by the Goths, Germans, and Vandals, under Alaric, Radagaisus, and Genseric.

SECTION II.

Second Trumpet—Invasion of Atilla and the Huns.

"And the second angel sounded, and as it were a great mountain was cast into the sea; and the third part of the sea became blood; and the third part of the creatures which were in the sea, and had life, died; and the third part of the ships were destroyed." A mountain, we have seen, represents a government, and a mountain in motion must represent a government in motion. The sea represents people in commotion, or disorganized, and most probably those upon the sea-shore, or who are a maritime power. The Roman empire, in the previous trumpet, had been called earth, because it was yet consolidated, but, the northern invasions having disorganized it, the sea became a proper symbol of it. Ships symbolize the merchandise they bring; the thing containing being put, by synecdoche, for the thing contained. A mountain being cast into the sea, and destroying one third of the ships, and turning one third to blood, will represent a kingdom moving violently into the disorganized empire, and desolating it with terrible war, and destroying its remaining wealth, and wasting the substance of the people in one continent of the Roman empire. This trumpet, therefore, predicted the invasion of the Huns under Atilla, as we shall see. The Huns from Asia, under Atilla, were a mighty government, and mustered 700,000 warriors in the field. All northern Europe had bowed before them; and the Ostrogoths, the Gepidæ, and Scandinavian kings, owned the supremacy of Atilla. This awful power now turned its course from the north, and hurled its burning legions into Europe. "The whole breadth of Europe, from the Euxine to the Adriatic, was at once invaded, occupied, and desolated, by the myriads whom Atilla led into the field. Words the most expressive of total extirpation and erasure, are applied to the calamities they inflicted on seventy cities of the Eastern empire." In 450, the Hun threatened the east and west, and "mankind awaited the decision with awful suspense."—(*Gibbon.*) He ravaged the east, and turned toward the west, and changed it all to blood, and boasted that "the grass never grew on the spot where his horse had trod." Thus, by this burning warlike mountain of fire, was the third of the Roman world changed to blood, and its merchandise destroyed. Atilla is commonly called "the scourge of God."

SECTION III.

Third Trumpet—Invasion of Genseric.

"And the third angel sounded; and there fell a star from heaven, burning as it were a lamp; and it fell upon the third part of the rivers and fountains of waters; and the name of the star is called wormwood; and many men died of the waters because they were made bitter." A star represents a king, and, by synecdoche, a kingdom; a burning star descending represents a kingdom coming upon the empire, bringing fire or war. A lamp, also, represents a government, as we find in I. Kings xi.—(*Sym. Dic.*)

A river symbolizes a variety of things, according as it is connected with the text, and, with the old prophets, represented a king or kingdom. As it is used here with reference to the Roman world, it must bear the relation to the empire of a leading power; and so, fountains must signify the heads of government. The rivers and fountains will therefore represent the controlling powers of the empire, or its political seats of power. It is evident that the rivers and fountains do not represent as large a portion of the empire as the earth or sea, but rather the head of the empire. The star like a burning lamp, is not by any means so extensive a destroyer as the hail-storm or burning mountain. A lamp, we remark, is a symbol of religious power, and descending in fire, must represent a politico-ecclesiastic fanaticism. This burning, or warlike power, in its destruction of the heads of empire, exactly coincides with Genseric and the Vandals, in their invasion and subjection of Rome and the powers of Italy. This power espoused the Arian religion, and was the only one of the barbarous nations which invaded the empire, that propagated its religion by fire and sword. In 455, this people, under Genseric, invaded Italy, and, for fourteen days, Rome, once mistress of the world, was given up to the licentiousness of the Arian Vandals and Moors. It was plundered of all its wealth that remained after the northern invasion. "By former ravages the power of Rome had been greatly weakened, but, by Genseric, it was so completely broken, that in a little time it was utterly subverted."— (*Gibbon.*) The waters were made bitter by the invasion, for the remains of the Roman Christian and pagan religions were almost entirely ruined.

For a full account of this invasion, see Gibbon's Roman History.

SECTION IV.

Fourth Trumpet—Fall of the Western Empire.

"And the fourth angel sounded; and the third part of the sun was smitten, and the third part of the moon, and the third part of the stars; so, as the third part of them was darkened, and the day shone not for a third part of it, and the night likewise." The sun, we have seen, represents the civil power; and the stars represent princes of provinces; and the moon represents the church.

FALL OF THE WESTERN EMPIRE.

The sun and moon of the Roman empire coincide with the iron and clay of the great image. A third part of these being smitten, shows that one third of the empire would be eclipsed. The day and night relate to the time of the duration of this eclipse of the sun by day, and the moon and stars by night. As a day of twenty-four hours represents a year, by analogy, a year represents a prophetic year, and two thirds of such a year will equal three hundred and twenty-five and one third solar years. At the end of this time the sun and moon, and stars, were to shine again, since they were only to be eclipsed for one third of a day, and one third of a night.

This vision plainly represents the overthrow of the seat of power of the empire in Europe under Romulus Augustus, by Odoacer. By this the Roman civil power, and the Roman church, and all their principal dignities and provinces, were subjugated, and placed under the feet of the northern invaders. This overthrow is commonly stated to have been in 476, but Gibbon says there is no certainty about this date, but that the event happened about this time. Now, on Christmas day of 799, or about 800, A. D., the Western empire was restored by Charlemagne, and the church, and princes, and provinces, were restored to splendor again. If, from this epoch, we subtract three hundred and twenty-five and a third years, we are carried back to the 25th of August, 474, A. D. This is certainly a very close coincidence, and is as conformable to history, as history is to truth.

Daniel described the broken state of the empire; and John, in these four trumpets, gives us the modes by which it was broken.

SECTION V.

Fifth Trumpet—First Woe, or Saracenic Invasion.

The predictions already given, related wholly to the European part of the empire; we now come to predictions of the breaking up of the Eastern empire, which stood longer than the Western. The breaking is by more permanent agencies than those which broke the Western, and by way of pre-eminent distinction, are called woes. Three of these eras of woes are announced; two of them apply to the east, and south of the empire, as originators of these woes; and the third begins at the fall of the empire church, and thence extends to the destruction of monarchy.

"Wo, wo, wo to the inhabiters of the earth, by reason of the other voices of the trumpet of the three angels, which are yet to sound."—Rev. viii. 13.

1. "And the fifth angel sounded, and I saw a star fall from heaven, unto the earth." A star is a symbol of some power; and its falling to the earth from heaven, denotes the descent of new calamities to the empire. Heaven, ordinarily denotes the church, or its place; but in the political world, it denotes the symbolic region where political clouds, and storms, and meteors form, and descend to the world.

2. "And to him was given the key of the bottomless pit." A key symbolizes power; as the "key of David." "The bottomless pit," is a prophetic symbol, and indicates some place in the world, which may properly be symbolized by the term used. It means a deep of innumerable desperate spirits, or barbarians.

3. "And he opened the bottomless pit." That is, the way of invasion was opened to barbarians.

4. "There arose a smoke out of the bottomless pit, as the smoke of a great furnace, and the sun and the air were darkened by reason of the smoke of the pit." Smoke symbolizes several things, but is used to represent the coming of war; it also represents false doctrine in motion. Isaiah foretold war by this symbol; as " out of the north there cometh a smoke."—(*Sym. Dic.*) The sun being darkened by the smoke, symbolizes that the civil power of the empire would be greatly disturbed by it. The air symbolizes the place of evil spirits, or an evil people generally, throughout the empire. A great and warlike error is, therefore, to be understood by the symbols, as threatening the empire generally, and the eastern empire particularly; as the sun, or civil power, was already observed in the west.

5. "And there came out of the smoke locusts upon the earth, and unto them was given power as the scorpions of the earth have power." Locusts symbolized hostile armies, among the prophets.—See Jer. xlvi.; Na. iii.; Deut. xxviii.; Ps. lxxviii.; Amos vii.; Ex. x.; Judges vi. and vii. Scorpions are wicked or impious enemies, Ezk. ii.; Eccl. xxvi.

6. "And it was commanded them that they should not hurt the grass of the earth, neither any green thing, but only those which have not the seal of God in their foreheads." The seal of God plainly represents true Christians, in opposition to the impious professors of Christianity in the empire.

7. "And to them it was given not to kill them, but that they should be tormented five months; and their torment was as the torment of a scorpion when he striketh a man. And in those days shall men seek death, and shall not find it; and shall desire to die, and death shall flee from them." This shows that the government

would not be overthrown, but that it would be terribly afflicted.

8. "And the shapes of the locusts were like unto horses prepared unto battle; and on their heads were, as it were, crowns like gold; and their faces were as the faces of men, and they had hair as the hair of women; and their teeth were as the teeth of lions. And they had breastplates as it were breastplates of iron; and the sound of their wings was as the sound of chariots, of many horses running to battle. And they had tails as the tails like unto scorpions, and there were stings in their tails; and their power was to hurt men five months. And they had a king over them, which is the angel of the bottomless pit, whose name in the Hebrew tongue is Abaddon, but in the Greek tongue hath his name Apollyon. One wo is past." This whole account is plainly doubled, as the mention of the five months twice clearly shows. The whole prophecy represents plainly the Saracenic conquests and empire. The locusts represent the militant Mohammedans, and the king symbolizes the civil authority under which they were organized. Newton and others have interpreted this trumpet so well, that their views need but little revision. The reader can see our improvements, by comparing our points of difference. These hosts sprung up from Mahomet, but, in his day, no attack was made upon the empire; but the smoke had ascended from him, and filled the empire with fearful forebodings. In 632, the invasion of the empire began; and the last attempt of the Saracens was made against Rome about A. D. 848. From the first invasion to the last, as near as can be estimated, was $215\frac{1}{2}$ years, and the five months during which this scourge was to continue, equal 215 years and 175 days.

SECTION VI.

Sixth Trumpet, and Second Woe—Turkish Invasion.

"Behold, there come two more woes hereafter. And the sixth angel sounded, and I heard a voice from the four horns of the golden altar which is before God, saying, to the sixth angel, Loose the four angels which are bound in the great river Euphrates." The Eastern empire had stood firm amid all the assaults of the Saracens, for their commission was to torment the empire, but not to overthrow it; but now comes up a power to annihilate it.

1. The four angels in the Euphrates find a full coincidence in the four sultanies of the Turks; the capitals of which were Bagdad, Damascus, Aleppo, and Iconium. In the year 1299, A. D., these were combined, under Othman, and began their conquest and destruction of the east. The sultanies were near, and on the Euphrates. Gibbon says, the first attack of this power on the eastern empire was " on the 27th July, 1299 ; " and that, from the conquest of Prusa we may date the true era of the Ottoman empire.

2. "And the four angels were prepared for an hour, and a day, and a month, and a year, to slay the third part of men." The third part of men means the third part of the empire; and as the west was already slain, or broken down, the eastern, or Asiatic, empire must be meant; and it was here the Turks prevailed, and do prevail at the present day. The period of this prevalence over Asia, or the eastern empire, was to be for $13_{1\frac{2}{6}}$ months, or for 561 years and 357 days.—(*See discovery*.) If we date this on the 27th July, 1299, we are brought down to the year 1861, and about the fourth of July, for the date is old style, or eleven days too much.

3. "And the number of the army of the horsemen were two hundred thousand, and I heard the number of them." The Turks were generally horsemen, and hence, their whole host or population is represented by that symbol. As to the great number of them, it may have had a literal accomplishment by the time the empire falls. They boasted that they produced cavalry by the million.

4. "And thus I saw the horses in the vision, and them that sat on them, having breastplates of fire and jacinth, (or hyacinth) and brimstone; and the heads of the horses were as the heads of lions; and out of their mouths issued fire and smoke and brimstone. By these three was the third part of men killed; by the fire and the smoke and the brimstone, which issued out of their mouths." Here is an evident allusion to the use of gunpowder and ordnance, which were first used extensively, by the Turks, in the subjection of the east and attacks upon the west.

5. "For their power is in their mouth and in their tails; for their tails were like unto serpents, and they had heads, and with them they do hurt." The mouth here represents civil and military authority, and their tails represent doctrine, or their church, as the tail of the dragon. The Turkish government was an absolute despotism, and exceedingly cruel, and their church was the Mohammedan. The horses' heads and tails are a collective representation of the whole Turkish system, civil, military, and ecclesiastical. They fully overturned the eastern empire and Africa, and were the heirs of the Saracens; so that they may be properly said to have destroyed the third part of the Roman empire.

6. "And the rest of the men that were not killed by these plagues." That is, those parts of the old empire in the west, which were not overturned by the Turks

"Yet repented not of the works of their hands, that they should not worship devils, and idols of gold and silver, and brass and stone, and of wood, which neither can see, nor hear, nor walk.' These symbols are put for the idolatry of the western church. The Mohammedans and Jews both charged upon the west, that, in the worship of saints they were idolaters. "Neither repented they of their murders."—The murder of true Christians. "Nor of their sorceries."—Their deceptious arts over the people. "Nor of their fornication."—Monachism was the universal and fruitful source of this sainted crime in Europe. "Nor of their thefts."—They "stole the livery of heaven to serve the devil in," and swindled the people out of their money, under pretense of giving them salvation in exchange.

7. "The second woe is past." That is, it will be past at the fall of Turkey, and not before. It certainly will not close till after the rise of the witnesses, and the fall of one of the principal or tenth parts of Europe, at the coming insurrection; because the end of the woe is placed in the text as occurring there.—Rev. xi. 14. The fall of Turkey is to be simultaneous with this rising of the witnesses. We have placed it in 1861, but, unless we are greatly mistaken, the witnesses will rise much sooner. But we can not be far in error. We have been less particular than usual in explaining these trumpets, because they have, for the most part, been properly explained by Newton, Faber, and others.

SECTION VII.

Seventh Trumpet—Rise of the United States and Fall of Monarchy.

1. "And the seventh angel sounded." This period of prophecy had already been announced by the great angel who came down with the little book. He said "in the days of the voice of the seventh angel, when he shall *begin* to sound, the mystery of God should be finished, as he declared to his servants the prophets." The mystery referred to, must be the development of the nationality of God's Israel; for this is the great mystery that has been concealed from Christians and the world. The disciples had asked Christ, "if he would at that time restore the kingdom to Israel," and he had replied, that it was not for them to know the times and seasons which the Father hath put in his own power." Here, the restoration to nationality is the object and answer of the question proposed, and hence the mystery was to be solved at the *beginning* of the seventh trumpet period.

2. "And the seventh angel sounded, and there were great voices in heaven, saying, The kingdoms of this world are become the kingdoms of our Lord, and of his Christ; and he shall reign forever and ever." As we have already seen, in the vision of the woman and her man child, that the kingdom of God and Christ had come, the beginning of the seventh trumpet must coincide with it. But as the kingdoms that came after the three and a half times were composed of twelve stars, or the confederacy of God's Israel, so must these kingdoms be twelve; and as the former did not fill the world at their origin, but divided it with the dragon, so must these new kingdoms This truth is further decisively settled, by the facts tha

the seventh trumpet period was to be a long one, and, during its progress, the seven vials of wrath were to be poured out on the earth, and the dragon was not to be chained till its close; and these kingdoms are announced as occurring at its beginning, and the great angel said, that at this beginning, the *mystery* should be finished, and not at its *close*. Again; the very text itself is proof of our position, for in the original, the words are *hai basileiai tou kosmou tou kuoiou humon;* these, translated literally, signify the kingdoms of the world of our Lord. The word kosmou, translated world, has thirty-five definitions, and one of them is "world," and another is "the people or territory of Israel."—(*Greek Lexicon*.) As the prophecy is symbolic, the term world can not be forced into a literal signification, but must coincide with the context and the nature of things among which it appears, and must harmonize with them. And as it can not, when taken in a literal sense, at all harmonize with succeeding prophecies, it must have the symbolic sense we give it. Again; if it were literally true, then it would be the Millennium or final kingdom, which it certainly is not, as the succeeding revolutions among the nations show. That it is the vestibule of the Millennium, we freely admit.

3. "And the four and twenty elders, which sat before God on their seats, fell upon their faces, and worshiped God, saying, We give thee thanks, O Lord God Almighty, because thou hast taken to thee thy great power, and hast reigned." Here the dual symbols of Israel give God glory for the great restoration, and the establishing of a nationality on the earth, with himself and Christ as head.

4. "And the nations were angry." That is, they were greatly disturbed at the rise of the new order of things,

and provoked to great hostility, and prepared for revolution. "And thy wrath is come:" that is, the threatened judgment of God upon the destroyers of his people. "And the time of the dead, that they should be judged:" that is, the time for pouring judgments on account of the souls slain and under the altar, as seen in the fifth seal. "And that thou shouldest give reward unto thy servants the prophets:" a prophet is the common scriptural appellation of a teacher of God's truth. The reward may be the elevation of this class in society. "And the saints:" that is, Christians generally. "And to them that fear thy name, small and great:" that is, to the observers of God's practical laws, by mankind generally; it is a comprehensive and emphatic repetition of the reward to all true Christians, of every name. "And shouldest destroy them which destroy the earth:" that is, the whole Roman power, the church and state, or all the iron and clay.

The affirmation of these elders, after the coming of the nationality to Israel, is a full prophetic programme of the whole of the seventh trumpet period. We can not well imply from it a literal resurrection and spiritual judgment day and second advent, for the symbolic terms are not strong enough to give grounds for such opinion; besides, the prophecy is generally political, rather than spiritual.

5. "And the temple of God was opened in heaven, and there was seen in his temple the ark of his testament; and there were lightnings, and voices, and thunderings, and an earthquake, and great hail." This is immediately introductory to the vials of wrath and the angels from Mount Zion, and is prophetic of their introduction. The temple represents the nationality of Israel, as we have shown; and the ark must represent

the promises that it should be restored. The lightnings, thunderings, and voices, symbolize the preparation of the political heavens for the changes about to transpire; and the earthquake announces the first great shock that overturns the scepter of monarchy, and opens the way for its final doom. The seventh trumpet, being the final period of the sufferings of the church, it is twice predicted, and each panorama of the era will claim our attention.

Paragraph I.

FIRST PANORAMA OF THE SEVENTH TRUMPET.

CLAUSE I.

First View. United States.—"And I looked, and lo, a lamb stood on mount Zion, and with him a hundred forty and four thousand, having their Father's name written in their foreheads."—Rev. xiv. "And they sung, as it were, a new song before the throne, and before the four beasts, and the elders. And no man could learn that song, but the hundred and forty and four thousand, which were redeemed from the earth." "These were redeemed from among men, being the first fruits unto God and the Lamb." This is so poetic, that we dislike to translate it into matter of fact on earth. But it was a prophecy of things on earth, for Christ said so to John. The order of its realization is placed before the conversion of the world; for the angel, with the gospel to convert all the world, goes out after it was fulfilled. As it came at the sound of the seventh trumpet, and before the evangelization of all the world, it coincides with the rise of the kingdom of Christ, at the end of the 1260 days of the witnesses, and the three and a half times of the woman with twelve stars; and must coincide, therefore, with the United States.

1. *The Lamb.*—This, as we have seen, represents Christ and his government. A lamb, wounded and restored, shows that the nationality had been dead, but, like Jesus, had revived again.

2. *The Company of the Lamb.*—As the lamb symbolizes the rise of a great Christian nationality, with Christ as its only head, the company properly represents the church of Christ. Twelve thousand being from every tribe, makes one hundred and forty-four thousand, which indicates Israel restored.

3. *Mount Zion.*—This is the city of David, and was called Ariel, or the double city. So that this new kingdom, now come, is twice doubly represented; once by the lamb and his company, and again by the double city. Mount Zion may also represent the religion upon which the new government stood, and in that case the lamb coincides with the temple; his company with the worshipers in the court of Israel, or court of the altar; and Mount Zion will coincide with the altar which symbolizes religion.

4. *The New Song.*—This symbolizes the different condition of Christians in the free country of Christ, from that elsewhere. The song of the Christians in America, at our nation's birth, was, indeed, a new song. Never, since Miriam tuned the timbrel of redemption, and led the host, singing the song of Moses, had such a scene been witnessed, as that when our fathers entered the temple of God, and exulted over the dragon, and sung the new song of honor to the Lamb. Through seas of blood the church had sailed; moldering arches of ages had darkened it with woe; flanked by dungeons; obstructed by fires of martyrdom; hunted in the wilderness; chased by the wolves of hell; driven to ocean; pursued by the dragon and his angels, it conquered; it

was free; it was redeemed; it stood on Mount Zion, and shouted salvation to God!

The first fruits means the first people in the realizing age that had chosen God as their only king. The first fruits were those old pious men from Plymouth rock to Georgia's glades, who cast the dragon from the church, and spurned a human head from the altar of their God. None upon earth can sing the song we sing, but those who deny prelates and kings the headship of the church.

5. *One Hundred and Forty-four Thousand.*—From close calculation, we find, there were just about this number of adult professed Christians in our country at its organization.

CLAUSE II.

Second View. The Church and State Free.—The next vision in the panorama is one of great glory. "And I saw another angel fly in the midst of heaven, having the everlasting gospel to preach unto them that dwell on the earth, and to every nation, and kindred, and tongue, and people, saying, with a loud voice, Fear God and give glory to him, for the hour of his judgment is come, and worship him that made heaven and earth, and the sea, and the fountains of waters." This preaching of the gospel is symbolic, for it had been preached from the days of the Christ. The angel had, however, been bound, and in the wilderness; and the holy city had been trodden under foot for ages; and it was not till the rise of our country that the gospel was preached with freedom. The flying of the angel in the heavens, symbolizes that preaching and the church were now free, and would continue so. This preaching symbolizes all gospel agencies, such as the press and pulpit, and missionary and bible operations. As the angel went through the heavens or church generally, this going forth to all nations represents the universal agency of the awakened church to evangelize the world. It is also remarkable, that just as soon as the church has been ready to send the gospel abroad, the old barriers have been broken down, and the door to its preaching has been opened. But this angel, at this period, coincides with the fiery stream from the throne of the ancient of days, and must represent a political gospel also. This view is confirmed by the declaration of the angel, that the hour of God's judgment was come. This is no other than the political judgment of the ancient of days, that was to destroy the Roman monarchy. It is also confirmed by the destruction of Babylon, which followed, and which was the result of the doctrines of this angel.

CLAUSE III.

Third View. Fall of the Western, or Latin Church. "And there followed another angel, saying, Babylon is fallen, that great city, because she made all nations drink of the wine of the wrath of her fornication." Babylon coincides with the beast with a wounded head, and with the harlot on the beast from the pit, and is the imperial church of Italy and Europe. This will be overthrown before Europe and England, for such is the chronological order in which its destruction is placed. It is the third great work in this seventh era, or time of the end.

CLAUSE IV.

Fourth View. Threat Against Great Britain.— "And the third angel followed them, saying with a loud voice, If any man worship the beast and his image, and receive his mark in his forehead, or in his hand, the same shall drink of the wine of the wrath of God, which is poured out without mixture into the cup of his indignation. * * And they have no rest, day nor night, who worship the beast and his image, and whosoever receiveth the mark of his name." As these particulars designate the British empire, and this threat is first addressed to those who honor the Roman church, and those who sustain the English church, or to Romish Ireland and Puseyite England, Scotland comes in for its share, as having in its imperial church the "mark of his name." As this threat follows the doom of Romish Europe, it must allude to the new and threatening attitude affairs will then assume, with regard to the church question in England and Ireland, and, finally, in Scotland. The utter destruction of these churches will follow, as is indicated by the spiritual torments they will receive in the world to come, which symbolize annihilation forever. "Here is the patience of the saints;" that is, the end of their waiting. "Blessed are the dead who die in the Lord from henceforth:" this passage is peculiarly appropriate to this period, or it would not have been asserted here. Why it should be so, let events determine. Doubtless it signifies that the laborer's works will never be interfered with, but will prosper in accumulating usefulness, without any interruption, to the end of time.

CLAUSE V.

Fifth View. Overthrow of Europe by America.—"And I looked and behold a white cloud, and upon the cloud one sat like unto the Son of man, having on his head a golden crown, and in his hand a sharp sickle." This symbolizes the United States. A cloud represents a body of power and people; as "a great cloud of witnesses." Being white, it denotes a Christian people; and, being raised from the earth, shows its superiority over all opposition. A man symbolizes a body of government resting on Christianity; the diadem of gold on his head, shows his imperial or supreme power over the nations; the gold of his crown shows that his government is a unity and precious; his sickle shows his warlike power, and preparation for the harvest of war. The cloud, and the man upon it, coincide with the dual form of Israel restored; and, being in the image of the Son of man, confirms its application to the Israel of Christ. As he was to reap the earth, or Roman Europe, he coincides with the stone from the mountain; the ancient on his throne; the man child from the woman; and the man with many crowns, on the white horse; and, as these coincide with the United States, so must he also.

"And another angel came out from the temple, crying with a loud voice, to him that sat on the cloud, Thrust in thy sickle and reap, for the time is come for thee to reap, for the harvest of the earth is ripe." The angel from the temple is an agency from the civil government, calling upon the United States to strike for the world's redemption from monarchy. The time being come, shows that the war would not have been seasonable at an earlier period, but that now forbearance was no virtue.

"And he that sat on the cloud thrust in his sickle on the earth, and the earth was reaped." This single thrust of the sickle coincides with the single stroke of the stone upon the feet of the image, and is the battle of the great day. How swift the work of overthrow will be! how dreadful the fray when the thrones shall be cast down by our republic!

CLAUSE VI.

Sixth View. Overthrow of Britain.—"And another angel came out of the temple which is in heaven, he also having a sharp sickle." As the temple represents the civil department of Christ's Israel, this other angel with a sickle must represent some warlike Christian power, about to attack England. This angel must be identified with the man on the white cloud, since, in the taking of the beast, the false prophet is taken with him, by the man on the white horse, who coincides with the man on the cloud. Attempts may be made by the liberals of England to change their monarchy, and we shall be involved. The Irish, or Scotch, it would seem, then, may coincide with this angel primarily, or the liberal party in England.

2. "And another angel came out from the altar, which had power over fire." That is, a war-producing agency was to be manifested from the religion of the country. "And cried with a loud cry to him that had the sharp sickle, saying, Thrust in thy sharp sickle, and gather the clusters of the vine of the earth; for her grapes are fully ripe." This was a call from religion, or a Christian people, to the civil power of Christianity, to enlist in war, or in a revolution.

3. "The vine of the earth," must be that empire which grew up from the Roman empire, and coincides with the two-horned beast from the earth, or the British empire. This application must be correct, for the reaping of the earth and the vine, coincides exactly with the taking of the beast and false prophet. A vine represents a church, and its clusters represent the government which grows up out of it. The gathering of the clusters will, therefore, represent the overthrow of the British monarchy. Its grapes will soon be fully ready to be trodden out.

4. "And the angel thrust in his sickle into the earth, and gathered the vine of the earth, and cast it into the great wine-press of the wrath of God." This reaping

implies the declaration of war, and grappling with the mighty power of Britain. The wine-press of the wrath of God, symbolizes the most terrific destruction by war.

5. "And the wine-press was trodden without the city." This represents that the great war would not be on the continent of Europe, but outside of it. The term city is, throughout Revelation, used to designate Roman Europe, in one of its forms, either the church or state; hence, the war was not to be in its limits. Perhaps it will be on the island of England.

6. "And the blood came out of the wine-press, even unto the horse-bridles, by the space of a thousand six hundred furlongs." This represents the greatest slaughter spoken of in the history of the world. The extent of the country over which it spreads, or the real battle-field, is stated to be 1600 furlongs, or 200 miles. This will coincide with the length of England, but, if a furlong be taken for a mile, it will coincide with the United States, as the battle-field. These two great battles coincide with Joshua's two, in the conquest of Canaan; in the first, he met the five powers of Canaan, and afterward the remnant, in confederacy; and so the United States will meet five great powers of Europe, and then the rest in confederacy, and slay them all.

CLAUSE VII.

Seventh View. The Millennium.—One of the seven angels, at the pouring of the last vial, gave John a full description of Roman Europe, church and state, and also of the powers that were to destroy them; and gives two descriptions of the opening of the Millennium; one by a view of the chaining of the dragon, and the other by the symbol of the marriage supper of the Lamb. Now, one of these two views appropriately belongs to each panoramic history of the seventh trumpet period, to complete the harmony; and the marriage supper, appropriately, belongs to the panorama we are now viewing. It is recorded in the nineteenth chapter, beginning with the sixth verse.

1. "And I heard as it were, the voice of a great multitude, and as the voice of many waters, and as the voice of mighty thunderings, saying, Alleluia, for the Lord God Omnipotent reigneth. Let us be glad and rejoice, and give honor to him, for the marriage of the Lamb is come, and his wife hath made herself ready." This represents the end of the time of the end. Monarchy in Europe was now overthrown; Babylon was in ashes; the nations were free, and a new order of things appears; and, at the dawning glory, the millions of the liberated fill the world with songs of thanksgiving to God; the battle was over, the victory gained, and the saints possessed of the kingdom, and the Christians ruled the world, and each man was now himself a king and priest to God, and the Christians " reigned on the earth." This period is the Millennial one, because it can be nothing else. The lamb symbolizes, as we have seen, the civil government of Christianity, with Christ as its only head. The lamb's wife, most appropriately symbolizes the true universal Christian church, as all will allow. As the harlot and beast, or imperial church and state, were removed, a new church and state necessarily and naturally succeed in their room; the former had lived together incestuously, but the new relationship of lawful union is represented by marriage. The union of the lamb and the bride represents, therefore, this new government, in which the Christian church and state fill their own sphere without unholy interference. The bride making herself ready, represents that the church

had purified itself from all Roman idolatry, and that she taught and received the gospel in truth.

2. "And to her was granted that she should be arrayed in fine linen, clean and white, for the fine linen is the righteousness of saints." This shows that the bride represented the saints or Christians. The righteousness of the saints, represented by the fine linen, coincides with the freedom from the scarlet dress of Rome and all her idolatry.

3. "And he saith unto me, write Blessed are they which are called unto the marriage supper of the Lamb." That is, happy are they who then shall live and participate in the new order of affairs in the world.

> "And who shall see that glorious day,
> When throned on Zion's brow,
> The Lord shall take the vail away,
> Which blinds the nation's now."

So ends this panoramic history of the revolutionary period, called the seventh trumpet, or time of the end. The era began with 144,000 worshipers, but ends with countless millions. This vision of the period has given a full view of its spiritual matters; and we now turn to the other panorama in which political visions predominate.

Paragraph II.
SECOND PANORAMA.

The Seven Vial Periods.—These prophecies are announced as beginning at the rise of the United States, as did the other panorama.

CLAUSE I.

First View. United States.—1. "And I saw another sign, great and marvelous. Seven angels having the seven last plagues; for in them is filled up the wrath of

God." That is, all the curses of God upon his political foes, were to be poured upon them during the seventh trumpet era.

2. "And I saw, as it were, a sea of glass mingled with fire; and them that had gotten the victory over the beast, and over his image, and over his mark, and over the number of his name, stand on the sea of glass, having the harps of God." As the two panoramas of the seventh trumpet coincide upon the same epochs, the Lamb and his company on Mt. Zion, must coincide with these victors upon the sea of glass and fire. A sea represents a body of people, or a particular sea represents a particular nation. Jeremiah compares the Medo-Persian power to a sea. Glass denotes purity and consistency, and fire denotes either the word of God or vengeance. As the Lamb and his company, therefore, coincide with the Israel of Christ restored, so does this dual or trinal nationality, composed of a state of Christian churches and the true religion.

We have already shown that the beast, the mark, and his image, taken together, symbolized the trinal form of Great Britain; and these victors were, therefore, those who had conquered Britain. Thus, again, the coincidence of these victory symbols with our country is remarkably accurate. From the revolutionary war, therefore, we shall look for the fulfillment of the vial's curses which were to be of a political character.

3. "After that, I looked and behold the temple of the tabernacle of the testimony in heaven was opened, and the seven angels came out of the temple, having the seven plagues." As the temple represented the civil power of Christ's Israel, these vials proceeding from it must be political curses, and as the tabernacle of the testimony was opened, we see the fact disclosed, that

God had not forgotten his promise of old, to recompense judgment upon the heathen for their treatment of his people, but was now going to be as good as his word. After these angels came out of the civil department, one of the four beasts gave them seven vials of the wrath of God: that is, these agencies were put into operation by the civil government of Christ's Israel, and which is symbolized by all or one of the beasts.

The temple being filled with smoke, so that none could enter till the plagues were fulfilled, shows, that after the rise of the United States, no other people could establish a Christian republic, until the end of the seventh trumpet era.

First Vial. Curse on Britain.—"I heard a great voice out of the temple, saying to the seven angels, Go your ways, and pour out the vials of the wrath of God upon the earth." This expresses that the curses should proceed from civil considerations.

"And the first went and poured out his vial upon the earth; and there fell a noisome and grievous sore upon the men which had the mark of the beast, and upon them which worshiped his image." That is, this vial was poured out upon the British nation, which was represented by the image and mark of the beast. A sore symbolizes a great affliction, and one of long continuance; and the grievous sore is a national calamity of great and continuous extent; and the sore of Great Britain was the loss of her most glorious jewels, the thirteen immortal stars that will forever adorn the temple of the free. Never did a nation suffer such a grievous sore and still survive, without prodigious feeling on account of the loss.

Second Vial. Reign of Terror in France.—"And the second angel poured his vial upon the sea, and it became as the blood of a dead man; and every living soul died in the sea." The sea, generally, represents a body of people in a state of fusion or agitation. The changing of the sea to blood, shows terrible devastation and bloodshed in the community called the sea. The death of living creatures symbolizes not mere individuals, but minor supports, or orders of state; such as nobles, dukes, counts, earls, etc. This vial finds a coincidence in the reign of terror in France, which succeeded the British losses, and which also succeeded the revolution of 1789. During this whole period the whole of France became a scene of slaughter, and all vestiges of the former government perished. Who is not familiar with this dreadful era of blood?

Third Vial. German and Mountain Countries.—"And the third angel poured out his vial upon the rivers and fountains of waters, and they became blood. And I heard the angel of the waters say, Thou art righteous, O Lord, which art, and wast, and shall be, because thou hast judged thus. For they have shed the blood of saints and prophets, and thou hast given them blood to drink, for they are worthy. And I heard another out of the altar say, Even so, Lord God Almighty; true and righteous are thy judgments." The rivers and fountains, we have before shown, were the heads of empire in Europe. Now, as the last head of the dragon in Europe was the German and Spanish empire, we look to this for its remaining strength, as coinciding with the rivers and fountains of waters. Now, this vial coincides with the terrific desolation carried into the Germanic body and Spain, by the French. The German empire was shaken to its center by war, and was compelled to sue the French for its very existence. Savoy, the great destroyer of the Waldenses, was wrested from it; the

United Provinces, and the Helvetic Confederacy, and Spain, were filled with blood by the French. These regions, and others not mentioned, were all great murderers of Christians; and God, through France, gave them blood to drink. These countries were, literally, countries of rivers and fountains; and, figuratively, were fountains of people, and heads of government.

Fourth Vial. French Empire.—"And the fourth angel poured out his vial upon the sun; and power was given unto him to scorch men with heat. And men were scorched with great heat, and blasphemed the name of God, which hath power over these plagues; and they repented not, to give him glory." The sun is the civil power of greatest magnitude in a firmament of states, and, as these vials were to be poured out upon the state system of Europe, the principal state in Europe, at the time of the vial, must be meant; and this could be no other than France, when it was changed to an empire in 1804. The scorching rays of this sun were felt by France itself, by Holland, Switzerland, Italy, Spain, and the west of Germany, and, indeed, by all Europe.

Fifth Vial. Russia Invaded.—"And the fifth angel poured out his vial upon the seat of the beast; and his kingdom was full of darkness; and they gnawed their tongues for pain." As there were two beasts, the question is difficult to decide which one is referred to; we think, however, that it was Russia, or the beast from the pit, from the close coincidence in fulfillment, and from the fact that the forty-two months were expired. The seat of a beast is his empire; and the filling of his seat with darkness, is the filling his empire with great affliction; darkness, with the old prophets, symbolized war and ruin. The French invasion of Russia is one of the most famous in history, and filled it with darkness: and the people literally gnawed their tongues for pain, in a wide spread degree.

Sixth Vial. Battle of Waterloo.—1. "And the sixth angel poured out his vial upon the great river Euphrates, and the water thereof was dried up, that the way of the kings of the east might be prepared." 1. A flowing river is a nation in motion. Now, as the river Euphrates was the ancient river of Babylon, so this nation must bear a similar relation to the great Babylon, or Europe. At this era, the French was the great moving nation of Europe, and the cause of all its curses; and, to check their career, would be to dry up the great river Euphrates. This drying up of the Euphrates, coincides with the battle of Waterloo, by which the tide of war, in Europe, was checked, and was followed by a comparative peace, of thirty or more years. 2. This cessation of war was to allow the kings of the east to be prepared for the final battle of the world. Now, by this cessation of the French empire, the kingdoms of eastern Europe have grown into great power; but especially has Russia gathered the eastern kingdoms under its wings, and will gather more and more until the war.

2. "And I saw three unclean spirits, like frogs, come out of the mouth of the beast, and out of the mouth of the dragon, and out of the mouth of the false prophet." A spirit, we have seen, symbolizes a doctrine, and an unclean spirit symbolizes an un-Christian doctrine. A frog has no scriptural exposition among the prophets, except that of a destroyer.—Psa. lxxviii. The ancients considered them inhabitants of the Stygian lake. The dragon represents the civil or monarchical power in Europe; the beast from the pit coincides with Russia; and the false prophet coincides with the fifth head of the dragon, or England. Now, the year following the battle

of Waterloo, the sovereigns of Europe agreed to the doctrines of the holy alliance. "The professed object of this triple alliance was to preserve the peace of Europe on the principles which God, in his revelation, has pointed out, as the source of tranquillity and prosperity But the parties understood by these principles the maintenance of despotic power, and made their engagement a pretext for resisting the efforts made subsequently by several nations, to establish constitutional freedom."— (*Taylor's Hist.*) The sovereigns of Russia, Prussia, and Austria, signed, at Paris, the league called the holy alliance. They declared in this their determination to make Christianity the basis of their actions, domestic and foreign. They asserted their divine right to govern "*three branches* of one and the same Christian nation." They invited England to become a party; the regent declined his signature, but expressed his APPROVAL.

Legitimacy, church supremacy, and the divine rights of kings, were the three horrid doctrines really taught by Britain, Russia, and European monarchy, after the war with France. England spent $1,000,000,000 to establish these three principles in the war with France; and yet England talks of being the bulwark of freedom, while she has been to the world the bulwark of hell; she holds these doctrines now in full, and will fight to uphold the most degraded despotism on earth.

3. "For they are the spirits of devils, working miracles, which go forth unto the kings of the earth, and of the whole world, to gather them to the battle of that great day of God Almighty." These doctrines have been proclaimed to monarchs as the true basis of their thrones, and they are now ready to sustain them by the sword against the rights of men; and, undoubtedly, will ultimate in a confederacy of monarchs in Europe, for a

common cause and a common danger will drive them together. That battle of the great day is the one predicted at the beginning of time, and is now near at hand.

4. "Behold, I come as a thief. Blessed is he that keepeth his garments, lest he walk naked, and they see his shame." This, doubtless, is a figure of speech, referring to the coming of a people of Christ, that should break this grand coalition to atoms. The United States, as a legitimate child of God, has never been recognized by the Europeans; it is stealing upon them as a thief. The passage can not refer to the second advent literally.

5. "And *he* gathered them into a place, called, in the Hebrew tongue, Armageddon." The three spirits are here represented as one power, which shows a consolidation of the beast, dragon, and prophet. Armageddon, or plain of Esdrelon, or valley of Jezreel, was the greatest plain in the Holy Land, and where many great battles were fought. As the term is here used metaphorically, it must represent a great place in the land of Christ's Israel, which coincides with the literal term. Now, as the European power was to perish between the seas, this battle-field seems to coincide with the valley of the Mississippi. This battle, it is plain, was not fought in this vial era, but the preparations, and calculations, and initiatory preliminaries, had been taken, that were soon to result in it; and that, too, rather unexpectedly.

Seventh Vial. Overthrow of the Western Church. The Great Battles. Third War.—This era will close the warfare of the world, and work its great release. We are now within its limits, and shall soon hear the clang of Michael's trumpet, that shall fill the earth with trouble, such as was never dreamed of here below. Great God! prepare us against the deadly tide of woe that must roll over us soon, and deluge the globe with blood.

1. "And the seventh angel poured his vial into the air." The air symbolizes the whole political firmament of Rome, or the whole region of Satan's political rule in the old empire in Europe; hitherto, the disturbances had been rather local, but now they were to be general.

2. "And there came a great voice out of the temple of heaven, from the throne, saying, It is done;" that is, the last curse of God on men has begun, and will soon close the drama of the strife for freedom.

3. "And there were voices, and thunders, and lightnings." These are the symbols of a coming political storm.

4. "And there was a great earthquake, such as was not since men were upon earth; so mighty an earthquake, and so great; and the great city was divided into three parts;" or, more literally, (according to Griesbach,) "was affected in three parts;" that is, three great parts were prominently affected by the shock. Now, if we look to the political earthquake in Europe, in 1848, we find it the greatest period of insurrection ever known upon earth; and, also, that Europe, or the great city, was mostly affected in three great parts, the German empire, France, and Italy, by these insurrections. The coincidence is remarkably accurate.

5. "And the cities of the nations fell." It is also remarkable that, in 1848, the cities were universally overthrown; and the cities, generally, took the lead in the great uprising and overthrowing. As the shock of a natural earthquake soon passes away, so this political one ceased, and only its traces of destruction are visible, for the natural order of things has been resumed.

6. "And great Babylon came into remembrance before God, to give unto her the cup of the wine of the fierceness of his wrath." By comparing this last vial

period of this panorama with the events of the first panorama, we shall see that the gospel angel filled an era from the rise of our country to the fall of Babylon; and, by consequence, the angels and events which follow him, all coincide with the era of the seventh vial, beginning with the fall of Babylon. Babylon is the state church in Europe, of which the papal power is the head. This whole power is now to be overthrown with terrible slaughter. "And every island fled away, and the mountains were not found;" that is, all the state church institutions are to be overturned; not a parish, nor a bishoprick is to remain; all of its glory is to perish.

7. "And there fell upon men a great hail out of heaven;" that is, a terrible destruction by war fell upon the minions of Babylon, the officers and establishments of the church. "Every stone about the weight of a talent." Nothing can intimate a speedier and more complete overthrow than this. Hail like this, falling thick as rain-drops, would, in ten minutes, demolish all creation. "And men blasphemed God, because of the plague of the hail; for the plague was exceeding great." The term men symbolizes a collective body; and here it represents the people of Babylon who were not involved in the immediate destruction. At this annunciation the prophet receives a full description of the two great powers which are to be overthrown, and also of their destroyers.

To these we shall now turn. We must, however, enumerate the great occurrences belonging especially to this vial. It begins with the earthquake, or insurrections of 1848, and then discloses the fall of Babylon, or the western state church; and then the conquest of Europe and Britain by the United States. The fall of Babylon, in the first panorama, coincides with its fall here; the troubles of England also coincide with the fall of Babylon; the reaping of the earth, by the man on the cloud; and the reaping of the vine, by the angel from the temple, coincide with the taking of the beast and false prophet, by the man on the white horse. Keep these points in view. We now turn to the description of the great subjects of destruction, and their destroyers; they are as follows: Babylon and its destroyers; the ten kingdoms and Russia; the beast; and the man on the white horse.

CLAUSE II.

Second View. Babylon and the Beast, or the State Church, and Russia and Europe.—"And there came unto me one of the seven angels which had the seven vials, and talked with me, saying unto me, Come hither, I will show unto thee the judgment of the great whore which sitteth upon many waters." This declares that he will show the destruction in a clear light. "With whom the kings of the earth have committed fornication, and the inhabitants of the earth have been made drunk with the wine of her fornication. So he carried me away into the wilderness; and I saw a woman sit upon a scarlet-colored beast, full of names of blasphemy, having seven heads, and ten horns, &c., &c. And upon her forehead was a name written: *Mystery, Babylon the Great, the Mother of Harlots, and Abominations of the Earth.* And I saw the woman drunken with the blood of the martyrs of Jesus." After this description, an interpretation, or another view is given of four particulars. "I will tell thee the mystery of the woman, and of the beast that carrieth her, which hath seven heads and ten horns."

1. *The beast.*—"The beast thou sawest was, and is not." A beast, we know, represents an empire; and

the seven-headed beast with a wounded head, and the seven-headed dragon coincide, in their great features, with this beast from the pit; but as the seven-headed beast, with the wounded head, was the Roman universal church, it here coincides with the harlot Babylon; and this beast from the pit must coincide with the dragon; and, therefore, it represents the Romish empire. This empire, says the text, " was and is not." The symbol is constructed so as to take in the whole history of the empire, from the day the harlot was seated upon it, or the church was united to it: it " was and is not," shows that the empire, as originally formed, had ceased to exist at this time. The time of the seeing of this vision was in the seventh trumpet period, and in the last vial period of it; for so the text states, and, of course, the condition of the Roman empire in that period, is the one in which the apostle stood, looking backward to the past, and forward to the future.

"And shall ascend out of the bottomless pit." This we have seen coincides with Asia, or barbarism. The empire of Rome is, therefore, to arise again, and the origin of this last formation is to be in Asia, or, perhaps more properly, among endless swarms of barbarians. With this description, Russia exactly coincides. " It began in 1462, with Ivan, of the family of Ruric; and up to this time, the different parts of those vast regions had been ruled by many petty chiefs."—(*Taylor*.)

"And go into perdition." That is, the empire shall be reformed in its original dimensions, and then be destroyed. " And they that dwell on the earth shall wonder," (whose names were not written in the book of life from the fall of the world). That is, all, but true Christians, shall wonder at the domination of Russia over Europe.

"When they behold the beast that was and is not and yet is." That is, when they shall see the empire, now broken but still existing, arising to its original extent. From this it is clear that the empire, in its broken condition, is still regarded as the Roman empire; this will be further evident from what follows.

"And here is the mind which hath wisdom. The seven heads are seven mountains on which the woman sitteth." A mountain always signifies a superior and great empire or kingdom : the woman, therefore, or Roman church, was to rest upon seven great governments. To make these mountains coincide with the seven *little* hills of the city of Rome, is the lowest depth of absurdity.

"And there are seven kings." This is but a repetition, or double declaration, of the fact that the Roman church would rest upon seven great heads of empire. These seven mountains, and seven kings, coincide with the seven heads, for the text says so ; and, as the heads represented the great successive forms in which the empire would exist, the mountains and seven kings do the same.

"Five are fallen, and one is, and the other is not yet come." This at once shows that these heads, or governments, were to succeed each other chronologically. Five were fallen; that is, had ceased to be " lords of the ascendent." The sixth was dominant at the time of this vision, and must have been the British empire. Another supreme autocracy was to arise before the destruction of Babylon. "And when he cometh he must continue a short space." The last head will continue as an empire but a very little time.

"And the beast that was and is not, even he is the eighth, and is of the seven." That is, the old empire which was broken, and is now broken, will be united

CHURCH AND STATE UNION.

is one head or government, which will constitute the eighth form in which the empire shall appear. As it was to be of the seven, and yet was the eighth, and as the eighth was to be as the first empire in magnitude and power, it follows that it thus would be the seventh empire in one sense, and the eighth in another. Now, the Roman empire before it was divided was represented by a beast with a single head; but as it was to be existent in seven other forms, the seventh of these divisions would be the eighth, counting in the original head or universal consolidated empire. And as the last head of the seven was to coincide with the first beast, (verse 8,) which is not reckoned among the divided seven heads, it follows that the seventh autocracy of the heads would really be the eighth as well as the seventh. Each head of the beast represents, for the time being, the whole empire, but the seventh head alone coincides with the original empire. The original empire existed in three continents, and the last, or seventh head, was also to extend to three. The first head was the empire during church and state union, and before the breaking of the empire. The vision only goes back to the union of church and state, for it does not exhibit anything anterior to the time when the harlot Babylon sat upon the beast.

The whole meaning of the beast, therefore, amounts to this: the Roman empire existed as a unit in three continents, and the church was then united to it; after this it was broken up, and was represented by seven successive empires, which were not as great as the original one; but the seventh after its rise, was to extend to three continents, as did ancient Rome. These heads were also to exist in Europe, but the last was to be of Asiatic or barbarous origin. Hence, the terms, "was and is not and yet is," represent the original Roman empire, and its broken state, in which the original monarchy was represented by lesser heads or empires, in the old territory of Rome. The seven we have seen were, the Western empire, Charlemagne's empire, the papal empire, the empire of Charles V., the British empire, the French empire, and the Russian from Asia, and, counting the original empire, we have eight heads upon the beast We also learn from this, that Russia will equal in extent the old empire of Rome, and will possess Africa, as well as Asia and Europe. This confederacy is further or expressly stated.

As the seven-headed dragon coincides with this beast, we learn that each head of the dragon represented, for the time, the whole dragon, or each smaller empire of the seven represented, for the time, the whole empire of monarchy. Hence, Britain, as one of these seven heads, represented the whole dragon, or all monarchy, in its attack upon America in the revolutionary war.

2. *The Ten Horns.*—" And the ten horns which thou sawest, are ten kings (kingdoms) which have received no kingdom as yet." That is, ten kingdoms in Europe will receive strength from Russia. The next clause explains the term kingdom to be power or stability. "But receive power as kings one hour with the beast." That is, according to the analogy of the symbol, about twenty-one years, or sixteen years, or less. The term, "ten kings," relates to ten kingdoms in the last stage of the history of monarchy. Now, according to Daniel, ten were to begin at the breaking up of the empire. It is possible that there have been seven periods in which ten kingdoms have been found, in Europe, coeval with each other.

" These have one mind, and shall give their power and strength unto the beast." That is, they shall unite their forces or confederate with Russia. This would be natural, as they were upheld and preserved by Russia. We may, therefore, look for these in the south, and east, and middle of Europe. What powers they are, or will be, let time determine.

"These shall make war with the lamb." The lamb coincides with the man with many crowns; and of course these European states, backed by Russia, will make war upon the United States. "And the lamb shall overcome them." Europe will be defeated by us. "For he is Lord of lords and King of kings." The name* or attributes of God are here given to his Christian Israel, and shows that he will be with us. "And they that are with him are called, and chosen, and faithful." As this combat is a military one, the true and faithful symbolize the American people, ever true and faithful to Christian republicanism.

3. *The Harlot Babylon.*—"The waters which thou sawest where the whore sitteth, are people, and multitudes, and nations, and tongues. And the woman which thou sawest, is that great city which reigneth over the kingdoms of the earth." Church and state union in the Roman empire, are, in these descriptions, mentioned twice: first, the whore in many waters; and second, the woman on the scarlet-colored beast. It includes the papal power and all of Christianity, united to the state in any form or kind, and in all stages of the empire. A harlot is, among the prophets, a common symbol of a corrupt church. Extended proofs of our position here are useless; for all can see that the dragon and beast with a wounded head, coincide with the beast and harlot, and that church and state in union, are represented by them

---

* Numbers vi. 27.

severally. The capital of the harlot's empire is Italy "And the ten horns which thou sawest upon the beast, these shall hate the whore, and shall make her desolate and naked, and burn her with fire." These are symbols of terrible destruction. Observe, then, that the European kingdoms will destroy this church and confiscate its property; and as Italy is its capital, we may expect the destruction to begin there. "For God hath put it into their hearts to fulfill his will, and to agree to give their kingdom unto the beast, until the words of God be fulfilled." Here, a confederacy of these European kingdoms with Russia is distinctly announced, and the destruction of the state church in Europe will be the consequence. It is the will of God that this should be, so as to execute judgment on the corrupt church. We may remark that the term city symbolizes all Europe; the term great city symbolizes the whole political church system.

4? *Destruction of Babylon.*—The destroyers of Babylon, the harlot, we have seen, will be the European kingdoms in conjunction with Russia: the destruction itself most demands attention; the description is too lengthy to copy, and we refer the interested to it, as detailed in Rev. xviii. An angel came down and filled the world with glory, and "cried mightily with a strong voice, Fallen, fallen, is Babylon the great." "Come out of her, my people, that ye be not partakers of her sins." Although the political church of the Roman empire has been very corrupt, yet thousands of the pious have lived and do live in its communion. This call is to all of them to reject it and leave it quickly. "Her plagues shall come in one day, destruction and mourning and famine." "For in one hour is so great riches come to naught.' "And a mighty angel took up a stone, like a great millstone, and cast it into the sea, saying, Thus with violence shall that great city Babylon be thrown down and found no more at all." The destruction will not only be terrific, but it will be sudden. "And in her was found the blood of prophets, and of saints, and of all that were slain upon the earth." It has been computed that not less than 50,000,000 of Christians have been put to death by the church since its union with the state, and this is a small estimate. God has not forgotten this long career of blood, and he calls upon all to reward this church as it rewarded Christians in past ages. He says, "Rejoice over her, thou heaven, (or church,) and ye holy apostles and prophets, for God hath avenged you on her." And who would not rejoice on an occasion when God rejoices to avenge the sufferings of helpless innocence for ages. Immediately on the destruction of this power, we find the nations filling the world with shouts of salvation and alleluias, on account of this destruction. As soon as this event transpires, the gospel will fly like lightning over Europe, and prepare its way for republicanism. We have seen, in this episode, the two great characters to be destroyed in the seventh vial period, and also their destroyers, but we now come to a full view of the destroyer of the beast.*

---

* Trinal and absolute sovereignty over the earth is the faith of Rome, and whatever disasters may befall her, she will still anticipate real supremacy in the end. Her confidence that she will be in the ascendant in the United States, is not likely to be shaken, and this faith will affect her conduct and lead to the subversion of religious liberty here, if in her power. We may, therefore, well suppose that she is now laboring to establish her throne among us, by becoming a politico-religious element in our elections, and at her fall in Europe we may anticipate that she will redouble her efforts to destroy Bible democracy. She will fail of her ends, for Providence will bring means to thwart her; Jesuits will be met by organizations possessed of as much intelligence as themselves; and American shrewdness

CLAUSE III.

Third View. The Man with Many Crowns on a White Horse, or the United States of America.—1. "And I saw heaven opened, and behold, a white horse, and he that sat upon him was called Faithful and True." A man, we have seen, symbolizes a body of government, and a white horse the Christian religion. These two, therefore, represent a Christian nationality, and the terms faithful and true, symbolize the truthfulness of the civil power to the principles of Christianity.

2. "In righteousness he doth judge and make war." The term "doth judge," signifies that the mode of his government is just, for a nation judging, is a nation ruling. This could not be a monarchy, for God hates monarchy as the spawn of the devil. The making war in righteousness, or on account of right principles, is another characteristic of this nation, and indicates its disposition to treat all nations uprightly, but to fight them if they do not reciprocate righteousness.

3. "His eyes were as a flame of fire." Eyes symbolize watchfulness; and eyes as a flame of fire, symbolize the activity of his vigilance; as, "eternal vigilance is the price of liberty."

4. "And on his head were many crowns," (diadems) A diadem signifies a sovereign power. A head symbolizes the ruling power; and the "symbols about the head

---

will foil the jugglery of priestcraft; and European fanaticism will quail before the common sense of our countrymen. We must be up and doing; we must fight with their armor; we must meet fire with fire, and secrecy with secrecy, and dexterity with dexterity; and ever remember that "eternal vigilance is the price of liberty." We long for some scheme to be organized that shall "take the beast and give its body to the burning flame."

show the extent and power to rule."—(*Sym. Dic.*) Many crowns about the head show that the ruling power of this Christian nationality was made up of distinct sovereignties united, or confederated states.

5. "And he had a name written that no man knew, but he himself." "The name of a person, or thing, according to the Hebrew style, frequently imports the quality, or state thereof."—(*Sym. Dic.*) This name, therefore, imports that the great quality possessed by this nation, was possessed by no other nation upon earth.

6. "And he was clothed in a vesture dipped in blood." This symbolizes that his origin was through blood. A garment signifies character; and a vesture dipped in blood shows past scenes of warfare, to attain redemption for himself, and his preparedness to be the political redeemer of others.

7. "And his name is called the *Word of God.*" "And they shall put my name upon the children of Israel, and I will bless them."—Numb. vi. 27. As a symbol, the word of God is called the "sword of the Spirit." This nation was, therefore, to be the great agent of God, in avenging his cause on earth. The name may, and does, imply its Christian character.

8. "And the armies which were in heaven." Heaven symbolizes the place of the church on earth. The armies coincide with the many diadems, or sovereignties, for there were many; the states are thus doubly symbolized.

9. "Followed him upon white horses;" this shows that all of the states held to the true religion.

10. "Clothed in fine linen, white and clean:" this symbolizes the practically Christian character of the states composing the nation; and that their governments were just.

11. "And out of his mouth goeth a sharp sword." The mouth symbolizes doctrine and authority, and a sword represents magisterial and martial power.

12. "That with it he should smite the nations." Here, we see he is to be a destroyer, for the term "smite" is a figure of warlike destruction.

13. "And he shall rule them with a rod of iron:" this symbolizes the most absolute authority over the world, and coincides with the ancient promises to Christ and his people. "Let the high praises of God be in their mouth, and a two-edged sword in their hand, to execute vengeance upon the heathen, and punishments upon the people; to bind their kings with chains, and their nobles with fetters of iron; to execute upon them the judgment written: this honor have all his saints.—Ps. cxlix. "Thou shalt break them with a rod of iron; thou shalt dash them in pieces like a potter's vessel. Be wise, therefore, O ye kings."—Ps. ii. "He that overcometh, to him will I give power over the nations, and he shall rule them with a rod of iron; as the vessels of a potter shall they be broken to shivers." The above expression also identifies this symbol in signification with the man child of the woman; for he, also, was to "rule all nations with a rod of iron." Both symbols represent, therefore, the very same agent, or nation. The symbol here, at the close of the seventh trumpet, is of the same nation that was born at the beginning of the trumpet; then it was an infant, but now it is a man grown, on horseback, and a hundred years old.

14. "And he treadeth the wine-press of the fierceness and wrath of Almighty God." The political church received only "the cup of the wine of the fierceness of his wrath;" but the civil monarchy of Rome is to suffer in the wine-press itself. The wine-press is that battle in

which the vine of the earth, or Great Britain, is to be trodden, in the final war; hence, the man on the white horse is to destroy Britain. The destruction of all monarchy is, indeed, comprehended in the quotation, as we shall presently see.

15. "And he hath on his vesture, and on his thigh, a name written, KING OF KINGS, AND LORD OF LORDS." The names of Jehovah attributed to his people, is what God himself affirmed should transpire. Thus it is written, "they shall put my name upon the children of Israel, and I will bless them."—Numb. vi. 27. The Israel of Christ is, therefore, properly called by the names or attributes of Christ; thus, God's people are called godly, and Christian is derived from Christ; and, in general, the name of the sire is attributed to his offspring; and God's ancient people, according to this custom, were "called gods." This is a symbolic expression, denoting the power of this nation over all others. It is an attribute which many monarchs have assumed, and has been true, literally, of some of them. Thus closes this sublime description of a Christian nation. It coincides with some nation, and that one is our country, and no other. No one can deny but it represents a great political power, as it was to destroy Europe and Britain in battle. As this nation was to be a true Christian one, so is the United States; as its government was a just one, so is ours; as it only made war for just causes, so our nation never unjustly made a war; as it was a confederate government of many sovereignties, so is the United States; as it had a national quality distinguishing it from all others, so civil and religious liberty is alone possessed by us, among all nations; as it was to be stained with blood of war, for its own release, so was our country, for it is the finale of the long martyrdom of

Christianity; as it was to be the sword of God, so is our country, in a gospel sense; as many armies with a pure religion followed and sustained this nation, so many true Christian states sustain our union; as it was to rule all nations with supreme control, so, prospectively, our country will; and, as it was to overthrow European monarchy, so it seems our country will. In all points, down to the present, our country coincides with this nation; and, hence, it is fulfilled in us.

But, again, this nation was to overturn European monarchy forever; hence, as the stone cut out of the mountain was also to do this very work, and also the ancient of days, and Michael, and the man child of the woman, and the reaper on the white cloud, and reaper from the temple, it follows that all of these symbols represent but one and the same great Christian republic of the United States of America. Here close these episodical views of the actors in the last vial of the drama, and we resume the descriptions of the events in that period.

CLAUSE IV.

Fourth View in the Seventh Vial. Third Woe.— We have seen in this vial, first, the earthquake of 1848; second, the earthquake and fall of Babylon, about 1865; third, a full picture of the European church history, and the Roman empire in all stages of this history, the kingdoms that will destroy the church, and that will attack us, and a full view of Russia, and a view of the United States. We now come to a fourth view:

1. *France.*—"And I saw an angel standing in the sun." The sun of the European system, we have seen, was France; and, no doubt, this is France. "And he cried with a loud voice, saying to all the fowls that fly in the midst of heaven." Birds of prey symbolize armies,

and these, in the midst of heaven, are the advocates of Christian liberty. "Come and gather yourselves together unto the supper of the great God." This symbolizes the great slaughter of the battle of the great day of God Almighty. "That ye may eat the flesh of kings, and the flesh of captains, and the flesh of mighty men, and the flesh of horses, and of them that sit on them, and the flesh of all men, both free and bond, both small and great." This call to destruction of kings by France, shows that she will make another desperate revolution for freedom, and invite all to join in the crusade against monarchy. This opens the way for the European kingdoms to begin their attack upon us: then Michael's trumpet shall call his legions to the charge, and the Reign of Terror will begin.

2. *The Battle.*—"And I saw the beast, and the kings of the earth, and their armies:" that is, Russia and its ten allied kingdoms and confederates. "Gathered together to make war against him that sat upon the horse, and against his army:" that is, against the United States and its states. The French will be with us then, as they were at first. "And the beast was taken:" the beast is Russia, and coincides with the fourth monarchy of Daniel. Its being taken, shows it was overthrown. The taking of the beast coincides with the reaping of the earth, in the first panorama. "And with him the false prophet, that wrought miracles before him, by which he deceived them that had received the mark of the beast, and them that worshiped his image." This identifies that false prophet with Britain. And the taking of the prophet coincides with the reaping of the vine. As the prophet and beast are both taken together, it is plain that the reaping of the earth and vine, in the first panorama, must be simultaneous occurrences, and that the wine-press

battle, Armageddon, and the battle of the great day, all symbolize but one and the same dreadful war. As the battle was to be out of the city, or Europe, and, as Ezekiel places it on the mountains of Israel, the United States must be the battle-field. Our policy will be to let them enter the country, and reach the Mississippi, or Ohio valley, and then pour hail and brimstone into them. We shall fight with certainty of success.

"Yes, the day is coming fast; earth, thy mightiest and last,
It shall come in blood and toil, in glorious victory and spoil;
It shall come in empire's groans, blazing temples, crashing thrones,
Broken Gentile, rue thy lust; earth to earth, and dust to dust."

"These both were cast alive into a lake of fire, burning with brimstone." Here the figure of the spiritual punishment of the wicked is used to represent the terrible destruction that England, Russia, and their confederate powers will meet.

"And the remnant were slain with the sword of him that sat upon the horse, which sword proceeded out of his mouth." The remnant must relate to some monarchial remnants in Europe, that struggled to exist after the great powers were defeated. They will, however, be subverted.

"And all the fowls were filled with their flesh." That is, the republican armies gained the fullest victory. This taking of the beast under his seventh head, coincides with the destruction of the heathen by Israel restored; the destruction of Gog, in the land of Israel; the smiting the feet of the image of iron and clay; the casting down of thrones by the ancient of days; the taking of the kingdom by the people of the saints; the slaying of the beast, and destroying of his body; the end of the willful king; the "time of trouble," and the last battle of the world; and the blood of Armageddon; and the great day of the wrath of the Lamb.

CLAUSE V.

Fifth View. Chaining of the Dragon.—1. "And I saw an angel come down from heaven, having the key of the bottomless pit." In the fifth trumpet we saw that Mohammedanism had "the key of the bottomless pit," and opened it, and let in the Asiatics upon the Roman empire. The term is, therefore, symbolic of Asia, and the swarms of barbarous tribes out of the limits of the old empire. The angel with the key of the bottomless pit, therefore, symbolizes an agency that will shut up the dragon in the wilds of Asia.

2. "And a great chain in his hand." "A chain signifies hindrance from action."—(*Sym. Dic.*)

3. "And he laid hold on the dragon, that old serpent, which is the devil and Satan, and bound him a thousand years." At the beginning of the war declared by God against sin and hell, or between the woman and the serpent, the woman's seed and serpent's seed, and "he" and the head of the serpent, we saw that the serpent symbolized the religion of its head, or of the devil, literally; and we have seen that the seven-headed dragon represented Roman monarchy, being the seed or spawn of the symbolic old serpent; and, as the child bears the cognomen of its sire, so monarchy is called a dragon, from the paternal cognomen of its sire, the old serpent. In the text, the distinction between the old dragon and the Roman dragon is clearly drawn; for it is called the old serpent, or Satan, in contradistinction to its seed. The name devil and Satan is added, because he was the head of it, and, of course, a part of it; the prime instigator and establisher of false religion. The binding of

the dragon is, therefore, the binding of false religion, that great agency of its head, the devil. This religion was to be bound, and kept from prevalence for a thousand years, in Europe. It will be remembered that it had before been cast out of the United States. Its being now cast out of Europe and the United States, or abandoned by the race of Japhet, and cast into the pit, shows that the bottomless pit refers to all the rest of the barbarous world. The thousand years of binding, is called the Millennium. It will, therefore, be seen that the Millennium embraces the Japhetic race, as Noah predicted, and does not extend over the whole world: it is but the prevalence of a pure Christian religion, and Christian democracy, in the bounds of America and the old Roman empire, embracing Europe, the south-west of Asia, and north of Africa. During its continuance the Shemites and Hamites, as a mass, will be gradually Christianized, and elevated to the condition of dignified men; but they will not be admitted to political equality, generally, among the white race.

4. "And cast him into the bottomless pit, and shut him up, and set a seal upon him that he should deceive the nations no more, till the thousand years should be fulfilled." Upon the definition of the term "nations" hinges the extent of the false religion. As it is ordinarily used in a limited signification among symbols, it, doubtless, here refers to those nations which had rejected it. It is possible that it may refer to a more extensive giving up of idolatry, over Asia and Africa.

5. "And after that he must be loosed a little season." This symbolizes the degeneracy of Christianity, after a thousand years prevalence. This loosing is further enlarged upon in a few sentences following. Thus, John says, "When the thousand years are expired Satan shall

be loosed out of his prison. And shall go out to deceive the nations which are in the four quarters of the earth, Gog and Magog, to gather them together to battle; the number of whom is as the sand of the sea." The prevalence of a decayed Christianity, among the Asiatics and Europeans, represented by Gog and Magog, will lead them to prefer monarchy to Christian republicanism, and they will conspire together to overthrow the great system of freedom and pure Christianity. "And they went up on the breadth of the earth:" this shows that all of the old world will be engaged in the fray. "And compassed the camp of the saints about, and the beloved city." This camp coincides with the seat of the ancient of days, or of the United States, or America, which was never to be entered again by the old serpent, as we saw, in treating of the revolutionary war. "And fire came down from God, out of heaven, and devoured them." This represents their total discomfiture by America, the heaven, or place of the church *on earth*. Mark this, the dragon was to be cast out of America forever; but out of Europe only a thousand years. "And the devil, that deceived them, was cast into the lake of fire and brimstone, where the beast and false prophet are, and shall be tormented day and night forever." In one respect this must be symbolic, but that which is symbolized must itself have a fuller meaning than can be now understood. The beast, or monarchy, the false prophet, or British monarchy, and the serpent, or false religion, all symbolize political bodies, and their punishment as such must consist in utter annihilation as political bodies. But the fact of their perpetual torment, after this overthrow, is only consistent with the punishment of their individual supporters, for spiritual crimes. It follows, therefore, that this general overthrow, by fire from heaven, was accomplished at the time of the final judgment, which is then immediately announced.

The triumph of God's dominion was predicted at the fall of the world, but the details of the mode of its accomplishment were left to later ages. It was predicted to Abraham, by Moses, by David, and other prophets, but especially by Isaiah, Ezekiel, Daniel, and John. The prophets, also, of each later age, enlarged upon the details of its accomplishment given by his predecessor. Daniel and John give their statements with such chronological accuracy, that they may be regarded as our chief guides in determining the future. John gives us the successive stages of the approach of the complete regeneration of the world with elaborate distinctness, yet he and Daniel must coincide, because they cover the same field and events. Daniel does not dwell upon a Millennium as antecedent to the full and eternal establishment of Christ's dominion, but he embraces it in the final kingdom, in one vision, and simply alludes to it in another; but John shows the length of the duration of the preparatory periods of triumph. Daniel gives the length of "the time of the end," and also two epochs at the inception of the final dominion. First, the coming of the ancient and giving of judgment, or democracy, to the saints or Christians. The first evidently coincides with the time of the end, the last with the close of that time. John shows that the political empire of the world will fall into the hands of the Christians at the Millennium, but that the spiritual empire will be delayed one thousand years longer. We shall treat of John's epochs in this kingdom particularly.

CLAUSE VI.

Sixth View. The Millennial Democracy.--1. "And I saw thrones, and they sat upon them, and judgment was given unto them." A throne symbolizes a government, or state, or dominion, and thrones signify countries, or states, or dominions. "They sat upon them." The term they, is a symbol of multitude, and the sitting of the multitude on thrones, shows that this passage agrees with Daniel's account of the government of the world falling into the power of the Christian people. "Judgment was given unto them," is a stronger expression that the government was in the hands of the people, and is explanatory of the symbol before expressed. Daniel and John must agree on this point, for they both treat of it. The Millennium is a political redemption rather than a spiritual one, though it includes both to a certain extent.

2. "I saw the souls of them that were beheaded for the witness of Jesus and for the word of God, and which had not worshiped the beast, neither his image, neither had received his mark upon their foreheads, or in their hands." The generality of the European world were embraced in the preceding sentence, as having political emancipation given them, but here a distinct class of persons is cited as enjoying superior favors. Now, as the British empire is designated by the beast, his image, and mark, these persons who had been slain must be those overcome and crushed by the British power. These persons, it appears, had suffered martyrdom, and, as we understand it, they or their religion had suffered political martyrdom. Some persons will understand these passages as purely literal and spiritual, but certainly such a view is not in harmony with the general scope of the prophecy, which, having described the overthrow of monarchy in Europe and Britain, now treats of the organization of the government that succeeds monarchy. It is, however, possible, that as at this period

the 1335 days have an end, that Daniel may "stand in his lot" at that time. "And they lived and reigned with Christ a thousand years." This may refer to the fact they will live with Christ as merely their sovereign head or governor; yet it seems difficult to give this expression an entirely figurative sense from what immediately follows. The second advent will occur in the United States, either at the beginning or during the Millennium, or at its close, no telling when positively. "But the rest of the dead lived not again until the thousand years were ended." A distinction is here drawn between the martyrs living for a thousand years, and those who were not martyrs. Now, it seems utterly impossible to interpret this passage politically, because all persons in Europe and America are to enjoy political redemption, while those that will live afterwards are the dead generally. The resurrection, it seems, therefore, must be something more than a political restitution of rights to man. "This is the first resurrection. Blessed and holy is he that hath part in the first resurrection; on such the second death hath no power, but they shall be priests of God and of Christ, and shall reign with him a thousand years." Here, the conviction is resistless almost, that the first resurrection will be literal, and will embrace the martyrs and noblest servants of Christ who have lived in the world. This resurrection must be that which Paul endeavored to attain unto. Yet, after all, as symbols are mostly exaggerated and political representations, the first resurrection may relate to a general resurrection of a political nature in the main. The second advent of Christ, and the first resurrection, are subjects on which we are not clear, and can not be till the events shall determine the time of the one and the nature of the other

Understand us, then, to teach that the Millennium will be a Christian republic of the Japhetic race only, and of some few Shemites, within the Roman empire, and that the Asiatics, generally, will hold to the Millennial, or Japhetic race, the relation of a younger brother to a king, and the Hamitic race will hold the relation of a ward to a guardian, or servant to his master. The perfection of the spiritual kingdom of Christ will not occur till after the regeneration of nature by fire. The United States will, in the Millennium, be the great ruling power of the world, and it will never apostatize. It is likely a confederacy of the United States with Europeans, will occur; but the Europeans will, after a thousand years, apostatize, and gather the world against America; and in the midst of their war, the spiritual judgment will come, and the earth will be burnt up, and changed into the paradise of God, and the full glory of God shall be forever manifested. This period coincides with the sealing of the twelve tribes, after the sixth seal, and with the marriage supper of the lamb.

CLAUSE VII.

Seventh View. The Spiritual Judgment-Day.—In the vision of the ancient of days, an exhibition of a political judgment-day was given, occurring at the close of the time of the end, and which coincides with the war of Armageddon. But here, a thousand years after that event, we have a full account of the great spiritual judgment of the dead and living. This is spoken of by all the Bible teachers of spirituality, but expressly, by none of the political symbolic prophets, except John.

1. "And I saw a great white throne, and him that sat on it, from whose face the heavens and the earth fled away; and there was found no place for them." This

is a generic description, extending over a wide compass, and includes the time of the judgment; for the heavens and the earth could not have passed away before its close, as the sea and earth were in existence during the judgment, and gave up their dead, and they were to pass away.

2. "And I saw the dead, small and great, stand before God." As nothing is said of the judgment of the living, in this judgment, may it not have already transpired, by the presence of Christ on earth? "And the books were opened, and another book was opened, which is the book of life, and the dead were judged out of those things which were written in the books, according to their works." As the literal dead are here judged, of course it was not a political judgment, but a spiritual one. "And the sea gave up the dead which were in it; and death and hell delivered up the dead which were in them, and they were judged every one according to their works." Death is, by a figure, put for the bodies destroyed by death, or the grave, and hell is put for the grave or receptacle of disembodied spirits. "And death and hell were cast into the lake of fire. This is the second death." This limits the terms death and hell to the bodies and souls of the wicked. "And whosoever was not found written in the book of life, was cast into the lake of fire." That is, all the wicked were sentenced to eternal punishment.

CHAPTER XIV.

THE NEW HEAVEN AND EARTH—THE VICTORY.

"The earth and heaven fled away;" "and I saw a new heaven and a new earth, for the first heaven and the first earth were passed away, and there was no more sea." This is literal, because the term sea, in the connection in which it stands, can not be made to receive a symbolic sense. This was the long promised regeneration of the globe. Some severe destructionists have been advocates of the total annihilation of the globe, from a strange misconception of the meaning of this, and other passages of scripture; but no theory can be more destitute of truth and good sense. The truth is, the destruction of the present heaven and earth is necessary to accomplish the promise of the full glory of God, by preparing the globe for the erection of the throne of David and of God upon it forever. We will briefly meet the theory on its merits. It is affirmed that the heaven and earth that are to be destroyed, signify the globe. This we deny most positively. 1. The term earth, has at least twelve significations; and the term, world, has twenty-two. Now, it is not by any means necessary to give the signification of globe, to the term earth, whenever it is used, and especially when the context does not require it. 2. The terms heaven and earth, as used by Moses, most certainly do not signify the globe; for he expressly defines them to signify only parts of the mundane system. Thus, he says, "God called the *dry land* earth, and God called the *firmament* (or atmosphere) heaven," "and the *gathering together* of waters called he seas." Here is as clear a definition of these terms, by inspiration itself, as could be desired. Now, as it is illogical and falsifying to give the terms of an author a different sense from that he has expressly given them, so is it falsifying God's word to insist that he means the destruction of the globe, when he speaks of the destruction of heaven, and earth, and sea, which he had defined to be but exterior parts of the globe.

3. St. Peter, who gives a description of the heavens and earth, literally by fire, teaches plainly that he does not mean a destruction of the globe, but only a renewal of it by fire; and Moses, in his description of the destruction of the earth by the deluge, concurs with our views. Thus, he says, "I will destroy them with the earth;" "a flood to destroy the earth." Peter says, "by the word of God, the heavens were of old, and the earth standing out of the water, and in the water, whereby the world that then was, being overflowed with water, perished; but the heavens and earth which are now, by the same word are kept in store, reserved unto fire against the day of judgment." Nothing can be plainer than that the old heavens and earth, before the flood, perished, and that the globe did not; and nothing can be plainer, than "that the heavens and earth which are now," are as much different from the globe, as were the heavens and earth before the flood. It is as clear as light, that the heavens and earth destroyed by water, have the same signification as the terms heaven and earth, which are to be destroyed by fire. So that the destruction announced by Peter, has no sort of reference

to a destruction of the globe, but only to its external organization. Besides, he says, "according to his promise, we look for new heavens and a new earth." Now, the only special promise upon this subject, was given by Isaiah, and he locates them upon the present globe. It therefore follows, that when Christ said, "the heaven and earth shall pass away," he referred to the present heaven and earth, erected upon the globe, and not the globe itself.

4. The reason for the passing away of the heaven and earth. There is good sense in every act of God, and hence there is a good common sense reason for the destruction of the present heaven and earth, and that reason is as obvious as it is sensible: it is to restore the world to its pristine glory. The war which God declared in the beginning, was for the conquest of the world; to restore man upon earth to subjection to his government. Now, the curse upon the ground was a great act of war, to aid in the subjugation of the race; and the curse on the earth was a double one; the first at the fall, and the second by the flood. After the conquest of man, this curse would, according to the promise at the beginning, be removed; and this removal would require as great a change in the heaven and earth, at such renewal, as took place when they were changed at the fall and the flood: that is, to remove the curse, the heaven and earth would need to be removed or changed. The promise of the final removal of the curse, on all things, was made at the first, and repeated in all subsequent ages. The removal of the curse of death implies a resurrection; and the removal of the curse on the heavens and earth, implies their removal, and the erection of a heaven and earth without imperfection, and not the annihilation of the globe, which would be the severest curse ever inflicted on it.

5. The annihilation of the globe implies that God entertains spite against inanimate matter, which is most absurd to suppose.

6. God has engaged in war for six thousand years, to establish his kingdom on the globe. Now, what good sense is there in fighting for ages, through the most awful scenes of affliction, to regain a revolted province, on purpose to annihilate it as soon as it is possessed? Tell us, ye wise! say, is there reason in the baseless assumption you make?

God swore to Moses that the whole earth should be full of his glory; and the prophets say that it shall then endure forever. Does this look like annihilation of the globe? Does it not look like its regeneration at the final "restitution of all things?"

7. John says, that after the old heaven and earth were gone, that the new Jerusalem descended to the new earth, and to the region where the curse had prevailed. The words, "there shall be no more death, neither shall there be any more pain; for the former things are passed away," are applicable to a world where these things had prevailed, and from which they were banished, and not to a world where they had never been known. "Behold, I make all things new," can not refer to the third heaven, but only to a world where every thing needed reorganization. "There shall be no more curse," applies only to a world where the curse had prevailed. But, again; all these things were prophecies, to be fulfilled after the days of John, and they must refer to this globe, and not to the third heaven, which existed before John's day. Besides this, the new Jerusalem came down from God, out of heaven, to men, and men did not go up to it; which shows, again, that this globe was to be the

throne of God and the Lamb. Daniel, and Isaiah, and all the prophets, make the world redeemed to abide forever; and after the Millennium is ended, and the judgment is past, John shows the state of the world in the full blaze of celestial glory. Whoever heard of Christ's returning from the earth after his second advent to it? And who has not read that the *tabernacle* of God shall be with men after the new Jerusalem descends, and that they shall reign with God and the Lamb forever and ever, in the new Jerusalem, and in the heavens and earth, from which the curse had been removed?

The truth is, the regenerated globe is to be the battle-monument of eternity; the seat of government of Jesus, head over all things; the holy of holies of the universe. As the believers shall come from the dust, where the curse had laid them, and shall wear the image of Jesus, and shall be adorned with all the glory which infinite skill can compass, or Omnipotence create, so also shall their residence, freed from the curse, appear in all the splendor commensurate with its citizens and King. As the throne of the Son of Mary will shine with all the splendors of the Deity; as it will be the supreme expression of all the concentrated excellence with which matter can be clothed by Jehovah's limitless resources and power, so this poor blood-stained globe will shine, wrapped in the uncreated blaze of God's robe of royalty; so it will be filled with eternal music and delight; so it will be holy, holy, holy to the Lord God of hosts; so it will be an eternal honor to the Captain of our salvation. When the serpent's head is bruised, when the curse shall fly from earth, and hover forever over the lost, in the night of their woe, may you and I, dear reader, have a shelter beneath the jasper skies and trees of life, beside the living streams o. joy. Then from our central home, upon Jehovah's wing, O be it ours to visit every home of angels, and know, in person, every creature of his love, in every world of his own universe, and pass eternity delightfully! This regeneration of the globe completes the victory foretold to the serpent; it is the "kingdom come on earth, as it is in heaven."

PART SECOND.

THE DISCOVERY—COMPLETED JANUARY, 1852.

A veil is on the prophets, and clouds are on the page of unquestioned revelation; the light shines in the darkness, but the darkness comprehends it not; symbols glow on the doors of the temple, but the language of divinity is a mystery to the cherubim; prophecy is a dream, and realization a conjecture; the world waits impatient for the breaking seals, and longs with eagerness to behold the shadows of mountains condense into sublime reality, and conjecture to the truth of God. Since the fall of Judea not a prediction is, with certainty, known to be either interpreted or fulfilled; all theories of that era are false, in the main, and only "darken counsel by words without knowledge." Yet an age of knowledge was to break from the dungeon of doubt; a day was to dawn when the book was to open, the seals be disclosed, and the words of the Lord be made known by his ways. The sublime work, now undertaken, is to point out his footprints, and by their light interpret the ancient words of Omniscience. An achievement so stupendous, so honorable if successful, might challenge the effort as impious, were not the risk of infamy so great in case of defeat; or that a blessing is pledged to him who hears, and reads, and keeps the awful oracle. Let us proceed promptly to our work. We propose to give a key to all the mysterious prophecies of the past, and open up some relating to the future. The last vision of Daniel, or that portion stretching from the "desolation" to the resurrection, is a key to all others covering the same field: its sealing implied that of all its collaterals, and its re .... in volves their simultaneous manifestation. To get fairly at our work we transcribe the symbolic portion of this vision. "But thou, O Daniel, shut up the words and seal the book, even to the time of the end; many shall run to and fro, and knowledge shall be increased. * * * How long shall it be to the end of these wonders? * * * * * * It shall be for a time, times and a half, and when he shall have accomplished, to scatter the POWER of the holy people, all these things shall be finished. And I heard, but I understood not; then said I, O my Lord, what (when) shall be the end of these things? And he said, go thy way, Daniel, for the words are *closed up* and *sealed* till the time of the end. * * None of the wicked shall understand, but the wise shall understand. And from the time that the daily sacrifice shall be taken away, and the abomination that maketh desolate set up, there shall be a thousand two hundred and ninety days. Blessed is he that waiteth and cometh to the thousand three hundred and five and thirty days." Daniel xii. Let the following particulars be noticed with great attention.

1. What was to be sealed? The answer is, only those things relating to the period following the destruction of Jerusalem, or desolation. That this view is correct, is evident, because all of the first part of the vision, down to the desolation, is but a literal prophetic history of Syria, Egypt, and Judea. Thenceforward, all else is wrapt in symbols. The term "wonders," manifestly begins at the "desolation," for the $3\frac{1}{2}$ times begin there, and both were to be co-eval. The $3\frac{1}{2}$ times were especially to be sealed, for while the closing and sealing are, at first, applied to all the vision from the desolation, they are yet repeated and directly referred to these times.

2. The terms "sealing," and "closing," "the words and book," most unequivocally affirm that mystery was to be upon the meaning of the prophecy, by divine decree; the repetition of the sealing, is to emphasize this truth with the greatest force.

The sealing of this vision necessitates that of all other coeval prophecies, because only the greatest events of time are predicted. All prophecies limited to the same field coincide, therefore, in descriptions of the same great subjects. Hence the other co-eval prophecies of Daniel, St. John, Isaiah, and Ezekiel, are also sealed; and universally it is agreed that they are mysterious. Is it not, however, very strange, that expositors have been so thoroughly blinded, as not to see with what emphasis the sealing of these visions is affirmed? Let the reader fix the truth firmly in his mind, that the vision was to be a mystery for ages.

3. The beginning of this sealing was to be at the fall of Judea, for the beginning of the 1290 days, and 3½ times, and 1335 days, is either *declared* to be at the cessation of the daily sacrifice, or is located at that point by the vicinity of the case.

4. The end of the sealing was to be at the "time of the end," or at the close of the 3½ times, or 1290 days, or gathering of the power of Israel. The certainty, therefore, of a discovery is positively asserted.

5. The discovery of the meaning of the prophecy was to be understood by the WISE only. This term being one of multitude, from its connection in the text, implies a body of people, synonymous with Israel restored, or with true Christians generally.

6. The WICKED, or foes of Israel, or civil and religious liberty, were not to receive the discovery as a reality. It seems that the European nations generally, will scout the discovery whenever it is made.

7. "The *power* of the holy people" represents government or nationality, as "the powers that be," &c.

8. "The time of the end." This does not refer to the end of time, that not being mentioned in the text. It coincides with the period after the sounding of the 7th trumpet, when "the mystery of God shall be finished, as God declared by the prophets." It was to be characterized as an age of great locomotion, and intelligence, for

the words "many shall run to and fro, and knowledge shall be increased," is added immediately after the term "time of the end," as explanatory of it. It seems also to be that period between the end of the 1290 and 1335 days, or between the two endings of the 3½ times, hereafter to be noticed.

9. As each prophetic symbol has uniformly a symbolic explanation, the 3½ times seem to be interpreted by the 1290 and 1335 days.

Hitherto none have been able to solve the mystery. The reason for the failure is the decree of God. Most men who have studiously attempted it, with philosophic coolness, lived several centuries since, and their inevitable errors, descended to our age, form the basis of recent and now general fancies. Is it not plain that any theory of exposition is in error, if proposed prior to the "time of the end?" Among these errors are those of the carnal restoration, and esteeming a symbolic day as a solar year. As these are the pivots of all great systems of exposition now received, all must be fallacious. Should a true theory be offered, it must deny these errors a place, direct attention to another than carnal Israel, and give a new mode of computing days and times. It would show the realization of prophecy in a new and unexpected direction, and seem as eccentric and luminous as a comet lighting all the heavens with its train.

For such a theory we inquiringly seek, and our age being one of great locomotion and intelligence, it coincides with "the time of the end," in which the discovery is to transpire, we may inquire hopefully. The symbolic days and times of Daniel's last vision, being a key to all its arcana and of all other sealed visions, and days and times or years, being convertible, we shall direct all of our attention to the determination of the meaning of symbolic days, to ascertain, with mathematic precision, the exact amounts of solar time they represent. Now, then, arises the momentous question, how can this be known? The answer is very simple; it must be known either from scripture or from fulfillment, or from both. What, then, does scripture say? It answers darkly; it gives no general or specific *precept* to guide us; yet it affords two *examples*, in which the term day symbolizes a year. Thus: "After the number of days in which ye searched the land, even forty days, (*each day for a year*,) shall ye bear your iniquities." Numbers xiv, 34. "Thou shalt bear the iniquity of the house of Judah forty days; I have appointed thee *each day for a year*." Ezek iv, 6. These examples, though applied to specific cases, allow us the privilege of counting other symbolic days as years, if need require; yet they do not *prove* that we would be positively correct in so doing. Again, as there were different kinds of years in use among the Hebrews, it is impossible to affirm, *a priori*, which kind is symbolized by a day. All that can be inferable from these examples is, that a day *may* symbolize a year of any kind known to the Mosaic ritual. We are, therefore, still unable to determine, from anything in scripture, the exact number of solar years that are symbolized by the $3\frac{1}{2}$ times or 1260 days or 1290 days. Yet as we know the lengths of several kinds of Hebrew years, and as the examples quoted allow these days to be esteemed as years, if need require, and this need existing from the very nature of the case, we know certainly that these days represent some kind of years. The next query is, what kind of years is intended? To this the Bible gives no reply. How then shall it be determined, or shall it be at all? If not answered, then realization cannot be known, and prophecy is an inanity, which is absurd to suppose. Again, it is clearly declared that an answer shall be given, and that a fulfillment shall be patent and unequivocal to all the wise. Reason and scripture both declaring that fulfillment shall perspicuously transpire, it follows that a satisfactory mode of explanation is to be found. Now, then, how is it to be discovered? We answer, on the same principles that any other obscure prophecy is shown to be fulfilled. And what are they? Pay attention to the following things and you will know. There are two characters of prophecies; the first is literal and unequivocal, as that of Christ's declaration to the disciples, "they shall be led away captive into all nations." A coincidence of events with such a declaration is an indubitable fulfillment; and this was fulfilled at the destruction of Jerusalem. The other class of prophecies may be termed obscure. By far the larger number of predictions are of this kind. The obscurity arises from (1.) the nature of most words. Scarcely a word, in any language, but is possessed of several meanings, and in many compositions it is impossible to determine, either from the nature of things or from the context, what the word was intended to signify. (2.) Obscurity arises from the common use of a term in either a figurative or literal sense; here it is sometimes impossible, *a priori*, to fix the sense intended by inspiration. (3.) Obscurity often arises in prophecy from the use of symbols. The meaning of a symbol never changes, it is always determinate, but it is always generic and not minutely specific; it cannot therefore be known, prior to the chronologic appearance of its antitype, what it represented. For this reason a symbolic vision cannot by possibility be fully and definitely understood prior to a partial fulfillment, at least, unless interpreted literally by inspiration itself. Many symbols may have the same sense, but no one symbol ever has two senses; a simple figure may have many. (4.) Obscurity is a quality of prophecy by divine decree, and for wise ends. Prophecy, however, is never so obscure as to detract all significance from it; *a priori*, enough meaning attends it to create expectation and encourage the church; enough to stimulate hope without ministering to a vain curiosity; sufficient ultimately to see and admit an unequivocal and striking fulfillment, and demonstrate the divinity of inspiration. By a lack of obscurity the proof of a prophetic spirit had been weakened rather than improved. Understanding a prediction, men wishing it true would attempt to realize

.t; were it opposed to their selfishness they might hinder its easy completion. How earnestly those Christians and Jews, who believe in the carnal theory, labor to secure the restoration of the Jews; should they succeed, they might claim their fanaticism a fulfillment predicted antithetic to this; had Europe believed it foretold that our country would rise and destroy the scepter of monarchs, would they have connived at our republic or fought for our independence? Their ambition had rather been to crush and bind us, and only miracle had prevented their overpowering hostility in our infancy. The original obscurity of prophecy was intentional and useful; but it is yet inquired, may not this obscurity prevent the realization from being clearly shown? We answer no. It is then asked how we make this appear? We reply: 1. All prophecy forms but one system of predictions; that each major subject is predicted many times, either by one or by several prophets; and that each important prediction, taken separately, is composed of several prominent parts, and that in the fulfillment a realization of all things, foretold of a single subject, transpire simultaneously. Thus, there are many predictions of Christ, quite a number of Israel, Egypt, Persia, and Rome, and when one is fulfilled the realization of each separate prediction forms a part of the strength of proof of inspiration; but all combined produce overpowering demonstration. The seventy weeks uttered by Gabriel, form a part of a detailed historic prophecy of the Jewish state, and the realization of one part, though clear in itself, is yet so joined with other parts, that their simultaneous fulfillment with it, confirms its truth, and all taken together, remove all ambiguity either with reference to fulfillment or the original intent of the prophecy. 2. As from the nature of obscure prophecy, it is susceptible of various, *a priori*, meanings, there is no way of arriving at the only, *a priori*, meaning of the text intended, except by fulfillment. This is self-evident. The true meaning of the text will, therefore, lie between several meanings, each of which may be legitimately attributed to the text. Now, fulfillment will accord with such, only, of these meanings, as was originally intended; by consequence, fulfillment in determining the exact meaning of the prophecy must determine which, *a priori*, sense is the correct or intended one. This, also, is self-evident. In showing that an obscure prediction is realized, all that can be required of an expositor is for him to show that his interpretation is legitimate. A legitimate, *a priori*, exposition is one which opposes neither the context nor the nature of things existing, prior to the realization. Now, then, upon these self-evident principles, if we show that events coincide with our expositions, and that our expositions are legitimate, we shall prove that they were intended by inspiration, and also exhibit an unequivocal fulfillment. With these premises we proceed another step. We showed that it was legitimate to suppose, that in a chronologic prophecy, a day might stand for a year of some one kind or more known to the Hebrews. We may now ascertain its exact length as intended by inspiration, if we can, a prophecy in which it exists whose fulfillment is certainly known to have transpired. But one such fulfilled prophecy is known, and that is the famous one of Gabriel to Daniel, concerning the restoration and final desolation of typical Israel. It contains a chronologic prophecy of weeks, which measure accurately the space of time transpiring between certain great historical epochs. As days, weeks, months, and times, or years, are mutually convertible, if we find the intended length or lengths of weeks in solar time, we shall find a key which will, *a priori*, unlock the symbolic days, months, and times of both Daniel and John.

We here quote the prophecy and inquire with what legitimate, *a priori*, expositions it coincides.

CHAPTER I.

INTERPRETATION OF THE SEVENTY WEEKS.

1. "UNDERSTAND the matter and consider the vision. Seventy weeks are determined upon thy people, and upon thy holy city, to finish the transgression and make an end of sins." That this part refers, *a priori*, to the destruction of Jerusalem, admits of no question; hence the seventy weeks have an ending there.

2. "To make reconciliation for iniquity and to bring in everlasting righteousness; to seal up (VELACHTOM, *to finish or complete*) the vision and prophecy, and anoint the Most Holy." This refers to the crucifixion, (see various commentators.) Hence the seventy weeks were to end here also.

3. "Know, therefore, and understand that from the going forth of (by) the commandment to *restore* and to *build* Jerusalem, unto the Messiah, the Prince, shall be seven weeks and three score and two weeks; the street shall be built again and the wall, even in troublous times. And after three score and two weeks shall Messiah be cut off, but not for himself." Here the decree of restoration and the time of the appearing of Christ in his office of Messiah, and the length of time between them, are fully stated. The beginning of these weeks is at the decree of restoration; the end, at the beginning of Christ's ministry; the length of time, sixty nine weeks. The crucifixion is to transpire *after* the end of the sixty-nine weeks, and not *at* the end; keep this in view. That the seventy weeks are to begin at the same point as the sixty-nine, is plain; otherwise, they have no beginning point, which is not supposable.

Whatever may be the true, *a priori*, explanation of these weeks, one thing is clear, which is, that their exact length in solar time is determined by fulfillment. It devolves upon us, therefore, to ascertain the amount of this solar time. To do this, we must ascertain the time when the restoring decree took effect, and when the crucifixion and desolation transpired. As history does not record the date of Christ's entry upon his ministry, with exactness, we shall pay no attention to it.

4. "And the people of the prince that shall come shall destroy the city, and sanctuary, and the end thereof shall be with a flood, and unto the end of the war desolations are determined." This is explanatory of the seventy weeks ending " upon thy people and holy city," already quoted. The invasion of the Romans is here to be understood. "The end of the war," being spoken of, *after* the desolation of Israel, must refer to the long desolation of the true Israel's nationality.

5. "And he shall confirm the covenant with many for one week; and in the midst of the week (end of the week, says Prideaux) he shall cause the sacrifice and oblation to cease, and for the overspreading of abominations he shall make it desolate, even until the consummation, and that determined, shall be poured upon the desolate." Dan. ix.

The explanation of this one week being useless to confirm our theory, we shall not trouble the reader with it. We shall proceed, first, to determine the precise time of the restoring decree or decrees, and of the crucifixion and desolation; secondly, to show that the seventy weeks may be dated from two decrees of restoration; thirdly, to exhibit a number of legitimate, *a priori*, expositions of the text; fourthly, to show that fulfillment coincides with four of these expositions, thus demonstrating the true modes of interpreting symbolic days, and unsealing the last vision of Daniel, and all other sealed prophecies.

SECTION I.

The Decree of Restoration—The Crucifixion—The Fall of Judea.

History shows us that there were two principal decrees given for the restoration of the Jews; the first, and full decree, was by Cyrus; and the second was given to Ezra, by Artaxerxes Longimanus; by the first, *Jerusalem* and the *temple* were rebuilt, and the country *resettled;* and by the second, the Jewish ritual was reformed. We will consider each in order.

Paragraph I.

THE DECREE OF CYRUS.

This was given in the last part of the year 537, before Christ. In the first year of Cyrus, according to Ezra, first chapter, and the last of 2d Chronicles, the decree for Judea's restoration was issued. Keep it in mind, that it was the *first year* of Cyrus. Now, by the combined aid of astronomy, scripture, and history, we shall show, that this first year synchronizes with 537, B. C. There was an eclipse of the sun on the 20th of September, A. U. C., 601, which had been foretold by Thales, the Milesian, and this was the 147th year of Nabonassar, and the 9th of Jehoiakim, king of Judah.—(*Prid. Conn.* vo.. i.) Now, Daniel, in his first chapter, says that Nebuchadnezzar came against Jerusalem, and besieged it; and the Lord gave Jehoiakim into his hands, in the third year of his reign. Subtracting, therefore, the 3d year from the 9th, we have six remainder, and adding it to 601, gives us 607, B. C., as the date of this siege. The siege was in the latter part of the year; Prideaux says in October; and its conclusion must have been a month or two later, or about December. Earlier in the year, Nebuchadnezzar had made a conquest of Egypt, had taken Carchemish, and subdued Syria and Phœnicia, and he here finishes his campaign, and returns home with the Jewish and other captives. Of these, Jeremiah says, "These nations shall serve the king of Babylon seventy years. And it shall come to pass, when seventy years are accomplished, that I will punish the king of Babylon and that nation for their iniquity, saith the Lord."* Counting these seventy years, therefore, from the time of the beginning of this servitude, it is evident that it ended seventy years later than 607, B. C.; and also, that the king of Babylon was overthrown seventy years after this servitude began; hence, the conquest of Babylon, and the death of Belshazzar, was in 537, B. C.; and this, according to Ptolemy, was the first year of Cyrus, and, according to scripture, the first of Darius and of Cyrus conjointly. Why some chronologers should have placed the fall of Babylon in 538, B. C., one year before the seventy years were to be fulfilled, is very hard to divine; and is certainly an error, or else inspiration errs. The seventy years of the Jews began later in the year than that of other nations, and about December; and Prideaux states that their return must have begun in December; so that we may fully claim, that the going forth of the captivity, by virtue of the Cyrus decree, was in December of 537, B. C., just seventy years after it had left Jerusalem for Babylon. Prideaux thinks, that

---

* Jeremiah xxv.

ne first year of Cyrus was his third year from the taking of Babylon, as Tully reckons it; that is, the first of his sole reign, after the death of Darius, the Mede; but Ptolemy's canon reckons his first year with his conquest of Belshazzar; the scriptures speak of the reign of both monarchs; but it is easy to see that their first year synchronizes with all the statements of scripture. We strongly suspect Prideaux's theory of the seventy weeks led him into this error; for it would bring the date of the Ezra decree too early for him by a year, unless he made the first year of Darius to be in 538, B. C., and the first of Cyrus, two years after it. But, as 538, B. C., could not be the first of Darius, if he makes the first of Cyrus to begin two years later than Darius, his theory brings him too late in time for its own good. Mr. Prideaux's view seems to us very unreasonable, as well as impossible to receive; for, according to his notion, the Jews would have been detained in Babylon two years longer than the Gentiles, and two years longer than their appointed time; and God had said that Cyrus should overthrow Babylon, "for *Jacob, my servant's sake,* and Israel mine elect," (Isa.) and unless seventy years mean seventy-two years, we can not see how he can be correct; indeed, we know he must be erroneous.

Paragraph II.

DECREE OF ARTAXERXES LONGIMANUS.

This was given to Ezra, and published in Jerusalem, in the month of July; and in the seventh year of Longimanus, and in the year 456, B. C.

Prideaux places this decree in the year 458, B. C., and differs from Usher. Indeed each chronologer of this epoch differs arbitrarily from his compeers, and all depart arbitrarily from history, for the sake, as they say, of scripture chronology; but really to accommodate their several theories of the seventy weeks. Each fixes his theory, and then dates back his amount of years from the death of Christ, and wherever they end, there they place the date of the Ezra decree. A strange way indeed of showing the fulfillment of prophecy! Let history be true, though theories suffer! We can not and will not depart from history, and especially from Ptolemy, unless strongly biassed by opposing testimony; and it is singular that on the date of this decree, Prideaux and Usher both should have left the astronomic chronology of Ptolemy to follow a fancy.

According to Ptolemy, Cyrus reigned nine years from the conquest of Babylon; he was succeeded by Cambyses, who reigned seven years and five months, and he by Smerdis for seven months, and he by Darius for thirty-six years, and he by Xerxes for twenty-one years, and he by Longimanus, and in his seventh year the decree was given to Ezra for reforming Jerusalem. These amount to eighty-one years in all, and estimating, as reasonably we may, that the reign of Cyrus began about the middle of the year 537, B. C., and subtracting eighty-one years from it, we are brought down to $456\frac{1}{2}$, A. C.

Paragraph III.

YEAR OF THE CRUCIFIXION.

This was A. D. 29, and on the twenty-fifth of March. So it appears from the facts. Christ was born in the 5th year B. C., v. 3.; and was over thirty-three years of age, but not over thirty-four at his death; and by consequence must have died A. D. 29; and the scriptures say the crucifixion was on the fourteenth of Nisan which answers, in that year, to March twenty-fifth. To verify our position, we quote the authority and argument of Eusebius, the first ecclesiastical historian, and of the era of Constantine. He says, " it was about the fifteenth year of the reign of Tiberius, according to the Evangelist, in the fourth year, that Pilate was procurator of Judea, when Herod, Lysanias and Phillip, as tetrarchs, held the government of the rest of Judea, when our Lord and Saviour Jesus Christ was in his thirtieth year, that he came to the baptism of John, and then made the beginning of promulgating his gospel." The holy scriptures moreover relate that he passed the whole time of his public ministry under the high priests, Annas and Caiaphas; intimating, that during the years of their priesthood, the whole time of his ministry terminated. For, beginning with the pontificate of Annas, and continuing after that of Caiaphas, the whole of this interval does not give us four years. The rites indeed of the law having already been abolished since that period, with it, also, were annulled the privileges of the priesthood, viz: of continuing in it for life, and of hereditary descent. Under the Roman governors, however, different persons at different times were appointed as high priests, who did not continue in office more than a year.

Josephus, indeed, relates that there were four high priests in succession from Annas to Caiaphas. " Valerius Gratus having put a period to the priesthood of Annas, promoted Ishmael, the son of Baphi, to the office; and removing him also, not long after, he appointed Eleazer, the son of Annas, who had been high priest before, to the office. After the lapse of a year, removing him also, he transfers the priesthood to Simon, the son of Camithus. But he also did not continue to hold the honor longer than a year, when he was succeeded by Josephus, surnamed Caiaphas."—(*Antiquities*.) Hence, the whole time of our Saviour's ministry is proved not to embrace four entire years; there being four high priests for four years, from Annas to the appointment of Caiaphas, each of whom held the office a year respectively. Caiaphas, indeed, is justly shown by the gospel narrative to have been high priest in that year in which our Saviour's sufferings were finished, with which present observation the time of Christ's ministry is proved to agree.

Again; by reference to the scriptures it appears that Christ, after his baptism, at which he was thirty years of age, attended only four passovers, at the last of which he was the "Lamb that was slain;" so that he could not have been over thirty-four years of age. These four passovers are noticed at length in the indices of most family bibles. Secondly; that Christ was born four years before the common era, is agreed to by all writers. The proof of this is incontestable: for on the thirteenth of March, B. C. 4, there was an eclipse of the moon; and Herod was at that time suffering his last illness, and he died that year, so that his charge to destroy the innocents must have been of earlier date; which proves that Christ was born some months before this eclipse.—(*Prideaux, Josephus, &c.*) This point needed not to be proved, as few sane men will call it in question.

Again; Townsend, in his late profound work, the Chronological Bible, places the crucifixion in A. D. 29; as does Playfair also; and this is followed by the Comp. Comment., and is agreed to, latterly, by all men of chronological research. Gibbon says,* there is no reason to doubt that Christ died under the consulship of the two-

---

* Dec. and Fall, vol. i., 262; note 6.

Gemini, March 25th, A. D. 29; and an ancient and lately discovered, and well preserved medal, also states that it was on the 25th of March. It may be proper to state, that Usher and Prideaux, and all the seventy-week theorists, place the crucifixion in 33, A. D., because Christ was baptized, being thirty years old, in the fifteenth year of Tiberius, which, they say, began after the death of Augustus Cæsar, in August, A. D. 14, and which would make the year of Christ's baptism to have been in A. D. 29, and his death in 33, A. D. The solution of the difficulty is easy, for there were two epochs to the reign of Tiberius: the first, when he was made associate imperator with Augustus; and the second, after his death; and, by dating Luke's statement, of fifteen years from the first epoch, all the facts harmonize with each other.

These theorists make Christ to have been only thirty-three and a half years of age, at the crucifixion; and yet, also, thirty-seven years old. We have before us an ecclesiastical history, that states that Christ was born four years B. C., and was crucified in 33, A. D., and that then he was just thirty-three and a half years old! And is not Bishop Usher, the prince of chronologers, chargeable with the same inconsistency?

From the light we enjoy, it is a fair conclusion that Christ was about thirty-three and a half, or thirty-four years old, at his crucifixion; and that this was in A. D., 29, March 25th. That Christmas day was not his birthday, is susceptible of ample proof; Hebraic analogy, and circumstances, and history, combine to place his birth, either at the autumnal or vernal equinox, or at the beginning of the Hebrew civil or sacred year. If the nativity was at either of these epochs, and the crucifixion was at the vernal equinox, then was Christ either exactly thirty three and a half, or thirty-four years of age, as is generally supposed.

Paragraph IV.

YEAR OF JUDEA'S FALL.

The next epoch we are called upon to determine, is that of the desolation of Judea, the burning of the temple, and the beginning of the long captivity. This was the year 68, A. D. The last sacred year ended at the first of Nisan, of the year 68; the army of Titus entered Judea in this month, and encamped at Jerusalem on the 14th, when the passover was to be celebrated; on the 17th of Panemus, the daily sacrifice ceased; and on the 8th of Ab, the temple was burned; and on the 10th of Elul, the city was broken up, and its walls were broken down; and all things were desolated by the beginning of the seventh month, or the new year's day of the civil year. About this epoch, chronologers have given themselves apparently little concern, as their disagreements evince, for they variously place it in 68, 69, 70, 71, 72, and 73, A. D. The records of those most deeply interested in preserving a true account of the year of Israel's desolation, and upon whose memory it must have made the deepest impression, that is, of the Jews themselves, show that this event was in the Rabbinical year of the world, 3828, which coincides with A. D. 68. The Roman historians, upon whom many chronologers depend, differ among themselves in those accounts of the reigns of monarchs, essential to a true understanding of the date of the epoch we are seeking. But the case is by no means as hopeless a one to settle as might be supposed; for carelessness has evidently influenced chronologers, more than want of materials. Our materials, we believe, are chosen with the most candid and critical discrimination; and our results harmonize with the date the Jews assign to the fall of their commonwealth.

As the crucifixion was in A. D. 29¼, and Christ was then thirty-three and a half or thirty-four years of age, and was thirty years old at the 15th year of Tiberius, if we subtract the difference between thirty and thirty-three and a half, from twenty-nine and a quarter, we are brought to A. D. 25 and about nine months, which is about the time of year when Tiberius assumed the purple, or the anniversary of his reign. If we assume that Christ was born at the vernal equinox, B. C. 5, as Dr. Clarke, and many moderns and ancients teach, then, he being thirty-four years of age at the crucifixion, if we subtract four years from 29 A. D., eighty-five days, (or March 25) we are carried back to the month Nisan, A. D. 25, as the 15th of Tiberius. In either case, we are removed from this year of 25 to A. D. 10, by subtracting either fifteen full years, or fourteen and a half of Tiberius from it. If Christ was thirty years of age in the fall season, just at the anniversary of Tiberius' reign, it is very unreasonable to believe that Saint Luke would speak of the 15th of Tiberius, when that year had scarcely begun; but, as he does speak of it, the presumption is, that it either was about complete, or well advanced toward completion.

The notion that John's baptism of multitudes, and preaching to them in open fields, was in the frosts of winter, seems absurd, and we have no proof of it; and, more especially, as the manifestation of great personages and events was more likely to begin at the Hebrew new year, and at the feasts. We think no sensible scholar, of the Protestant school at least, will dispute about the time of Christ's birth; we are certain it would be to their shame to dispute his age; and we therefore conclude, that either fourteen and a half or fifteen years are to be subtracted from A. D. 25, to find the beginning of Tiberius' reign; and, by either process, we are carried to A. D. 10, and the latter or former portion of the year. Having this epoch, as a fair goal, we set out from it to reach A. D. 68. The length of the reign of Tiberius was from August 28th, A. D. 10, to March 16, or 26th, A. D. 37, a period of twenty-five years, six months, and twenty days; the length of the reign of his successor, Caius Caligula, was three years and eight months; and of his successor, Claudius Cæsar, thirteen years, eight months, and twenty days; and of his successor, Nero Cæsar, thirteen years and eight days; after him Galba reigned till the third of January following, and was murdered on the fifteenth; his reign was seven months and seven days; Otho next reigned, three months and three days; Vitellius next reigned, eight months and five days, and was killed on the third of Caslen, answering to November; Vespasian, however, began his reign on the fifth of the Nones, or Ides of July preceding, and in his second year, about the month of September, Jerusalem was destroyed.

While the historian allows seven months and seven days to Galba, we allow him but five months and nineteen days; and we assign Vitellius three months and six days, because they were cotemporary with other monarchs. This fact is admitted by historians, and is very manifest by a strict addition of the days and years of their predecessors, and seeing the time of the year when Nero ended his reign, and comparing this date with the known days when Galba and Vitellius ended their reigns, and the date of Vespasian's election to the purple. According to this, Nero ended his reign about the 14th of July, 66 A. D.; and Galba's images were thrown down, and Otho was declared emperor; and Vespasian was declared emperor in July following; but Vitellius was his cotemporary till November, or Casleu. Galba, Otho, and Vitellius, are omitted from Ptolemy's canon, showing that none of them reigned a single year; and Dio estimates the sum of their reigns, seriately, at about a year, which is close to what we reckoned it, before knowing his testimony. The sum of all the reigns, as thus explained, allowing one year and three months for Vespasian's, to the fall of Jerusalem, is fifty-eight years, one month, and fifteen days; and, adding this sum to the first year of Tiberius, August 28th, A. D. 10, or ten years, seven months, and twenty-seven days, we are brought to A. D. 68 and nine months. In this estimate there may be an excess of a few days, but we think no greater exceptions can be taken to it. The common epoch assigned to the associate reign of Tiberius, is A. D. 11, and we think we have shown good reasons for not adopting it; but if any think that this date is settled as much by testimony, as by the want of it, we would say, that though the epoch of the founding of Rome is supposed to be 753 years B. C., and, by consequence, the first of Tiberius synchronizes with 11 A. D., yet all must be aware that time never was measured by a more uncertain chronometer than the Roman year before the days of Julius Cæsar. Chronologers often rest content with assigning events to one year, which belong to another, because the want of time and facilities prevents their treating the subject with more accuracy.

The reader must perceive that we have spent much time and labor to be exceedingly accurate in our chronology; and that we differ from no chronologers of reputation by any large sum of years, but mostly about a year or two; and where we differ, we think he will allow that we do so for sufficient reasons. We are indebted mainly to Archbishop Usher, Prideaux, Josephus, Whiston, Townsend, and a few others, for our facts. We prefer to follow such profound men as these, to referring the reader to a host of almost irresponsible authorities. Whatever is excellent on the chronology of the eras reviewed, is embodied in the writings of these men. One thing we may be permitted to observe; that our chronology was not made to suit a theory, but, in the main, was decided upon before our theory was planned, and was, indeed, the very origin of it.

SECTION II.

Beginning of the Seventy Weeks.

1. *Epoch of the Cyrus Decree.*—The prophecy of the seventy weeks primarily designates the decree of Cyrus as their beginning epoch. In settling this point, we are necessarily governed by the strictest laws of just criticism, to avoid censure on the one part, and on the other to ascertain the truth. "To find the true sense of a written document, is often difficult and embarrassing, even when of recent date and in our own language, but the difficulty is greatly enhanced when it is of ancient date, and in a foreign tongue." Even the acts of our legislatures, framed with the most technical care, require judges of profound and discriminating learning to interpret them precisely. Yet there are rules of exposition which embody infallible principles of guidance to certainty; they are alike applicable to all species of writing, whether human or divine, and, if followed unvaryingly,

are certain to clear the meaning of the text of doubts, unless the composition be either ambiguous, or symbolic, or senseless. Two of these we introduce for our safeguards: the first is, that "the most simple and obvious sense of a passage is always its true one;" and the second is, that "no interpretation can be just which brings out of any passage a sense that is repugnant to the ascertained nature of things."—(*Stewart, Horne, Buck, Bib. Rep.*) In addition to these, another principle, of equal validity and importance, is, that every passage is to be taken in its literal sense, unless it be inconsistent with common sense to do so.

In applying these rules to Gabriel's annunciation to Daniel, it is at once obvious that if the words he uses are to be taken in their plain, obvious, and literal sense, then the decree of Cyrus, to *restore* and *build* Jerusalem, is that to which primary reference is had. Nothing can shake this position, unless it can be fully and unanswerably demonstrated, that, from the very nature of things, they can not by possibility apply to this decree.

In the first place, no one has ever yet attempted to deny this for any other reason than that, according to the common mode of interpreting the seventy weeks, they fail to equal the space of time between that decree and the death of Christ. But surely, every one can see that the simple and obvious meaning of the text can not be made to yield to a mere theory, however plausible. To allow this, is at once to abandon all hopes of arriving at the truth of any writing, and especially, to make the word of God of none effect. That it may be the more impressed upon the mind that the obvious import of the angel's message is a reference to the Cyrus decree, we would, secondly, place the case in its own simple light. More than one hundred and fifty years before the empire of Cyrus, Isaiah prophesied, saying, "thus sayeth the Lord to his anointed, to Cyrus, whose right hand I have holden, to subdue the nations before him: I will loose the loins of kings to open before him the two-leaved gates, and the gates shall not be shut, * * * that thou mayest know that I, the Lord, which call thee by thy name, am the God of Israel. For Jacob my servant's sake, and Israel mine elect, I have even called thee by thy name." "That confirmeth the word of his servant, and performeth the counsel of his messengers; that sayeth to Jerusalem, Thou *shalt be inhabited;* and to the cities of Judah, *Ye shall be built*, and I will raise up the decayed places thereof. That sayeth to the deep Be dry, and I will dry up the rivers: that sayeth to Cyrus, He is my shepherd, and shall perform all my pleasure: even saying to *Jerusalem Thou shalt be built:* and to the *temple*, Thy foundations shall be laid."—Is. xliv. xlv. Here is a plain statement, by God himself, that a great decree for the *restoring* and *building* of *Jerusalem* should be made by Cyrus: and the language is identical with that of Gabriel. Now, although there were three other decrees for the repairing of Jerusalem, yet none of them are rendered important by such pre--eminent prophetic emphasis as this of Cyrus.

Again; it is further evident, that this decree was to be given at the end of the seventy year's captivity; and for such a decree, Daniel was praying when Gabriel descended, as is evinced by the fact that he himself says, that he understood from Jeremiah, that at "the end of seventy years" the restoration of Israel should transpire, and he knew that it could not take place without an imperial decree to that effect. While praying, therefore, it is plain that he then expected the decree to be given by Cyrus, as he knew that the seventy years were about at an end. That he was preparing for such a decree, is not only intimated in the language of answer to his prayer, sent through Gabriel; (for he says to him, "from the going forth of the command to restore and build Jerusalem, &c.;") but it is as plain as need be, from the recorded portions of his supplications. Daniel knew, from the prophecy of Isaiah, that Cyrus was to give the desired command. Josephus, indeed, records that he showed that prophecy to Cyrus; and this is admitted by the learned. Everything conspires to show, that Daniel and Gabriel both referred to the same event. But, further, what great consolation could it be to Daniel, whom Gabriel came to comfort, to know that Gabriel had no reference to an immediate and anticipated decree, but spoke of some other one, to come eighty years after the captivity was to end. If Gabriel did not refer to the decree that Daniel did, it is plain that Daniel's prayer was not heard, which is contrary to the whole tenor of the angel's mission. The decree of Cyrus, recorded in the book of Ezra, was fully designed to embrace all that Daniel sought, and all that Isaiah foretold. But it is also clear, from history, that the Cyrus decree accomplished, ultimately, all that was predicted; this is allowed by Prideaux, who says that, " the publishing of the decree of Darius, A. A. C. 518, at Jerusalem, may be reckoned the thorough restoration of the Jewish state; and the people were in their cities, and the temple completed by A. A. C. 514." Had Gabriel appeared to Ezra, or Nehemiah, as he did to Daniel, there would be some propriety in limiting the weeks exclusively to their epochs; but as it is, there can be none. Besides these things, the decrees of Darius and Longimanus, were not for the restoring and building of Jerusalem, for Jerusalem was already built and restored; they were for carrying out the original decree of Cyrus, and for reforming abuses; they were but codicils to the will of Cyrus, inspired by the eternal Spirit. The decree to Ezra, was, however, more of the nature of that of Cyrus than any other; and if use is to be made of it, as a starting point for the seventy weeks, it must be simply as the finishing of a decree period, extending from Cyrus to Ezra. But after all, it is fully admitted that the decree of Cyrus coincides with the revelation of Gabriel, in every point save one, and that it does not amply coincide with any other decree. But it is also admitted, that this one excepted point may also coincide. Now, it is infallibly true, that perfect coincidence is perfect fulfillment, and as the most perfect coincidences exist between the prophecy of Gabriel and the decree of Cyrus, we must admit that the seventy weeks were to begin with the decree of Cyrus, or that they never have been fulfilled. But none will be so mad as to take so absurd a position; hence, the unknown period of seventy weeks will properly be begun at the decree of Cyrus, and end with the crucifixion and the fall of Jewry.

2. *Epoch of the Longimanus decree.*—This decree was a very important one, as it resulted in the restoration of the Hebrew ritual, and may be included in the meaning of Gabriel. It was given at the court of Persia, in Nisan, or March, B. C. 456, and took effect in the fifth month, or July following. The beginning of the weeks we place at the operation of the decree, because the word *of*, in the phrase "going forth *of* the commandment," is as properly rendered, by using the word *by* in its stead.

CONCLUSION—NEW THEORY.

It thus appears that from the Cyrus decree to the crucifixion was 564 years and some days; to the desolation it was 603 years and some days; from the Longimanus decree to the crucifixion was 483 years and some days; and to the desolation 522 years and some days. Now if the 70 weeks be reduced to days, and the days be taken for years, we have 490. But none of these periods coinciding with 490 years, the *a priori*, exposition which makes a day represent a solar year, is proved not to be intended by the prophecy. This theory totally failing, some other must be sought, whose legitimate, *a priori*, interpretation shall be realized in the fulfillment. We present the following as legitimate and sufficient: (1) The seventy weeks express *labor time only; seventy labor weeks of days or years, imply the co-existence of rest time; rest time consists of Sabbath days, regular holydays, and Sabbatic years; to obtain the full amount of solar time transpiring in seventy labor weeks, the co-existent rest time must be added; the amounts of such time to be added must be determined by the amount of rest time existing in the Hebrew calendar.* (2) The result of such additions will be symbolic or Hebraic years, and may be considered as representing solar years without any reductions, or they may be reduced to solar time. The year of 360 days is symbolic; the year of 364 days and that of 366 may be esteemed Hebraic. A time or year of years, may consist of as many years as there are days in a year. In section III we will show the various proportions of labor and rest time, and the length of years known to the Hebrews. In section IV we will show that the seventy weeks express only *labor time*.

SECTION III.

Hebrew Divisions of Time.

Paragraph I.

HEBREW WEEKS.

All Hebrew time, greater than a day, was divided into weeks of days, weeks of weeks, weeks of weeks of weeks, or 343 days, and weeks of months, and weeks of years. The Sabbatic year was the seventh year; and the jubilee was a Sabbatic year, and occurred every forty-ninth year. The first jubilee year, was the fiftieth after the possession of Canaan, the first being a rest year; but the jubilee period itself, was only forty-nine years long, and was made up of seven Sabbatic weeks; and the jubilee year coincided with the seventh Sabbatic year; so that there were not two rest years in succession.

Paragraph II.

SPIRITUAL AND CIVIL TIME.

In addition to the general division of time into weeks, it was further divided into spiritual and secular. Every seventh day was a holy day; and every seventh year was also a holy year; and every week of weeks of years, or every jubilee, closed with a year more especially sacred than any other rest year. They had also two kinds of calendar years: one began in the month Nisan, and was the sacred, or ecclesiastical year; the other began in the month Tisri, six months later, and was the civil year, at which the jubilee was sounded. The Sabbath, the Sabbatic years, and the jubilee years, were political, as well as spiritual, institutions. No division of the day into hours was known in the Mosaic economy; so that a part of a day was recognized as a whole day, or spoken of under that name. The amount of sacred time, in a jubilee period, was one and six-sevenths of all time.

Paragraph III.

LENGTH OF THE SACRED AND SECULAR YEARS.

1. *The Sacred Year.*—This was 364 days long. In proof, we adduce the following considerations: First, we claim, as confirmatory of this position, the general consent of Bible critics, that fifty-two weeks were reckoned

a year, among the Hebrews, as it is in all countries where time is computed by weeks. Second. The fulfillment of prophecy in a year of years, and fifty-two years, is proof that time was measured in this mode annually, and, also, that ages were thus measured. It was written in the law, that when Israel should disregard the Sabbatic years, that God would send them into captivity, until the land enjoyed its Sabbaths. Now, Jeremiah says, that the Babylonish captivity allowed the land of Judea to keep its violated Sabbaths. As the *desolation* of Judea continued only for fifty-two years, it is obvious that the neglect complained of, must have continued just 364 years. This fulfillment is full proof that God himself regarded the year of years, at least, as consisting of 364 equal parts, for his fulfillment endorses this view.

2. *The Civil Year.*—The civil year of the Hebrews, according to Calmet, was composed of twelve months. The length of this year coincided with the solar year, as near as it was possible for a year of days to coincide with a true solar year. It must, therefore, have coincided with the present Julian year, which was imported from Egypt, and, no doubt, derived from the Hebrews. It would then have been 366 days long, every fourth year, and 365 days every three years in four. Our reasons for this view are mainly these: First, There is no valid testimony against the position, nor can be. Second. The nature of the ceremonial law required the knowledge of an exact solar year. This all know, who have paid a moment's attention to the requirements of it. According to it, the sacrifices and triennial feasts were obliged to occur regularly, in the spring, summer, and autumn. Now, unless the year had been exact, there would have been such a shifting of these periods, in the course of ages, as to carry the vernal feast into the summer,

and to throw the autumn feast into the winter or spring. But, as we find these feasts, without any clashing, occurring at the same periods in the days of Solomon as in those of Moses, it is plain, that the Hebrew civil year must have coincided with the solar, as near as it was possible. Third. As these feasts were of divine origin, God knew that a perfect knowledge of the true solar year was requisite, to keep them up with regularity; and if the correct solar year was unknown, it is unreasonable to suppose that God would keep the Hebrews in ignorance of it, and yet require a close observance of it, as this would be preposterous.

Fourth. The Talmud, which is followed by most modern writers on Hebrew chronology, relates that the ancient Hebrew year consisted of twelve lunar months, which, falling short of the solar year, a month was intercalated whenever the 12th of Nisan happened to fall before the vernal equinox; and this month was called ve-Adar. This may have been their mode after the captivity, and after they became acquainted with the Grecians, but is plainly not of Mosaic origin. The *Comp. Commentary* remarks: "This arrangement of the Hebrew calendar, is made on the authority of (late) Jewish writers, who are not the best guides even in the affairs of their own nation. Their notation of the months has been implicitly followed by Christian critics and commentators universally; but we believe it to be incorrect; for, according to their distribution of the months, the religious festivals could never have been observed at the stated times; the seasons in Palestine not answering the purpose." In Carpenter's Calendarium Palestinæ, it will be seen that "the present Jewish calender is carried up a month too high." It is irrational to suppose that the Hebrew lawgiver, who regulated all things else with consummate skill and nicety of harmony, could have left the solar year in such an awkward and ungainly predicament as the Talmud represents it; for, according to its account, all of the fasts, feasts, sacrifices, ceremonies, summers, winters, harvests, and spring times, all of the Sabbatic years and jubilees were moving in a perpetual jerk, going hop, step, and jump, and jolting all civil business and sacred affairs into a perpetual jumble every three, or five, or eight years. A prelate, who was taught that the earth was the center of the universe, and that stars and suns rolled round it every day, impiously remarked, as he saw the absurdity of the doctrines, " that had he been of God's privy council, he would have advised him better." And many a prelate, in reading the Talmud, has felt that he could have advised Moses to adopt a more convenient year for his system to work by. The mechanism of the original Hebrew fabric can not be impeached of imperfection, for all its parts are of divine institution. But unless it was adjusted as near to the solar year as days can begin and end such a year, it was imperfect, as its motions were dependent upon a solar year to keep the machinery in well balanced operation. Springtime, and harvest-feasts were obliged to occur at precise seasons of the year, which could not have been the case, had these seasons been jostled about by the difference of a month or two almost every year. But Moses himself totally demolishes the Talmud fable, for he shows that he did not follow lunar months. The account of months and time, incidentally exhibited in the seventh chapter of Genesis, says Calmet, shows that he estimated the year to be 365 days long, (at least.) Scaliger, Prideaux, and Usher, inform us that the ancient Chaldean, Persian, and Egyptian year was 365 days long; and that some of them intercalated, to keep up with the sun. Their year, and that of Moses, seem identical in origin; and if his was so intercalated as to equal solar time, and thus to suit his system, we must suppose that he adopted it for general use; but if it was not so intercalated, he must have remedied its deficiency. Had it not approximated as near to solar time as a year can be made to do, his system would have become deranged by it, and hence, he must have adopted such a year, because the demand was imperious. But the nearest that a year of days can approach to the solar year, is to allow 365 days to three years successively, and give 366 days to the fourth. From the considerations, then, that the Mosaic law demanded a year as near to the Julian as is the solar, and that Moses knew of a year of 365 days long, it is a legitimate conclusion, that he intercalated one day in every four years, as his system imperiously required. The history of the Julian year is, that it was brought to Rome from Egypt by Sosigenes, and adopted by Julius Cæsar as the Roman year. But it is likely Sosigenes obtained it from books or traditions, rather than from observation. The famous astronomers of Greece and Rome, and other nations, were not able to ascertain the number of days of a solar year, nor to approximate closely to it; nor did ancient astronomy afford remarkable facilities for any correct knowledge on the subject. The fact, then, that a year of 365 days was known as early as Moses and Noah, is presumptive of a direct revelation on the subject. Indeed, as Moses gives the account of the deluge, and the time of its continuance, by immediate inspiration, and not from books, the revelation of the days and months of the year is certain.

Lastly. If prophecy is found to be fulfilled in years of this kind, it will confirm all our views indubitably. We have now seen, that all Hebrew time was divided into weeks, whether days or years, or years of years; and that a part of all their time was sacred time; and that the year was of two kinds, the sacred of 364 days, and the secular of 365 and 366. We now take another step, and will show that they had full and abbreviated time.

SECTION IV.

Abbreviated Time and Full Time.

We have already seen that the Hebrews had weeks of years, and we know that 70 weeks of years, or 490 years, will not fill the demand which the fulfillment makes, that they should equal 564 and 603 years. To these periods, we know they must be equal, from the absolute nature of the case. Now, as 70 weeks are less than 603 years, it is a plain case that a certain amount of time, not expressed by the 70 weeks, must be understood as connected with them, and that this must be added to them in order to fill the demand. It is also plain, that this time to be added, must be added in accordance with a clear and well defined principle. The next question, then, is, What is the principle? We reply, that the principle is this, That spiritual time is to be added to these weeks; that it is not expressed in them; and that the weeks are weeks of secular time. The weeks are, therefore, abbreviated weeks, and represent full time, but do not express it. We must, therefore, add spiritual or rest time to the weeks, in the proportions in which it actually existed in all Hebrew time, and then we shall reach the periods coinciding with the 564 and 603 years; and having done this, we not only show a fulfillment, but the fulfillment incontestably verifies the correctness of our interpretation.

A secular week will, it is obvious, contain a less number of days than a full week, which includes the Sabbath or Sabbatic year, and in order to get the full length of a Sabbatic week or jubilee, consisting only of secular time, a proper proportional of sacred time must be added to it. Because, during the existence of forty-two secular years, seven spiritual or rest years must also have transpired. It may be here observed, that in all Christian countries the rest days, such as Sabbaths and holy days, are unknown in law as days. So that a legal year is composed of not over 312 days, and generally, of not so many. To obtain then the solar time which transpired during 312, or less legal days, we must add in the uncounted, but understood, Sabbaths and holy days. Of this nature the seventy weeks partake; they are weeks of legal time, to which the Sabbath, or holy day time, must be added, in order to ascertain the full solar time that passed during their existence.

Besides the seventy weeks, there are other examples in scripture where abbreviated years are used instead of full ones. Thus, Moses and Paul both say it was 430 years from the Abrahamic covenant to the exodus; while Moses, in another place, shows that it was at least 603 years in full, from the covenant to the exodus. The book of Kings says that it was 480 years from the exodus to the foundation of the temple; while the books of Joshua, Judges, and Acts, show that it was over 600 years. Now, in each of these cases, both accounts must agree, because they are both inspired. The only way in which they can coincide is, by considering the shorter periods as consisting of secular time, and the longer, of both spiritual and secular time. These examples confirm our position with regard to the seventy weeks being abbreviated or secular time only. The position we here assume is also most completely sustained by the literal Hebrew text, which mentions the seventy weeks.

* In the phrase " seventy weeks are determined upon thy people, " &c., the English words " are determined " express the figurative sense of the Hebrew word NECHTAC, for which they are rendered; yet the word determined, in its etymological sense, coincides with the literal sense of *nechtac;* for it signifies *limited, cut short, abbreviated, decided, &c.* The word NECHTAC, which stands in the Hebrew text, and is translated " determined " in our version, literally signifies *cut short, cut, cut off, abbreviated, &c.*, and, figuratively, it means *decreed, divided, determined. &c.* In the Septuagint, NECHTAC is rendered into Greek by the word *sunetmethesan,* whose primary meaning is *to cut, to cut off, to abridge, to abbreviate, &c.* In the Vulgate NECHTAC is rendered by the words " *abbreviatæ sunt,*" which signify *abbreviated.* Here we have the fourfold testimony of four different languages, or rather the testimony of the most distinguished lingual scholars who have lived during the space of two thousand years, that the words of Gabriel to Daniel conveyed distinctly the notion that the seventy weeks were abbreviated weeks of years. Mr. Prideaux contended against this notion, doubtless, because it disagreed with his theory: but his argument is inadmissible; for it is in direct conflict with the signification of the word *nechtac* as laid down in the lexicons, and also with such a multitude of unbiassed scholars, who were more likely to be correct. In the

---

* We are indebted to Prof. SHELTON, of Union University, for assistance in this criticism.

Vulgate, the passage of the prophecy under consideration is rendered thus: "*Septuaginta hebdomades abbreviatæ sunt tuum populum*," &c.; which, being literally translated, reads thus, "*seventy weeks abbreviated are unto thy people.*" The early fathers, the Romish doctors, and a vast class of learned men, have approved of this rendering for ages past; and he who rejects it, must possess either uncommon erudition, or remarkable assurance. We maintain, therefore, that the literal meaning of the text teaches that our position is fully correct; that is, that the seventy weeks were of the abbreviated kind, and did not include Sabbatic years or rest time, but demanded their addition.

SECTION V.

Application of Principles.

Having shown that the seventy weeks must equal 564 and 603 years, and, also, that in the text they are abbreviated weeks, to which holy time must be added, we will now add the amount. The basis of this addition must be the relative proportion existing between sacred and secular time, as laid down in the Mosaic law. The sacred time is of two or three kinds, one consisting of Sabbath days, or holy days and of Sabbatic years. The Sabbath days are in the proportion of one day to six secular days; the Sabbatic years are in the proportion of one to every six. But, as one-seventh of all the Sabbatic years is composed of Sabbath days, it follows, that Sabbatic year-time would amount, in forty-nine years, to one-seventh less, in the aggregate, than would the whole number of Sabbath days in the same period; that is, in supplying the Sabbatic year-time required to complete the solar time, represented by the seventy weeks, we would add one year to every seven, and not one to every six, as in the case of Sabbath days. With these plain principles before us, we proceed to give various formulas by which the weeks may be interpreted.

Paragraph I.

SEVENTY WEEKS EQUAL TO FIVE HUNDRED AND SIXTY-FOUR YEARS.

FORMULAS.—1. If to 490 years we add one-seventh of it for Sabbatic time, we shall have 560 years.

2. An abbreviated week, we have seen, may consist entirely of secular time, or it may consist in whole or in part of it. Hence, if we take the Sabbatic year-time from a Sabbath week, and leave in the Sabbath days, we shall have $6\frac{1}{7}$ years. Now, if we multiply the 70 weeks by this, we shall have 430 years. As in this computation the Sabbaths of the Sabbatic year are taken out, the proportion to be added is less than one-seventh; and to obtain it, instead of dividing 430 by 7, we must divide it by 43, and take six parts of it. Dividing, therefore, 430 by 43, we have 10, and multiplying this by 6, we have 60, which, added to 430, gives 490; to this adding one-seventh, and we have 560.

3. By taking out all Sabbath days from a Sabbatic week, we have an abbreviated week of 6 years. Now, multiplying 70 weeks by 6, and we have 420; then adding one-seventh for Sabbatic time, we have 480, and then adding one-sixth for Sabbath-day time, and again we have 560.

4. By dropping both Sabbatic year and Sabbath-day time, we shall have an abbreviated week of $5\frac{1}{7}$ years. Now, multiplying 70 weeks by this, and we have 360. To this, if we add one-seventh for Sabbatic time, we

shall have 411⅔, and, adding to this Sabbath day time, or one-sixth, we shall have 480. To this again, we must add one-sixth, which gives us 560. The reason for three additions, when both Sabbath and Sabbatic time is taken from the multiplier, is found in the fact, that when we multiplied by the full week of 7 years, we then added one-seventh ; and when we multiplied by the week abbreviated by dropping only Sabbath day, or only Sabbatic time, we made two additions ; but, when we dropped both Sabbath day and Sabbatic year time, we must, of course, make one more addition of sacred time.

5. We have now shown, that by the various kinds of weeks multiplied into the 70, we obtain 560 years. We now show the same results, in another way, by estimating the weeks as years:

First. As 364 days make a year, and as 52 weeks also make a Hebrew year, it is obvious that 70 weeks will be equal to one year and 18—52. Now, 364 years plus 18—52 of 364 are just equal to 490, and, adding Sabbatic time, we have 560 years.

Second. It is well known that 49 weeks represented a Hebrew year; indeed, it is an abbreviated year, of a week of weeks of weeks, or of 343 days. Seventy weeks will equal one year and three-sevenths of a year of this kind; and one and three-sevenths of 343 are just equal to 490 ; and adding one-seventh, or Sabbatic time, and we again have 560 years.

Third. Forty-two weeks are, also, another form of an abbreviated year, and such a year consists, of course, of 294 days; and 70 weeks of this kind will equal one and two-thirds of 70 weeks ; and one and two-thirds of 294 are just equal, again, to 490 ; and, adding Sabbatic time, we again have 560.

Fourth. Thirty-six weeks are the lowest form of an

abbreviated year, and a year of this kind will consist of 252 days; and 70 weeks of this kind of year will make a year and 34—36; and once 252 and 34—36 of this, will just equal 490 again; and, Sabbatic time being added, will give us, again, 560 years.

Thus have we found eight modes of obtaining 560 years, and each one conforming strictly to Hebrew modes of estimation.

We remark, that 36 years of secular time are found to equal just 52 years, if we add to the 36 their proportional amount of sacred time. For example: in a jubilee period, there are seven Sabbatic, or rest years, and in the remaining 42 years, there are 12,348 days of secular time; for, in each of the 42 years there are 52 Sabbath days, and 18 extra holy days. Then, as 12,348 days of secular time imply a full period of jubilee time, or 49 years, we find that sacred time, added to 36 secular years in the same proportion, gives 52 years.

Example. $12,348 : 49 :: 364 \times 36 = 52$.

Or, as in 364 days, there are 18+52, or 70 sacred days, we will have the proportion of sacred time to secular as 70 to 294. Then, if 70 sacred days give 294 secular ones, or vice versa, then 42 years will give 10 years.

Example. $294 : 70 :: 42 = 10$.

Let this quotient be added to 42, and again we have 52 years. In these cases, the proportion of sacred to secular time, is as 1 to 6; 70 to 294; and 10 to 52. In these cases, the year of 364 days, or 52 weeks, is the basis of the results. We shall add several others.

First. As one kind of Hebrew year consists of 360 days, there will be in it $51\frac{3}{7}$ weeks, and 70 weeks will make one and a third years of this kind, which equal 480. Now, adding Sabbath day time, or one sixth, to this, and we again have 560.

Second. If we take one and one third of 364, as we did of 360, we shall have $485\frac{1}{3}$, and, adding to this Sabbath day time, we shall have $565\frac{2}{3}$.

It will now be seen, that we have obtained two periods of Hebrew years; one of 560 years, and another of $565\frac{2}{3}$. Neither of these amounts are in form exactly what we want, but they are in value precisely what we want, as we will now show.

1. The Hebrew year of 360 days, or years, is only a symbolic year, and was never in use as a civil year; it was used only among the prophets. It being a year, however, it must symbolize the kinds of Hebrew years which were in use. Now, as one kind of year consisted of 364 days, a year of years of this kind would equal 364 years multiplied by 364 days, and these days would, of course, be represented by the year of 360 years, or days. Now, 364×364 equal 132,496 days, or 362 years $278\frac{1}{3}$ days. Then, as 360 years equal 132,496 days, 560 will equal $206,104\frac{8}{9}$ days, which are exactly equal to 564 solar years, and 109 days.

2. We have seen that the 70 weeks are equal to $565\frac{2}{3}$ years. As these must be reckoned as consisting of 364 days each, by reducing them to exact solar time, they are equal to just 564 years, and 109 days.

3. We have seen that 70 weeks are equal to one year, and 18—52, and that $1\frac{18}{52}$ of 364 equal 490, and that this, by Sabbatic addition, equals 560.

Now, as 364 years, multiplied by 364 days, equal 362 years $278\frac{1}{3}$ days, if we add Sabbatic time, or one-seventh of it, we shall have 151,424 days, or $414\frac{4}{7}$ years; then adding Sabbath time or one sixth, and we have $176,661\frac{1}{4}$ days or 483 years, 250 days. Then, to this again, add Sabbath time, and again we have 564 years and 109 days. These three additions of sacred time, we have seen, are allowable, when we begin with the lowest amount to which 70 weeks are reducible.

4. A fourth mode of computing these weeks is very remarkable and exact, and confirmatory of all that we have said. A Hebrew year in one of its forms, consists of 49 weeks, or 343 days, and in another, of 364; making just 21 days difference between them. The former of these, is an abbreviated year, of course. Now, then, a Sabbatic week of years of this kind, would, when abbreviated by taking away the Sabbaths, be abbreviated by just one year and 21 days, or $1\frac{3}{9}$ years. Then, as one week must have $1\frac{3}{9}$ years added to it, seventy weeks would require the addition of $10\frac{30}{9}$ years, which would make $89\frac{30}{9}$ years. Now, multiply this by seven, and we shall have $564\frac{2}{3}$ years. This lacks only four days of equaling the other amount already obtained, and in so vast a period, so small a variation can be no sort of objection to it, especially as the coincidence was to be in weeks rather than in days. Having now, in a variety of differing ways, arrived at the fact that the 70 weeks were 564 years, and 105 or 109 days long, we proceed to show that this sum exactly coincides with the fulfillment of prophecy.

Paragraph II.

SEVENTY WEEKS EQUAL TO SIX HUNDRED AND THREE YEARS.

FORMULAS.—1. As 49 weeks are an abbreviated year, we may have the following formula:

49 : 360 ∷ 70 weeks equal to $514\frac{2}{7}$. Now add in Sabbath day time, and we have 600 years.

2. As 42 weeks are an abbreviated year, they may be equal to 360 days. Then we may have the following formula: As 42 : 360 × 70 = 600.

3. As 49 weeks may also represent a Hebrew year of 364 parts, we may have the following formula: As $49 : 364 \times 70 = 520$. Now, adding Sabbath time, we have $606\frac{2}{3}$.

4. As 42 weeks may also represent 364, we may have $42 : 364 \times 70 = 606\frac{2}{3}$,

Having now attained two periods from the 70 weeks, one of 600,* and another of $606\frac{2}{3}$ years in length, we are to reduce them to solar time. We here remark, that in computing the weeks which related to the spiritual matter of the crucifixion, we estimated them by years of years, of 364 parts each, but, in turning to civil matters, the use of civil time will be required. The longest year we have seen, was 366 days. Now, the text gives no intimation as to what kind of a year the 70 weeks were to be realized in; of course, therefore, we are to look to the fulfillment itself, to settle that matter, and in whatever kind it was fulfilled, that, undoubtedly, was the kind intended. The fulfillment will, and must, determine whether the years were to be reduced into solar years, or whether they symbolized solar years. With these things premised, we will reduce the $606\frac{2}{3}$ to years of 366 days. They may be considered as years of 364 days, as they stand.

---

* We may here observe, with reference to this great period of 600 years, that Josephus says it was recognized among the Jews in very ancient times, as the great astronomic year. We give his own words, "God afforded them a longer term of life on account of their virtue, and the good use they made of it in astronomical and geometrical discoveries, which would not have afforded the time for foretelling the periods of the stars, unless they had lived 600 years, for the *great year* is completed in that interval.

THE DISCOVERY.

1. Multiply $606\frac{2}{3}$ by 364, divide the product by 366 days, and we have 603 years and $128\frac{2}{3}$ days, or 129 days. A part of a day, with the Jews, was esteemed as a whole one.

2. A year of years of 364 days each, when reduced to years of 366 days, amounts to 362 years and 4 days. Then, as the symbolic year, or 360 years, represents any Hebrew year, it will represent 362 years and 4 days. We have then the following formula and result:

$360 : 362$ years 4 days $\times 600 = 603$ years 129 days.

3. As near as can possibly be ascertained, in addition to the exclusively Sabbath day time, one twelfth of all other time was sacred time, or, in other words, the days of fasts and feasts, which existed in addition to weekly Sabbaths, were also estimated as Sabbath or rest days. These amounted to just one month. Now, one-twelfth of 364 equals $30\frac{1}{3}$ days, and in a Sabbatic week there would be 7 times $30\frac{1}{3}$ sacred days. This sum would include the difference of 21 days, which exists between the year of 343 and 364 days or years. There would, therefore, in a Sabbatic week be one year and $\frac{131}{343}$ to be added to the secular time; for 343 becomes the divisor and representative year in these computations. We then have the following formula and result:

If 7 years, or one week, gives $1\frac{131}{343}$ years, then 70 weeks, or 490 years, will give $113\frac{1}{3}$. And this sum, added to 490, gives us just $603\frac{1}{3}$ years, or 603 years and 122 days. This will be found exceedingly accurate.

4. As 49 weeks represented a year, and as we find 28 days, or four sacred weeks of time in the year, besides the Sabbaths, if we add these to 49 we shall have 53

weeks. Now, as 70 weeks, or 490 years, are 49 weeks multiplied by ten, so multiplying 53 by 10, we shall have 530 years. Now, adding Sabbath time, or one seventh, and we have 605$\frac{5}{7}$ years. If now we multiply this by 1$\frac{3}{7}$, and divide by 366, and subtract the quotient from 605$\frac{5}{7}$, we shall again have 603 years and 129 days.

It is difficult to explain the reason for this multiplication satisfactorily, yet it is plainly correct. We know that 430 was one form of the 70 weeks. Now, if to this we merely add Sabbatic time, or one seventh, we have 491$\frac{3}{7}$ years. Now, we know that this is an excess of 1$\frac{3}{7}$ over the true value of the 70 weeks; and that is about all we know of it. Its conformity to some correct, yet unknown principle, is proved by its conformity to truth.

Paragraph III.

SEVENTY WEEKS EQUAL TO FOUR HUNDRED AND EIGHTY-THREE YEARS.

FORMULA.—70 weeks multiplied by 6, the number of days in an abridged or "cut short" week, will equal 420 days or years, and adding Sabbatic time, or one seventh of them, we have 480 years. Then, as the symbolic year of 360 years equals 132,496 days, 480 years will equal 483 years and 250 days.

Paragraph IV.

SEVENTY WEEKS EQUAL TO FIVE HUNDRED AND TWENTY-TWO YEARS.

FORMULA.—$70 \times 7\frac{3}{7} = 520$; and as 360 represents 362 years and 4 days, as already shown, then 520 will 522 years and 326 days.

CONCLUSION.

We have shown that seventy symbolic weeks may have seven, *a priori*, senses, legitimately, viz: $70 \times 5\frac{1}{7} = 360$; and $70 \times 6 = 420$; $70 \times 7\frac{1}{7} = 430$; $70 \times 7 = 490$; $70 \times 6\frac{6}{7} = 480$; $70 \times 7\frac{3}{7}$, and $70 \times 4\frac{6}{7} = 411\frac{3}{7}$. We have also shown that these may be considered abbreviated weeks, to which rest time may be added. We have, also, shown that upon reduction to solar time, the 70 weeks may equal 483 years and 250 days; 522 years and 326 days; 564 years and 109 days; and 603 years and 129 days. We now, then, inquire, do any of these results coincide with the fulfillment of the 70 weeks. As we know certainly that these weeks are fulfilled, and also the dates when they were realized, we will date them at one of these points, say at the crucifixion, and return into the past and see where they carry us. 564 years and 109 days, dated at the crucifixion, March 25th, A. D. 29, carries us back to the 6th of December, B. C. 537, right to the very week when Israel left Babylon by virtue of the Cyrus decree. Let us date the 603 years and 129 days at this point, and return, and we are brought to the 21st of Nisan, A. D. 68, and to the very day on which the desolator encamped at Jerusalem. Again, dating the 483 years 250 days at the crucifixion, and returning we are carried to 456, B. C., and the month of July, when Ezra, by virtue of the decree of Longimanus, began the restoration of the Mosaic ritual; and, dating the 522 years and 326 days in the month of July, 456, B. C., we are brought forward to A. D. 68, and to the month Sivan or June, when the great mount was built which brought the ruin of Jerusalem. Here, then, the fulfillment of the 70 weeks actually coincides with FOUR of our, *a priori*, expositions, and gives a quadruple sanction to the legitimacy of our expositions, and thus determines our accuracy infallibly. Nothing of this kind has hitherto been presented to the world, and we, therefore, may claim the discovery without any immodesty or injustice to others.

Observe, now, that our labor has not been to prove that the seventy weeks are fulfilled; this is an admitted fact; our object has been to ascertain from this fact, the mode of explaining the weeks, *a priori*, so that we might see how they coincided with fulfillment. We showed, upon self-evident principles, that any legitimate, *a priori*, expositions with which the actual solar lengths of the weeks would coincide, must be counted those which the prophecy was intended to fulfill; we showed that our expositions were as legitimate, *a priori*, as any others; and as God's own fulfillment endorses them, who will deny their validity? Who can show the illegitimacy of our interpretations? We challenge the world to the labor. We have not proved, *a priori*, that our expositions are those intended, by God, to explain the prediction; such a thing can be done by no mortal; we have shown the need of a new theory to explain the text, and the theory presented, *a priori*, perhaps as doubtful as any other, is yet changed to demonstration by the, *a posteriori*, proof of a divine realization. In the very same way, that every obscure prophecy is shown to be fulfilled, so our exposition explains the realization of the weeks. But again let it be emphasized with power, that our showing is not merely strong with the strength of a single overwhelming coincidence, nor only doubly strong to convict the mind of its veracity; its truth rushes upon us like the *four* winds of heaven, and besets with the might of a whirlwind; it sheds its light, not from one lone star of durable fire, but, with the quadruple splendor of the sun, it expels all darkness, and obscures only with its excess of brightness. It is as profound as mathematics, and as conclusive as geometry; requiring sense to comprehend it; only "the wise shall understand." From the demonstration here given, we possess, henceforth, four, *a priori*, expositions, as a key to the days, months, and times of Daniel and John.

We showed, 1. That all prophecy relating to the period from the desolation of Judea to the present age, was not to be understood "till the time of the end." 2. That the last prophecy of Daniel is a key to this general mystery. 3. That the chronologic days and times are a key to this vision. 4. That these days and times are to be understood by the wise only, and in such an age as ours. 5. That scripture allows a day to symbolize a year, but does not specify what kind of a year is to be understood. 6. That its exact and intended meaning can be known only by a realization of some one of the meanings which may be legitimately attributed to the term day. 7. That any meaning is legitimate which is not opposed to the context, nor to the nature of things, prior to fulfillment. 8. The only prophecy, containing symbolic chronology, which, being fulfilled, enables us, thereby, to determine the exact solar time symbolized by prophetic days, is that of the "seventy weeks." 9. The seventy weeks may be legitimately esteemed as "abbreviated or cut short weeks," expressing only labor time, to which proportional Hebrew rest time may be added, to obtain the full time they represent. 10. The time, thus obtained, may be considered as symbolic of Hebrew years of years of 364 or 360 parts each, and these may or may not be reduced to solar time; or the time obtained by these additions may be considered as true solar time, and not symbolic. 11. That we obtained by either of these modes of computation, 483 years and 250 days; 522 years and 326 days; 564 years and 109 days; and 603 years and 129 days, as legitimate meanings of the 70 weeks. 12. That the 70 weeks were fulfilled in four ways, and in four lengths, exactly coinciding with these legitimate, *a priori*, expositions, thus demonstrating that they were the exact lengths of the 70 weeks, or 490 days, intended to be taught by inspiration. The conclusion is, therefore, that knowing the mode in which God has, by fulfillment, explained the length of symbolic weeks and days, we have a key to the days and years of Daniel's last vision, and also of that entire vision, and of all its collaterals, whether delivered by Daniel, Isaiah, Ezekiel or St. John. If there is no mistake in the whole argument, and we think no serious one can be found, then our interpretations are of the utmost utility to our country. To all commercial, agricultural, manufacturing, legislative, mechanical and Christian interests, they are of incalculable importance, and especially to warn our country against that great war of Armageddon, or "battle of the great day of God Almighty," which is so near us. We now apply our principles to certain dark historical features of the Bible, and finding in their explanation a confirmation of our theory, we proceed to explain all the symbolic chronology of Daniel and Revelation.

SECTION VIII.

Four Hundred and Eighty and Four Hundred and Thirty Years.

Paragraph I.

FOUR HUNDRED AND THIRTY YEARS.

Moses and Paul say it was 430 years from the covenant with Abraham to the law, or exodus. But if we look back to the detailed account of this same period, we see that it was much longer than 430 years. For God assured Abram, at the making of the covenant, that his seed should be in bondage, in a strange land, for 400 years. Now, Jacob was 130 years old at the descent into the land of bondage, and Isaac was 60 years old at Jacob's birth. Now, these together, make 590 years. But the covenant was several years earlier than this, as it was just before the birth of Ishmael, (see Gen. 15th ch.); and Ishmael was 13 years old at the birth of Isaac.

As these years are given in round numbers, there is, doubtless, a little excess over the true solar time, for it was customary with the ancients to call a part of a year a whole year. So, that Jacob's being born when Isaac was sixty, might be when he was *in* his sixtieth year. The whole amount can not rationally exceed 604 solar years, and was, doubtless, somewhere between 603 and 604 years. Now, we have seen, that 430 years is one form of the 70 weeks, and that 70 weeks were just equal to 603 years and 129 days. The 430 years, and the detailed chronology of the same period, are thus reconciled by our mode of exposition, and can not be satisfactorily explained in any other.

Paragraph II.

FOUR HUNDRED AND EIGHTY YEARS.

In I. Kings vi., it is stated that the foundation of Solomon's temple was laid in the 480th year after the exodus from Egypt, and in Solomon's fourth year. Josephus says, the period was 592 years long, but his detailed accounts vary a little from this aggregate. St. Paul says, the judges continued for 450 years; and after them David and Saul reigned, each 40 years, and Solomon $3\frac{1}{3}$, to the time of the foundation. These together, make $533\frac{1}{3}$ years, to which must be added the 40 years in the wilderness, making $573\frac{1}{3}$; to this must be added the days of Joshua and Samuel; these are reckoned, by some, to amount to 30 years; so that all taken together, will amount to $603\frac{1}{3}$ years.

Now, we have seen that 480 years was one form of the 70 weeks, which we know to equal $603\frac{1}{3}$ years. These explanations of these two periods are confirmatory of the correctness of our principles of interpretation. We could proceed, also, to show that all the great eras of the Hebrews are measured by some form of the lengths of the seventy weeks or Sabbatic weeks of years.

CHAPTER II.

DAYS, YEARS, MONTHS, AND TIMES.

Having ascertained the principles by which symbolic time is to be estimated, we proceed to apply them to the great prophetic periods predicted in the books of Daniel and Revelation.

SECTION I.

Twelve Hundred and Sixty Days.

In the eleventh chapter of Revelation, it is said that the two witnesses shall prophesy, clothed in sackcloth, for 1260 days; and in the twelfth chapter, it is said, the woman fled into the wilderness, with twelve stars upon her head, for 1260 days. That the two witnesses, and the woman, and stars coincide, no one can doubt; and their period of humiliation, in each case, being the same, the 1260 days of each must begin at the same points, and end in the same. That their beginning is at church and state union, we have already shown. We have seen, also, that this union is to date from the 19th of June, 325, at the Council of Nice; and, also, that the revision of the law completing this union, in detail, took place under Justinian, somewhere between 529 and 534, A. D. We saw, also, that the 70 weeks had two double modes of fulfillment; one set of modes being spiritual, and the other secular. We may also anticipate the same kind of twice double fulfillment, in the 1260 days. We shall proceed now to ascertain both kinds.

Paragraph I.

TWELVE HUNDRED AND SIXTY DAYS—SPIRITUAL LENGTHS.

1. As 490, or 70 weeks, equal 564 years and 109 days, 1260 days, or 180 weeks, will equal 529,984 days, or 1451 years and 17 days. Now, from the beginning of church and state union, June 19th, 325, down to the beginning of the disunion of church and state, at the rise of the United States, July 4th, 1776, was just exactly 529,984 days. And, as the humiliation of the woman and witnesses was to be during this union, and was also to be for 529,984 days, the coincidence is mathematically perfect. Nothing could be a more perfect demonstration of a fulfillment of a prophecy, than that here given. In this computation, it must be remembered, that the year 1776 was a leap year, and that there is a difference of about six hours between the meridian of Nice and the United States; and, also, that a part of a day, by Hebrew measure, is taken as a whole one. The 19th of June, 325 is, also, to be included. We estimate by true solar time, or 315,659,277 tenth seconds to the solar year.

2. As 70 weeks were also equal to 483 years and 250 days, or 176,661¼ days, 1260 days, or 180 weeks are equal to 1243 years and 267 days. If, now, we subtract this from July 4th, 1776, we are carried back to 532 A. D., and 274th day, or 1st of October. This is as near the date of the framing of the empire church laws, by Justinian, as can possibly be estimated from the knowledge we have of history. If some European scholars would search and look, doubtless, our exposition here would be found to coincide with the events exactly to a day, as it does in our previous exposition of the 1260 days.

Paragraph II.

SECULAR LENGTH OF THE TWELVE HUNDRED AND SIXTY DAYS.

1. Seventy weeks are equal to $603\frac{1}{8}$ years, and 1260 days, or 180 weeks, will equal $1551\frac{3}{7}$, and adding this to 325, A. D., and we are carried down to 1876 or 1877.

2. As 70 weeks are equal to $522\frac{6}{7}$ years, 1260 days, or 180 weeks, will equal 1344 years and a little over three sevenths, and dating this at 532, A. D., we are again brought to 1876 or 1877, A. D. Of course we may look for the overthrow of state dominion in the church universally, by about this time. There may, however, be another spiritual interpretation of the 1260 days, and it is very possible they may end from about 1862 to 1865, if not earlier; we have no certainty of this, and can only reason upon it by analogy. As this present time is the last vial period, we need be astonished at nothing occurring in the way of revolutions in Europe. The destruction of the empire church throughout Europe will certainly transpire before the fall of monarchy; and as monarchy will all go down before 1878, we may look for the overthrow of the Roman church very soon after Russia conquers Turkey.

SECTION II.

1290 Days—1708 Years.

These days are spoken of in Daniel xii. They are there shown as a partial interpretation of the three and a half times, and represented the time during which the POWER of the holy people, or Christian Israel, was to be depressed. At their end this power or nationality was to revive, and ultimately fill the world. Their end is the beginning of "the time of the end," which extends to the end of the 1335 days. The time at which they were to be dated, is stated to be at the cessation of the daily sacrifice. This occurrence took place on the 17th of Panemus, A. D. 68; that is, on the 189th day of that year. We place the date at this day because the seventy weeks ended on the 97th day of A. D. 68; and that day coincides with the 14th of Nisan, when the last passover of the Hebrews was celebrated at Jerusalem; and on which day, according to Josephus, the Romans encamped at the city. History does not state positively, that this 97th day of A. D. 68, was the 14th of Nisan, nor does it deny it; and it is certain that the date can not be from the true point more than twelve days. For the Grecian mode of intercalation, then prevailing in Judea, and the 14th of Nisan having been on the 25th of March, or the 85th day of the year A. D., 29, as we have seen, there could be no greater variation. Now, as the 70 weeks were to end at the invasion of Judea, and as they end on the 97th day of 68, and, as the Roman army camped at Jerusalem on the 14th of Nisan, the 14th of Nisan must coincide with the 97th day of 68, where these weeks ended. Again; the perfect harmony of this assumption, with all the interpretations of the other symbolic periods, is a full confirmation of this position.

First Interpretation.—The 1290 days are composed of three times 430 years, or of $3\frac{7}{3}$ times 360 years. Now, the 70 weeks, we know, are resolvable into 430 years, and, of course, the 430 years must equal some value of the 70 weeks. Now, 70 weeks are equal to 490 years, and three times this equals 1470; then, adding Sabbatic time, or one seventh, and we have 1680. Then, as 360 stands for the year of 366 days, if 360 equal 366, then 1680 will equal 1708 years exactly.

Second Interpretation.—As all the forms of the 70 weeks are resolvable into each other, and as 480 is one form, we may multiply it by $3\frac{7}{3}$, since 1290 is $3\frac{7}{3}$ of

360; we then have $480 \times 3\frac{7}{12} = 1720$. Again, if to 430 we add Sabbatic time, or one sixth, we have $491\frac{2}{3}$; and, multiplying this by 3, we have $1474\frac{2}{3}$ years; and, adding Sabbatic time, we have 1720 years. From this we see, again, that the values of the weeks are interchangeable. Now, as the 70 weeks equal 520 years, and, as 3 times this equals 1560, if we add one seventh of it to 3 times 490, or $3\frac{1}{2}$ times 420, that is, to 1470, we shall have $1692\frac{6}{7}$; now, dividing 1560 by 104, for extra sacred time, and we have 15, which, added to the above, gives $1707\frac{6}{7}$ years, or 1707 years 314 days. Now, the 1290 days were to be dated from the setting up of the abomination of desolation, as well as from the cessation of the daily sacrifice; and this may well be settled as having fully occurred at the burning of Jerusalem, on the 8th of Elul, or 239th day of 68, A. D. The two dates at which these 1290 days were to begin are, then, respectively, the 189th day, and 239th day, of 68. Dating the first length, or 1708 years, at the former, and we are brought exactly to July 4th, 1776; and, dating the latter at the 239th day, we are also brought to July 4th, 1776.

SECTION III.
Thirteen Hundred and Thirty-Five Days.

If to 1335 we add Sabbatic, and then Sabbath time, we shall have 1780 years. Then 360 stands for 366 civil years; 1780 will stand for $1809\frac{2}{3}$. Now, if this be dated from the attack and burning of the city, or 68, A. D., 239 days, we are carried down to A. D. 1878, and to the 117th day. At the close of these days, the scattering of the power of the Christians was to be entirely completed, so that the governments of Europe will be changed into a Christian democracy by that year. The last end of the three and a half times will also close with them, as the 1290 and 1335 days are but an interpretation of the three and a half times of the Gentiles.

SECTION IV.
Forty-Two Months.

Revelation xi., xiii. This period is said to be the length of time the Gentiles should tread the holy city under foot, and the time during which the beast with the wounded head was to continue. These months are plainly an abbreviated year of months, for their very number indicates this fact. If we add to these Sabbatic time, we have 49 months, and if we add other sacred time, or 3 months, we have 52 months.

First Interpretation.—If we estimate the 52 months as consisting of four weeks, or 28 days each, we shall have 1456 days or years. Then, esteeming these as representing years of 364 days each, and multiplying them by this sum, we have 529,984 days.

Second Interpretation.—If the months be supposed to consist of 30 days each, we shall have $42 \times 30 = 1260$ days, and $49 \times 30 = 1470$ days; and $52 \times 30 = 1560$ days.

Then, as 70 weeks equal 483 years 250 days, 1470 days, or 210 weeks, will equal 1451 years and 17 days, or 529,984 days. And, as $70 = 411\frac{3}{7}$, and as this equals 151,424 days, then 1260 days, or 180 weeks, will equal 1243 years 277 days. And, as 70 weeks equal 490 years, and as 490 equal $176,661\frac{1}{4}$ days, then 1560 will equal 562,132 days, or 1539 years and 312 days.

Third Interpretation.—As in the interpretation of the 70 weeks, we saw that 7 weeks were equal to an additional value of $1\frac{7}{10}$ weeks, then 42 months will equal $48\frac{1}{5}$.

Now, multiplying this sum by 30 days, the number of days in a month, and we have 1451 years and one week.

Fourth Interpretation.—As 132,496 days are a year of years, or 364×364, the one month will equal one twelfth of this value, or 11,041⅓ days. If, now, we add Sabbatic time to the 42 months, or one seventh of 42 to itself, we shall have 48 months; then multiplying 48 months by 11,041⅓ days, and we again have 529,984 days.

The time when the spiritual Gentiles began to tread down the true church of God, and the time when the beast with the wounded head received a seat from the dragon was, unquestionably, at the union of church and state. This union had two great epochs; the first begins at the session of the first Nicene Council, June 19th, 325; and the second was at the reorganization of Roman law, between A. D. 529, and 534. Now, in 529,984 days after this union began to exist, it was to begin to cease; and, as from this 19th of June, 325, to 4th of July, 1776, was just exactly 529,984 days, and as on that day church and state union did begin to cease, on a most tremendous scale, at the declaration of American independence, it is inevitably true that the rise of the United States was looked to, by prophecy, as the great beginning of the cessation of spiritual and, also, of political despotism. This last must be true, because political despotism can not exist without spiritual despotism of some kind, as its great coadjutor. If, now, we subtract 1243 years and 277 days from July 4th, or 1776 and 186 days, we are carried back to the last day of September, or first of October, 532. And as consummation of church and state union was between 529 and 534, it seems that 532 is the date, or epoch, at which prophecy begins the 42 months. Again; as 42 months equal 1539 years and 312 days, if we date them at June 19th, 325, we are carried forward to the 27th of April,

1865. As we could identify but two spiritual fulfillments of the 70 weeks, this giving three values to the 42 months is purely analogical, and can not be relied upon. It seems to us, the present empire church of Europe must fall before that time, though, possibly, it may be later. There are some modes of computation, that bring the time to 1861 or 2, but they are not endorsed by past fulfillment.

SECTION V.
Three and a Half Times—1243, 1451, 1708, 1810.

The word *time* is used as a prophetic measure of years in the seventh and twelfth chapters of Daniel, and in the twelfth chapter of Revelation; it is synonymous with the term year, as we find by reference to Daniel iv. 16. As it is used by the symbolic prophets, in preference to the term year, there must be some reason for it, and that reason consists in the peculiarity of the year it represents. We saw that the seventy weeks represented seven kinds of year, as 360, 411¾, 420, 430, 480, 490, and 520 years. Now, these 3½ times must coincide with one of these kinds of years. Indeed, it seems, that there are four classes of great years of years: First, the day year of years, consisting of 360 years, represented by days; second, the week year of years, represented by 52 weeks of years; third, the month year of years, or 42 months; and the year year of years, or 360 years × 360 years. Now, before fulfillment of the three and a half times transpires, it is impossible to determine with certainty what kind was intended by the prophet; but, when a fulfillment of them is seen in part, the whole fulfillment is easily calculated. We shall now take up these times, and give a twice-doubled interpretation of them. It is obvious, that as the seventy weeks had a twice doubled exposition, and that, as one pair of these applied to the civil department of Israel, and the other to the spiritual, so, also, these times may be interpreted. In the seventh chapter of Daniel, and in the twelfth of Revelation, the times are plainly applicable to spiritual matters; and in the twelfth of Daniel, they refer to civil matters primarily. As the spiritual lengths of the seventy weeks differ from civil time, so will the lengths of times also differ. We shall first interpret their spiritual lengths.

Paragraph I.

SPIRITUAL LENGTH OF THE TIMES.

1. 360 being one form of the symbolic times, or years of years, if we multiply it by $3\frac{1}{2}$, we have 1260 years. If to this we add Sabbatic time, or one seventh, we shall have 1440. Then, as $360=132,496$ days, or 364×364, 1440 will equal 529,984 days, or 1451 years and 17 days.

2. As $411\frac{3}{7}$ are another form of symbolic year, if we multiply this by $3\frac{1}{2}$, we again have 1440. Then, as $360=132,496$, 1440 will equal 529,984 days.

3. As 420 is another form of 70 weeks, or a time, and as this is equal to 151,424 days, or 132,496 plus one seventh of it, and as $3\frac{1}{2}$ times $420=1470$, then 1470 will equal again 1451 years 17 days.

4. As 364 years are a time, or year of years, if we add Sabbatic time to it, we have 416. Then, multiplying this sum by $3\frac{1}{2}$, we shall have 1456 years. Then, multiplying this sum by 364 days, the number in the sacred year, we have 529,984 days, or 1451 years and 17 days. In the same way we may deduce 1243 years and 277 days, as the value of the $3\frac{1}{2}$ times.

Now, as the little horn, or empire church in Europe, was to domineer over the church 529,984 days, and for 1243 years and 277 days, and as this domination ceased, in part, at the United States, these days must and there. Now, as this domination began on the 19th of June, 325, and as from that time to the 4th of July, 1776, was exactly 529,984 days, it is evident that here is a fulfillment, shown on a great scale, in part, and that a part remains yet to be realized.

Again; as the three and a half times of the woman in the wilderness, began also at the same date, her time of deliverance, also, began to end where the 1451 years ended; that is, at the rise of our country, July 4th, 1776.

Paragraph II.

SECULAR LENGTHS OF THE THREE AND A HALF TIMES.

First Length.—1. As 70 weeks, or 490 years, are a year of years, or a time, $3\frac{1}{2}$ times, this equal 1715 years. Then, as 490 equals 488 year, 1715 will equal 1708. 490 is equal to 488, because 360 equals 366, and as by consequence, 480 will equal 488, and 480 and 490 are equal to each other.

2. $480 \times 3\frac{1}{2} = 1680$. Then, as $360 = 366$, 1680 will equal 1708 years.

Second Length.—1. Seventy weeks are equal to 520 years, and 520, multiplied by $3\frac{1}{2}$, equals 1820. Now, multiply this by 2, and divide by 366, and we have 1810 years and 20 days. The reason for this is, that 2 is the difference between a year of 364 parts, and one of 366; and the 1820 years are years of 364 days long, and these are to be reduced to years of 366 days. We have an example of the propriety of this mode of reduction in the 70 weeks. There it was seen, that by adding Sabbath time to 520, we had $606\frac{1}{2}$ years, and multiplying it by 2, and dividing by 366, we obtained 603 years and $128\frac{2}{3}$ days. Indeed, if we multiply this by 3, we obtain 1810 years and 20 days.

2. We saw that the 70 weeks were just equal to $603\frac{1}{3}$ years, by the addition of Sabbath time. Now, if we

subtract Sabbath time from it, we have 517½ years as the length of a "time." Then multiplying this sum by 3½, we have just 1810 years, or 1810 years and 20 days. These times are evidently to be dated, according to Daniel xii., at the overthrow of Judea by the Romans. They will, therefore, naturally begin at the last passover, and the last daily sacrifice. Now, the last daily sacrifice was on the 17th of Panemus, or 189th day of A. D. 68, and just 1708 years after that date, exactly, a Christian nationality arose, answering to the Israel restored described by the literal prophets. From A. D. 68, and 189th day, to July 4th, 1776, was exactly 1708 years. So that the three and a half times began to be fulfilled at that point. Again; if we date the other length of the times at the last passover, or 97th day of A. D. 68, we are carried down to A. D. 1878, and 117th day.

SECTION VI.

Twenty-three Hundred Evening Mornings.

Paragraph I.

THE EPOCHS OF THEIR BEGINNING AND ENDING.

Daniel viii. "How long shall be the vision concerning the daily sacrifice, and the transgression of desolation, to give both the sanctuary and the host to be trodden under foot? And he said unto me, Unto two thousand and three hundred morning evenings, then shall the sanctuary be cleansed."

"And the vision of the evening and the morning which was told, is true; wherefore shut thou up the vision: for it shall be for many days." "By him the place of his sanctuary was cast down; and an host was given him against the daily sacrifice, by reason of transgression." "And shall destroy the mighty and the holy people." This prophecy is found in one of the four prophetic histories of the world related by Daniel. Accompanied with the application of it, by Christ, to the destruction of the temple, and the long captivity of his people and the Jews, together with its literal fulfillment in these events, its meaning can not be mistaken. The casting down of the sanctuary is synonymous with the burning of the temple, and the taking away of the daily sacrifice, with the cessation of national worship; but in speaking of the treading of the sanctuary and the host under foot for many days, the reference is plainly to the long humiliation of the two departments of the nationality of God's Israel. The sanctuary and the host are metonymic figures for the Hebrew church and state; the sanctuary signifies the church, and the host the commonwealth of Israel. The cleaning of the sanctuary at the end of the 2300 days, represents the removal of the desolator that polluted it; and can not refer to the temple as a house, because it does not exist, and no mention is made of its rebuilding; but a cleansing of something, still in being, is mentioned, and, therefore, it must signify the true system of divine worship, purified from the control of secular authority; in other words, a free church. The 2300 morning evenings are rendered in two ways by our translators, one of which is the above, and the other is by the term days. But the former is the literal meaning of the passage, and the latter is more of an inferential character. The daily sacrifice, mentioned so often, became a real measure of Hebrew time, as it never ceased; and, for the same reason, the double sacrifice on each Sabbath, and the hebdomadal sacrifice every two months, conjoined with the daily, made their aggregate number a most accurate reed for the measurement of solar time. It required two lambs to constitute one sacrifice, or to equal one day; for one was sacrificed in the morning, and the other in the evening; and on every Sabbath they killed four lambs; and at the beginning of every month seven more were added; and the year, according to Moses, (says Calmet) was just 12 months, and contained 52 Sabbaths; and, as two lambs made but one sacrifice, there were 52 and 42, or 94, more sacrifices than there were days in a year.

It would be an endless task to review all the fanciful expositions given to these days. Those who fix upon 606 as the epoch from whence the 1260 days are to begin, are brought down to 1866; and they subtract this from 2400 days, the reading of the seventy, and are thus carried back to the third year of Cyrus, when, instead of destruction to Israel and the temple, we find them just rising from ruin. Deserting this period, therefore, they seek to prove that 2300 days is an improper rendering of the passage, and follow the reading of Jerome, or 2200 days, and this brings them to A. C. 334. But this, though the epoch of Alexander, is not an epoch of the destruction of Jerusalem and the casting down of the sanctuary, and, therefore, it is utterly impossible to date these days at 334, A. C. It is very remarkable, that expositors should not here have seen, and given up their error, after such plain disagreement between their epochs and that so plainly stated by scripture. If they subtract 1866 from 2300, they are as deep in trouble as ever; for that lands them at 434, A. C., at which time the sanctuary and the host still stood in glorious majesty. Yet **all** affirm that the 2300 and the 1260 days ended together, in the freedom of Israel, and in this they are plainly sustained by the text. There is not the least agreement between these expositions and the prophecy: the epochs they choose for beginning the days, is one directly at variance with the prophecy, and the facts which fulfilled it. Nothing can be plainer to mankind, since the fall of

Jerusalem, than that the prophecy and the 2300 days are pinned down to that epoch as strongly as language can convey meaning, without mentioning names and times right out, in full and minute detail. No fall of Jerusalem and a long captivity ever occurred after the prophecy, but the one in A. D. 68; and the fall and captivity were to continue from that period, says the angel, for 2300 mornings and evenings. To begin the days then, before the captivity and casting down of the sanctuary, is flatly to contradict the angel, who says they begin there. Another mode of interpreting the prophecy, is that adopted by the book of Maccabees, which refers the days to the profanation of the temple by Epiphanes. But while some men agree with it, it is so obvious that this profanation does not coincide with any two features of the prophecy, that the exposition must be considered an extravagance; for, when a prophecy is fulfilled, it coincides with history in all points, with exactitude; which was not the case, in that simple pollution of the altar and temple.

It being agreed on all sides, that the three and a half times and 2300 days must end together, and the scriptures equally as clearly placing their beginnings together, it follows, inexorably, that they are of equal lengths when reduced to solar time, and if three and a half times and 1290 days equal 1708 years, and refer to the restoration of a free church and Christian or Hebrew commonwealth, the 2300 morning evenings must equal 1708 years also.

Paragraph II.

THE EXPOSITION.

Having seen that the daily sacrifice, from its nature and associations, was a measure of Hebrew time, and that it is so used by the angel, and that 2300 morning evenings are equal to 1290 and 1260 days, and that there were 188 more lambs, or 94 more daily sacrifices than there were days in the year, we must subtract this difference from the 2300 days, and the result will in solar time (taking a day as a year, as hitherto,) be equal to that of the three and a half times, &c.

The reduction $2300 \times 94 = 186,796,800,000$ tenth seconds, and divided by a solar year, or $315,569,277$ tenth seconds, equals 591 years, 343 days, 8 minutes, $49\frac{3}{10}$ seconds. Subtracting this sum from 2300, and considering these 2300 as years of 343 days, and we have 1708 years remainder; or, considering them as solar years, and we have 1708 years and 22 days. Dating one of these at the 189th day of 68 A. D., or at the cessation of the daily sacrifice, and we have 1776, July 4th; and subtracting the other from July 4th, or 1776 and 189th day, we are carried back to 68, A. D., 167th day, or to the month Sivan, when the great mount was built around the city, which wrought its destruction. These days have another interpretation, which ends between this and 1878, or about 1861—5.

SECTION VII.

Fall and Rise of the Western Empire—One Third of a Day and One Third of a Night.

These are predicted in the eighth chapter Revelation, and under the fourth trumpet. The fall of the Western empire, was to continue for one third of a day and one third of a night, or for two thirds of a symbolic day According to the analogy of symbols, this may represen a year, and that year may again represent a year of years. Now, as a year of years is equal to 488 years. two thirds of this will equal $325\frac{1}{3}$ years. Now, the fan of the Western empire, under Augustus, took place some time between 470 and 476. Mr. Gibbon says the date is uncertain. We, however, know that it was restored, and that Charlemagne was crowned at Rome, on Christmas day, 799. Subtract, therefore, 325¼ from this, and we are carried back to 474, and to the latter part of the year.

SECTION VIII.

Five Months—Duration of the Saracenic Invasions.

"Their power was to hurt men five months." The attacks of the Saracens upon the Roman empire, are to be dated after the death of Mahomet, in 532 or 3. Now, as 42 months equal three and a half times, or 1708 years, then 5 months equal 203¼ years. Dating this at 632¼, and we are brought down to 835 or 6. Again, as 42 months equal 1810 years, 5 months equal 215¾ years, and this lands us in 849. At this epoch, the Saracens were defeated in their invasion of Italy; and this was the last of their disturbance of the Roman territories. The great difficulty of obtaining correct dates in Saracenic history, prevents great accuracy in fulfillment being seen. The five months may have three other lengths: one of about 183 years, another of 172, and another of 148 years.

SECTION IX.

Day—Hour—Month—Year.

Duration of Turkey.—"An hour and a day, and a month and a year, to slay the third part of men." This sum makes $391\frac{1}{4}$ days. And, as $360 = 488$, $391\frac{1}{4} = 530$ years and 29 days. Mr. Gibbon dates the true epoch of the Turkish empire in 1299 and 1326. He says, "It was on the 27th of July, in the year 1299, A. D., that Othman first invaded the territory of Nicomedia; and the singular accuracy of the date seems to disclose some foresight of the rapid and destructive growth of the monster." The conquest of Brusa, which became the capital in 1326, is, possibly, an epoch at which to date the day, month, and year. The first attack of the power on the east, would seem the most proper epoch at which to begin. If we date on the 27th July, 1299, we are carried down to September, 1829. It was in this month, on the 14th day, that the treaty of Adrianople was made, which resulted in the loss of a great portion of the empire. Greece was fully separated from it, and much, also, was ceded to Russia, and the destruction of Turkey fully began. If we date the 530 years at the establishment of the capital at Brusa, about 1324, 5, or 6, we are brought to A. D. 1855, 6, or 7; otherwise, to 1861. But another length of the day, month, and year, is also found. Thus, if 42 months equal 1810 years, 391 years will equal 551 years and 271 days. Dating these in 1297, July 27th, and we are carried forward to 1861. Much discrepancy exists among historians, as to the time when Brusa became the capital of Turkey, some placing it as late as 1328, and others as early as 1298. The fall of Turkey is certain, but the time is uncertain, though it can hardly be placed beyond 1861.

SECTION X.

Synopsis of Days, Months, and Times.

1. The 1260 days, 42 months, and spiritual 3½ times are equal to 1451 years and 17 days, and, also, to 1243 years and 277 days. They measure the duration of church and state union, from June 19th, 325, and from 532, October 1st, and ended the 4th of July, 1776, when church and state union began to cease, on a most extensive scale. The end of this union is not complete, nor

will it be till the end of the Greek church and Russia. The Roman, and, perhaps, the English church, will fall before Russia does. The period is, doubtless, very close at hand, but we can not be certain in what year; yet we may look for it soon.

2. The secular three and a half times are equal to 1810 years and also to 1810 years and 20 days; and, also, to 1708 years. Dating these severally, at the last passover, 14th of Nisan, or 97th day of A. D. 68, and the first victory over the Jews or 117th, or 120th, and the 17th of Panemus, or 189th day, when the daily sacrifice ceased, and we are carried forward to the 4th day of July, 1776, and the 117th day of A. D. 1878.

3. The 1290 days are equal to 1708 years, and, also, 1707 years 314 days. Dating one of these on the 8th of Elul, or 239th day of 68, A. D., and the other, at the 189th day, or 17th of Panemus, and we are brought down to the 4th of July, 1776.

4. The 1335 days are equal to 1809 years and 244 days. Dating these from the setting up of the desolator, on the 8th of Elul, or the day of the burning of Jerusalem, or the 239th day of A. D. 68, and we are carried down to the 117th day of 1878. Thus, do the 3½ times, and 1290, and 1335 days, end in the very same years, and on the very same days in those years. Within twenty-six years, then, from the date we are writing, the most awful tragedies ever imagined will be realized by the world! The scene is too vast and terrible to dwell upon; its realization will be enough, without any description.

CONCLUSION.

We have, in this discovery, shown the following things:

First. That the seventy weeks, nor any other symbolic period, were ever correctly interpreted.

Secondly. We proved, positively, that the weeks were abbreviated, or consisted of secular time, to which sacred time was to be added, to obtain their full value.

Thirdly. We showed, in four different ways, that by a four-fold method of adding sacred time to the seven-fold forms of the seventy weeks, that they coincided with history, in a four-fold way.

Fourthly. The showing of these fulfillments, not only demonstrates that the prophecy was fulfilled, with amazing accuracy, but it also demonstrates the correctness of our theory, with *mathematical* precision.

Having, therefore, a key to the interpretation of symbolic weeks, we were possessed with a key to symbolic months, and days, and years. This key has unlocked for us all the symbolic prophecies, with wonderful exactness.

Thank God, that we have succeeded in this mighty work! "It was good for me to draw near to God; I have put my trust in the Lord, that I may declare all thy work."

THE END.

www.ingramcontent.com/pod-product-compliance
Lightning Source LLC
Chambersburg PA
CBHW030322020526
44117CB00030B/366